CREATING CONSERVATISM

RHETORIC AND PUBLIC AFFAIRS SERIES

CREATING CONSERVATISM

POSTWAR WORDS THAT MADE AN AMERICAN MOVEMENT

Michael J. Lee

MICHIGAN STATE UNIVERSITY PRESS • *East Lansing*

∞ The paper used in this publication meets the minimum requirements of ANSI/NISO Z39.48-1992 (R 1997) (Permanence of Paper).

 Michigan State University Press
East Lansing, Michigan 48823-5245

Printed and bound in the United States of America.

20 19 18 17 16 15 14   1 2 3 4 5 6 7 8 9 10

LIBRARY OF CONGRESS CATALOGING-IN-PUBLICATION DATA

Lee, Michael J., 1979–
Creating conservatism : postwar words that made an American movement / Michael J. Lee, Michigan State University Press.
        pages cm.—(Rhetoric and public affairs series)
    Includes bibliographical references and index.
    ISBN 978-1-61186-127-3 (pbk. : alk. paper)—ISBN 978-1-60917-414-9 (pdf)—ISBN 978-1-62895-002-1 (epub)—ISBN 978-1-62896-002-0 (mobi) 1. Conservatism—United States. 2. Rhetoric—Political aspects. 3. United States—Politics and government. I. Title.
    JC573.2.U6L435 2014
    320.520973—dc23   2013046121

Book design by Charlie Sharp, Sharp Des!gns, Lansing, Michigan
Cover design by Erin Kirk New
Cover art is ©istockphoto.com/firebrandphotography

g green press INITIATIVE Michigan State University Press is a member of the Green Press Initiative and is committed to developing and encouraging ecologically responsible publishing practices. For more information about the Green Press Initiative and the use of recycled paper in book publishing, please visit www.greenpressinitiative.org.

To Sam,
Who thought trust falls were funny

Contents

⌘

Acknowledgments

⌘

I began writing this book in late 2005 when the nation's domestic and foreign policies, not to mention the conservative movement, were shaped by social conservatives and neoconservatives. I completed this book in late 2013 when resurgent libertarians sought to revolutionize the nation's domestic and foreign policies and, of course, conservatism itself. I had lots of help along the way.

This book, which analyzes conservatism over these and the many other years since World War II, would not have been possible if not for the guidance of several exemplary scholars including Karlyn Kohrs Campbell, Ron Greene, James Farr, John Murphy, Ed Schiappa, and Jarrod Atchison. Two scholars deserve special mention for their influence on this book. Kirt Wilson was an unfailing source of creativity and inspiration as a dissertation adviser; Marty Medhurst was consistently thorough, thoughtful, and fair in his evaluations of the book manuscript. I am deeply grateful for the assistance provided by this model group of scholars.

My thinking about conservatism was sharpened by innumerable conversations with colleagues and students at the University of Minnesota and the College of Charleston. This book has also benefited from the suggestions of several anonymous reviewers both for this book series and at *Rhetoric & Public Affairs*, where portions of chapters one and five were published. That material is reprinted here courtesy of the Michigan State University Press journals program. Heartfelt thanks are also due to several people at Michigan State University Press. Julie Loehr, Kristine Blakeslee, Elise Jajuga, Robert Burchfield, Annette Tanner, Travis Kimbel, and the production team as a whole have been prompt, perceptive, and insightful.

I am also grateful for the generous financial assistance provided by both the University of Minnesota and the College of Charleston. I was awarded the University of Minnesota's Doctoral Dissertation Fellowship during 2007–2008. The College of Charleston invested in this research project in several forms including a first-year faculty summer stipend, a Faculty Research and Development Grant, and an award through the Dean's Discretionary Fund. This financial assistance allowed me time to write the book that I wanted to write.

I am especially lucky to have had the support of two wonderful parents, Steven and Frances Lee. They taught me to love learning; they taught me, sometimes to their chagrin, to criticize commonplace assumptions; they taught me, most importantly, how to be a compassionate parent.

I am most indebted to my wife, Erin Benson. Her patience was unyielding even as this project stretched on year after year; her encouragement was galvanizing especially in those moments when I was not sure what else I had to say; her criticisms, most importantly, were precise especially in those moments when I said too much. All told, she has sacrificed greatly in support of my work. I love her dearly.

The Old Argument Comes Full Circle

⌘

M uch later in life, William F. Buckley recalled an odd meeting he had in the mid-1950s. After delivering a lecture at Smith College, a man approached him abruptly: "I came out of the lecture and this thin, angular man bounded over and said, 'My name is Peter Viereck. Can we talk?'" In a hurry, Buckley answered that he only had time to talk while walking to his waiting car. Viereck agreed. Off the two went, Buckley on foot, Viereck on a bicycle. "So we chatted for about five minutes and then he fell," Buckley remembered. "So I dragged him out of this sort of ditch. It didn't interrupt his talking for one second!" Unfazed by his brief encounter with the pathway ditch, Viereck explained that Buckley's upstart magazine, *National Review*, was a valuable but flawed contribution to U.S. politics. "America need- ed a conservative magazine," Viereck stressed, but *National Review* should acknowledge that the "true conservative" in national politics was Adlai Stevenson, a Democrat. To Buckley, the conservative wun- derkind, this suggestion was "just preposterous."[1]

Although this was their first face-to-face meeting, these two conservatives had crossed paths before. In 1951, the *New York Times* asked Viereck to review Buckley's first shot across the bow, *God and Man at Yale*. In the review, Viereck rejected what would become a mantra of conservative thinking in later years: the Cold War was a zero-sum conflict, and no ground should be given to potential enemies. This assumption shared much with Winston Churchill's lesson on appeasement. Speaking of Neville Chamberlain, Churchill argued that accommodating Hitler was "a bit like feeding a crocodile, hoping it would eat you last."[2] To Viereck, however, the postwar expression of this style of prewar thinking was a non sequitur. The Left was not monolithic; some were allies, and others were enemies. Of Buckley's famous attack on the Yale humanists, Viereck wrote, "The author irresponsibly treats not only mild social democracy but even most social reform as almost crypto-Communism."[3] Viereck denied the premise that collectivism of any variety allowed Communists a foot in the door. These two conservative claimants, however, traveled a two-way street. After *God and Man at Yale*, Buckley spoke to his publisher and proposed a book that would examine Viereck's work and, in so doing, challenge his claim to represent "legitimate conservatism."[4] Sensing that his services were required elsewhere, Buckley abandoned his critique of Viereck to write *McCarthy and His Enemies* (1954) instead.

Before the Smith lecture, before *Up from Liberalism* (1959), before *National Review* (founded in 1955), before *God and Man at Yale* (1951), and before the American Right called itself "conservative," Viereck was the author who fired shots across bows and challenged the dominant assumptions of U.S. political culture. In 1940, the twenty-three-year-old Harvard graduate was approached by the *Atlantic Monthly* to write an essay about the "meaning of young liberalism." Viereck accepted the offer and wrote "But—I'm a Conservative!" instead, which the magazine published in its April 1940 issue. Viereck's conservatism was politically prudent rather than rigidly devoted to sacred first principles. He was a Christian and rejected collectivism, but he was neither a religious nor a laissez-faire literalist, the uneasy combination of Christianity and capitalism, the space "between Jesus and the market" as one scholar put it, that would become a quintessential conservative position as the twentieth century progressed.[5]

For Viereck, conservatism was an alternative to the ambitious and destructive radicalism of the previous century. "Revolt," he explained, "now has its hierarchy of saints. . . . It has its elaborate, formalized incantations, its holy slogans." According to Viereck, responsible political actors should resist Communism, the Popular Front Left, and the Liberty League Right, but also resist the "smug convention" that the only alternative to "fascist terror" is Marxism. Against the Marxist "materialistic assault" on "non-economic values of the spirit," Viereck advocated "conservative values." "Conservatism," as he defined it, "must include what Thomas Mann calls humanism: the conservation of our cultural, spiritual, and individualist heritage." He couched "common sense" as "the oracle of conservatism."[6] His was a political philosophy most closely associated with the European conservative tradition generally and Edmund Burke's suspicion of the radicalism of the French Revolution specifically. Viereck's treatise about this "common and universal sense of mankind" was, in the historian George Nash's estimation, the first call for a "new conservatism in America."[7]

The conflicts and odysseys experienced firsthand by several generations of Viereck's family may help explain his commitment to conserving tradition amid revolutionary fervor. His grandfather, Louis Viereck, was friends with Marx and Engels, and was a socialist discussion group leader in Munich before being jailed for violating antisocialist laws.[8] No doubt seeking a warmer political climate for their beliefs, the family moved to the United States following the birth of their son, George Sylvester. Sylvester, as his intimates called him, developed a flair for the intricately metaphoric style of the Romantic tradition and, like his father, a radical streak. Unlike his father, however, he was more taken with ethnic nationalism than class politics. He was suspected of pro-German espionage in 1915; he was convicted of accepting Nazi money and financially supporting pro-Nazi groups in 1941. He spent four years in federal prison.[9]

Just a few years after his father was imprisoned for supporting the Third Reich, Peter Viereck published *Conservatism Revisited: The Revolt against Revolt*, his attempt to sketch a philosophical alternative to ideological dogmatism. Although *Conservatism Revisited* did more than most postwar books to create "the new conservatism as a self-conscious intellectual force," many of Viereck's claims were not unique.[10] His advocacy for the dignity of individual souls, anticollectivist politics, antinominalism, Aristotelian self-restraint, and political humility in light of human imperfection had been theorized before. Nevertheless, Viereck united these themes into a coherent set of arguments, and he gave this ideology a tidy label: "conservative." The little-used political term connoted a perplexing range of meanings in the midcentury.[11] When Richard Nixon and John F. Kennedy first ran for Congress in 1946, "the former ran as a 'practical liberal,' the latter as a 'fighting conservative.'"[12] Henry Regnery, the influential publisher of several canonical conservative books, later said that he began publishing in 1947 not "with the idea of publishing *conservative* books, but books which didn't necessarily fit the liberal ideology" instead.[13] Even in the Regnery-published *God and Man at Yale* in 1951, Buckley identified as an "individualist."[14]

The word "conservative," a neologism in England's late Georgian era, was initially used favorably by those hoping to protect established institutions and social traditions from protesters and reformers.[15] Viereck employed the word in a similar sense, but he recognized it to be "among the most unpopular words in the American vocabulary."[16] To infuse it with fresh cultural force, Viereck envisioned conservatism as a sensible alternative amid the senseless upheavals of the age. As much as any rival, Viereck succeeded in popularizing the once-sullied term and in naming a "nascent movement."[17] In a telling assessment written fifty-five years after Viereck's article first appeared, a *National Review* writer and no fan of Viereck's reluctantly conceded him conservatism's "naming rights."[18] This kin of the kaiser, grandson of a revolutionary, son of a traitor, had found his cause. Conservatism, not monarchism, socialism, or nationalism, would be his contribution to the progression of ideas in U.S. political culture. He was a poet and a poet's son, and his pen produced many enchanting words, even Pulitzer Prize–winning verse, but none was more important than "conservative."[19]

Several years after his most formative work, however, Viereck was lifted from a campus ditch by a prominent conservative who, he believed, misunderstood the true meaning of conservatism. Viereck had written insistently that although the political label meant a refusal to collectivize, it did *not* mean McCarthyism. His denunciations of the zealous witch hunt for un-American activities were met with incredulity by conservative supporters of the Wisconsin senator. When, in 1962, Viereck thought his moderate, integrationist, anti-laissez-faire conservatism represented Barry Goldwater's coalition of big business leaders, states' rights supporters, and virulent anti-Communists, his bright blue eyes must have stared in bewilderment.[20] Viereck picked up the weapon he knew best and published a *New Republic* essay called "The New Conservatism: One of Its Founders Asks What Went Wrong." In an interview several decades later, he remembered clearly when the movement started to pass him by. He explained that in the late 1940s, *Conservatism Revisited* "opened people's minds to the idea that to be conservative is not to be satanic." But, he continued, "Once their minds were opened, Buckley came in."[21]

William F. Buckley Jr. was not a poet, nor was his father. When Sylvester Viereck was suspected of treason (for the first time), William F. Buckley Sr. also found himself involved in revolutionary politics. Specifically, he invested in counterrevolutionary politics. He had made a fortune in the 1910s oil boom in Mexico. When Pancho Villa, Alvaro Obregon, and other revolutionaries demanded taxes from oil expropriators in Mexico and denounced Buckley Sr.'s spiritual anchor, the Catholic Church, he began supporting measures more friendly to U.S. business interests, private land ownership, and clerical politics. He was expelled from Mexico in 1921.

Although he never wrote poetry, William Buckley Jr.'s words would make him famous. Rich Lowry, editor of *National Review*, said, "Bill is the Michael Jordan of language. He does things that no one will ever do again."[22] In addition to considering him an "intellectual godfather," James Roberts, former president of the American Conservative Union, called Buckley "a virtuoso with the English language."[23] Buckley, an admiring conservative touted, "knew what Shakespeare knew: There is a time to write fancy, or sophisticated; and there's a time to write plain, low."[24] Buckley's dazzling rhetorical style, with its muscular vocabulary and barbed sentences, evinced that, as *Time* proclaimed on a 1967 cover, "Conservatism Can Be Fun."[25]

Through numerous media outlets, Buckley personified the conservative cause for nearly six decades. One commentator described the growth of Young Americans for Freedom on college campuses in the 1960s this way: "A flock of little Buckleys now torment social scientists in colleges large and small."[26] In 1955, he founded *National Review* as an explicitly conservative magazine that targeted a bourgeoning conservative intelligentsia. Under his editorial control, *National Review* became a big tent under which disparate political groups experienced revival. The magazine featured libertarians, Christians, Burkeans, traditionalists, hybrid conservatives, borderline anarchists, and borderline monarchists in regular columns, yet Buckley managed to focus these writers' energies on external enemies rather than on one another.[27]

Because of his successful efforts to fuse lines of libertarian, traditionalist, and anti-Communist thought under a single label, the meaning of conservatism was always more than the sum of his efforts. The
more "fun" he made conservatism seem, the more Americans understood their ideas about law and order, Communist threats, or Social
Security as conservative. Between *National Review*, scores of books,
his *Firing Line* television punditry, dozens of speeches per year, and a
weekly syndicated column, Buckley campaigned on behalf of conservatism for millions of hearts and minds. Before Buckley, conservatism
meant many things: the defense of the status quo, the defense of the
aristocracy, the defense of capitalism, and the defense of tradition.
After Buckley, conservatism still meant all of these and more, but there
was nothing defensive about it. For Buckley, being conservative meant
attacking the status quo and standing, as he urged in *National Review*'s
first issue, "athwart history" yelling "Stop."[28] Buckley's efforts to shape
a conservative coalition produced paradoxical results. The more he did
on conservatism's behalf, the less its meaning was manageable.

Buckley and Viereck, two erstwhile rivals, helped save conservatism from midcentury idiosyncrasy. Alongside their efforts, Russell
Kirk's resonant, voluminous *The Conservative Mind* appeared in 1952.
Scores of books and magazine articles, including *The Conscience of a
Conservative* in 1960, affirmed the term proudly within the next decade.[29] The start of conservatism's cachet as a political identity can
be located in the early 1950s.[30] Cachet, however, is only one facet of
meaning. The term's postwar genesis was not a period of uniformity;
it was, instead, the starting point of a disagreement among conservatives, ongoing still, over the meaning of conservatism. Jonah Goldberg,
a self-described ideological "hit-man," noted matter-of-factly at a 2008
National Review seminar that conservatism "remains unsettled" after
all these years and considered what course of action, if any, was appropriate to resolve the conflict. Short of the *National Review* editorial
board "issuing *diktats*" to rein in conservatives, impossible on multiple
accounts, Goldberg recommended, somewhat sarcastically, a bloody
purge to help refocus conservatism. The prospect, he admitted, was
appealing; Goldberg loved the "old argument" over conservatism, and,
he beamed, "we keep having it over and over again."[31] This book is
about that "old argument" and its role in shaping conservatism in the
United States.

Conservatism and Its Discontents

When examining a debate over a complex political phenomenon such as conservatism, the gateway question that precedes all others is how the concept in question should be defined. Which definition or, better yet, whose definition of conservatism should be privileged? To appreciate conservatism as a highly trafficked intersection, rather than a clean-cut ideology, the lesson learned by Mary Shelley's Dr. Frankenstein is instructive. We work tirelessly and often give much of ourselves to make and use tools. The tools that we create may be the products of our efforts, but they are also available for purposes contrary to our own. "Conservative" is such a tool, useful in various political projects.

Creating Conservatism is a unique approach to the history of conservatism. *Creating Conservatism* highlights the process by which conservatives of many different stripes have generated the resources for partnership despite sustained disagreement since World War II. Many scholars agree that conservatives of various prefixes—neo-, paleo-, cultural, economic, and compassionate—hold doctrinally disparate beliefs, yet the most basic question when considering modern conservatism is among the least considered: what holds conservatism together?[32] The resources of the conservative coalition, I argue, have been symbolic. The shared symbols of its lingua franca were generated in part by galvanizing texts within the conservative movement's print culture, a small group of midcentury books that have been essentially canonized by subsequent generations of conservatives. The circulation of these common texts was formative in the creation of conservatism as a political identity that housed differing ideological traditions. Rather than follow one strain of conservatism, I take an expansive approach to document the wide influence of the conservative canon and the labyrinthine development of its political language, including what I call its traditionalist and libertarian dialects. Ultimately, I analyze conservatism in many of its manifestations and contradictions, its cautious suspicion that speaks to a human desire to conserve, and its impetuous attitude that demands considerable change in the political world.

At its most basic, *Creating Conservatism* is a book about books and their readers. I aim to locate the scriptural force of American conservatism's secular canon. *Creating Conservatism* establishes the vital role played by a small collection of writings published between the end of World War II and Barry Goldwater's losing presidential bid in 1964 in generating the keystone expressions of conservatism, their god and devil terms as Richard Weaver put it.[33] This is a story about how conservatives seized conservatism in powerful midcentury books, how they later employed these books to infuse the term with new meanings, and how these books abetted conservatives' attempts to purge heretics at some points and adopt ecumenicalism at others. Although I stray from the 1945–1964 period sporadically by, for instance, including Friedrich Hayek's *The Road to Serfdom* (first printed in England in 1944), my larger point should be clear: many conservative arguments—their capacity to polemicize, to moralize; their cautious, suspicious tones and their righteous indignation; their beloved "freedom," "tradition," and "order"; their fears of government, Communism, decadence, and cultural decay; and their penchant to approach politics religiously—are traceable to a small set of postwar texts and the reverential discourse each has inspired.

In order to establish how a more-or-less shared symbol system emerged among such a heterogeneous political grouping, this book is structured around one central dialectic: the potential for symbolic *fusion* and *fracture* within the conservative coalition. Fusion represents a stitched, stable consensus about the broader meaning of the conservative political project; fracture denotes seam-splitting separatism in which factions fight to define conservatism or secede to form a new political identity. At its base, this collision between conservatisms is a collision between two sects of "true" conservatives who look back fondly to founding texts from the midcentury. Traditionalist founders, like Russell Kirk and Richard Weaver, affirmed that societies should honor social tradition and hold fast to a vision of the good; libertarians, like Friedrich Hayek and Barry Goldwater, believed that one vision of the good was the whole problem. All told, combative conservatives have turned to canonical texts to establish their bona fides and to protect authentic conservatism from impostors and apostates.

Coalitional conservatism, especially among bedfellows as hostile toward one another as libertarians and traditionalists, required not only reasons to justify the wedding but tools to weather a rocky marriage. With conservatives claiming exclusive legitimacy on both sides of the line separating the belief in a transcendent moral order and the commitment to expanding individual freedom, the movement's political future rested on the persuasiveness of the fusionist project. Fusionists had to step in and reconcile absolutism and relativism, freedom and virtue, individual rights and social duty, and argue forcefully that one clear synthesis rose from this rancor: conservatism was the belief in free markets and free people under a watchful God. Writers such as Frank Meyer, William F. Buckley, Jr., and Whittaker Chambers fused conservatives by creating a common argumentative repertoire, a storehouse of powerful narratives, concepts, and ideals conservatives used to settle disagreements and identify common enemies. Although the philosophical compatibility of traditionalism and libertarianism remains questionable, their synthesis has proven to be a successful basis for political activity. A fusionist conservative could value freedom and virtue in tandem and validate, as a Ronald Reagan adviser once put it, "libertarian means for traditionalist ends."[34]

Storytelling is like cat-skinning; it can be done in different ways. After years as a misunderstood and understudied subject, explaining the rise of conservatism has become a cottage industry. Scholars and commentators have interpreted the ascent of free market economics, religious politics, and bellicose foreign policy as ostensibly conservative trends.[35] A number of scholars have emphasized several significant cultural and political trends when explaining conservatism's post–World War II growth: demographic changes, the catalyzing force of electoral campaigns, the political impact of racial resentment during the civil rights era, and anti-Communism.[36] Nevertheless, scholars have noted only in passing that a small set of postwar books were "critical to the success of the GOP Right" without detailing their influence or their rhetorical function as a canon.[37] The full story of the canon's role in shaping philosophical conservatism and influencing political conservatism remains untold.[38] With a few notable exceptions, analyses of conservatism undervalue the role of rhetoric and media in the creation of conservatism as an appealing political identity.[39] What Buckley named "the conservative demonstration" was not, I argue, an ethereal phenomenon or an abstract set of political ideas; conservative arguments were modeled in canonical texts and enacted rhetorically by adherents.[40]

Creating Conservatism charts the role of pivotal postwar books in the creation and evolution of the meaning of conservatism among conservatives. This book does not devote significant space to topics that have been covered capably elsewhere. This is not, in other words, a book about any particular conservative intellectual, any particular conservative politician, or any particular conservative organization. Although the majority of this book establishes the importance of core texts in conservatives' quarrels over conservatism, I also contend that a doctrinally and rhetorically diverse canon significantly aided the development of conservatism as a powerful yet adjustable political language. Within the movement, these books have become classic expressions of absolute, sacred values and emotionally resonant symbols that, some scholars conclude, secured conservatives' political advantage.[41] I do not, however, spend substantial portions of the book analyzing *all* conservative rhetoric on issues like civil rights, antifeminism, or anti-unionism that contributed to the movement's ascendancy. This book paints the period since the end of World War II with broad brush strokes to show the persistent features of the bookish political language that inspired these organizations, that supplied advocates resonant rhetorical resources for use in these and many other political controversies. Conservatives have turned to canonical works as guidebooks so consistently in periods of triumph, defeat, stability, and division that the canon resembles the protean force of the Bible among Christians, an anchor for communal identity and a wellspring of interpretive disagreement simultaneously.

   Creating Conservatism unfolds in three parts: *identity, fracture,* and *fusion.* The first section, identity, theorizes political language and print culture, the concepts I use to frame the symbolic movement culture of conservatism. In the book's second section, fracture, I examine the opposition between conservatism's traditionalist and libertarian dialects. In the third section, fusion, I analyze three rhetorical strategies that created an appealing identity across conservative camps and helped many put messy doctrinal differences aside and press the conservative case forward.

   My goals in this book are expository, not critical. I evaluate conservative arguments as is fitting, but I am not out to endorse free markets or to heighten awareness of theocrats in conservative clothing. I am interested in what "people who identify themselves as conservatives habitually do."[42] This is a story about the evolution of conservatives' conception of conservatism, not my conception of the worth of conservatism, for better and for worse.

Political Language and Print Culture

Since George Nash's influential *The Conservative Intellectual Movement in America since 1945* (1976), "conservatisms" has been a more appropriate descriptor than "conservatism" for a complex political phenomenon that does not proceed from identical first principles.[43] Traditionalists, to summarize Nash's parsimonious categories, held that social traditions should guide the creation of moral politics and feared that factions guided by "reason" would create hell on earth by attempting to upend natural social hierarchies. Libertarians, conversely, believed moral politics were possible only when individual freedom was protected. Anti-Communists considered Communism an immediate and existential threat and shelved other political issues as secondary. Nash's tripartite conception of conservatism has prompted many writers to create similar classification schemes rather than hazard a one-size-fits-all definition of conservative.[44] The agreement, however, regarding the complexities of conservatism ends there; analysts differ on how many conservatisms there are and what to call each camp.[45] Given its variations and inconsistencies, I argue that an exclusive focus on ideology is a limited way to explain conservatism.[46] The conservative coalition, a strange, often strained partnership, "cannot help but contain contradictions."[47]

Creating Conservatism accounts for the rise of American conservatism as a range of doctrinal commitments tethered to a political identity by employing two conceptual lenses: political language and print culture. Political language refers to the symbolic practices of a community organized around a shared political label. The popular narratives, standard idioms, dominant lines of argument, de rigueur tropes, and god and devil terms of a group with a common term of self-identification ("conservative") constitute their political language.[48]

More specific than the general political language that characterizes a historical era, an individual political language, in sum, is a political community's standard argumentative stock, a communally specific collection of rhetorical resources in which ideological and symbolic diversity can yield potency, flexibility, and combustibility.[49] Political languages are spoken by groups who accept a common term of identity, cultivate common narratives about themselves, contest the philosophical boundaries of their identity, interpret their history, attempt to manage internal deviation, protect against splinter identities, and develop argumentative styles suitable for these tasks.[50] The results of these communal efforts are relatively settled codes that become, to varying degrees, "institutionalized."[51] The language's conventions are "capable of being 'learned,'" reflected upon, adjusted, even mocked.[52] Self-reflective members of political communities, a "Monsieur Jourdain" in J. G. A. Pocock's terms, occasionally step outside their political culture in order to comment on its rhetorical conventions, admitting, "We seem to be talking in such and such an idiom, whose characteristics are such and such."[53] Using this analytical approach, I treat conservatism not as a uniform set of policy positions grounded in consistent philosophical doctrines but rather as the symbolic patterns by which a community voiced its varied, sometimes inconsistent, political commitments.[54] This perspective on political language aims at analyzing doctrinal traditions but also goes further to assess the resources that doctrinally diverse communities use to create, sustain, strain, or destroy a coalition.[55]

The language heuristic not only aids in identifying rhetorical similarity; it also highlights clear differences over the proper performance of an identity.[56] As with formal languages, political languages are governed by social conventions that are contested intensely. Languages denote both wide verbal conformity and, in the case of dialects, patterned deviations unique to subcommunities. A linguistic dialect is a language variation that is intelligible to speakers of the same language.[57] Speakers of what I treat as different dialects of a political language do not contend with differences in phonology, morphology, and syntactical arrangement as American southerners and London's East Enders would, but they do employ distinct families of arguments, specialized idioms, and guiding narratives about the political world that are, nevertheless, recognizable parts of the same political identity. In terms of political language, what distinguishes dialects from separate languages is the common allegiance to a shared political identity across dialects. Traditionalists and libertarians have fundamental disagreements about social order and individual freedom, yet each casts their politics as conservative. As different performances within the same community, dialects afford a versatile range of rhetorical resources to a political community, but they also portend the possibility of communal splintering, or, as with ancient European languages, speakers of dialects might grow so different from one another that common bonds fray.[58]

The argumentative and syntactical patterns of political languages do not necessarily appear randomly; they are influenced by a community's media practices. Communities "establish conventions that are largely tacit and negotiable as to how community members can 'recognize, create, experience, and talk about texts,'" and, in turn, communities use texts to establish conventions about how community members should speak.[59] Part of speaking the conservative political language is learning to talk about valued texts and employ their key terms. Few canonical accolades offer more significant testimony of these texts' power than one from 1981. One of their own had been elected president; America's Bastille had been seized, yet Ronald Reagan grew nostalgic. Ticking off nearly every canonical writer, conservative "leaders" like Buckley, Russell Kirk, Friedrich Hayek, Frank Meyer, and others, Reagan credited each with shaping "so much of our thoughts" and, more dramatically, rescuing the nation's "sense of mission and passion for freedom."[60] Reagan performed a particularly reflective conservatism, a political identity bent on figuring its future in terms of a storied printed past.[61] Beyond Reagan, praising canonical texts in awed terms became a frequently invoked rite of conservatism among Ann Coulter, Rush Limbaugh, Pat Buchanan, William Kristol, Grover Norquist, and numerous other conservative pundits, activists, writers, politicians, and movement insiders. Patterns of reference were, in one sense, patterns of reverence; the conservative community consecrated valued ideals through acts of rhetorical remembrance.

The development of political language is, then, partly a matter of the relationship between a stable set of texts and receptive audiences, talking about the right books with the right audiences. Common media furnish shared reference points, ideological authorities, and argumentative topics that enable and enliven communal life. What I refer to as a print culture is one account of shared media practices; print culture means a culture that venerates print materials, books, magazines, and more, rather than a culture whose principal means of communication is print. Canonical books, more specifically, are salient media in a culture dedicated to preserving prized print sources.[62]

A canon is a set of texts that a community, implicitly and explicitly, didactically and organically, links to its identity. Canons are "complicit with power."[63] After all, canonization is a decisive expression of authority, of those texts considered timeless, prophetic, or prescient, but they do not function monolithically. The content of canonical literature may be subject to disputatious interpretations; nonetheless, much like constitutional disputes in the United States, participants widely acknowledge that *this* document, and no other, must form the basis of proper interpretations. Accordingly, social movement advocates may put "sacred" texts to fusionist or fractious purposes: adjudicating competing claims, resolving crises of legitimacy, charting movement history, forming coalitions, silencing off-key performances, and excommunicating the unrepentant. Common textual practices can become cardinal features of a community's identity, both "a shared matrix for a diverse tradition" and one of its "central operative concepts."[64] As references to source material accumulate in print and public address, the community's text-centered practices become a ritualistic rhetoric. If the variety of Christian doctrines and worship practices can serve as an example of the interpretive range of such a tradition, then canons "can be much more flexible, and less ideologically binding, than prevalent conceptions allow."[65] As one locus in contests between ecumenical and exclusive conceptions of conservative political identity, canonical questions are communal questions and, quite often, vice versa.

The Canon: An Inventory

Before Fox News and dozens of conservative media outlets created an "echo chamber," in Kathleen Hall Jamieson and Joseph Capella's terms, a group of ten select texts published between World War II and Barry Goldwater's defeat in 1964 became the de facto canon of conservatism, defining elements of the movement's media culture.[66] Some of these works, like Goldwater's *The Conscience of a Conservative* (1960), defined and defended conservatism rather defiantly; some, like Friedrich Hayek's *The Road to Serfdom* (1944) and Whittaker Chambers's *Witness* (1952), were written by intellectuals who later resisted association with conservatism. *The Conscience of a Conservative*, *The Road to Serfdom*, and *Witness* joined tracts like Richard Weaver's *Ideas Have Consequences* (1948), William F. Buckley's *God and Man at Yale* (1951) and *Up from Liberalism* (1959), Russell Kirk's *The Conservative Mind* (1953), Robert Nisbet's *The Quest for Community* (1953), Milton Friedman's *Capitalism and Freedom* (1962), and Frank Meyer's *In Defense of Freedom* (1962) as conservatism's most frequently celebrated texts.[67] A more generous account of the conservative canon beyond these "true classics" might expand the list to roughly fifteen and include second-order postwar texts by James Burnham, Willmoore Kendall, Ludwig von Mises, Leo Strauss, and Eric Voegelin.[68] Lines from these books acquired long lives as each was transported from its original context through citation, quotation, and appropriation into a coiling, widening circle of aspirants' prose.

I concentrate on how the canon has shaped the rhetoric and tactics of prominent conservative politicians, activists, and organizations, but I do not claim that all conservatives have studied the canon. To be sure, these books circulated widely outside the rarefied worlds of Republican politics, *National Review* contributors, and the members, donors, and seminar and conference attendees associated with organizations like the Heritage Foundation, Young Americans for Freedom, the American Conservative Union, and the New Centurion Program.[69] Books like *Up from Liberalism*, *Ideas Have Consequences*, *The Conservative Mind*, *Witness*, and *The Road to Serfdom* have been printed, reprinted, and distributed en masse and often free of charge by conservative organizations of postwar vintage like the Foundation for Economic Freedom and the Intercollegiate Society of Individualists.[70] Books like *The Conscience of a Conservative* and *Witness* were best sellers but also were promoted in local conservative bookstores.[71] These and others were "handed out like party favors" at grassroots counter-counterculture rallies of the 1960s.[72] One Goldwater activist testified after reading *God and Man at Yale*, "Reading was extremely important [to us]. . . . There had to be a coming forth of good conservative writers that could express the view, there had to be a legitimate voice of the conservative position before there could be a growth of the conservative movement."[73] Nevertheless, this book does not examine the meanings local, everyday readers made of these formative texts.[74] That strategic choice on my part should not, however, suggest that a book like *The Road to Serfdom* was influential only among conservative office-holders, office-seekers, and well-heeled donors and not at dinner tables, school board meetings, and neighborhood reading groups.[75]

First-order canonical books are those that prominent conservatives have read, studied, memorized, applied, debated, cited, invoked, and quoted persistently since the midcentury.[76] Nevertheless, I have not treated as canonical every book that conservatives bought in great numbers or described as influential. For instance, I have not identified many popular midcentury books, like Phyllis Schlafly's *A Choice Not an Echo* (1964) or John Stormer's *None Dare Call It Treason* (1964), as canonical because conservative reverence for them peaked long ago.[77] Edmund Burke and other continental conservatives of the eighteenth and nineteenth centuries loom large for some in the movement, but a long-standing dispute among conservatives over whether American and European conservatism shared political dispositions or responded to similar historical circumstances mitigated the impact of books like Burke's *Notes on the Revolution in France*, Bastiat's *The Law*, or Smith's *The Wealth of Nations*.

Canonical texts have not been the subjects of occasional or pro forma praise, and few conservatives would bristle at the notion that these ten books were foundational. To that end, I have also excluded books like Ayn Rand's *Atlas Shrugged* whose classification as canonical or even conservative is highly contentious among conservatives.[78] Although Rand remains a foremost advocate for individual liberty and figures in my analysis of the libertarian dialect of the conservative political language (chapter 3), "many conservatives," one writer observed, treat her "philosophical ideas as, well, nutty."[79] Ranging from celebratory to ambivalent to outright hostile, the reception of Rand's ideas, particularly her militant atheism, by preeminent conservatives distanced *Atlas Shrugged* and *The Fountainhead* from the devotion consistently shown to canonical texts.[80] In an infamously acerbic rebuke of *Atlas Shrugged* in *National Review*, Whittaker Chambers likened Rand to the twentieth-century's worst butchers. Her atheist materialism was so dogmatic that Chambers sensed the horrors of the gas chamber "from almost any page of *Atlas Shrugged*."[81] "Chambers," Buckley concluded, "did in fact read Miss Rand right out of the conservative movement."[82] For legions of conservatives, reading Rand has been a "gateway drug to life on the right," provocative, rebellious, and largely unsanctioned.[83]

Independent of their distinct ideas and the question of who represented genuine conservatism, audiences have used canonical books to unite in the belief that "conservative" was a term of inspiration whose intellectual tradition required rescue and whose political future required shepherding. These books were remarkable not just because each enumerated conservative political positions but also because their memorable language demonstrated *how* to take those positions. They were, in essence, debate handbooks, displays of a style of verbal combat that became essential to the public performance of the conservative political language.

CHAPTER ONE

The Conservative Canon and Its Uses

⌘

To Pat Buchanan, his was "the voice in the desert" whose defeat in 1964 was a "baptism of fire." This politician-prophet left a sacred text, a "sermon of fire and brimstone." The blessed document, Buchanan said of Barry Goldwater's *The Conscience of a Conservative,* was conservatives' "new testament," and "we read it, memorized it, quoted it."[1] William F. Buckley, whose writings also enthralled conservatives, agreed with Buchanan; *The Conscience of a Conservative,* he wrote, held "near scriptural authority" in the community.[2] Yet Goldwater's was not the only book that acquired transfixing power among conservatives. Milton Friedman praised Friedrich Hayek's *The Road to Serfdom* as a "revelation."[3] Ronald Reagan could quote lines of Hayek's from memory as well as those warning of the "evil" of Communism from Whittaker Chambers's sullen memoir, *Witness.*[4] When George W. Bush alleged evil, he also used Chambers as source material. Michael Gerson and David Frum, the authors of "axis of evil" in Bush's 2002 State of the Union address, knew *Witness* well; they attended a posthumous 100th birthday party for Chambers held at the White House in 2001.[5]

Many of the post–World War II texts conservatives canonized—ten first-order texts by Buckley, Chambers, Friedman, Hayek, Goldwater, Kirk, Meyer, Nisbet, and Weaver as well as second-order books by Burnham, Kendall, Mises, Strauss, and Voegelin—forward different, even antithetical, versions of conservatism. Since the postwar era, however, each of these texts has been touted over others with remarkable consistency in prominent conservatives' editorials, speeches, polemics, campaign books, memoirs, testimonials, obituaries, and histories. *National Review* (founded by Buckley in 1955) became both a laboratory for conservative ideas but also the premier venue in which these midcentury books were promoted, reaffirmed, and canonized. The magazine's masthead became a Who's Who of conservative authors, yet each developed a distinctive conservatism.[6] For all its internal rancor, *National Review* organized scattered groups on the right under the common sign of conservatism.[7] Common books played a significant role in this coalescence. Conservative writer Rich Lowry remembered that citations in *National Review* led him "to certain books, which led in turn to more books." He started with "the basics": *The Conscience of a Conservative, Up from Liberalism,* and *The Conservative Mind.*[8]

The canon, I argue, creates and manages the potential for symbolic *fusion* and *fracture* among conservatives. The canonization of books defending a range of philosophical commitments eased the fusion of dissimilar and contradictory conservatisms both within and beyond the Republican Party: traditionalist and libertarian, populist and elitist, religious and secular, agrarian and corporatist, and principled and adjustable.[9] In addition to furnishing doctrinal and political resources for activists, writers, and politicians, the canon was a resonant symbol of conservative synergy as well as a constituent element of political identity. But in a larger sense, the development of a political identity with a shared history, a trove of insider references, a set of common heroes and enemies, and a repertoire of preferred argumentative forms was aided significantly by an organic canonization process in which conservatism's long-standing ideological and rhetorical traditions merged after World War II.

Although the canonization of divergent philosophical conservatisms generated versatile symbolic resources useful in fusing a political coalition, persistent differences in philosophical first principles and political priorities contributed to conservative fracture by rendering a precise definition of conservatism difficult.[10] Philosophical diversity in the movement's midcentury symbolic foundation has legitimized a protean conservatism that shifted between emphases on small government libertarianism, social tradition and the establishment of a Christian moral order, and a forceful nationalism.[11] These oscillations resulted in regular reckonings in which conservative critics lamented conservatism's leadership and published paeans about canonical wisdom. The canon has become a storehouse of symbolic capital useful in disputes over the meaning of philosophical conservatism and the direction of political conservatism.

This chapter is not an analysis of specific books per se but is a demonstration of the rhetorical function of the canon within the conservative political community as an illustration of the variety of rhetorical and political practices it enabled and constrained. I establish the central role of the canon in a decades-long controversy over conservatives' communal identity. To demonstrate the sheer variety of conservative commemorative practices, I open this chapter by detailing how conservative organizations have constituted canonical texts as a Great Books tradition within the movement. Then, I analyze two common narratives in conservative literature that exemplify the symbolic power of the canon: genesis claims with mythic depictions of founding conservatives, and vitriolic jeremiads defending the one true conservatism. I conclude by analyzing the link between the principles of classical conservatism and canonical politics.

Creating and Conserving the Canon

Like other communities, conservatives have used their canon variously as "a standard, a sublime truth, a rule, a master-work, an artistic model, and . . . a book-list for educational use."[12] These consecrated texts remain more than resources for pithy proverbs; they are primary teaching tools of conservative organizations, and audiences are encouraged to imitate what they read. Leading conservative organizations invested considerable authority in promoting canonical works both as the origin of the movement and its enchiridion. Conferences at the Heritage Foundation, seminars at the Reagan Ranch, and scores of reading lists and would-be syllabi promoted canonical works by gallant midcentury wordsmiths who forged a political movement, faced down Communism, and stemmed New Deal liberalism.[13] One 2009 panel cosponsored by the American Enterprise Institute and the National Review Institute illustrates the power conservatives attributed to their canon: "On the Ropes: What William F. Buckley Can Teach Today's Conservatives."[14] At the event, one author urged conservatives to reach back to Buckley and "the founders of modern conservatism" and "apply them to contemporary problems."[15]

In the decades since each founding book was published, conservatives have parsed the canon to reprint memorable portions in encomiums with telling titles like *Did You Ever See a Dream Walking?* (1970), *Keeping the Tablets* (1988), *The Conservative Bookshelf* (2004), and *The March of Freedom* (2004).[16] As distillations of conservative beliefs, each canonical book held doctrinal appeal. As lodestars of how to make a persuasive conservative case, each book held literary appeal. The accolades conservatives heaped on these texts and the communal events conservatives dedicated to their study suggested a talismanic appeal as well.

Contemporary conservative speakers and writers displayed fealty to postwar sources through noticeable exhibitions of canonical writers' standout terms and lines.[17] Numerous American writers have energetically updated Hayek's midcentury argument that England's planned economy denied political freedom by limiting economic freedom. These American Hayeks alleged that America was "hurtling down," "speeding down," and merely "traveling down the road to serfdom."[18] The nation's economic policies risked Keynesian malaise at best or economic despotism at worst, and Hayek's metaphor was most appropriate to describe excessive government involvement. Similarly, when surveying the state of higher education or religious freedom, Buckley's *God and Man at Yale* was the rhetorical standard; the title's basic form and rhythm remained, but the nouns did not in articles like "God and Man at Columbia," or "GOP and Man at Yale," or "God, Man, and Green at Yale," or "God and Man in the Conservative Movement."[19] The vocabulary Buckley used in 1951 to call Yale to task for abandoning its Christian roots in favor of secular humanism was a benchmark of cultural criticism, especially when impugning religious or educational decline. These were liturgical acts; they mirrored public worship rituals.

By parroting the style, tone, and topic of canonical sources, conservatives sought canonical cachet unsubtly. One writer admitted to forcing awkward "prose gyrations" in college papers in "shameless" attempts to imitate canonical writers like Buckley.[20] Alfred Regnery, a conservative book publisher, recalled assessing "no fewer than fifty manuscripts and book proposals that began, 'This book picks up where *God and Man at Yale* left off.'"[21] Conservative writers dressed their case in a canonical vernacular in more furtive ways as well. Conservative advocates bonded with knowing audiences over pedantic noms de guerre for canonical writers: Russell Kirk as "the Sage of Mecosta," William F. Buckley as "WFB" or "Chairman Bill."[22] Playful uses of enigmatic and unwieldy lines from second-tier canonical writers—Eric Voegelin's "immanentization of the eschaton" from *The New Science of Politics* (1951) was emblazoned on T-shirts and bumper stickers—indicated that even the most opaque and peripheral canonical works contained symbolic sway.[23] All told, in such a text-savvy movement culture, recitations of Kirk or Buckley demonstrated that the writer or speaker was both a knowledgeable advocate of core conservative ideas and that he or she was a willing conservationist of the movement's text-centered tradition.

Beyond references, both obvious and otherwise, conservatives have employed various commemorative practices to shepherd readers to the canon. Suggested reading lists, frequently lists that ranked canonical texts, became ubiquitous in conservative literature. Notable conservatives weighed in on the best ways to read the canon.[24] Ann Coulter, for instance, preferred to "snuggle up" with the classics in their entirety. *Witness* was her favorite.[25] Conservative magazines such as *National Review* and *Human Events* published commemorative lists like "The 100 Best Non-Fiction Books of the Century" and "The Fifty Worst (and Best) Books of the Century."[26] Conservative authors generated even more specific lists featuring canonical texts of the "Top 10 Books Liberals Want to Burn" and the "Top 10 Books Every Republican Congressman Should Read."[27] In essence, conservatives competed to commemorate canonical texts in new ways; they ranked and reranked books in comprehensive lists, subclassified and ranked within genres, and ranked by decade.

These argumentative patterns reveal a connection between the mastery of conservative political thought and proclamations of membership within the conservative community. Performing canonical proficiency signified adroit conceptual familiarity *and* genuine identity. The canon, in short, became a measure of authority and authenticity, and conservatives often displayed their rhetorical plumage. Since these texts were indelibly linked to communal identity, canonical knowledge, narratives, and rhetorical forms were valuable and fungible cultural capital. In a general sense, allusions to sanctioned sources, whether Shakespeare or *SportsCenter* depending on the community, affords both "*linguistic* capital," the ability to speak in the rhetorical forms of authorities, and "*symbolic* capital, a kind of knowledge-capital whose possession can be displayed upon request and which thereby entitles its possessor to the cultural and material rewards of the well-educated person."[28] In the conservative context, there was a performative dimension to canonicity. Adept canonical rhetoric signified both education and acculturation. Similarly, conservatives employing canonical allusions wrapped themselves in the authority of an authentic conservative identity; their politics were the natural result of internalizing not just any philosophically libertarian or traditionalist works but, more specifically, treasured books within the community's postwar textual tradition.

On the one hand, the postwar period was a galvanizing era for long-standing political traditions of the American Right.[29] Classical liberals, individualists, capitalists, defenders of civilization, religious traditionalists, states' rightists, Jeffersonian agrarians, distributists, and an assorted throng of ardent critics inveighed against New Dealism, socialism, Communism, secularism, and civil rights during the mid-century. On the other hand, the postwar period, the 1950s in particular, was a moment of tremendous change both in the creation of conservatism as a term of American political identity and, as Martin Medhurst put it, "the evolution of conservative ideas."[30]

Before World War II, rhetorical and ideological traditions like classical liberalism offered inventional resources to diffuse advocates.[31] There was not, however, any stable body of doctrines organized under a consistent political label; there was no "cohesive conservative tradition."[32] Propelled by galvanizing tracts, postwar advocates converged under the conservative banner. For members of this nascent political community, *The Road to Serfdom*, rather than William Graham Sumner's *What Social Classes Owe Each Other*, became the most valuable symbolic capital of classical liberalism; the agrarian tradition of small, rural property owners opposed to industrial capitalism was encapsulated for conservatives by *The Conservative Mind* far more than nineteenth-century English distributists like Hilaire Belloc or G. K. Chesterton. The view of America as the fulfillment of a political tradition begun in Greece, continued in Rome, and preserved by Christian societies since was voiced for postwar conservatives by Meyer's *In Defense of Freedom* more than Orestes Brownson's *The American Republic*. Before World War I, Brooks and Henry Adams wrote expansive intellectual histories that depicted the Middle Ages as a lost Eden compared with modern decay, but Richard Weaver and Eric Voegelin became the primary points of post–World War II articulation for the civilizational decline narrative.[33] In sum, formative texts helped mid-century conservatism become a symbolic junction of the historically disparate American Right by renewing, renovating, and reenergizing the rhetorical resources of its particular traditions.[34]

Older, engrained texts and traditions certainly remained vital resources for canonical writers and other conservatives. Postwar conservatives like Russell Kirk were, in fact, careful conservators of these writers' ideas. Nevertheless, these older traditions acquired a new name, new saints, new reference points, and new vocabularies. When conservatives glorified canonical texts, they glorified a political idea epitomized. Authors and their books were masters and masterpieces or, put differently, the embodiment of and metonym for conservative concepts of freedom, religion, tradition, markets, and nationalism. In celebratory discourse about the canon, books and authors were corporeal referents and material emblems for ethereal ideas. To share the book was to share the idea; discussing the idea meant citing the text. More important, citing, referencing, or republishing a canonical text meant preserving conservative political thought for a future audience. Canonical texts arranged timely cases for timeless ideals so memorably that these books were metonymic of conservative ideas, but not as simple, physical stand-ins. Canonical books were the most eloquent, thorough account of the concept, the idea in its most resplendent rhetorical form. The concept, moreover, before its postwar emblem was an inert abstraction searching for a moving rhetorical form. Like the holy tomes of religions, the text and the idea become permanently yoked for their communities. In Weaver's *Ideas Have Consequences*, a broad political idea like the preservation of tradition found, conservatives argued, its fullest, most forceful expression in Weaver's ruminations about the decline of musical tastes, language purity, the sanctity of private property, and Western civilization. When Frank Meyer dubbed

Weaver's book the *"fons et origo"* of American conservatism, he intimat-
ed that traditionalism was inchoate without *Ideas Have Consequences*
as its apotheosis.[35]

Reading like Reagan

Beginning in the postwar period, conservative writers, magazines, publishers, and organizations like Young Americans for Freedom (YAF),
the Foundation for Economic Freedom (FEE), and the Intercollegiate
Studies Institute (ISI), became dedicated to conserving conservative
ideas by introducing young conservatives to these textual totems and
guiding their reading experiences.[36] These organized efforts to nurture
what forerunning conservative Albert Jay Nock called "the Remnant,"
an elite group that would preserve the conservative case for future
generations, have continued apace.[37] Aspiring conservative politicos
have availed themselves of a variety of workshops devoted to the canon
and its famous readers. "Everywhere young conservatives turn," the
New York Times reported in 2006, "there are conferences, seminars
and reading lists that promote figures from the movement's formative
years."[38] One young participant excitedly called her monthlong experience "conservative boot camp."[39] ISI regularly convened national and
international conferences, colloquia, half-day seminars, and weekend
and weeklong retreats to discuss the enduring relevance of canonical
texts.[40] In 2005, for example, ISI invited fifty-four select undergradu-
ates for a two-week study session on "order and liberty" at Oxford organized around four anchor texts: *Witness, The Road to Serfdom, Ideas
Have Consequences*, and *The Conservative Mind*.[41]

These promotional efforts were billed as both essential to countering progressive educational trends and, more broadly, to cultivate a
new generation of intellectual conservatives capable of leading examined lives. The Young America's Foundation's reading list, prominently
displayed on its website, aimed to counter liberal pedagogy: "This list
of books is only a sampling of the best books available to help you
balance your education with conservative ideas."[42] The conservative
historian Lee Edwards made the case for rescuing students from a low,
liberal culture while he moderated the instructively titled "Great Books
to Read in College" panel at the 2009 National Conservative Student
Conference (NCSC).[43] These commemorative practices provided

models of text-centered behavior to students to school them in the movement's learned past, a Great Books tradition specific to American conservatism.

As canonical novels by Dostoevsky or Tolstoy purportedly improved the cultural literacy of the general reader, conservatives claimed that the movement's canonical texts enhanced the conservative reader's philosophical literacy. Conservatives have borrowed this cultural "uplift" argument from high culture defenders such as Matthew Arnold, F. R. Leavis, and Harold Bloom to justify preserving their version of the conservative movement's Great Books. Contemporaneous with most books of the conservative canon, Great Books of the Western World, the 32,000-page brainchild of Mortimer Adler and Robert Hutchins, appeared in 1952. This collection of 443 works by seventy-four white male writers ostensibly made the best of Western knowledge available for mass consumption.[44] Through the Great Books collection, midcentury audiences could put their jumping beans aside and get a dose of culture by entering the erudite realm of Goethe, Byron, and Hume. The connection between the midcentury marketing of the Great Books and conservatives' more recent commemoration of their canon was far from accidental. Great Books devotees and some prominent conservatives, such as Adler and Leo Strauss, shared elitist sensibilities; they cast aspersions on mass culture as a breeding ground for mob rule. Adler cotaught selected canonical works with Whittaker Chambers in a class called Renaissance and Modern Thought in 1926, and, still a disciple nearly seventy years later, he discussed the Great Books with William F. Buckley on *Firing Line* in 1993.[45]

In their efforts to mold young conservatives into eager, canon-focused readers, several conservative writers have taken cultural cues from notable aesthetes and steered audiences to "classic" conservative books that improved, or "lifted," the reader and thereby made the model conservative a sophisticated polymath.[46] Some conservatives have essentially rewritten movement-specific versions of Bloom's *How to Read and Why*, encouraging conservatives to read the right books to attain a more "capacious" sense of conservatism.[47] In so doing, they have cultivated themselves as "arbiters of bibliographic taste."[48] Dinesh D'Souza, for example, concluded his *Letters to a Young Conservative* (2002) with an Arnoldian warning: to be an "educated conservative," he wrote, aspirants must "be familiar with 'the best that has been thought and said' of modern conservative thought."[49] D'Souza, however, went a step further into the high culture lexicon and, channeling Adler's *How to Read a Book*, offered a suggested reading list for those hoping to refine their conservatism.[50]

As conservatives imbued their canon with the renown of Great Books, they also framed trailblazing conservatives as canonical disciples with the implication that the latter station caused the former condition. In *Reading the Right Books: A Guide for the Intelligent Conservative* (2007), Edwards injected conservative saints into Adler's famous compilation of reflective reading strategies from *How to Read a Book*. Edwards recalled visiting Ronald Reagan's house in 1965 and discovering "works of history, economics, and politics" in his library. Naturally, Reagan read as Adler instructed. He was no "passive reader"; the shelved books in his home, "conservative classics such as F. A. Hayek's *The Road to Serfdom*," among others, "were dog-eared and annotated, obviously read more than once."[51] Consuming the Great Books of conservatism was, by Edwards's reasoning, Reaganesque. Reagan's political legacy was intertwined with reading habits and the philosophical lessons of the canon.

Edwards's encomium to Reagan-the-reader was not anomalous. Conservative organizations located him within the canonical tradition that students could easily access. At the 2006 Young America's Foundation convention, noteworthy young activists earned membership in "Club 100." New "Club 100" members were invited to a retreat at the Reagan Ranch Center, "where the foundation conducts summer workshops instructing students in public speaking, media relations, and the fundamentals of conservative philosophy" including the writings of Goldwater, Kirk, and Buckley.[52] One Reagan Ranch lecturer informed students that Reagan "gained strength from Russell Kirk and Friedrich Hayek." In case the moral of the story was unclear, he exhorted them to follow in the footsteps of the presidential reader in order to be "as good and decent and helpful as Ronald Reagan."[53]

Scholastic retreats on liberty and order, Great Books panels at conservative student conferences, and stories about Reagan-the-reader were designed to shape the way conservative readers encountered this group of texts. Whether they read each canonical text or not, conservative audiences came across these books, as Stanley Fish puts it, "*in media res*": "they go about their business not in order to discover its point, but already in possession of and possessed by its point."[54] These authors and organizations preconstituted the canon as well as potential readers; appeals to canonical texts and their model readers established the beau ideal of the conservative sophisticate who located the core of his or her political identity in fundamental texts and who slogged through often ornate prose to find enduring conservative truths.

A Useful Canon

Two patterns in conservatives' canonical discourse reveal the varied communal uses to which the canon has been put. Some conservative stories about the canon were a kind of folklore about the movement's origins; other stories pursued a divisive revanchism and urged the purging of interlopers. All of these stories, nevertheless, were rooted in the canon, and such shared practices were essential to the creation of conservatism as a protean political experience shared through common texts. The conservative canon provided the resources for constituting the political community as well as the means to contest its boundaries.

The Genesis Claim

Ranging from recollections of Barry Goldwater's presidential campaign to the unheralded financiers of the early movement, conservative discourse was replete with tales from the postwar period.[55] One tale, however, is noteworthy because its form was replicated by many conservative writers and politicians. What I term the genesis claim was a text-centered account of the movement's post–World War II origins. Part history, part historiography, part hagiography, the genesis claim was conservatism's origin myth. Conservatism, the genesis claim stipulated, was the product of print, not a march, a protest, or a pivotal moment of persecution.[56] The claim explicitly invoked canonical texts as near-holy books penned by ideological warriors.

The argumentative structure of the genesis claim was causal, and its form was that of exaltation. *American Conservatism: An Encyclopedia* introduced its 626 entries spread over 1,000 pages noting that "postwar conservatism was launched through the publication of groundbreaking books."[57] Regnery, to take another example, thought conservative ideas languished during the midcentury before the conservative movement developed in keeping with an "old maxim" in the publishing industry: "everything starts with a hardback book." "Hayek, Mises, Buckley, Chambers, and Kirk," he asserted, framing canonical texts as causal agents, "ignited the conservative cause with books, and over the coming decades, books would be at the heart of the growth of the movement."[58] Regnery's assessment of the searing power of books was not unique. The conservative movement grew, Richard Viguerie and David Franke contended, because "avid book readers . . . acted out the title" of Weaver's *Ideas Have Consequences*.[59] In genesis claim accounts, authoring an influential book amounted to a heroic, even legendary deed.

There were small variations in the form of the genesis claim. Some advocates briefly name-checked midcentury conservatives; others gave book-by-book delineations of the role each played in fusing the conservative ideological coalition. These variations were different takes on the same story, one in which dedicated, midcentury writers connected with midcentury readers, and together they created conservatism as a self-aware political community. This founding story allowed members of the conservative ideological coalition, despite frequent fractious disagreements, to identity a common heritage and bond over shared texts.

The genesis claim exhibited both the content and structure Mircea Eliade attributes to myth. "Myth," Eliade defines, "narrates a sacred history; it relates an event that took place in primordial Time, the fabled time of the 'beginnings.'" Myths develop the "deeds of Supernatural Beings" who brought "reality into existence."[60] Myths are stories that serve a basic existential purpose, providing an account of "creation," of how a world and a community "began to *be*."[61] The repetition of the origin myth, its public performance, ritualizes those roots and signals that the performer possesses valued knowledge. Eliade explains, "He who recites or performs the origin myth is thereby steeped in the sacred atmosphere in which these miraculous events took place." Mythic recitations renew the "fabulous time" and permit the performer to summon "the presence of Gods or Heroes."[62] The performer of the origin myth conjures paragons to interpret the community's past and future.

In several conservatives' version of the genesis claim, the two decades following World War II were Eliade's "primordial Time," a portentous period featuring a disconnected, sporadic, and beaten Right. Free thought was restricted in the midcentury in this account; political ideas that did not emerge from secular, collectivist principles were shunned. Regnery depicted a condition of ideological homogeneity:

"The press, the intelligentsia, the publishing companies, the universities, and virtually all parts of the culture that disseminated ideas were left of center."[63] Other conservative chroniclers framed this stifled intellectual environment as a form of domestic totalitarianism, "the sort of monopoly enjoyed by Pravda in its Soviet heyday."[64] Conservatism's exile from political culture was compounded by a liberal, New Deal orthodoxy shared by both political parties. The Republican Party, "shaped in the luminous but nebulous image of Dwight Eisenhower," offered no recourse.[65]

With vivid details of fledgling conservatives' political desperation during the postwar era, conservative canonists enhanced the power of founding texts to the transcendent by intensifying the drama of the genesis claim. Those few daring to call themselves conservative after World War II had "no organizations," "no networks," "no voice," and "no power."[66] Like Eliade's mythic Gods, conservative founders had few resources with which to bring conservatism into existence; risking much, they composed plangent texts out of sheer will. One writer depicted the publication of these texts in salvific terms; marking the beginning of the end of their midcentury plight, these books were an "escape from bondage." Laying these intellectual foundations was, he continued, "an astonishing achievement" amid the "long reign of doctrinaire liberalism."[67] The founders composed textual talismans when conservatism's prospects were darkened by total ideological isolation.

Mirroring Eliade's notion that myths identify the founding moment of communal existence, the genesis claim advanced a causal relationship between conservative books and growing legions of conservatives. Sacred, pathbreaking tracts enabled the growth of "articulate, self-confident conservatives."[68] These genesis claims employed the tropes of epic battle sequences to amplify the competition between liberalism and conservatism into a postwar ideological war. At the last possible moment when liberalism looked most dominant, most capable of ending ideological competition in the United States, and most friendly to the nation's Soviet enemy, a band of elite ideological warriors stepped forward in revolt. A small coterie of heroic conservatives, the movement's "own greatest generation," as Edwards named them, arrived to face the "prevailing liberal orthodoxy."[69] They sought to win the war of ideas, and, outnumbered, they stocked up on ideological ammunition in preparation for a protracted siege. Regnery's rendition of the genesis story portrayed the suddenness of these heroes' daring intellectual gambit: "But then, out of the blue, during the 1940s and 1950s, a few articulate and outspoken conservatives began to challenge the status quo." Men like Hayek, Kirk, Chambers, and Buckley, "lonely" and "intrepid" men, throttled the nation's political culture by introducing conservatism in the 1950s, gained a foothold in the Republican Party by 1964, and, by 1980, saw a president elected because of ideas they developed.[70]

As these books were treated as ideological touchstones, the unprecedented and irreplaceable outcomes of single moments of inspired genius, their authors became legendary founding figures, Eliade's "Supernatural Beings," capable of producing masterpieces and much more. Genesis claim accounts reached for metaphoric language appropriate for idols. In Edwards's version of the genesis claim, postwar conservatives produced a print deluge: "Indeed, books poured forth from right-thinking men and women . . . like a mighty river."[71] Where Edwards employed naturalistic imagery, other conservatives magnified the genesis claim with martial metaphors. According to John Engler, former governor of Michigan, Russell Kirk defended the "permanent things" by brandishing the "'Sword of Imagination' against an 'antagonist world.'"[72] Other metaphoric accounts of the founders' greatness were just as martial if also more visceral. By one account, Buckley was "Braveheart lopping off the heads of one faculty lord and knight after another."[73] Other writers reached for holy metaphors figuring founding texts as Bibles and the founders as divinely inspired seeders of the gospel like Paul.[74]

Whereas conservative historiographers asserted these books' national force, first-person narratives afforded the canon considerable power in the lives of individuals. Several conservatives' odes to canonical texts exemplified the anecdotes that animated these personal versions of the genesis claim. In *Right from the Beginning* (1988), Pat Buchanan remembered how he devoted himself to canonical texts, developed an irrepressible conservative zeal, and was made anew. To depict his transformation, Buchanan borrowed the imagistic language Keats employed to describe reading Chapman's Homer: "Yet did I never breathe its pure serene/Till I heard Chapman speak out loud and bold: Then I felt like some watcher of the skies/When a new planet swims into his ken."[75] Tales like these were enculturation exercises bound within insider anecdotes and personal narratives; these stories showed conservatives the importance of testifying about the transformative power of conservative texts and ideas.[76] Reading the canon was positioned as a religious experience that changed the reader's political identity.

Many of these sample genesis claims privilege the operatic over the ideological—that is, some conservatives rehearse their origin myth quickly as an ingratiating prelude to a speech, article, or book; others, however, forwarded claims that valorized the ideological content of canonical texts more specifically. These enhanced versions featured founding deeds no less mythic in nature; conservatives recognized canonical texts as forming conservatism as a multifaceted ideology, a big tent sheltering conservatives of many types including, at least, traditionalists and libertarians.

Reagan, for instance, waxed nostalgic about the books that sparked his conversion so often that he even, in a speech to a *National Review* audience, reflected on the communal value of such rhetorical practices. He gave it a romantic name: "The Portuguese have a word for such recollection—*saudade*—a poetic term rich with the dreams of yesterday. And surely in our past there was many a dream that went a glimmering and many a field littered with broken lances."[77] In 1981, he framed his election as a "victory of ideas" rather than a "victory of politics" in a speech at the Conservative Political Action Conference. Alluding to the "fabulous time" of conservatism's founding, he recognized the founding writers for nourishing these ideas "through many grim and heartbreaking defeats."[78] Yet canonical texts for Reagan were not all conservative in the same sense. Variations in the ideological content of each signified that canonical conservatism was not monolithic. For Reagan, the founding conservatives' efforts deserved continued tribute because they both created and connected potentially separate ideological threads. The founders' works of philosophical invention as well as synthesis allowed midcentury conservatism to develop one philosophy with two manifestations in libertarianism and traditionalism, not two philosophies combined awkwardly under one name.[79]

In similar fashion, William Rusher's *The Rise of the Right* (1984) modeled the historiographic genesis claim as a mythic origin story featuring a coalition of Supernatural Beings rather than a single act of creation. Rusher used his midcentury conversion to conservatism as symbolic of the development of each camp in the "conservative triptych" of libertarians, traditionalists, and anti-Communists.[80] Beginning with libertarianism, Rusher was captivated by *The Road to Serfdom*, the

"Bible and battle cry of postwar classical liberals."[81] In the early 1950s, Chambers's *Witness* taught Rusher the same lesson Reagan learned from canonical texts: in lieu of an unwavering commitment to any first principle, conservatism meant ideological parity between liberty, tradition, and security.[82] As Rusher completed his depiction of the conservative coalition, his conversion narrative reached its final moment of clarification when the clouds parted. Kirk's *The Conservative Mind* gave him traditionalist precepts to explain his suspicion of "scientists" and his hatred of "all forms of Marxist socialism, including communism."[83] These three conservative traditions yielded Rusher a complete worldview and, as he harkened to Constantine's martial, genre-defining conversion tale, "a new sign under which to conquer."[84] His satisfaction with the "Republican" label, "whatever that meant," had worn off during his formative years, and he discarded it for something more potent. "I was something else," he wrote with a heightened sense of melodrama, "something with a longer tradition, a richer heritage, a deeper significance. I was a *conservative*."[85]

As Reagan and Rusher did, several conservative historians recount the history of postwar conservatism using canonical texts to represent the founding and fusion of conservatism as a philosophical network.[86] Although these texts insisted that conservatism was a coherent philosophy, they also framed differences among conservatives as necessary to produce a larger movement that was not philosophically slavish to any one premise. The canon became the fused doctrinal core that balanced individual freedom, social custom, and a Judeo-Christian heritage.[87] Conservatives have made sure that mythic textual memory, Reagan's *saudade*, was an important ritual in the performance of conservatism.[88]

The Canonical Jeremiad

When rhapsodized in the genesis claim, the canon fused. The genesis claim rehearsed a common history and set of founding documents for an often argumentative political community. But contemporary conservatives also used a transformed version of the genesis claim as a more divisive tool to highlight breaches separating different types of conservatives; the canon's sacred message was once written in stone, and conservatives who have departed from those truths have been called false prophets ever since. "The young men and women of the Right," one writer howled in the pages of the *American Conservative*, "aren't reading much Richard Weaver these days—nor much Robert Nisbet or Russell Kirk." "College Republicans" favored lower formulations like "'George W. Bush is My Homeboy'" instead.[89] When conservatives failed, it was not a sign that conservatism needed updating or wholesale reinvention; it needed recovery, which only happened when conservatives recommitted to "the writings of the passionate original thinkers and scholars who helped found the modern conservative movement."[90] The canon had been extolled so frequently in conservative discourse that it has become plain that following its lessons was critical to maintaining one's conservatism. Accusing other conservatives of discarding canonical texts was a potent argument that simultaneously reinforced the conservative credentials of the accuser, placed others' pedigrees in doubt, and resituated the canon as the measurement of true conservatism.[91] The canon, in short, provided the basis of another hallmark performance of postwar American conservatism: the canonical jeremiad.

A product of Puritan New England, the rhetorical form of the jeremiad followed the structure of Jeremiah's ancient plea for Jews to forsake false idols. Puritans found meaning in Jeremiah's simultaneous lamentation of communal activities and exaltation of communal traditions. The jeremiad featured a "Biblical precedent" once accepted by the community, detailed the consequences of the community's failure to stay true to the precedent, and promised a utopia if the community could return to its spiritual roots.[92] In its modern uses, the jeremiadic form allowed dissenters to encapsulate their criticisms of a community's practices within norms the community itself has sanctioned. The conservative Jeremiah was a reformer, not a revolutionary, and the people needed only to return to their roots to save the community.

Since the conservative canon included ten first-tier texts, it was a flexible standard that conservatives adopted to censure a variety of objectionable practices. Conservatives issued canonical jeremiads to critique conservatism's leadership and media culture, but, ultimately, the elasticity of the canon was exhibited by the multitude of political lessons devotees drew: axioms on limited government, justifications for increased government intervention on issues of public morality or military action, tenets on individualism, articles of an interconnected society, and teachings on the combination of social traditions and free markets.[93] Although conservative Jeremiahs blamed conservatism's drift on different impostors, the use of the canonical jeremiad by both libertarian conservatives and traditionalist conservatives demonstrates both the frequency and plasticity of the return-to-roots form.

Traditionalists isolated those canonical tracts, *God and Man at Yale*, *The Conservative Mind*, and *Ideas Have Consequences* in particular, that helped sustain the claim that conservatism privileged morality over economics. Denouncing excessive defense spending, expansions of entitlement programs, and attempts to legislate morality, libertarian conservatives chastised conservatives for backsliding from limited government lessons in canonical books like *The Conscience of a Conservative*, *Capitalism and Freedom*, and *The Road to Serfdom*. Whether these texts were selected individually or spotlighted as a group or whether original doctrinal tensions among canonical works were obfuscated or highlighted, the function was similar: the political community agreed that present practices should proceed by past principles.

Traditionalist and libertarian conservative infighters in the 2000s had one thing in common as well: conservatism, they agreed, needed to be saved from conservatives. In *Modern Age*, "the principal quarterly of the intellectual Right" since Russell Kirk founded the journal in 1957, George Panichas hoped to restore this conservatism to its traditionalist roots.[94] True conservatism, Panichas demanded, began with a reverent posture toward inherited social values; it was suspicious of mass politics, political fads, and, contra libertarianism, individual freedom. The lessons of *The Conservative Mind* and *Ideas Have Consequences* had been discarded as the formerly fixed term "*conservative*" experienced "diverse changes in meaning and value."[95] Panichas amplified his jeremiad by framing the struggle over conservatism in terms of the virgin-whore dichotomy. Traditional conservatism was pure; modern conservatism was perverse. To ignore charlatans who theorized conservatism as the pursuit of private freedom without consideration of public virtue was "to prostitute the ethos of conservatism." To allow transgressions against conservative ideals yielded to "a cheapness that not only smothers the very soul of the conservative idea but also deconstructs it beyond recognition."[96] Real conservatives were forced to compete with libertines who did not acknowledge an objective morality for control of conservatism.

Rather than entrust inherited moral standards to markets or governments, conservative politics required, Panichas argued, the active conservation of "time-tested traditions and time-honored customs." To do less would cede conservatism to the hubristic traitors.[97] As conservators of social conscience, conservatives performed a "critical function," to recommend "deliberation" and "inner searching" about what was good for society while "opportunists and nihilists" engaged an "idolatrous *Zeitgeist*" and promised to free individuals from any and all social strictures.[98] The chief lessons Panichas drew from Weaver and Kirk, the source texts he leaned on most, were of a conservatism deeply suspicious of individual freedom that tolerated political change only glacially.

This term warfare could have been avoided, Panichas explained, if conservatives learned from Richard Weaver, the "rhetorical theorist *par excellence*," that "improper changes" in the use of terms, the abandonment of "ontological referents," preceded the breakdown of civilized communities. Closer attention to Weaver's warning in *Ideas Have Consequences* may have protected conservatism from the nihilists who misappropriated conservatism as they pleased.[99] Against the "false conservatives in sheep's clothing" and their relativist morality, Panichas advocated the permanence of moral truth and the conservation of social tradition.[100]

Contrary to the traditionalist take on the canon, other conservatives mined the canon for lessons on limited government and individual freedom. George W. Bush–era conservative polemics like *Reclaiming Conservatism, Invasion of the Party Snatchers, Impostor, Conservatives Betrayed,* and *Take Back the Right* claimed that philosophical conservatism was once a gospel of individual freedom, but conservative politicians grew fat with power and the conservative movement grew lazy with age. A return to the founding ideals was necessary to rescue conservatism from social conservatives, anxious to use government to install a national religion domestically, and neoconservatives, inclined to pursue a wide-eyed quest for global democratic order.[101] The biggest factor, Michael Tanner argued in *Leviathan on the Right* (2007), in the degradation of conservatism from its individualist foundation was the idea that "big government can be used for conservative ends." Isolating his canonical heroes, Tanner concluded that the oxymoronic big-government conservatism actually "ridicules F. A. Hayek and Barry

Goldwater while embracing Teddy and even Franklin Roosevelt."[102]
Following his favored guidebooks, Tanner urged sweeping tax cuts, increasing state jurisdiction, and massive entitlement reform as quintessentially conservative remedies.[103]

Similar to Panichas's jeremiad, Tanner's book took aim at conservative factions that deviated from canonical lessons. To recover
conservatism's moorings, Tanner hoped to excommunicate "neoconservatives," "national-greatness conservatives," "the religious right,"
"supply-siders," and "technophiles." Also similar to Panichas's jeremiad,
when Tanner sketched the ideological development of these faux conservatives, he did not link them to any hallowed postwar texts.[104] They
were deviationists, pure and simple, with no claim to conservatism's
postwar ideological heritage. As Panichas did not pin pernicious libertarianism on Friedman's or Goldwater's books, texts many of his fellow conservatives idolized, Tanner's version of conservatism's postwar
origin story was a simple lesson about free markets and individualism
with no debate, discord, or extraneous interpretations of conservatism
from which later interlopers might have found inspiration. The disparate philosophical factions on the right—traditionalists, libertarians,
and others—only unified in the postwar period because of a common
belief in "small government conservatism," Tanner summarized.[105]

Panichas and Tanner's shared reluctance to impugn canonical authors and texts, even those least harmonious with their preferred conservatism, confirmed that while the jeremiad demanded social change,
it also set "limits on reform."[106] Put another way, even when used in
factional conflict, the canonical jeremiad had limited explosive potential because it left a forgiving foundation in the form of diverse texts
intact.[107] Partitioning canonical books or sequestering one founder's
ideas from those of his midcentury colleagues in order to argue for
a more streamlined conservatism was beyond the pale. Even while
pressing contentious, even sectarian, cases in jeremiadic form, these
conservatives countenanced, one tacitly, the other explicitly, a potentially multivocal canon. The canonical jeremiad was particularly important within the conservative coalition because it allowed for a process
of reflection and controlled critique within circumscribed boundaries.

Conserving Conservatism

Although the canon has inspired and given legitimacy to different schools of conservatives, its constituent books have remained, as I have shown, relatively static in the rhetoric and rituals of many prominent conservatives. The conservative canon thus contains a paradoxical balancing act between order and flexibility, permanence and reinvention. In fact, as an important part of conservatives' "Sisyphean" quest for philosophical order, the canonization of postwar texts has been an appropriate rhetorical practice for a movement that has attempted to square freedom with order.[108] Whereas the flexible and insouciant canon symbolized choice among conservative doctrines and pragmatism about their political application, the whole notion of canonized masterworks conveyed authority and order.

As flexible as the canon has been, the creation of a canon of venerated political thought resembled, in both ideological content and rhetorical practice, a classical British conservatism that predated its American counterpart. Justifications for the conservative re-creation of the Great Books replicated the watchwords of the conservatism of Edmund Burke, a conservatism whose first principle was conservation.[109] Although U.S. conservatives disagreed vociferously about whether Burke was an "appropriate patron saint," the bedrock values motivating Burke's fears of the destructive force of unguided reason, science, and political equality were safely reaffirmed in many canonical texts.[110] Independent of the doctrinal impact Burke had on some American conservatives, his concerns about a modern world that, in Kirk's gloss, "damns tradition, exalts equality, and welcomes change" mirrored the concerns that conservative canonists cited when recommending canonical texts to young readers.[111] On a basic level, canonicity itself proceeded from a respect for the conservative ideological tradition, the need to provide philosophical order to an often pliable movement, and a deferent relationship to the touchstones of prior generations. The canon, preserved in countless citations, references, and larger acts of reverence, was the vehicle by which conservatives conserved their ideological tradition. In articulating a timeless idea in moving terms—the dangerous coupling of absolute power with human frailty in the nation-state, for example—a canonical text warranted preservation. As conservative individuals and organizations repeatedly held up timeless exemplars of the wisdom of past generations, they modeled corresponding classical conservative values as well: an understanding of heritage, a social authority, and individual humility. The conservative canon, in short, was the bibliographic form of order and tradition.

As contemporary conservatives treasured postwar texts and encouraged different types of conservatives to do the same, they worked as custodians to cultivate a usable American conservative past centered on ideas and their textual exemplars. These books have been enshrined as intellectual founts because conservatives saw them as brilliant guides through dark times. As such, many conservatives argued as if their political thought risked impoverishment without rapt devotion to their ideological forbearers. Yet many conservatives did not seek to preserve tradition for tradition's sake, because of some nostalgic sentimentality, or out of blind fealty to mandarin midcentury conservatives. The diverse conservative ideological tradition was worth preserving for a more pragmatic reason: casting the classics aside meant abandoning useful rhetorical prototypes. The movement's canonical practices were direct endorsements of Harold Bloom's more artful aphorism about classical texts as intellectual models. "Without the Canon," Bloom declared, "we cease to think."[112] Conservatives afforded their own canon a similarly constitutive force; to neglect its insights was to abandon the myriad ways in which political actors could make sense of their world and still call themselves conservatives. These were texts that both formulated a doctrinal inventory for conservatives and, one conservative concluded, taught them *"how to think."*[113] One could not engage the legacy of conservative thought, much less be a thoughtful conservative, without a degree of mimicry.

CHAPTER TWO

The Traditionalist Dialect

⌘

"Am I Conservative?" was the title of Max Eastman's last *National Review* article in 1964. (The magazine's cover phrased the title a bit differently: "Max Eastman Says We Should Impeach God.") It was the first time Eastman published such an existential question about his relationship to conservatism; it was not the first time Eastman expressed grave reservations about his politics. He had a touch of political wanderlust. As a young writer, he identified as a "democratic radical," but by the time World War I broke out, he preferred "scientific socialist." When that one no longer fit, he opted for "libertarian conservative."[1] Eastman's latest label began troubling him in the 1960s because many Christians began calling themselves conservative as well. He opened his final article with the frustration of a writer who realized that the meaning of political labels changed faster than his politics did. Eastman felt immersed in a total crisis of political meaning, one he made sense of in Old Testament terms: "I find

myself somewhat bewildered in the Babel of Labels that prevails since
'Liberals' went in for the all-powerful state and 'conservatives' came
out for individual liberty."[2] At heart, Eastman was an Enlightenment
rationalist hoping to liberate individuals from the tyranny of old world
myths and arbitrary cultural hierarchies.

An early advocate of sexual liberation, woman suffrage, and any
action that did not "encroach injuriously upon the lives of others,"
Eastman was no stranger to the libertarian defense of free choice
across the board. Yet the simultaneous conservative defense of freedom *and* a transcendent universal order governing right and wrong
struck him as strange. Of these incongruous claims to freedom and
divine order, Eastman declared, "To advocate freedom, and then lay
down the law as to how men 'should' use it, is a contradiction in
terms." These pseudo-conservatives promoted an "ecclesiastical authoritarianism"; their talk of "objective moral order'" was nothing more
than "pedantic pulpiteering."[3] Eastman thought conservatives faced
a forced choice: either they accepted individual freedom in a broad
sense, relied on human reason to sort through political problems, and
pushed a scientific worldview stripped of backwards religious customs or they acknowledged an attentive God as the maker of all things,
accepted social traditions as heirlooms of accumulated wisdom, and
distrusted individual reason as a license for short-sighted hubris.
Eastman thought these factional belief systems utterly negated one
another; conservatism was not big enough for both the Enlightenment
and the Counter-Enlightenment. Eastman closed his column not
with the venom of someone with nothing left to lose but by pressing
the meaning of conservatism: "Whether a person, because his goal is
freedom for every individual, ensured by the market economy, and
protected against the incursions of an overgrown state, can be called
conservative—this is my question."[4]

The growing Christian chorus was loud enough for Eastman to
reconsider his conservative membership. Many of conservatism's most
popular midcentury writers were "heavily Roman Catholic, Anglo-
Catholic, or critical of Protestant Christianity."[5] "God or Man" was how
Whittaker Chambers saw the Cold War.[6] Buckley's breakout study of
Cold War politics on a smaller scale, *God and Man at Yale*, made only
a minor change to the refrain.[7] Buckley's and Chambers's point was
clear enough; for many conservatives, politics was inescapably intertwined with religion. Eastman feared that conservatism was becoming

dominated by theocrats and technophobes insisting on "an emotional turning back on all subjects, to Edmund Burke, and beyond Burke to the Middle Ages?"[8] He left *National Review* on good terms.[9] For all his political meanderings, one belief remained intact throughout his fifty-year public career: Eastman was an "impious moralist whose politics needed no invisible means of support."[10]

When Eastman asked whether conservatism stood firm against the state or turned back to the Middle Ages, he assumed that it could not tolerate doctrinal contradiction. He assumed that what was true of the part must be true of the whole; religious tropes must represent essential conservatism. "Sooner or later," Jeffrey Hart wrote, "the question had to arise of whether it was possible to be conservative *without* being religious."[11] Eastman's defection raised the question, and Buckley felt compelled to answer it. Addressing the Eastman affair in *National Review*, Buckley acknowledged the conflict within conservatism but disagreed about the import of contradiction. Buckley was not doctrinaire, and walls were not his preferred method of policing the borders of conservatism. Careful to note natural boundaries where the soil changed, he responded to Eastman's defection by issuing an encyclical on conservatism and religion.[12] Buckley's Golden Rule on religion held that conservatives did not have to be religious, but conservatives must not despise religion.[13] In essence, Buckley proclaimed that the meaning of conservatism was both communal and doctrinal; he welcomed a broad conservative alliance, including atheists, as long as its members welcomed one another. "The freeway," he wrote, "remains large, large enough to accommodate very different players with highly different prejudices and techniques."[14]

Buckley's easy tolerance was an effective coalition-building tactic, but it did not eliminate the possibility of a libertarian-traditionalist schism. When conservatism is treated as an identity with a set of expressions adherents protect, controversies like the Eastman affair resemble linguistic controversies that pit users of an evolving language against one another. Which side had claim to the purest expression of conservatism? Eastman's resignation and Buckley's proclamation were pivotal moments in the development of conservatism, but each also highlights a significant concept in the operation of political languages: dialects. Libertarians of Eastman's ilk and traditionalists like Russell Kirk and Richard Weaver represented different performances of conservatism that have coexisted uneasily since World War II. To highlight the competition between these two internally consistent symbolic systems, I treat traditionalism and libertarianism as separate dialects within the conservative political language. The traditionalist and libertarian argot makes it possible for conservatism to contain distinct sets of ideas and for the conservative community to venerate different books within a larger canon.

Libertarians and traditionalists engaged one another in a profound argument over human nature, the most basic element of any political theory. This argument was conducted in a dialect unique to each camp whose key phrases were derived from separate canonical sources. Each camp held such antithetical conceptions of human beings, their tendencies, their desires, their abilities, and their organization that each side generated different vocabularies and argumentative styles as well as assigned dissonant meanings to terms in common usage like freedom, tradition, individual, community, God, and government. To detail how varied dialects may perform the same political identity and exist in the same political language, chapters 2 and 3 feature an economy of the traditionalist and libertarian dialects. Each chapter delves deeply into the fretwork of traditionalist and libertarian books and their standout phrases in order to track two symbolic trajectories within conservative rhetoric.[15] All told, these two chapters explicate durable rows from the midcentury that have, when inflamed, threatened the survival of the conservative coalition but, when managed, have provided conservatives a versatile set of traditionalist and libertarian rhetorical resources.

This division of a larger political language into constituent dialects borrows basic ideas about the structure of language from linguistics without transposing a linguistic framework onto political languages. To clarify, I do not inventory the traditionalist or libertarian dialects by cataloguing linguistic components like diphthongs, triptychs, or their grammar. One learns a political dialect, I suggest, by learning an argumentative pattern, not an inflective one. To analyze a dialect within a larger political identity as opposed to a larger formal language is to attend to frequently invoked topics, lines of argument, dictums, and narratives of a subgroup within a political movement or organization.

More fundamentally, dialects maintain distinct vocabularies composed of, as Richard Weaver named them, "god terms," sacrosanct words with the "capacity to demand sacrifice," and "devil terms," vehicles for communal contempt of a repulsive enemy that may also fulfill a "tribal need for a scapegoat."[16] The traditionalists' favored terms—

"tradition," "hierarchy," "order," and "transcendence"—were not shared by speakers of the libertarian dialect, which repeated a different set of terms: "freedom," "liberty," "reason," "individual," and "markets." These recurrent terms have relatively clear points of origin in canonical texts. Central terms of the traditionalist dialect, words like "tradition" or "order," might become central in the wider political language, but these develop in a niche network of far more obscure and specialized terms, references, and lines of argument that fewer are fluent in. Advancing an argument about, for example, the decline of Western civilization while quoting Weaver's *Ideas Have Consequences* as source material signified two types of group membership simultaneously, a conservative argument rendered via the traditionalist patois.

The Hedgehog Argument

Isaiah Berlin began *The Hedgehog and the Fox*, an extended meditation on two competing theories of history, by quoting the ancient Greek poet Archilochus: "'The fox knows many things, but the hedgehog knows one big thing.'"[17] What Berlin was after, by way of examining Tolstoy's *War and Peace* and Joseph de Maistre, the French royalist, was a distinction between a view of history that saw events unfolding according to a pattern and those that regarded history as merely one thing after another. A "great chasm," Berlin wrote, separated hedgehog historians' "single central vision" and fox historians who were guided by "no single moral or aesthetic principle."[18] Conservatives have noticed the prominence of hedgehog arguments among traditionalist canonical writers and their acolytes; they searched endlessly for a "Big Idea" or "Holy Grail" to explain politics, culture, and history.[19] Some traditionalists, for example, even describe their entire philosophical enterprise as premised on "the demonstrable existence of *Absolute Truth* and *Absolute Power* forever unchanged and unchanging" that was communicated to humans "by natural law" and "Divine Revelation."[20]

The traditionalist dialect was typified by what I, following Berlin, call the hedgehog argument, an assertion of one core truth that explained the sweep of history and a tragic narrative about the collapse of that truth in the modern world. This hedgehog argument about the rise and fall of a sacred political value was accompanied by pinpoint historical claims identifying falls from grace as well as a nostalgic sense that life was lived better in premodern times. Before demonstrating how each traditionalist canonical text employed hedgehog language, in this section I sketch the dialect as a whole.

Traditionalists, chiefly Russell Kirk, Richard Weaver, Eric Voegelin, Willmoore Kendall, Robert Nisbet, and Leo Strauss, took it as axiomatic that totalitarianism had a spiritual cause.[21] Kirk credited Voegelin with identifying "the great line of division in modern politics," and it was not between the local and the national or the indigenous and the institutional. It did not, Kirk summarized, divide authoritarians and libertarians, groups that differed over the amount of individual freedom desirable in a polity. Instead, the line fell "between all those who believe in some sort of transcendent moral order, on one side, and on the other side all those who take this ephemeral existence of ours for the be-all and end-all—to be devoted chiefly to producing and consuming."[22] When those who refused to accept a universal moral order pronounced God dead, the resultant anarchy made them vulnerable to absolutist secular religions.

The traditionalists, "New Conservatives" in 1950s parlance, were coiners of eccentric phrases, and popularizers of murky terms, each of which became the telltale hedgehog rhetoric of traditionalism. "Immanentizing the eschaton," "Gnosticism," "nominalism," and the "permanent things" coincided with less offbeat language of authority and truth; each was a different name for the same thing: metaphysics was the heart of politics, and everything else was symptomatic. Unlike the libertarian dialect that was bisected by skeptical and absolutist versions, the traditionalist dialect was consistent; it performed what it preached: order and stability. Each traditionalist byword derived from these six foundational writers could be substituted for the other without marking much doctrinal or rhetorical distance. The hedgehog argument was made with words that refused context, opposed contingency, and denoted objective forces independent of eras, cultures, or individual perceptions.[23] Edwin Feulner, president of the Heritage Foundation, wrote in this stead when he portrayed conservatism as a basic law of nature: "The conservative case for freedom and markets, virtue and families, has been proven like Copernicus's case for the movement of the earth: because it corresponds to the unavoidable reality."[24] Whether one sought to understand the reorganization of Europe after the Treaty of Westphalia, the ascension of Enlightenment thought, or twentieth century fascism, the one big truth illuminated virtually any period of social change.

For all their universalist language, traditionalist writers, as the name implied, also celebrated social traditions, a concept tethered to ideas of particularity, locality, even relativism. Put simply, different communities erected different traditions to address particular political and social controversies; to understand the possibilities for political change within a society, one must take inventory of the local traditions, the resources through which a culture made sense of its world. A static conception of human nature, however, was embedded within the traditionalists' language of local tradition. Communal folkways were shaped by universal human needs. The central organizing principles of traditional communities, "family, religious association, and local community" in Nisbet's language, were not rational innovations of individual minds; these were natural outgrowths of the human condition, how we were meant to live.[25] Communal and familial bonds were "essentially prior to the individual" and provided the "indispensable supports of belief and conduct."[26] A society organized by individual pursuits may be seductive, but the a priori need for specific forms of kinship was ineradicable.

The traditionalist rationale for local traditions thus blurred and merged with universal ideals. Traditionalists often treated tradition and religion as indistinct, as if traditions were imbued with divine designs. As Kirk wrote, "All culture arises out of religion."[27] Social order was preserved by a "fixed social hierarchy sanctioned by divine will."[28] Political systems could be judged by the values they encouraged, even enforced, among the citizenry. For Kirk, spiritual values were separate from and opposed to material ones, and any political change could be judged by the side it veered to most clearly.

In contrast to the libertarians, the free individual was not the traditionalists' end game. Individuals had in their basic constitution a capacity for folly and excess but also a deeply felt desire for direction and regulation. All communities, traditionalists thought, regulated individual conduct to some extent; it was only a question of the regulator. Communities, at least the premodern kind traditionalists pined for, were composed of rigid classes in which each person knew his or her place; they were headed by aristocrats who provided behavioral exemplars for the community and who carried a sense of noblesse oblige to protect the lesser lot. The central role of the church provided additional order; the community orbited the church, and religious customs and rituals structured daily life.

Traditionalists' respect for the ordering power of social hierarchy sprung from their understanding of the needs of a properly functioning society. Societies were fragile ecosystems, not just an assemblage of individuals who happened to live in close proximity. Society was, as Berlin described this view, "a thick, opaque, inextricably complex web of events, objects, characteristics, connected and divided by literally innumerable unidentifiable links—and gaps and sudden discontinuities too, visible and invisible."[29] Societies risked social stability and engaged a fanciful cult of individual power by assuming that changing old traditions was the logical, forward-thinking response to new and difficult circumstances. Tides of change arose and washed away old habits, customs, and political norms whose functions may have been both vital and non-obvious, like removing a fence without knowing its original purpose.[30] The proper posture toward society as a whole was to treat all of its parts as organically interconnected; upsetting one instrument could throw off the entire operation.

The traditionalists treated society as a somewhat mysterious, inexplicable organism; they treated individuals as simple and predictable. All individuals had a feverish need for order, and, as per Voegelin and Nisbet, without genuine religious order, individuals accepted impersonal, violent, and centralized order. A social vacuum was created in the absence of traditional communities, and primal human desires for meaning and order manifested in self-destructive pursuits. Nisbet, who distinguished between two types of social restraints, genuine "authority" and coercive "power," saw the two as linked.[31] "Power arises only when authority breaks down," he summarized. Minus a godhead, humans made gods out of demagogues; flights of revolutionary fervor took the place of real communal connections; cults of personality filled religious voids. Individuals needed something from above to give meaning to the seemingly random, to explain both good fortune and suffering, to afford life a purpose, something, ultimately, to lean on. Spectacular displays of state power provided the order and structure that humans craved, and individuals gave in to "political mysticism" driven by unprecedented "fanaticism."[32] More mindful of aphoristic appeal than his like-minded contemporaries, T. S. Eliot, Kirk's idol and friend, put the choice between communal restraint and outright terror most succinctly: "If you will not have God (and He is a jealous God) you should pay your respects to Hitler or Stalin."[33]

When individuals became enchanted by their own powers and arrogant enough to assume that the inscrutable and inexplicable were transparent and antiquated, they convinced themselves they understood true community and ended up, rather quickly, destroying it. This twentieth-century traditionalist position followed in the vein of the French counterrevolution. Maistre chalked up the failure of the Jacobin revolution to, in Berlin's words, "the incurable impotence of human powers of observation and of reasoning, at least when they function without the aid of the super-human sources of knowledge— faith, revelation, tradition, above all the mystical vision of the great saints and doctors of the Church."[34] In contrast to the Enlightenment-Communist-liberal call for progress and liberation, the traditionalists' ideal individual was demure. Their "hero" knew that hubris had unpredictable consequences. The traditionalists' idealized individual was obedient, but to the extent that this timidity was trumpeted by traditionalist writers, the individual acquired a bifurcated character, both righteous and self-denying.[35]

Traditionalists, accordingly, adapted a view of history that minimized the power of individual choice. Whereas historical materialists or hard determinists might position economic resources or technology as the prime cause of historical change, traditionalists' one big idea held that ideas were history's prime movers. Weaver's much referenced title, *Ideas Have Consequences*, was the argument in its simplest form. Ideas acted; they took hold of individuals, even entire cultures. Once an idea ensnared a culture, it guided the habits and practices of both adherents and the apolitical alike. Like a self-replicating virus, influential ideas reproduced themselves over generations to better suit the emotional needs or political environment of cultures and nations.

To write as a traditionalist was to write about great dichotomous contests of ideas—individualism versus tradition, secularism versus religion, and so on—but it also meant writing from the position of the vanquished. That is, the one big idea, the hedgehog truth, had been desecrated. Although traditionalists hoped that local, hierarchically organized communities respectful of timeworn traditions could be restored, traditionalism was not a hopeful dialect generally. Traditionalists' cherished beliefs had been eclipsed, and they fought on as lost cause warriors. To that end, they employed a surfeit of pessimistic words like "decay," "rotting," "demise," and the ever-present "decline" to describe a contemporary age that was both drunk with decadence and moribund. They chafed against the prurience of their era and urged the restoration of values from a bygone premodern age that was more reverent, more religious, and less consumptive.

The traditionalists belonged to a generation of critics, not just on the right either, who looked upon the wreckage of World War I, World War II, and the bloody interwar years and judged the whole era a natural conclusion to intellectual and scientific trends since the Enlightenment.[36] The transformation of farm fields into bloodlands was quickened because scientific advances produced unprecedented killing powers. Ancient architectural heirlooms were ruined in the blink of a modern eye. Across Europe, entire populations were ripped apart, extricated, or exterminated. The idea that an entire era had lost touch with core human values, principles that might make for a stable, peaceful coexistence, became attractive to those who saw Hitler, Stalin, and mechanized mass destruction as symptomatic of a deep emptiness in the modern human experience.

The midcentury traditionalists' declinism was also an inherited rhetorical tradition as old as the word "conservative."[37] The notion that the "Western world" was in "rapid decay" was, as Berlin described, first crafted by "Roman Catholic counter-revolutionaries" who considered the French Revolution "as a divine punishment visited upon those who strayed from the Christian faith and in particular that of the Roman Church."[38] To implore cultural rot in the twentieth century, however, raised the issue of its origins. When, precisely, did the rot start? Maistre and other conservatives of Europe's revolutionary era blamed the cult of reason and its hostile anticlericalism for the excesses of the French Revolution. When Kirk called the automobile a "mechanical Jacobin," he carried on the legacy of conservative reaction even while imploring technology of the Industrial Revolution.[39] Other traditionalist conservatives theorized answers of pinpoint historical specificity, which touched off a somewhat competitive affair to see who could locate the first moment when the premodern ideological edifice began to decay because of an insidious idea.[40] Locating the very first articulation of this idea, its absolute point of origin, became a traditionalist penchant.

Three traditionalists in particular, Strauss, Weaver, and Voegelin, posited clear historical division points, B.C. to A.D. shifts gone horribly wrong. Strauss tracked the transition from natural law to natural rights back to Nicolo Machiavelli and Thomas Hobbes.[41] To understand the roots of Renaissance heresy and Enlightenment impiety, Weaver reached back to medieval England. He identified the destructive root idea, nominalism, as well as a chief culprit, William of Occam, on whom the downfall of the Western world could be pinned.[42] As far as Voegelin was concerned, Weaver's division point was a millennium late. Before attacking medieval thinkers, Voegelin theorized the origins of modernity in the irreverence of Gnostic Christians of the second century.[43]

Arthur Schlesinger Jr. dismissed the "New Conservatism" of the early 1950s, with all its fondness for distant yesteryears, as "the politics of nostalgia" and the "ethical afterglow of feudalism."[44] Schlesinger was on to something fundamental about traditionalism, even if he was not a political ally. "Adherence to the old and tried, against the new and untried," as Abraham Lincoln once put it, was a vital component of traditionalism.[45] With frequent and radical change figured as flirtations with Jacobinism, several prominent conservatives affirmed that "the traditionalist conservative's first feeling . . . is the sense of *loss*, and hence, of *nostalgia*."[46] Although Nisbet intended no "lament for the old" or "nostalgia for village, parish, or other type" of past social arrangement when he juxtaposed the "corporate church," "extended family," and "village community" of the Middle Ages to individualist, statist Enlightenment, his comparison was heavily tilted in favor of the medieval and against the modern; he strummed the same nostalgic chords other traditionalists did.[47] He looked fondly on a premodern "orthodoxy" with the power "to inspire and integrate" communities through "ritual and symbolism."[48]

Traditionalists generally did not use this nostalgia to recommend turning back the historical clock or restoring the entire social organization of a former age both root and branch.[49] "Maistre," Berlin explained, "sighs for the Dark ages," but he did not really think the status quo ante could be copied, only modeled.[50] The same was true of Strauss, Weaver, and Voegelin. Each located historical division points, exact moments of decline, but each spent little effort defending the lost order of feudal Europe or Bishop Irenaeus's Roman Gaul with any specificity. For Kirk and Weaver, erstwhile students of the Southern Agrarians, the antebellum American South also loomed as a lonely modern example of ancient social practices, but, in *Ideas Have Consequences* and *The Conservative Mind*, neither explored this affection as thoroughly as they did in other books.[51] In the end, their canonical works leaned on a cultivated allure of feudal and southern traditions to lament a lost order without recommending their revivification.

In sum, the traditionalist dialect was a symbolic system composed of Manichaean opposites: decadent modernity and austere premodernity, the virtuous community and the sinful individual, and faith versus reason. For all the traditionalists' declinist, nostalgic rhetoric and identification of fixed historical division points, traditionalism was less a whole-hearted call to restore a past age and more an argumentative style reliant on the aura of an unpretentious, orderly past. It was not that traditionalists actually desired ancient forms of anesthesia, although some came close to Luddism. Goaded to greater and greater "progress" and abetted by scientific "advances," hubristic and imperial modern civilizations mutilated the social fabric. A pious orientation toward the world, one reverent of social authority, could be regained despite rampant individualism, unbridled consumerism, and coercive egalitarianism.

Gnosticism

In 2002, conservatives marched together, but not in lockstep, in the national debate over the legalization of gay marriage. In a rebuke of several conservatives' support for gay marriage rights, *National Review* editor Jonah Goldberg paused for reflective explanation: "My position on homosexuality might lead some folks to charge that I am *immanentizing the eschaton*."[52] Goldberg reached deep into traditionalism's rhetorical inventory and selected a phrase whose nine syllables and foreign sound had simultaneously confused and intrigued *National Review* readers for decades. Encountering articles with coy uses of the phrase, particularly when *National Review* writers made sport of accusing one another of "insufficiently deimmanentizing the eschaton," the magazine's readers routinely queried about the shibboleth's meaning and origin.[53] Eventually, organizations like the Young Americans for Freedom marketed the torturous phrase as a showy slogan on bumper stickers and other conservative paraphernalia.[54]

The bulky arrangement was, after all, a fancy way of decrying human attempts to build a heaven on earth to perfect themselves, their social order, or their political system. "Immanent" meant earthly achievement; "eschaton" meant pinnacle or end point. In total, the phrase denoted a foolish pursuit of perfection in the here and now, the blowback from dreaming fantastical dreams. The opposite of an immanentized eschaton was the humble recognition of a transcendent eschaton that awaited sinners who earned an escape from a sinful world. Or, as Buckley, who frequently borrowed the phrase, explained in *The Unmaking of a Mayor* (1966), "Conservatives believe that there are rational limits to politics, that politics should not . . . attempt to 'immanentize the eschaton.'"[55]

"Immanentize the eschaton" seeped into the wider conservative political language alongside a related term with similarly obscure origins: "Gnosticism." Demonstrating their tandem usage, Goldberg explained that modern liberals shared an ideological heritage with ancient Gnostics. Both "had figured out God's plan"; both believed they could "perfect the inherently imperfectible"; both were "very, very smug and more than a little annoying."[56] Gnostics held a naive faith in the possibilities for human advancement and, accordingly, used the power of the nation-state to immanentize the eschaton.

Gnosticism and its knotted, sidekick phrase were bound firmly within the traditionalist dialect because they expressed a centuries-old argument, faith before reason, in terms unique to a specific political subcommunity and its canonical literature that was rich with communal capital. But these terms were not of Buckley's making, and they did not originate in *National Review* or from a masthead writer's pen. Their author was a German-born émigré, Eric Voegelin, whose *The New Science of Politics* (1952) contributed mightily to the development of traditionalism alongside more "seminal thinkers," Kirk and Weaver, and their standout tracts, *Ideas Have Consequences* and *The Conservative Mind*.[57] Voegelin, who was later friendly with both Hannah Arendt and Strauss, was schooled in the United States during the 1920s. He took classes with John Dewey and studied the work of George Santayana. He left the United States a firm antiracist and published two books, heretical in *Anschluss* Austria, attacking the "scientific" study of race. Voegelin was spirited away by train while Nazi authorities searched his apartment in 1938.[58]

If Voegelin shared anything in common with fellow European intellectual transplants to the United States such as Hannah Arendt, Max Horkheimer, and Theodor Adorno, it was that ideas were not epiphenomenal to events: entire nations, even epochs, could be hoisted on their own ideational petards. In a few of his completed books, most notably *The New Science of Politics*, Voegelin sought to find the primary source of Western degeneration after the tumult of two world wars in thirty years. Although he styled his cultural criticisms with considerably less panache than other conservatives of the age, *The New Science of Politics* was an important part of a larger midcentury merger between Christianity and Cold War politics. From rising church membership to the addition of "under God" to the Pledge of Allegiance to the increasing visibility of Fulton J. Sheen, Norman Vincent Peale, C. S. Lewis, and Billy Graham, the early 1950s was a hotbed for religio-political ideas.[59] In this religious climate, *Time* devoted an unheard-of five pages to investigate what the magazine called "pre-Gnostic views of the world."[60]

Although *The New Science of Politics* was a convoluted text comprised of multiclaused sentences thick with philosophical nomenclature, its basic point was plain enough: Voegelin distinguished the ideal political order in classical Greek and Judeo-Christian political theory from that of modernity. In one of his abstruse lines, Voegelin explained, "The attempt at constructing an *eidos* of history will lead into the fallacious immanentization of the Christian eschaton."[61] Modernity, Voegelin claimed, was a sort of "dreamworld" that existed parallel to but not in accordance with reality in which there were limits to human achievement.[62] Gnosticism was Voegelin's hedgehog legend, his key to understanding cycles of war and authoritarianism.[63]

In 1945, just a few years before Voegelin laid every conceivable modern disaster at Gnosticism's door, a young Egyptian boy's accidental desert find set off a spiritual and scholarly conversation about the Gnostics, an early Christian sect scattered throughout the Middle East and North Africa. While collecting fertilizer, the fourteen-year-old Muhammad Ali Samman found several parchments that became the Nag Hammadi, or Gnostic, gospels. New gospels such as Thomas and Truth contained stories of Jesus's death and resurrection that affirmed not sin and the need for redemption but "enlightenment overcoming ignorance and suffering."[64] The Gnostics did not perceive humanity and divinity as separate. They believed that through secret knowledge, or gnosis, individuals could directly access divinity. Human divinity was caged within mortal bodies by an evil creator deity.[65] These gospels also challenged other Christian norms; Mary Magdalene was celebrated as a church leader; God was feminine; the Apocalypse of Peter reversed the conclusion of Mark by portraying Jesus "glad and laughing on the cross."[66] These stories, to say the least, have not become Sunday morning lessons.

Among other long-held notions that the discovery of the Gnostic Gospels upended was the treatment of Bishop Irenaeus's second century *Adversus Haereses* (Against Heresies) as the authoritative source for understanding Gnostic Christianity. "Gnostic" meant one who "knows" or "seeks experiential insight," but Irenaeus thought of them as "people claiming to 'know it all.'"[67] Irenaeus likely knew of the Gnostic gospels of Judas and Thomas as well as the Gospel to the Egyptians.[68] Suspicious of Christian communities finding different lessons in different gospels, he insisted on canonization to control Christianity's message. He was the first to insist on "only *four* gospels, not more and not fewer."[69] As Elaine Pagels and Karen King explain, "Irenaeus planted the seeds of what would become the Christian New Testament by arguing that 'orthodox' believers must read during worship only books that he and other bishops approved; others, which he called 'secret, illegitimate' books, were to be rejected like poison—for heresy, he admonished, can draw people away from the truth."[70]

Voegelin gravitated toward Irenaeus's authoritative insistence on a singular religious experience as an antidote to the social disintegration of his lifetime. He used Irenaeus's terms to decry the political climate of the modern world. The "growth of Gnosticism," Voegelin proclaimed, was the "essence of modernity."[71] Modern Gnostic practices varied in operation, but a central theme predominated. Whether Gnosticism was a "primarily intellectual" conception of humanity and divinity or the destructive politics of "revolutionary activists like Comte, Marx, or Hitler," its basic aim was reversing the biblical "fall" without looking to God.[72] Irenaeus's rebuke of Gnostics closely resembled the traditionalist attack on the Left nearly 2,000 years later. Pagels and King paraphrase, "You think that you are saved because of your spiritual nature and heavenly origin, so you don't need faith in Christ. Instead, you claim to have special knowledge revealed to you alone."[73] This argument both lauded the humble citizen who knew her or his station and denied that scientific, authoritative knowledge could be possessed by anyone. To Voegelin, the spread of scientific knowledge was tantamount to "the redivinization of society." Those who fell prey to its appeal substituted "faith in the Christian sense" for self-worship.[74]

Voegelin traced several high points of antiauthoritarian Gnosticism through the Middle Ages and the Enlightenment, but he was not interested in the general intellectual history of these periods as much as he was in chronicling the destruction of piety. *The New Science of Politics* was a comprehensive genealogy more than an exhaustive history of Western civilization. The lessons of first-century heretics were periodically revived over the next two millennia and extended radically during the Reformation, the Renaissance, and the Enlightenment.[75] In a characteristically panoptic hedgehog line, Voegelin linked social classes across countries and centuries by their shared Gnosticism: "In the early phases of modernity they were the townspeople and peasants in opposition to feudal society; in the later phases they were the progressive bourgeoisie, the socialist workers, and the Fascist lower middle class." The rise of the scientific method in the sixteenth and seventeenth centuries was, in his historical narrative, "the symbolic vehicle of Gnostic truth," and it "reached its extreme when the positivist perfector of science replaced the era of Christ by the era of Comte."[76] Western Christian society, Voegelin theorized to the delight of traditional Catholic intellectuals in the postwar period, was based originally on the organizing principle that the "pope and emperor" were "supreme representatives in both the existential and the transcendental sense."[77] The Catholic culture of Christ—reverent, ritualistic, hierarchical, and mediated—was toppled by the scientific culture of Comte, empiricist, nihilistic, individualistic, and anarchic.

Although Voegelin gave no quarter to many religious and scientific thinkers, especially Comte and the Gnostics, he tried a specific culprit for reintroducing dormant Gnostic ideas in the Middle Ages. Voegelin faulted Joachim of Flora, a twelfth-century theologian, for the annihilation of church hierarchy and social authority in later centuries. Joachim was a debauched Gnostic legatee; he represented a pivotal inflection point in the spread of Gnosticism, a historical actor who preserved and expanded an ideological system for future inheritors. He took the dispersed theological musings of an ancient Christian cult and transformed them into fuel for the entire Reformation. Although Voegelin did not specifically fault Joachim for the dissolution of Henry VIII's marriages, Martin Luther's theses, the destruction of England's monasteries, or the rise of Protestantism, he lamented Joachim's role in creating a world in which a destabilizing Reformation became a distinct possibility. Joachim's idea that the "spiritually perfect" could "live together without institutional authority" became an infinitely variable idea fomenting everything from "Renaissance sects," to Puritan churches, to democratic credos, forward to the "Marxian mysticism of the realm of freedom and the withering away of the state."[78]

The religious culture of the Middle Ages was a check against social disharmony. Voegelin "valued the power of religion itself as a vitalistic force shaping human society, a force that could be directed to good ends so long as its proper function was respected." Religion fulfilled a preprogrammed psychological need; minus formal religion, societies turned to "grotesque secular deities like Hitler, Stalin, and Mussolini."[79] As Voegelin put it, once Gnostic societies "sacrifice God to civilization" their leaders, always "divine redeemers" promising followers they will inherit the world, were free to deal with enemies "with a bullet in the neck."[80] Voegelin's political theory was clearly a Christian political theory rather than a generic, more tepid endorsement of the social value of any religion. Nevertheless, although he called himself a "pre-Reformation Christian," Voegelin never identified and defended a particular Christian theological program as an alternative to secular "political religions" like Communism or fascism.[81] His admiration of the Christian Middle Ages or Irenaeus's world was explicit but undeveloped.

When he partially specified the biblical roots of "the oldest wisdom" or cycles of "growth and decay," he turned to Ecclesiastes: "To every thing there is a season, And a time to every purpose under heaven: A time to be born and a time to die."[82] It is safe to say that Voegelin's Christianity was not a midcentury version of a prosperity gospel in which God rewarded those who worked hard; to him, Christianity demanded recognition of one's station and, eventually, an acceptance of suffering. The church offered few comforts, no ready salves for sick souls, and the Christian pilgrim's progress was measured only in time's passage. In dense prose, Voegelin posited, "The soteriological truth of Christianity, then, breaks with rhythm of existence; beyond temporal successes and reverses lies the supernatural destiny of man, the perfection through grace in the beyond."[83] Put differently, obeying a properly Christian worldview meant casting a suspicious eye toward political gains or scientific achievements because the fate of faithful individuals was to achieve perfection in heaven. Christianity's great teaching, one that Voegelin wanted to sustain, was that blessed eternity awaits the faithful. The faithful must also wait for eternity.

Revelation

Voegelin's division of politics into a war between the here and the hereafter aligned perfectly with the hedgehog arguments of other conservatives writing in the early 1950s. Buckley remembered that the most
"galling" line of his *God and Man at Yale*, published one year prior to
The New Science of Politics, made the intellectual environment at Yale
a combat zone in the global war between God and man. Buckley declared, *"I believe that the duel between Christianity and atheism is the
most important in the world. I further believe that the struggle between
individualism and collectivism is the same struggle reproduced on another level."*[84] Like Voegelin, the young Buckley encouraged readers to
reduce manifold political disputes of the era to the choice Eve faced
in the Garden of Eden. This most hedgehog notion was suggested by
his mentor, Willmoore Kendall. Buckley knew the line would provoke
"difficulty," but he let it pass because "there was a nice rhetorical resonance and an intrinsic, almost nonchalant suggestion of an exciting
symbiosis."[85] That Kendall would prod Buckley to dramatize his first
book with stark terms inspired by Voegelin was hardly a coincidence.[86]
Voegelin was not just a mirror of other argumentative practices of the
age. His influence on Kendall, as well as on Buckley and wider conservatism, was direct and indelible.[87]

Kendall was a bona fide original, and not just among conservatives. After publishing *John Locke and the Doctrine of Majority Rule* as
a young professor, Kendall came to Yale a political theorist with a formidable reputation; he did much to sully it during his stay. The "wild
Yale don" never threatened interlocutors with a fire poker as Ludwig
Wittgenstein purportedly did; he did, however, argue first principles
with such ferocity that Yale paid him *not* to work every other year.[88]
When Yale and Kendall could not continue their uneasy partnership,
the institution bought out his tenure.[89] To Yale, it was worth the steep
price because Kendall, Buckley confirmed, was a "most unmanageable
human being."[90]

The same passion for heated argument that often repulsed his
colleagues at Yale and *National Review* drove Kendall's desire to be
"the theoretician of the American conservative movement."[91] In *The
Conservative Affirmation* (1963), Kendall based much of his conception of a society organized by conservative political theory on Voegelin's
earlier work. Like Voegelin, he understood politics as a binary: tran-

scendent metaphysics versus immanent empiricism.[92] He phrased Voegelin's ideas slightly differently; "reason" versus "revelation," Kendall wrote, was "*the* issue at stake" in American politics.[93] Kendall's book, unlike *The New Science of Politics*, was a work of political theory rather than history. His premise was that open democratic societies in which evidence was judged by scientific standards were intolerant of arguments based on revealed truth. If John Stuart Mill had his way, religion would have no public influence. If every question was settled through debate, every claim tested by empirically verifiable evidence, then there was no room for revelation. To him, Moses would have been shunned as a lunatic because he could not *prove* God's presence atop Mount Sinai. Empiricists spurned "Revelation" and "Authority" as modes of proof; the principle of falsifiability denied all religion.[94]

Kendall's ideal polity was organized around a common moral commitment. It was, in essence, more a cause than a society, and that cause was weakened by skepticism and debate. Fittingly, Kendall characterized the U.S. Constitution as "all sail and no anchor."[95] In other words, the Constitution furnished a legal and political process of competitive debate without specifying the point of forming a nation in the first place. Reason needed moral guidance; it needed grounding in a system of right and wrong. In democratic societies, no ultimate truth existed beyond the outcomes that were chosen freely, but these decisions were often constrained by ignorance, popular passions, and political expediency. To him, this sidestepped the basic question of governance: what moral end does a society seek? For Kendall as well as Voegelin, humans created government according to their conception of the divine, and "the kind of order they create, therefore, depends upon their relatedness to God, which in turn depends upon (a) the extent to which He has revealed Himself to them, and (b) the response to His revelation."[96] Secular societies erected weak governments.

What Kendall queried was how a society could remain,open to a multitude of political possibilities and remain safe and secure at the same time; he did not think it could. Nations without a shared value system, like Weimar Germany, "descend ineluctably into ever-deepening *differences* of opinion" and inevitably settled "public questions by violence and civil war."[97] Open political debate and ordered security were mutually exclusive. Voegelin conceptualized the need for order similarly if less clearly: "Central to every political *cosmion* is an understanding of the right way of living and the right ordering of society."[98]

Deepening Voegelin's contribution to the traditionalist dialect, Kendall used his concepts to attack cosmopolitan, pluralistic political values that empowered those intolerant of revelation. Strong government secured the fragile public. Like its biblical antecedents, Kendall's revelation was experienced and expressed by the chosen few. In the language of Jose Ortega y Gasset, Kendall defended the stability provided by a governing "select minority" whose allegiance to an accepted public orthodoxy of values was unwavering. "To ask more than that," Kendall wrote, "to ask that it give that select minority freedom to publicly treat all questions as open questions . . . is Utopian in the worst sense of the word."[99] Kendall's program, as well as his opposition to comprehensive free speech, was intended to protect the polis from Gnostic liberalism. If it seemed that Kendall's anti-Gnosticism also justified fascism, that enforced truth guaranteed coercive control, Kendall countered that he erected a barricade against violent social disintegration.

Nominalism

Richard Weaver was receptive to evidence based on revelation; he had, in fact, some experience with it. It was on a road in Texas, rather than one to Damascus, that Weaver said he converted to conservatism: "It came to me like a revelation that I did not *have* to go back to this job, which had become distasteful, and that I did not *have* to go on professing the clichés of liberalism, which were becoming meaningless to me."[100] Weaver was introduced to leftist ideas while attending the University of Kentucky, but he became disillusioned with the "shallow objectives" of the socialist rank and file. His tutelage under Southern Agrarian writers and theorists at Vanderbilt and Louisiana State University accelerated his political conversion.[101] His teachers' idyllic vision of small-property holders living close to nature in tight-knit communities, the "Agrarian ideal," was "powerful."[102]

Like Kendall, Weaver measured the virtues of small communities against a disaggregated world of isolated individuals. He thought societies and nations worked best when some set of revelatory truths exerted a centrifugal force in communal life; communities that swore fealty to common truths also swore fealty to one another. As M. Stanton Evans, an early conservative organizer and an admirer of Weaver's, quipped, when "the central precepts are lost, then all the rest is chaos."[103] Like

Voegelin's *The New Science of Politics*, Weaver's masterwork among conservatives, *Ideas Have Consequences* (1948), lamented the modern hubris that viewed communal bonds, especially religious bonds, as oppressive.

Aside from their complementary aims, *The New Science of Politics* and *Ideas Have Consequences* read quite differently; the first was styled as a thick work of intellectual history far removed from concerns of the present; the second, though it was no supermarket thriller, was not short on fulsome contemporary commentary. *Ideas Have Consequences* reads as an unsparing polemic warning of imminent civilizational collapse. Thinking its strident style and incendiary rebuke of modern culture would rouse public discussion, the University of Chicago Press's editor gambled on Weaver, then an unknown professor, and doubled the initial press run.[104] Four years prior, the press learned with the reception of *The Road to Serfdom* that polarized responses generated sales. Early reader reports suggested that *Ideas Have Consequences* had such an inflammatory capacity. Its release was backed by the press's biggest promotional effort to date.[105] Weaver's book was reviewed over 200 times within two years of its publication.[106] *Ideas Have Consequences* boosted Weaver to an "iconic status" among conservatives.[107] That the short text was vital to conservatism's philosophical ascendancy became a matter of "universal agreement among conservatives."[108] The depth and daring of the book left some conservative readers "awestruck."[109]

Ideas Have Consequences so enchanted conservatives in large measure because of its temerity. Weaver's was no localized critique of a political party, limited assessment of foreign policy, or even a broad critique of contemporary political ideas. Weaver alleged the collapse of the West and produced a trenchant, ambitious attack on all modernity: the Renaissance, the Enlightenment, the Industrial Revolution, mass democracy, individual rights, and beyond. Weaver penned ruthless assaults on nearly every facet of modern life: progress, science, technology, material prosperity, consumerism, pragmatism, mass education, literacy, equality, and mass media. He reviled the decline of interpersonal decency and the growing acceptance of obscenity. Even jazz music came in for rebuke as a cheap, inartistic jolt of sensory stimuli. Weaver put the ideas of an epoch "on trial," and, by doing so, "dramatically extended the mental horizon of the postwar Right."[110] Descent and restoration, integral features of the hedgehog style Weaver developed alongside midcentury traditionalists, were so powerful in his thinking that he originally chose to title his book *Steps toward a Restoration of Our World* before opting for *The Adverse Descent*. The publisher mandated *Ideas Have Consequences*, and Weaver threatened to walk before coming to his senses.[111]

Weaver was no populist pinning the failures of an age on enemies of the sanguine people. The modern masses were "moral idiots," and their "deep psychic anxiety" was evidence of "mass psychosis."[112] The middle class's obsession with comfortable living revealed their "spoiled-child psychology."[113] Searching through two millennia of intellectual history for the exact moment of rupture with sacred ideals, the primary source of Western decline, just as Voegelin did, Weaver arrived at a division point roughly contemporaneous with Joachim of Flora but postdating Voegelin's hated Gnostics by over a millennium. "Like Macbeth," he wrote early in *Ideas Have Consequences*, "Western man made an evil decision, which has become the efficient and final cause of other evil decisions." The medieval breaking point was the triumph of the "nominalism" of William of Occam over Thomas Aquinas's "realism" in the fourteenth century.[114]

Nominalism was a belief about the nature of beliefs; it held that humans had only sensory data to consult when making sense of the world around them. With only a limited ability to perceive and catalog the world, the words people used to represent things became momentary coordinates in a bewildering environment. Nominalists saw such labels as pragmatic tools and concluded that the meaning of words must be a matter of context and use. It was an idea with explosive potential in a world ruled by religious truths. Weaver objected that when the meaning of language became a matter of expediency, concepts like truth or universal validity were then not descriptors of actual conditions but just temporary names given to ideas people found important in the moment. As Weaver put it, nominalism left "universal terms mere names serving our convenience."[115]

The issue of meaning extended all the way up. Weaver thought that one's worldview determined the meaning of otherwise unintelligible events, behaviors, and phenomena. So-called facts meant nothing without an interpretive heuristic to make them signs of something larger. But Weaver was not interested in teaching cultural semiotics. He thought social paradigms were inseparable from theological concerns: how we viewed the world indicated what role we afforded God. "The issue," Weaver declared, "ultimately involved is whether there is a source of truth higher than, and independent of, man."[116] He saw no hope for any notion of right or wrong in a world of nominalist flux.

Nominalism functioned for Weaver as Gnosticism did for Voegelin. Each paradigm was a convenient demon that established a kind of second sin after humanity's original sin. Nominalism and Gnosticism were identifiable forces in history and could be blamed for all manner of catastrophes. Each was tied together only by a collection of premises about rationality, the possibility of collective action, and human perception; each was represented only in the work of a small group of infamous thinkers: William of Occam for Weaver and, after the Gnostics, Joachim of Flora for Voegelin. Each intellectual was like a second serpent in a medieval Eden who interrupted the natural bond between humanity and the divine by luring individuals to see themselves as gods in training. Each fostered a big truth about historical decline that explained disparate events occurring centuries apart. "Modern decadence," Weaver wrote, resulted from the turn toward nominalism, and the tragedy of modern Germany followed in due course.[117] His or Voegelin's readers can find traces of Joachim in Adlai Stevenson or William in John Dewey's *Democracy and Education*.

The understanding of history forwarded in *Ideas Have Consequences* aligned closely with a "Roman Catholic intellectual tradition" that reversed the formulaic narrative of modern history as progressive. Specifically, this view of history upended the idea that Rome's fall led to an illiterate and violent "Dark Ages," which concluded with the Renaissance, the Reformation, and the Enlightenment.[118] These periods were not breakthroughs in which hoary superstitions were done away with; these were regressive periods. The Middle Ages was not brutish, backward, and pestilential; the period was, one Weaver disciple declared, "the high synthesis of Western thought and practice," a civilizational zenith preceding a turn to barbarity.[119]

Weaver lionized the pre-Reformation church's capacity to produce a socially unified and properly reflective Middle Age order. Weaver's political goal, like Voegelin's and Kendall's, was the establishment of social bulwarks against individualism and relativism. For too long, Weaver wrote, "every man has been not only his own priest but his own professor of ethics," and the relativist condition produced extraordinary violence and mass mania that was inimical to an orderly society.[120] In a sense, Weaver's great hope was that the criteria by which people made personal decisions would become more public and less private.

Private choices should adhere to publicly accepted norms issued by moral authorities.

Weaver equated the presence of such a public religion with social strength. In a line rife with restorationist language, he argued, "The prospect of living again in a world of metaphysical certitude—what relief will this not bring to those made seasick by the truth-denying doctrines of the relativists!"[121] As Kendall did, Weaver's nautical metaphor decried the same process of endless, rudderless, back-and-forth debates in a polity without common goals and shared beliefs about the purpose of politics. Nominalism and its modern offshoots, empiricism and relativism, were childish and hysterical ideas. For Weaver, the current trajectory of human knowledge trended toward ignorance because universal knowledge of first principles, the only true form of knowledge, had been replaced. The idea of a single authoritative fount of acceptable knowledge took on masculine characteristics for Weaver. Real strength was required to stave off temptation, refuse immediate gratification, and accept discipline. "The very notion of eternal verities is repugnant to the modern temper," Weaver explained.[122] "A process of emasculation" commenced as humanity turned away from first principles; modern humans became fanatics and ethical eunuchs.[123]

Oddly enough, Weaver was not a Catholic or even particularly religious for that matter. Despite its vociferous criticisms of rationalism, biblical language and Christian icons were noticeably absent from *Ideas Have Consequences*. Weaver wrote only sporadically about explicitly Christian concepts in the book. He implored, for instance, the "relativism of 'man is the measure of all things'" because it implied a reversal of original sin, a concept he mentioned in passing.[124] Weaver did not elucidate church history as he surveyed Western history; he did not directly assert that the purpose of political action was to honor God. Some conservatives have even noted that his defense of Christianity was more "subliminal" than anything else.[125] He did, however, theorize natural law, and his take "entailed an acceptance of the notion of a Creator."[126] Generally, however, Weaver preferred to talk about "essences" and "universals," not "God."

Yet among many conservatives, Weaver's attempt to resuscitate the transcendent in modern culture was read as a mission to make sure religion was, once again, the center of both private and public life. "Universal truth" was interpreted as a religious doctrine cloaked in philosophical code. The "undertone of Roman Catholicism that many readers have noted in *Ideas Have Consequences*" was vital both to the book's appeal and its synergy with other religiously minded texts of the midcentury.[127] Nominalism, former North Carolina senator John East wrote in a hagiographic portrait of Weaver, overturned "the Platonic-Christian heritage" of universal authority.[128]

Although the form of Weaver's traditionalism, his universalist language, his declinist interpretation of history, and his emphasis on ideological pivot points, remained static after *Ideas Have Consequences*, his thinking on these subjects evolved after the publication of his most famous work. In *Visions of Order: The Cultural Crisis of Our Time* (1964), an influential and polemical follow-up, Weaver explored the real sources of the "revolt" against truth.[129] The book showed how Weaver had adapted many of his early ideas to Voegelin's rhetorical framework. As Weaver's cultural criticisms matured from *Ideas Have Consequences* to *Visions of Order* fifteen years later, his fulminations against many of the same enemies remained, but they were represented as Gnostics in the latter book. In *Ideas have Consequences*, for instance, Weaver blamed the conquest of the natural world on modernism. In *Visions of Order*, he identified this conquest as Gnosticism run amok.[130] "Science" and "rationalism" were the chief enemies of *Ideas Have Consequences*; these became signs of the Gnostic offensive in *Visions of Order*.[131] Appropriately, his emphasis on nominalism and William of Occam gave way to Bishop Irenaeus's battle with ancient heretics. Praising Voegelin's hero, he wrote, "We find further that St. Irenaeus, in his writings against the Gnostics, insists that some mysteries be left unsolved. . . . Modern man, however, has reached the critical point at which he feels no qualms about demanding that nature give up all her secrets."[132] Without vigilant monitoring of cultural and ideological trends, "the millennial dream of the modern Gnostic," atheist Communism, would become a reality.[133] Small decisions like changes to educational curricula were globally decisive in that each choice moved the cultural pendulum to a religious order on one side or to an immanentized eschaton on the other.

The Permanent Things

Russell Kirk, a man of letters in a modern world, wrote in ethereal, archaic terms that harkened back not just to older ways of speaking but bygone paradigms as well. Eugene Genovese called him a "creature of the mothballs."[134] Kirk styled himself "the last bonnet laird of the stump country."[135] Conservatives dubbed him the "sage of Mecosta."[136] He delighted in nostalgic allusions in his personal life, his politics, and his writing style. For instance, he relished comparisons of his Mecosta, Michigan, home—it was called "Piety Hill"—to Rivendell, the Elven villa in Tolkien's *Lord of the Rings*."[137] A writer of ghost stories and a reader of Tarot cards, Kirk's technophobia made Weaver's look tame by comparison.[138] Kirk had what one writer soft-pedaled a "carefully crafted eighteenth-century persona," but, as the first American recipient of the Doctorate of Human Letters from St. Andrews, a medieval university, his public image bore even older raiments as well.[139]

His persona matched his politics. Kirk valued unbroken, amaranthine social traditions as the movement of high ancestral wisdom across the ages.[140] When, in 1960, just fewer than 100 students gathered at the Buckley estate in Connecticut to codify the basic premises of conservatism, one student found a simple line Kirk borrowed from T. S. Eliot befitting the occasion.[141] Upon arrival, the new member of the new political community looked at the palatial estate, the manicured grounds, and the commitment shared by the young gatherers and reportedly said, "Now I know what Russell Kirk means by 'the permanent things.'"[142] It was one of Kirk's favorite phrases, and in tandem with *The Conservative Mind* (1953), his opus, it was how conservatives knew him best.

The permanent things were ideals Kirk thought modernity had abandoned, ideals he historicized in *The Conservative Mind*. Trademarks of a "civil social order," the permanent things included "aristocracy, church, guild, family, and local association."[143] Kirk hoped a revival of the permanent things in the public consciousness could stave off his and other traditionalists' worst fear: social rootlessness. Kirk argued that relativist science, the modern *cosmion*, as Voegelin would phrase it, provided no fixed grounds from which to argue, no communal bonds, and promoted a protean existence in which each day was a transformation of the previous. Without "institutional religion," "old-fashioned economics," "family authority," and "small political communities," the individual was unfastened from all meaningful continuities and set adrift to support "any fanaticism that promises to assuage their loneliness."[144] Accepting the permanent things meant resisting modern comforts, eschewing political fads, casting a wary glance at claims grounded in reason and science. The permanent things were, in short, the only sustainable political arrangement: "What revelation, tradition, and normative insight dictate often is highly inexpedient for a particular person at a particular time, or indeed for certain communities; yet those commands must be obeyed. . . . We cling to the permanent things, the norms of our being, because all other grounds are quicksand."[145] Echoing other traditionalists, Kirk's permanent things vaunted local orders and customs as well as universal moral direction, timeless truths blended with indigenous customs.

Kirk's coinage would live a symbolic life as glamorous as that of "immanentize the eschaton" or "nominalism." Ronald Reagan signified his affection for *National Review* by subtly nodding in Kirk's direction as he extolled the magazine's virtues: "We know that the permanent things this journal stands for, if given only the slightest bit of breathing space, must and will triumph."[146] Other writers, conversely, worried that *National Review* forgot the permanent things as it published essays on time-sensitive political controversies.[147] All told, whether in rebukes or affirmations of contemporary conservatism, many conservatives invoked Kirk's hedgehog formulation to symbolize timelessness, universal truth, and social stability.[148] Whereas Kirk's phrase affirmed what traditionalists valued and summoned a program they accepted rather than ideas, like Gnosticism, they abhorred, his ideal polity did not depart much from his traditionalist contemporaries. What set Kirk's contribution apart from those of Voegelin, Kendall, Weaver, Nisbet, and Strauss was that he, in his expansive *The Conservative Mind*, identified, historicized, and practically invented an American traditionalist tradition, a long lineup of American intellectuals dedicated to theorizing the permanent things in social life.

Alfred A. Knopf originally accepted *The Conservative Mind* for publication with one condition, that Kirk cut its length by three-fourths.[149] Henry Regnery, who agreed to publish the book without taking the ax to it, urged a new title, however. Kirk wanted to keep his declinist dissertation title, "The Conservatives' Rout." Instead, *The Conservative Mind: From Burke to Santayana* appeared in 1953 as one of the first books to use "conservative" in its title since World War II.[150] Some, Kirk's friend T. S. Eliot most prominently, wondered whether the atheist Santayana was a proper codicil. In subsequent editions, Kirk expanded the book and found a new subtitle as well: *From Burke to Eliot*.[151] The initial impact of *The Conservative Mind* was "hard to imagine" for Regnery. It "came like rain," he remembered, to end the drought of liberalism.[152] Laudatory reviews followed in the *New York Herald-Tribune, Washington Post, Saturday Review*, and *Fortune. Partisan Review* discussed the book extensively in two issues. *The Conservative Mind* would eventually be released in seven revised editions, numerous printings, and Spanish and German translations.[153] Although Peter Viereck had a legitimate claim to resuscitating the conservative label after World War II, many conservatives credited Kirk. Regnery trumpeted, "It would be too much to say that the postwar conservative movement began with the publication of Russell Kirk's *The Conservative Mind*, but it was this book that gave it its name, and, more important, coherence."[154] Whittaker Chambers went further; to him, *The Conservative Mind* was the book of the century.[155]

Kirk invested conservatism with considerable philosophical puissance. The term, nearly left for dead in midcentury American political discourse, was, after *The Conservative Mind*, freighted with the historical weight of the European antirevolutionaries like Burke but, more important, a new and sizable American cargo as well. Where Strauss, Voegelin, and Weaver found old thinkers to excoriate, Kirk erected a pantheon of American intellectual heroes for conservatives to venerate. Kirk took his Burkean notions of social tradition and hierarchy and combed through the pages of American intellectual history looking for homegrown matches. The result was a thick roster of thinkers, both well known and arcane, who Kirk called conservative, though none used the term with any regularity. *The Conservative Mind's* 500 pages spanned nearly thirty thinkers such as John Adams, John Randolph, Brooks Adams, Paul Elmer More, Walter Scott, John C. Calhoun, Nathaniel Hawthorne, Benjamin Disraeli, and Irving Babbitt. Schlesinger called it "an unconvincing and thoroughly artificial genealogy," merely a "collection of incompatible names," but the criticism did not stick among conservatives.[156] The book, a careful rendering of a conservatism shorn of monarchist, nationalist, and laissez-faire tendencies, showed conservatives the varying styles and political contexts in which "custom, convention, and old prescription" could check against, as Burke would have put it, "man's anarchic impulse."[157]

Kirk needed to find a "historical basis for a viable American conservatism," and, aside from the midcentury unpopularity of the term "conservative," another sizable factor stood in his way.[158] Schlesinger leveled "New Conservatism" as "the wrong doctrine in the wrong country in the wrong century directed against the wrong enemies."[159] Other influential midcentury historians, including Richard Hofstadter and Louis Hartz, made similar points about American conservatism.[160] America had no ancien régime, no aristocracy, no monarchy, no established church, no rigid class structure, and, obviously, no revolution that overthrew these institutions. America, therefore, did not and could not have a conservative tradition. After all, how could a capitalist nation whose history was colored by stories of mobility, alteration, and innovation maintain a static social hierarchy? Even some conservatives found Kirk's attempt to domesticate conservatism the politics of pure fiction. Kirk's longtime conservative rival Frank Meyer called Kirk's imagined society some amalgam of "eighteenth-century England" and "medieval Europe."[161]

Familiar with these arguments, Kirk was more sensitive to the distance between the nation's borders and European philosophical conservatism than his conservative contemporaries were. If conservatism meant a respect for local tradition, then he knew that being an American traditionalist mindful only of historic European customs was unworkable. To counter the claim that conservatism was un-American, Kirk sought to uncover, even discover, a common thread among many American thinkers, a domestic intellectual traditionalist tradition.

The book's imposing length was actually part of its argument; the more thinkers Kirk assembled under the conservative aegis, the more of a claim to a genuine American conservative tradition he had. The book's length also became part of its appeal; its thickness signaled intellectual heft. The more intellectuals Kirk gathered, the more conservatism was a stirring tradition rather than an ideological flash in the midcentury pan. As Jeffrey Hart argued, "When it appeared, *The Conservative Mind* enabled many bright young people to entertain the idea of being a conservative for the first time, so pervasive was liberal intellectual authority at that time. . . . Thus, there *had* been conservatives of majestic intellect, and so who could say that there was no serious conservative stance toward the world even today?"[162] The size and historical scope of *The Conservative Mind* helped Kirk create this new political community as members of a thoughtful lineage, caretakers of a once-honored tradition. He gave an upstart identity "an intellectually formidable and respectable ancestry."[163]

Kirk began *The Conservative Mind* defensively. Enumerating a string of historic insults laid on conservatives—that they were "stupid," stubborn, and reactionary—Kirk set out to prove that conservative ideas have "been defended, these past hundred and fifty years, by men of learning and genius, as well."[164] Kirk then made a strategic move to present American conservatism as a natural extension of British conservatism and to present both as natural extensions of a small set of transhistorical ideas. This tight "system of ideas" stood as bulwarks against modernist forces of destruction in England and the United States since the French Revolution. When Kirk surveyed the tradition of American conservatism, he did not see what Hartz saw in *The Liberal Tradition in America*, an idea that died "without impact on the mind of a nation."[165] That Kirk opened his opus tethering American conservatives to English conservatives was a powerful, if contentious, retort to liberal consensus historians who treated conservatives in the United States as isolated, peculiar, and obsolete. Kirk's conservatives were none of those things; he injected them into a cross-continental intellectual tradition of "conservation" opposed to "innovation."[166]

One portion of the book, the short introduction, stood out from the rest. Composing only a brief portion of *The Conservative Mind*, Kirk's "six canons of conservative thought" became the "most well-known touchstones for conservatism."[167] Kirk's canons included the belief in a transcendent order, the acknowledgment of inevitable variety in human life, faith in natural hierarchy among humans, a recognition that freedom and property were interrelated, confidence in social traditions, and the acceptance that political innovation must work within cultural customs. These were essentially rephrases of the growing traditionalist corpus of Voegelin's, Weaver's, and Kendall's work as terse dictums. As such, Kirk's canons covered a massive swath of intellectual territory; Kirk spent the most space, however, developing the first few of these canons. The permanent things were evident especially in the first canon, a transcendent order whose mark was felt through every phase of human history. For Kirk, like Voegelin, Weaver, and Kendall, all politics was "religious and moral."[168] "Justice" was not a human creation, some artificial contrivance, but rather was built into the basic structure of the universe. Like a collective conscience, justice was embedded within the relationships that constituted real hierarchal communities. Politics, then, was simply the art of "apprehending and applying" this antecedent justice.[169] To Kirk, this transcendent order was not a belief system imposed on the world. It accorded with the real world; it reflected the world. The permanent things and the six canons captured in words people's movements, rhythms, and needs, their nature.

Kirk's idealized conservative world, a world governed by these six principles, was a realm of commoners and lords; mystics and sages; long-held, deeply felt communal traditions; country manors and cathedrals; druid ruins; and court culture, where normal people stood in awe of the world rather than over it. It was a world where communities composed of religious families restrained and guided one another. Community was an anchor for individuals, and not just in the sense that it is nice to have some company once in a while. Community entailed obligation to the whole; when individuals genuinely belonged to a community, they knew its institutions, its customs, its internal organization, its very sense of itself. They respected its norms and ways of life, which meant that the community regulated and chastened individuals. In short, individuals had asocial desires that communities checked. Individuals can no more check their passions than they can develop social customs by themselves. Freedom from such a community was a "terrifying thing, the freedom of a baby deserted by his parents to do as he pleases."[170]

A conservative polity steered by Kirk's canons embraced the permanent things against the "demands of eager ideology."[171] Ideology, which Kirk defined as a dogmatic belief system imposed inflexibly, was the greatest threat to the permanent things. Ideologists were Kirk's Gnostics; they were acquisitive self-worshippers, base materialists like socialists and anarcho-capitalists consumed by considerations of wealth. Like Voegelin's Gnosticism, ideology promised "the Terrestrial Paradise to the faithful" and asked that the paradise "be taken by storm."[172] Conservatives realized that humans could fashion their "own Terrestrial Hell through infatuation with ideology."[173] Whereas ideology was a conscious rationalization of a set of experiences through a prefabricated lens, traditions evolved from unexamined and largely unseen cultural practices and social relationships. In Kirk's intellectual history, conservatism was the intellectual's faith, principled yet adjustable. Radicalism was more suited for emotional spasms of rage.[174]

Capitalism and Conservatism

To the traditionalists, Western civilization was rootless and rotting because modernity extracted people from traditional communities

and shoehorned them into an ersatz, valueless world governed by ex-
perimentation, speed, and mobility. State control, scientific "progress,"
and forced democratic egalitarianism all contributed tremendously
to the downfall of the traditionalists' ancien régime, a universal-local
trinity of religion, class hierarchy, and family. But the ascendance of
modernity was not just the philosophe's fault, and the mechanical
techno-dystopia of the modern world could hardly be pinned on the
nation-state. Consumerism, the transformation of people into zombie
spenders craving their next purchase, had much to do with the decline
of traditional values. When traditionalists identified and criticized the
capitalist root cause of consumerism, they threatened to splinter the
conservative coalition.

Suspecting that the traditionalists were rent-seeking capitalists
disguised as medieval monks, Arthur Schlesinger Jr. argued that their
politics would never "upset a landlord," that their ethereal language
gave capitalism some religious gloss.[175] Schlesinger's point is worth
consideration, especially given that the traditionalists, Kirk and Weaver
more than the others, went out of their way to defend private property
as a lodestone of philosophical conservatism. To confuse their "real
politics" as libertarianism concealed behind a theological veneer, however, misunderstands how traditionalism would translate into practical
governance.[176] To put the matter succinctly: traditionalists' dismissal
of individual freedom not only terrified libertarians, but traditionalist
economics would end modern capitalism. The traditionalist ideal of an
antistatist community was achievable only by eliminating the forces
of modernity that disintegrated communities, forces unleashed by an
overweening state but also the social impact of capitalist economics.
True communities regulated capitalism; they blunted it by introducing
controls on labor, production, competition, consumerism, and class
mobility.

Traditionalists took aim at capitalism both by implication and directly. Nearly all of the traditionalists lionized vanished societies, the
antebellum South and medieval Europe, whose practices a libertarian would refuse to call capitalist. Voegelin reached back nearly two
millennia to recover eternal verities that had become fully eclipsed in
the consumerist West. Nisbet, for instance, explained how premodern
families, churches, and local communities dealt with "social problems
of birth and death, courtship and marriage, employment and unemployment, infirmity and old age," spheres now presumably left to the

impersonal force of market fluctuations or government policy.[177] As traditionalists praised precapitalist societies, they also developed a philosophical vocabulary that was not just different than classical liberalism but adamantly opposed to it. Community, hierarchy, and authority, the cherished terms by which traditionalists made sense of society as an interlocking whole, were anathema to a vocabulary consisting of "*individual, change, progress, reason,* and *freedom.*" The buzzwords of capitalism took "the solid fact of the discrete individual" for granted and even deigned to liberate that "individual from the tyrannous and irrational statuses handed down from the past."[178]

Whereas much traditionalist writing took on capitalism without naming names—that is, by critiquing adjacent forces like materialism, individualism, and social mobility—direct, even acerbic, selections of *Ideas Have Consequences* and *The Conservative Mind* could not be explained away as purely nostalgic longings. The clarity with which Weaver and Kirk decried specific forms of capitalism left little doubt that they viewed the business of sparsely regulated buying and selling as one cause of the modern disease.

Weaver saw property rights as "metaphysical" rights. He explained elliptically that private property "rests upon the idea of the *hisness* of *his: proprietas, Eigentum,* the very words assert an identification of owner and owned."[179] Boiled to its essence, Weaver's metaphysical defense of private property was based on the requirement of "stewardship"; caring for a plot of land and preparing it for inheritance was a kind of spiritual conversation between past, present, and future generations.[180] But Weaver's validation of property and income stratification did not amount to a defense of capitalism generally. His neomedievalist, antimaterialist politics nurtured a "deep anticapitalism."[181] Weaver's desire to sanctify work and fundamentally alter the world of getting and spending advanced a restrictive notion of private property. Weaver valued the connection between individuals, families, and plots of land they knew intimately; he was no friend to real estate agents or to families looking at property as an investment.

Favoring tangible property cared for by an individual, not "the abstract property of stocks and bonds, the legal ownership of enterprises never seen," Weaver also took on finance capital and Wall Street.[182] He considered such ownership "a fiction useful for exploitation" in which anonymous shareholders pushed for short-term gains within their narrow "area of responsibility."[183] Weaver even went after the foundation of modern industrial capitalism: the corporation. Aside from its assault on the relationship between an individual and a tangible property, big business inevitably expanded the power of the state because it was to big business's financial benefit to shape a governmental apparatus friendly to its immediate needs. "Big business," he concluded dramatically, "and the rationalization of industry thus abet the evils we seek to overcome. . . . Respecters of private property are really obligated to oppose much that is done today in the name of private enterprise, for corporate organization and monopoly are the very means whereby property is casting aside its privacy."[184]

Kirk's writings were not apologies for capitalism either. Kirk's ideal economic order would likely leave the Chamber of Commerce aghast. In fact, Kirk's economics would upset the entire cycle of production and consumption; he wanted it that way. Daily life under industrial capitalism genuflected to consumption: trading labor for the means to buy products, acquiring products, amassing more products, and flaunting those products before peers. It was a superficial cycle indicative of humanity's powerful passion for immediate, fleeting pleasures. Pure capitalism, Kirk argued, was the perfect opposite of the permanent things: "The old *laissez-faire* was founded upon a misapprehension of human nature, an exaltation of individuality (in private character often a virtue) to the condition of a political dogma, which destroyed the spirit of community and reduced men to so many equipollent atoms of humanity, without sense of brotherhood or of purpose."[185] Kirk even hoped to create an overhauled laissez-faire in which the *"group,"* by which he meant "the family, the local community, the trade union, the church, the college, the profession," was treated as "the basic social unit."[186] It was still capitalism, but it was capitalism suited to static communities.

Communal bonds were not just a familial or a religious matter to Kirk; economics played a vital role in local relationships. One of the chief ways in which "mass industrialism" destroyed "traditional society" was by replacing "the old-guild organization" with corporate wage labor.[187] By setting limits on advertising, limiting work hours, and mandating particular production techniques, the guild system Kirk admired virtually eliminated market competition in parts of the medieval world. A shoemaker who decided to flood the local market with cheaply produced shoes in order to make a small margin on each sale risked personal exile. Guilds ensured that the lure of wealth or the demands of work did not revolutionize daily life and change how much time people spent with their families or reduce their church service.[188] Kirk longed for a society in which making money was deemed a depraved pursuit.

Where Weaver's anticapitalism softened as he aged, Kirk's hardened.[189] Nearly thirty years after *National Review* and Buckley helped broker an accord between traditionalism and libertarianism for the sake of conservatism, Kirk, in a withering *Modern Age* article, condemned the coalition as "inconceivable."[190] Kirk, quite boldly, would have sooner endorsed a "friendly pact" between traditionalists and socialists who both, at least, "declare the existence of some sort of moral order."[191] Traditionalism and libertarianism repelled one another at every political turn. Libertarians urged freedom; traditionalists pushed for order. Libertarians viewed the state as "the great oppressor"; traditionalists believed that "the state is ordained of God."[192] If Kirk harshly summarized libertarianism, he was outright demeaning in his depiction of actual libertarians. He hinted that beliefs showed the character of believers. The traditionalist was a "pilgrim in a realm of mystery and wonder."[193] Libertarians, by contrast, were "humorless, intolerant, self-righteous, badly schooled, and dull."[194] These inciting words, published in 1981 as a conservative secured the presidency, were the latest volley of incendiary intramural conflict among conservatives. Kirk hoped to cleave the partnership between traditionalists and libertarians, a thirty-year coalition that never made sense to him. When genuine conservatives accepted libertarians to widen their political coalition and face down a common enemy, he thought they replicated modernity's chief heresy: the abandonment of the sacred for material gain.

CHAPTER THREE

The Libertarian Dialect

⌘

In the late 1960s, the fragile peace between libertarian and traditionalist conservatives in Young Americans for Freedom (YAF), the conservative movement's first youth organization, collapsed. At its most ominous, this clash saw libertarians, or "Rads," as agents provocateurs defending radicalism, celebrating moral relativism, and otherwise irking the sermonizing traditionalists, or "Trads." Rads openly advocated market solutions to *every* social question. The market, the Rads agreed, could arbitrate fairly the price of sex just as it could the price of toothpaste. What right, the Rads asked, did some pampered bureaucrat have to force them to fight in Vietnam? From their bell bottoms to their bombast about Washington fascists, some Rads seemed to share more with the hated hippies than their conservative compatriots. Their ribald and rebellious permissiveness was best illustrated in a bit of libertarian humor from the time: A typical Trad chastised, "You libertarians are the types that would allow fornication in public parks!" A typical Rad answered, "What do you mean *public parks?*"[1]

The Rads had a well-earned "badboy" reputation among conservatives.[2] Following an uncompromising antistatist logic to anarchocapitalism, the end of the political line, the Rads argued that if social traditions or moral prohibitions were not marketable, they should not survive in an innovative market.[3] If it could be demanded, the market could provide it, for a price. Such Rad rabble-rousing threatened YAF's position as the clean-cut Christian counterbalance to vocal student activists on the left. YAF coffers could have suffered if wealthy donors considered young conservatives to be callow radicals.[4] Certain flash points—Vietnam was one—turned a feisty give-and-take between factions into naked hostility. One libertarian provided the spark when he lit a fake draft card at a 1969 YAF rally. Fights broke out; incensed Trads shoved Rads; libertarian allies rallied to protect the burning card from traditionalists' extinguishers.[5] Once the melee subsided, the Rads' "Laissez-faire! Laissez-faire!" chants were answered by the Trads' chorus of "Lazy fairies! Lazy fairies!" for the remainder of the convention.[6]

What seemed like a war over political doctrine was also a war over the authenticity of each camp's conservatism, and language was a primary battleground. Would conservatives rail against government of all sorts, or would governmental power be seen as an essential bulwark against international Communism and cultural decline? Which dialect would be recognized as the primary expression of conservatism? When, following the convention skirmish, YAF officially cracked down and began excommunicating Rads and decommissioning Rad-dominated YAF chapters, many libertarians thought the writing on the wall was composed in bold and decided to quit before they were fired.[7] This purge marked a new low in a volatile partnership that had already survived Whittaker Chambers's scathing critique of Ayn Rand's *Atlas Shrugged*, published in *National Review* in 1955, after which many libertarians and objectivists refused to associate with anything associated with magazine founder William F. Buckley.[8]

The clash marked neither a beginning nor an end but a continuation of ambivalence between libertarians and conservatives. Libertarianism has been both an independent force in U.S. politics with its own magazines, think tanks, and intellectuals as well as, for those who did not secede and were not exiled, a dependent political identity within conservative circles, a fuller explanation of what it meant to be a limited government conservative.[9] Like a smaller moon behind a larger sun, libertarianism has existed in a state of partial eclipse behind conservatism since the midcentury. To maintain distinct visibility, the diehard purists, those libertarians enamored with voluntary solutions to all political problems, wrote vicious assaults on conservatism. Fearing that upstart conservatism obscured classical liberalism, Rose Wilder Lane dissociated her cause from the "back-to-medievalism movement" of Russell Kirk in 1953.[10] Buckley and his followers, enemies of "true liberalism" a concerned contemporary of Lane's alleged, practiced a conservatism worthy of "the Inquisition," an ideology of "the rack, the thumbscrew, the whip, and the firing squad."[11] Unable to achieve full liberation from conservatism, libertarian authors wrote as the impetuous younger siblings of a "snide older brother," the "Buckleyite right."[12] Being confused with conservatives was supremely insulting to some libertarians, a casus belli to others.[13] It was Frank Chodorov, a Buckley family friend, pioneering pamphleteer, and author of such essays "Taxation Is Robbery" and such books as *The Income Tax: Root of All Evil* (1954), who appraised his relationship to conservatism most bluntly in 1956: "I will punch anyone who calls me a conservative in the nose. I am a radical."[14]

These stalwarts exhibited the now-familiar aggravation of other writers, such as Max Eastman, who simultaneously desired their linguistic tools to be privately defined yet publicly significant. Such attempts at unadulterated self-definition on the American right have been both frequent and frustrated. It has been a communal desire that is often impossible to satisfy; if a political identity is to speak meaningfully to a community, the community must have a say in its meaning. Language has a "certain refraction and recalcitrance"; labels can never be "fully controlled or individually owned."[15] What is common sense in neighborhoods also applies to political labels; tools used by neighbors are often returned in an altered form.

As the economic phalanx of postwar conservatism, libertarianism has achieved distinctive cultural and political saliency. Its logic was the logic behind deregulation, tax cuts, lessening federal bureaucracy, decreasing federal spending, and the equation of monetary contributions and protected political expressions. Try as they did to maintain a distinct identity, libertarian economics continued to be a main thrust of modern conservatism even if some libertarians wanted to opt out of the arrangement.[16] Brink Lindsey, a typical secessionist, urged libertarians to step out of conservatism's shadow and excoriate conservatives' acceptance of activist government in their social and foreign policies. Conservatives' antistatist rhetoric was more ruse than conviction, so, he bellowed, "It's time for libertarians to break ranks and stand on our own."[17] Yet secession was easy to urge and arduous to actualize. *National Review* editor Jonah Goldberg correctly identified the difficulty of detaching libertarianism from conservatism: "Economic libertarians, under the leadership of Friedrich Hayek and Milton Friedman, have been so successful in the conservative movement—and the conservative movement has been so successful because of them—that 'economic conservative' and 'libertarian' have long been synonyms."[18] More uncivilly, he said to libertarian critics of conservatism: "Grow up, you're stuck with us."[19]

Not all expressions of libertarianism have been co-opted by conservatives. Few want to dismantle the military-industrial complex. Few adopted the isolationism of the old, pre–World War II Right.[20] Few self-identified conservatives hoped consumer demand would separate legal activity from illegal activity. Even fewer would allow private markets to determine the acceptability of moral issues like abortion.[21] Just as with Buckley's tirade against the excesses of the John Birch Society, strategic police actions managed intemperate, unpalatable expressions of the conservative political identity by attacking groups and individuals, like anarchists and atheists, not concepts, like antistatism and individualism.[22] Mainstream conservatism advanced well into the conceptual territory of classical liberalism but stopped shy of expressions of libertarianism that most strained the bourgeoning coalition. The accepted performance of conservatism halted where libertarians became hostile to religion, where antistatism became antimilitarism, where libertarianism and libertinism became indistinguishable.

Since no other political label has competed for traditionalist concepts, the full range of traditionalist expressions has been unwaveringly conservative. The purpose of this chapter, then, is to explore the range of the libertarian dialect that remained within the conservative political language. In addition to its reverence for different god terms, the libertarian dialect featured different depictions of the typical individual and political enemies than those of the traditionalist dialect. Whereas writers in the traditionalist dialect consistently opted for transhistorical language to depict the timeless foundations of true communities, the libertarian dialect within the conservative political language was bifurcated between an *assiduous* and *audacious* libertarianism whose rhetorical divergences reflected substantially different conceptions of politics and citizens' roles in public life.[23]

Variations between a cautious, pragmatic libertarian cant and its polemical, principled counterpart are best viewed by exploring the subtle differences in the use of ostensible synonyms: "liberty" and "freedom." The space between these two terms is the blurry borderline between two renditions of the same dialect. Tracking the difference between freedom and liberty can be a tedious exercise in hairsplitting; the terms are used interchangeably as synonyms, and they issue from the same philosophical vein first ratified in the Magna Carta and fully expressed as classical liberalism in the nineteenth century.[24] Defining liberty without mentioning freedom, or vice versa, is a difficult prospect. Free people possess liberty; those with liberty are free.

The meaning of freedom and liberty, nevertheless, can be distinguished productively in the discourses of shrewd and absolutist libertarian-conservatives. These principal modes of expression in the libertarian dialect are typified by the two most influential libertarian-conservative sourcebooks of the midcentury: Friedrich Hayek's *The Road to Serfdom* (1944) and Barry Goldwater's *The Conscience of a Conservative* (1960).[25] "Liberty" was Hayek's god term. It was the end goal in *The Road to Serfdom* and defended even more fully in *The Constitution of Liberty* (1960). Goldwater's god term was "freedom," and, with a key exception, the word connoted the same idea of the public as atomized, disaggregated individuals. He defended freedom most resolutely in *The Conscience of a Conservative* where he proclaimed that the "overriding political challenge" for conservatives was "*to preserve and extend freedom.*"[26] The reserved, secular "liberty" protected imperfect individuals from social burdens, public attachments, political duties, and economic responsibilities; the pious, piquant "freedom" compelled ennobled individuals to accept two somewhat conflicting public responsibilities: to oppose government virulently and to risk personal sacrifice by protecting the nation from its enemies.

Each term became meaningful in separate libertarian-conservative rhetorical styles that modeled these doctrinal commitments. The

careful and cautious "liberty" was reflected in Hayek's qualified judgments, judicious distinctions, and refusal to hawk utopian alternatives;
the temerarious and rambunctious "freedom" was consistent with
Goldwater's combative development of absolute axioms in an ardent
rhetorical cast. Hayek and Goldwater also employed these key terms
in strikingly different narratives about politics, narratives in which the
typical individual, the starting point for libertarian political theory, possessed remarkably different characteristics. Hayek wrote about people
doing the best they could; Goldwater wrote about heroes. Although
Rand was never comfortable with conservatism and conservatives
never fully embraced Rand, her telling summary of her view of ob-
jectivism highlights this difference: "My philosophy, in essence, is the
concept of man as a heroic being, with his own happiness as the moral
purpose of his life, with productive achievement as his noblest activity,
and reason as his only absolute."[27] Goldwater's undaunted, self-suffi-
cient, downright muscular individual was decidedly Randian. Some of
Rand's devotees even pictured the chiseled former fighter pilot from
the Arizona desert as the personification of "Rand's iconography of the
independent, manly hero."[28] Hayek's middling individual, ambling ap-
prehensively through the political world, was not fit for the part. His
imagined everyday person was capable of rational judgment but was
often a bumbling gadfly, easily moved from cause to cause.

Hayek's and Goldwater's imagined political worlds were made up
by different heroes as well as different villains. The enemy of liberty
was, accordingly, not contained in an individual or an institution; it was
unchecked power. Goldwater's freedom was a final judgment made
about the size of government, period; it was tethered to nothing as
uncertain as Hayek's measured defense of the market and nothing as
weakly formed as his clumsy individual. There was more than a pa-
tina of galvanizing populism in Goldwater's conservatism; he turned
the typical individual into a romantic hero, and the straight-talking,
gun-toting Arizona senator personified the type and modeled an intrepid rhetoric to match. In Goldwater's conservatism, the only factor
suppressing the unlimited potential of individuals was government.
Americans became un-free because of Washington.

The following explication of the dynamics of the libertarian dialect is organized into two sections: the first on Hayek's *The Road to
Serfdom* (hereafter *Road*), the second on Goldwater's *The Conscience
of a Conservative* (hereafter *Conscience*). Beyond the importance of lib-

erty in Hayek's resonant work, I discuss its meaning in relationship to the "Rule of Law," "coercion," and the "knowledge problem." Beyond Goldwater's notion that freedom and government can hardly coexist, I concentrate on how Goldwater also saw victory in the Cold War as essential to preserving freedom.

Hayek's Skeptical Vision and the Knowledge Problem

Of the midcentury intellectuals who transformed conservatism in the United States, Friedrich A. Hayek was likely the most reluctant; he was surely the most annoyed. Richard Weaver, Russell Kirk, Willmoore Kendall, and Eric Voegelin could scarcely have predicted how successful their works would be in providing motivation to conservative activists and depth to conservative argument. The same was true of Hayek. His books, *Road* and *The Constitution of Liberty* in particular, catalyzed conservatives. When *National Review* published rankings of the best nonfiction books of the century in 1999, the signature titles of Buckley, Chambers, Kirk, and Weaver populated the list, but *Road* outranked them all. On *National Review's* list, Hayek had two entries in the top ten and was listed twice before others appeared once.[29] *Road*, in short, became "a bible to conservatives after World War II and throughout the Cold War."[30]

There was only one problem: Hayek did not call himself a "conservative." In fact, he wanted nothing to do with the term. When the paperback edition of *Road* appeared in the United States in 1956, Hayek, dumbfounded that people calling themselves conservatives cited him in earnest, made his choice of political identities plain: "I use throughout the term 'liberal' in the original, nineteenth-century sense in which it is still current in Britain. In current American usage it often means very nearly the opposite of this." "Liberal" had become "the camouflage of leftist movements." Clearly aware of the meaning shifts "liberal" was undergoing but unaware of the same shift in "conservative," Hayek maligned the terminological confusion of the midcentury. His own favored identity, liberalism, had completed a full migration from right to left: "I am still puzzled why those in the United States who truly believe in liberty should not only have allowed the left to appropriate this almost indispensable term but should even have assisted by beginning to use it themselves as a term of opprobrium." "True liberals," most regrettably, were describing themselves as "conservatives."[31] Conservatism, "by its very nature," defended privilege, something liberalism, by its "essence," fought.[32]

Hayek's distinction did not fend off the conservative colonists. Rand was a vehement free-marketer many conservatives kept at arm's length; Hayek was a sensible free-marketer conservatives had to have. In 1960, he tried to hold them off again. He concluded his massive *The Constitution of Liberty* with a chapter entitled "Why I Am Not a Conservative."[33] It did not work either.[34] Conservative opportunists claimed him in the name of conservatism.[35] Hayek's work was an essential rhetorical resource because he gave conservatives a way to talk about the public interest by talking about private enterprise.

Born in Vienna in 1899 to a wealthy family, Hayek was the third in a series of vaunted intellectuals to emerge nearly simultaneously from the city's imperial and cosmopolitan environment. Hayek's cousin, Ludwig Wittgenstein, would distinguish himself as the twentieth-century's preeminent philosopher of language. Hayek's later colleague and friend Karl Popper was one of the century's foremost social scientists. Hayek eventually made his name as an economist, but his dual doctorates from the University of Vienna, home of the Austrian school of economics, were earned in law and political science. It was only in a later post in the Austrian Office of Claims that Hayek would be influenced by Ludwig von Mises, the "the fountainhead of modern libertarianism" or a conservative before conservatism, depending on the author.[36] Hayek was also a devotee of fellow Austrian economists Eugen von Bohm-Bawerk, who argued that the price of goods resulted not from labor but from subjective marginal valuations (consumer desires), and Friedrich Wieser, who coined the phrases "marginal utility" and "opportunity cost."[37]

Road, a brief, lucid translation of liberal economic theory, first appeared in England in March 1944 and was released in the United States that September. Hayek discussed intricate economic theories, monetary policy, market processes, and efficiency problems in planned economies, in accessible terms. *Road*'s U.S. publisher, the University of Chicago Press, was the fourth to review the book.[38] While *Road* was growing in popularity in England, the U.S. version appeared with an introduction by influential columnist John Chamberlain and received substantial press attention. A lead *New York Times* book review by popular economist Henry Hazlitt likened Hayek's work to John Stuart

Mill's "On Liberty." Sales soared after Hazlitt's review.[39] They continued skyward when, in 1945, *Reader's Digest* published a serial version of *Road*, condensed by Max Eastman, and 600,000 copies of the compact book were distributed by the Book of the Month Club.[40]

The tolls exacted by the worst conflicts of the century were fixtures in Hayek's mind as he composed *Road*. He fought for Austria in World War I and was not exempt from the war that followed the war to end all wars. Not only was he a refugee from Nazism, Hayek wrote the book as somewhat of an academic refugee. When the London School of Economics, where he taught, moved north to avoid Hitler's blitzkrieg, Hayek maintained steady progress even though he completed duties as an air warden during the period as well.[41] Hayek's political philosophy was infused with a predictable skepticism toward concentrated power and largely dedicated to preserving a system in which authorities were held to a set of transparent guidelines. Hayek abandoned any hope that the rule of the powerful might be palatable. The title he chose for his book revealed his intellectual indebtedness to the skeptical political theories penned after the French Revolution turned tyrannical. "The road to servitude," the metaphoric phrase that Hayek found meaningful, was Alexis de Tocqueville's.[42] The chance that the benevolent dictator or rational planning committee would rise to power peacefully or that power would transfer bloodlessly through the magnanimous abdications of a series of Cincinnatus clones was not worth taking.[43]

Through *Road*, Hayek has become conservatives' herald of laissez-faire, but the book was neither doctrinaire nor friendly toward inflexible economics of any kind.[44] Hayek's concessions toward a government-enforced social safety net were striking not only because they blended classical liberal economics with modern liberal governance. Hayek opened the book with these allowances. He favored a regulated workplace including working hour maximums and safety provisions, as well as a social safety net including a minimum wage. Above all, Hayek sought to protect fair market competition, and government action was a necessary check on the gross competitive disparities and opportunities for deceit in a laissez-faire system. As Hayek stated clearly, "In no system that could be rationally defended would the state just do nothing. An effective competitive system needs an intelligently designed and continuously adjusted legal framework as much as any other."[45] John Maynard Keynes, Hayek's colleague, friendly nemesis, and co–air warden during the blitzkrieg, was surprised by Hayek's deviations from classical liberalism.[46] Rand was apoplectic. "The man is an ass, with no conception of a free society at all," she wrote of Hayek in her copy of *Road*.[47]

At first glance, Hayek's assumption that individual economic liberty was the backbone of a tolerant society did not square with his acknowledgment that government should redistribute wealth on a limited basis. This potential contradiction begged an important question about his political theory: how did Hayek tolerate some government actions but not others? Unlike other free market defenders, especially strict libertarians for whom liberty meant unrestricted personal autonomy, Hayek's political theory could not be reduced to a dramatic binary with government in the role of permanent villain and citizens playing the part of plucky protagonists. In *Road*, Hayek enumerated how government could be an effective guarantor of market fairness by limiting social "coercion" and enforcing the "Rule of Law."

Although Hayek's defense of the market, private property, and limited government was the most salient characteristic of his work, his perspectives on each of these stemmed from his epistemological pessimism about what humans could and could not reasonably know.[48] He called his approach to epistemology the "knowledge problem," and it may have been his most enduring legacy in economics.[49] Russell Kirk made an enemy of reason; Hayek was a cautious supporter rather than some tribune of pure reason from the early Enlightenment. Hayek applied his suspicion of the powers of reason to economic problems faced by individuals in their daily choices and governments in their yearly expenditures. He accepted the conclusion that humans were capable of folly and barbarianism and often perpetrated both in the name of reason. He did, however, conclude that decisions can be rationally guided and improved over time. His lukewarm assent to reason and market forces was an admission that even the most careful conclusions should be vigilantly checked and frequently revised.

The Austrian school of economics, of which Hayek was affiliated, held that market participants were fallible agents whose decisions were driven by local concerns and subjective decision-making criteria. Hayek's market did not transform ordinary people into gallant heroes by unleashing their untold creative potential. Markets only allowed the dissemination of information through economic exchange. For Hayek, "economic knowledge (i.e., information about price, costs, the state of technology, consumer preferences, and so on) does not exist in a centralized form precisely because a human society is inhabited by acting, choosing individuals who face a world of uncertainty."⁵⁰ Prices, for instance, were not some gluttonous capitalist's estimation of the maximum amount of money that might be extracted from poor sap consumers; prices were not arbitrarily chosen in large part because prices were not only the result of individual or organizational choices. Market prices were depositories of economic information.

Markets and prices were amalgams of a broader range of decisions other individuals made given similar economic indicators of relative scarcity. Prices enabled economic rationality; markets were the venue in which reasoned choices could be exercised. Reason was useful in governing social affairs only when the market produced the "limited knowledge" about "social and economic processes" that it could.[51] Prices reflected the availability of raw materials, costs of production, transportation difficulties, storing expenses, demand, as well as potential profits. Prices organically evolved as information accumulated, and they functioned as social signals about events in far away places. Without an understanding of natural fluctuations in, say, the quantity of a specific type of peaches after a frost, economic actors would be robbed of information that could be used to predict the price of other peaches as well as goods for which peaches were an ingredient. Nationalized industry, fixed prices, or forms of government aid to private businesses upset prices and accentuated the collective knowledge problem.

Average people were ill-equipped to ask the right economic questions, amass evidence, assess trends, and derive appropriate conclusions. Hayek hoped only to "enable" people to use whatever information they could amass to the "fullest," especially within "particular circumstances of time and place."[52] The individual did not possess some innate wisdom or benefit from some salt-of-the-earth common sense. She needed to be able to trust essential economic data. Hayek thus developed a political theory largely shorn of mythological components. Not some romanticized, square-jawed matinee idol, Hayek's typical individual was timid and tender, far more pathetic than iconic. Access to reasonably up-to-date and fairly accurate economic information was, to an average person easily overwhelmed by a torrent of information, essential to make well-informed predictions about an uncertain world. Unlike the near-divine characteristics of heroes in Goldwater's performance of conservatism, Hayek's central character was unromantic. His protagonist had qualities worth protecting, but these did not amount to anything truly grand:

> The point which is so important is the basic fact that *it is impossible for any man to survey more than a limited field*, to be aware of the urgency of more than a limited number of needs. . . . This is the fundamental fact on which the whole philosophy of individualism is based. . . . It merely starts from the indisputable fact that the *limits* of our powers of imagination make it impossible to include in our scale of values more than a sector of the needs of the whole society.[53]

The knowledge problem was a sober reminder that no person or organization could ever know enough to account for everyone's well-being. Hayek's skepticism about knowledge worked from the presumption that only the arrogant would claim to have gathered enough information about a product, say wheat, to set limits on production or consumption. Our mental measurements were too imprecise, our perspective was too limited, and our management of power was too fickle to presume that such central control with be either efficient or judicious.

Enemies of Liberty

Democracy, Hayek contended, flourished where capitalism did; self-determination was contingent on personal liberty.[54] The value of liberty for Hayek was not to free capable individuals from all restraints. For Hayek, liberty meant the limitation of uncertainty, the partial illumination of a dark world. How is it possible, a left-minded critic might ask, to rely on competitive markets, of all things, to maximize liberty and limit coercion? After all, is profit not the result of selling a good for more than it takes to produce the good, of extracting surplus value from workers? Hayek's own definition of coercion, "when one man's actions are made to serve another man's will, not for his own but for the other's purpose," could impugn the relationship between owners and laborers in private businesses.[55] The question concerning the coercive power of businesses as employers and owners of capital cuts to the heart of liberty in Hayek's system. Hayek was not an absolutist; an individual's liberty was not dependent on everyone's liberty. Perfect liberty, he conceded readily, was unattainable; the key was relative liberty. On balance, a competitive market system promoted more liberty than other systems. Moreover, and this was one of the central points of *Road*, the competitive market system did not run the same risk of totalitarianism as a planned economy.

Much like James Madison argued in *Federalist* 10 that passionate political factions would offset one another in a sizable democracy, Hayek perceived the best method to produce liberty was to balance innovation against innovation, greed against greed, and self-interest against self-interest. Liberty was produced by the set of institutional arrangements that pit the ambitions of individuals against one another to make private competition a public good. The basic aim was to preserve a private space beyond the reach of government where a variety of "views and tastes" could be expressed fearlessly.[56] "The classical liberal solution," Hayek's biographer Bruce Caldwell explains, "is to define a private sphere of individual activity, to grant the state a monopoly on coercion, and then to limit the coercive powers of the state to those instances where it is itself preventing coercion."[57]

The "Rule of Law" limited both the state's and the market's coercive powers. Official legality was not the sum of the Rule of Law. As Hayek asked in *Road*, would Hitler's accession by constitutionally sanctioned procedures suggest that the Rule of Law operated in interwar Germany?[58] Instead of valorizing any existing regime of semifunctioning legal rules, Hayek's Rule of Law consisted of the ideal legal restraints that protected competitive enterprise. The Rule of Law was a normative "doctrine concerning what the law ought to be, concerning the general attributes that particular laws should possess."[59] In *The Constitution of Liberty*, Hayek established that these "laws of liberty" should be designed to increase the free flow of information and ensure market participants some level of predictability. Such laws should be abstractly designed, constructed impersonally, enforced in all cases, and publicized. That is, laws were composed without regard to specific demographic groups or individual status, were enforced uniformly across social strata, and were available for public inspection.[60] Liberty was endangered not by the exercise of all centralized power, but by the ability to exercise arbitrary power; "*ad hoc*" actions stultified "individual efforts."[61] Although they would be couched in the language of "liberty" in his later work, these components are similar to the liberal principles established in *Road*: the promotion of competition, regulating fraud in the market, limiting arbitrary rule-making by government, and preventing favoritism in the enforcement of laws.[62]

Road was not just a rumination on abstract legal principles. Hayek wrote the book in response to specific atrocities perpetrated by over-reaching governments. Like Richard Weaver's *Ideas Have Consequences* and Peter Viereck's *Metapolitics: From the Romantics to Hitler, Road* of-fered an explanation of the rise of fascism with Germany most clearly in view. Hayek explained Nazism not as an outgrowth of Prussian mili-tarism, an extension of Romantic nationalism, or the rejection of higher moral law but as a consequence of socialism.[63] National Socialism, put simply, grew from philosophical socialism. Hayek cited Tocqueville's argument from 1848: "Democracy and socialism have nothing in com-mon but one word: equality. But notice the difference: while democ-racy seeks equality in liberty, socialism seeks equality in restraint and servitude."[64] Socialist tendencies were what Germany shared with Italy, Spain, and Russia. National Socialism opposed the liberal tradition that protected individual achievement in culture and respected indi-vidual liberty in politics: "The Nazi leader who described the National Socialist revolution as a counter-Renaissance spoke more truly than he probably knew. It was the decisive step in the destruction of that civili-zation which modern man had built up from the age of the Renaissance and which was, above all, an individualist civilization."[65] Hayek's book was more than an economic history of Nazism; he framed it as a warn-ing to Great Britain and, to a lesser extent, the United States. Students of the "currents of ideas" would note, he claimed, the parallel patterns in thought "in Germany during and after the last war [World War I] and the present current of ideas in the democracies."[66]

Hayek's warning that fascism could happen in the West gave *Road* tremendous rhetorical force, but Nazism was only the most recent, grotesque manifestation of an expansive ideological tradition. The great ideological enemies in the traditionalist dialect—socialism, lib-eralism, atheism, and scientism—could not see truths about human nature, community, and religion through their hubristic fog. Hayek viewed some of these same ideas as pernicious, but his rationale for opposing them was anathema to traditionalists. Although he invoked National Socialism as the consequence of government control of eco-nomic liberties, Hayek was neither a polemicist nor a scare tactician. The most salient enemy in *Road* was an idea, rather an approach to others' ideas, and everyone was vulnerable to its promise of security. Hayek's economic program was premised on protecting the variety of human experiences and imagining a political framework that checked rule-bound dogmatists, utopian social engineers, fascist nationalists, and any group that put the achievement of its ideological goals ahead of individuals' ability to follow their own vision of the good life. What Hayek's opponents had in common was not that they preferred the wrong political and economic arrangements but that they attempted to impose on others a political program based on their singular vision of a good life. Masses can be terrorized, one of Hayek's acolytes wrote, by those who would sacrifice individual life and liberty to achieve their "vision of the glory of a nation and a people."[67] Similarly, the villains in Hayek's work were not governments per se, but any set of political and economic circumstances that empowered unchecked inquisitors and enabled "the worst" to "get on top."[68]

Since Hayek's political theory lacked the narrative force of a personified enemy and an enchanting hero, it also lacked a dramatic resolution, one in which the two did climactic battle. Asserting the risk of Nazism in England and the United States was dramatic, but considering that he wrote while the Nazis bombed, Hayek can hardly be faulted for wild hyperbole. *Road* was more a sensible plea for understanding across political ideologies than a war cry against socialists of all kinds. Socialists, he argued, shared the same goals as classic liberals; they only disagreed about the means of their achievement, and, he wrote empathetically, most "would recoil" if they knew the disastrous consequences of their ideas in practice.[69] Since Hayek criticized not just socialism but the more general notion of a singular vision of order, he did not name names of planners or concentrate attention on an identifiable group of people (for example, Communists) hell-bent on destroying sacred values. Hayek thus reversed the pattern Kenneth Burke found in Hitler's rhetoric of national crisis. Whereas Hitler "materialized" a national scapegoat in the form of greedy, diseased Jews, Hayek took real groups of people—fascists, Communists, and liberals—and abstracted their similarities.[70] These were flesh-and-blood people with sympathetic motivations and recognizable concerns. Hayek humanized potential villains. An idea as an enemy definitely required vigilance because it could take root anywhere. An idea as an enemy could not, however, become a scapegoat.

What Hayek's liberty promised was actually quite limited. His arguments crested not with the salvation of a fully realized political dream or the conquering of an adversary, but with the cautious optimism that economic liberty underscored political liberty. The consummate realist, Hayek's liberty was defended in the careful terms of the social scientist, not the certain terms and tones of the righteous. As he argued in *Road*, "The attitude of the liberal toward society is like that of the gardener who tends a plant and, in order to create the conditions most favorable to its growth, must know as much as possible about its structure and the way it functions."[71] He admitted that the market price system often exacted "cruelly high" social costs by creating wealth disparities and producing classes of haves and have-nots. The market was often a world of "orders and prohibitions" in which "the favor of the mighty" lacked capable opposition.[72] The prospect of living in an era of high unemployment and cyclical recessions was daunting, but not as grueling as bread lines. Frugal spending and saving in preparation for hard times were better than being sent to the Gulag as an enemy of the people for reading the wrong book. As economic opportunities increased in traditionally restrictive societies, political controls would relax as well. Hayek assured nothing more than the liberty to make mistakes and the hope that others would do the same and mind their own business.

Hayek's Influence

Hayek's influence on public policy and political culture was greater than that of most intellectuals writing in the twentieth century. Milton Friedman reported that when he queried classical liberals in many countries about how they came to believe in market solutions, reading *Road* was the most frequent answer.[73] Friedman, recipient of the Nobel Prize and adviser to numerous politicians around the globe, authored the introduction to several editions of *Road*, including its fiftieth anniversary edition.[74] The first chapter of his *Capitalism and Freedom* (1962), entitled "Economic and Political Freedom," an essential linkage clarified by Hayek, asserted that "centralized control of economic activity would prove *The Road to Serfdom*."[75] Ronald Reagan was also an early devotee; he parroted Hayek's language ("State Socialism," "benevolent monarchy," and so forth) in letters to associates, like Richard Nixon, as early as 1960.[76] Reagan's first inaugural address reflected the reversal of decades of Keynesian thinking by declaring that "government is not the solution" to national problems. According to Newt Gingrich, another disciple, Hayek changed the world through Reagan.

The president was Hayek's "chief popularizer," promoting the same ideas with "better language."[77]

Although he protested the label, Hayek's message succeeded as a conservative message because it tacitly rebutted characterizations of conservatives as xenophobic, or theocratic, or just cruel capitalists. Conservatives could reposition themselves through Hayek as something other than greedy misers looking out for pecuniary interests. They were not Gilded Age holdovers going to battle for the Rockefellers, Carnegies, and Vanderbilts; conservatives were honorable, altruistic protectors of liberty whose prophecies about the dangers of government power were proven by the horrors in Europe. Hayek, in short, helped conservatives become humanitarians. Contrasting sharply with the perception that conservatism was worried only about private, pecuniary, and rent-seeking interests of the well-heeled, Hayek enabled conservatives to blend discussions of public and private welfare. Since the Hayek that conservatives appropriated spoke only about matters of the public interest, dismissing market economics as economic Darwinism or apologies for the wealthy became more difficult.[78]

Road was published during a powerful leftward turn in economics. Only ten years, for instance, separated Huey Long's "Share Our Wealth" program and the book's publication. By reframing the debate about private wealth and competitive markets, Hayek helped conservatives cultivate answers to postwar, post-Depression charges of economic unfairness. In Hayek's hands, private enterprise became public service. Entrepreneurs were not public servants in the sense that owning a successful roofing business created jobs and possibilities for economic advances in a local community, but that each exercise of financial liberty built the bulwark against economic despotism higher. In particular, Hayek's claim that state economic power traded off with individual political freedom allowed conservatives to advance a case for market economics with a benevolent rationale. In the wake of heartless midcentury killings, Hayek did not propose a solution that smacked of heartless disinterest in the less fortunate. Unlike Rand's superman, John Galt, and her broader defense of the morality of greed, Hayek's political theory held rhetorical appeal for conservatives because it began at the bottom, not the top.[79] Hayek imagined economic and political arrangements with each social strata in mind. His was a sober attempt to resuscitate the value of individual life in an age in which individuals had become thoroughly expendable.

The Goldwater Phoenix

Hayek made certainty an enemy: the sanctimony of the dogmatist, the certain dogmas of the fascist, and the certain conclusions of utopian planners. Barry Goldwater tolerated no trepidation; certainty was his rhetorical stock-in-trade. His most famous line, thundered at the 1964 Republican National Convention, "I would remind you that extremism in the defense of liberty is no vice," expressed this confident, assured tone. The line, a Henry Jaffa–authored late addition to the speech, was unrehearsed by Goldwater and unappreciated by Goldwater's campaign managers.[80] Richard Nixon, who introduced Goldwater with a big-tent Republicanism speech, said he felt "physically sick" after hearing the nominee's polarizing speech. Dwight Eisenhower even demanded an explanation for the vitriol.[81] Their fears about what his bravado might do to the party were not unfounded.[82] The hullabaloo had little to do with "liberty," Hayek's usual locution. "Extremism" was an especially acidic term in 1964. Even though President Kennedy's assassin was a former Communist, it was widely feared that a climate of extremism was partly to blame for the president's death.[83] As the historian Sean Cunningham writes, "To be an extremist in 1964 was almost as bad as being a communist in 1952."[84]

Goldwater was not much for following trends, and his followers were galvanized by his gall. A deafening roar required Goldwater to pause for nearly a minute after he embraced extremism so brazenly.[85] Goldwater was an atypical postwar Republican. He was one of a few Republicans to survive the lopsided midterm elections of 1958; he was nearly drafted to run for the presidency in 1960, and he resisted running in 1964. An insurgent conservative candidate in his own party then dominated by what he, Buckley, and others called Eastern Establishment Republicans, Goldwater was, in short, the consummate rhetorical iconoclast. He rejected the Republicanism of Eisenhower and Nelson Rockefeller as diluted New Dealism; Goldwater's star rose among conservatives looking for an anti-Establishment candidate. His iconoclastic persona was buttressed by a willingness to provoke scorn and an off-putting directness that signified his defiance of political convention.

The way that Goldwater approached extremism had an important precedent. When Young Americans for Freedom was established in 1960, adding "conservative" to the organization's title was rejected as "public relations poison."[86] *The Conscience of a Conservative*, which "altered the American political landscape" and transformed the Arizona senator "into the most popular conservative in the country," was published that same year.[87] His standing against the political tide inflamed enemies but energized acolytes. One University of Wisconsin student's words in the early 1960s typified the effect of Goldwater's brand of iconoclastic conservatism: "You walk around with your Goldwater button and you feel the thrill of treason."[88] The student identified with a misanthropic movement; but what made Goldwater likeable to followers made him unelectable to the nation. Goldwater was trounced by Johnson in 1964 (43 million votes to 27 million votes; forty-four states to six).[89]

As energizing as Goldwater's 1964 acceptance speech was, "extremism in the defense of liberty" was an insufficient indicator of Goldwater's conservative vocabulary. "Freedom," not "liberty," was essential to his take-no-prisoners conservative performance; it was Goldwater's jab, and he led most of his argumentative combinations, from his opposition to farm subsidies to federal civil rights law, with the word. Liberty was even overshadowed by freedom in his 1964 nomination acceptance address.[90] Freedom was not a simple political objective for Goldwater; it was an empyrean quest and the defining element of his rhetorical rebelliousness. Although his freedom retained its typical antipathy toward government regulation and concern for individual privacy, his version of freedom stood out among the litany of conservative promoters of the term because it demanded public performance through brassy acts. As its meaning took shape in Goldwater's iconoclastic style, freedom became something other than a quality or a status that could be privately possessed or secretly enjoyed. Goldwater's freedom conferred public duties on conservatives. It existed only where it was activated, and it was most potent when wielded at something, like government, or someone, like liberals, who might have been tempted to deny it. Freedom connoted both individual emancipation from restriction as well as a collective duty to find places where tyranny thrived and transform them in freedom's name. Free people and free nations knew that freedom required sacrifice; freedom had to be fought for.

Conscience, published four years before his Cow Palace address, was Goldwater's preeminent, and most popular, defense of freedom.[91] Its contents laid the groundwork for the "extremism" speech, the larger

Goldwater campaign, and, some said, Reagan's victorious campaign in 1980.[92] Few conservative books have attracted more attention than *Conscience*.[93] A runaway hit from the beginning with 85,000 sales in its first month and 700,000 sales by the end of 1960, *Conscience* amassed 3.5 million sales by the end of 1964. It even reached number six on the *New York Times* nonfiction bestseller list.[94] One conservative historian praised *Conscience* as the most popular political manifesto, with an estimated ten million readers, in twentieth-century America.[95]

The snappy language of *Conscience* moved conservatives in ways more intellectual conservatives discourses could not. As Pat Buchanan wrote of the book, "Like the man who produced it, the prose remains unembellished, simple, honest, straight, true."[96] Some remembered reading it and experiencing "a political awakening."[97] It spared the reader any discussion of specific policy issues until after the rousing, straightforward introduction in which freedom became the natural destiny of Americans. Readers could thus love its early lines "about permanent truths" or its overall "anti-authoritarian streak" without engaging Goldwater's more specific proposals about farm subsidies and military spending.[98] It was the galvanizing manifesto activist conservatives needed to take their case to the public. *Conscience* convinced "them that the time was ripe for a conservative counterattack."[99] Goldwater's conservative message, steadfast individualism, recognized the potential for greatness in every American citizen and presaged the transformation of conservatism into a winning electoral message. Overall, *Conscience* was a "brilliant rhetorical performance."[100]

The "rhetorical and intellectual" hold Goldwater had on followers inspired some to convert the bantam, catchy declarations throughout *Conscience* into explicit political goals.[101] For instance, the National Youth for Goldwater organization, founded just after the publication of *Conscience*, pursued two primary objectives: securing Goldwater's place on the Republican ticket in 1960 and creating a "a permanent, nationwide unity of youthful supporters" dedicated to pursuing maxims spelled out in *Conscience*.[102] Copies of *The Conscience of a Conservative* were like membership cards in YAF, the Right's equivalent to Students for a Democratic Society; everyone got their own when they signed up.[103] Youthful adherents in YAF even memorized portions of Goldwater's book.[104]

Such organizations found lasting success as the political culture became shaped by operatives and advocates who, as youths, had been shaped by *Conscience*. Karl Rove, for example, remembered being "wild" for *Conscience* as a teenager. "I loved," Rove said breathlessly, "that his philosophy celebrated freedom and responsibility, the dignity and worth of every individual, the danger of intrusive government, and the importance of politics to protecting those ideals."[105] For Rove and many others, *Conscience* was both a succinct explication of conservatism and a fetching demonstration of how to be conservative. "Reading it," one historian summarized, "conservatives felt born again."[106]

It took Brent Bozell only two weeks to write *Conscience*.[107] Goldwater possessed an unmistakable voice, but he balked at the chance at authorship, declaring, "I'm not a writer. I wouldn't know how to go about it."[108] Bozell, who also coauthored *McCarthy and His Enemies* with Buckley, his former debate partner, was a fellow student of Willmoore Kendall's at Yale. But Bozell did not argue as a traditionalist in *Conscience*; the solution he offered to every problem that vexed the nation, greater individual freedom, would have left traditionalists like Kirk and Weaver nonplussed. In one of the more powerful ironies of the split between traditionalists and libertarians, it was Bozell, the eastern-educated traditionalist and supporter of Catholic monarchist government, who penned the sine qua non of Western-styled, straight-talking, hands-off conservatism.[109]

Although Bozell actually put pen to paper, the young writer was familiar with the idioms of other, more libertarian *National Review* contributors as well as Goldwater's particular rhetorical style: an overriding suspicion of state power expressed in terse, principled shots. He wrote speeches for Goldwater in the late 1950s and studied many more to channel Goldwater's immoderate diction.[110] Bozell did trim, however, the sentimentality from some of Goldwater's formulations, calling them "a little poetic and corny."[111] One of the senator's highest levels of involvement with *Conscience* was sending a telegram demanding his 200 author's copies *after* it had been printed, but he was not entirely absent from the project.[112] He dictated preliminary ideas about the book to his secretary, who, in turn, delivered them to Bozell. The two also discussed the book's organization and royalties over lunch before Bozell began writing in earnest.[113]

Conscience was not even Goldwater's idea; it was Clarence Manion's. The prolific pamphleteer, radio host, and dean of Notre Dame's law school secured the funding, author, and publisher for *Conscience*. In a 1959 letter to Buckley, Manion said he had several reasons for publish-

ing such a book. Even though Goldwater had only, Manion cracked, a
"Chinaman's chance" at the 1960 Republican National Convention, he
wanted to give him an "authentic platform" to make a run at the nomination.[114] Its working title was "What Americanism Means to Me," and
Manion hoped it would "be purchased by corporations and distributed
by the hundreds of thousands."[115] He got his wish. In the early 1960s,
particularly in rural areas, local demand for books like *Conscience*, J.
Evetts Haley's *A Texan Looks at Lyndon*, and others was staggering.
Conservative demand equaled the production capacity of the nation's
two largest paperback printing plants, which were manufacturing all
of them.[116]

The Style of an Iconoclast

Conscience was stylistically unique among the books of the conservative canon. Several canonical texts, like *Witness* or *The Conservative
Mind*, would do well as doorstops; others, like Buckley's writings, were
multisyllabic exercises in rhetorical acrobatics; still others, like *Ideas
Have Consequences* or *Capitalism and Freedom*, posited a straightforward overall thesis but did little to aid a reader's understanding of their
manifold supporting arguments. Goldwater wanted conservatism to
jumpstart Americans' personal pride, to activate an undaunted self-
assuredness, and *Conscience* modeled a style fit for that purpose.

Traditionalists wrote as victims of historical circumstance, principled stalwarts born several centuries too late to enjoy the golden age
of humanity. Goldwater was a stalwart too, but he wrote confidently
of conservatism's self-evident ideological superiority. In his control,
conservatism was audacious, a brash welcome to all challengers, an
intrepid politics typified by the italicized, underlined points and short,
declarative sentences. His conservatism was, like a proper noun meriting textual designation, capitalized in all instances ("Conservatism").
"America is fundamentally a Conservative nation," Goldwater wrote
in the book's second paragraph; Americans "yearn for a return to
Conservative principles."[117] Only conservatives he asserted, understood the true meaning of the Constitution. Goldwater acted as if he
led a movement that was firmly entrenched within the U.S. political
consciousness, not as a representative of an upstart political identity
struggling to find national footing. His conservatism was not contested;

it had no history of disuse or misuse. Goldwater even criticized those conservatives who "apologize" for their "Conservative instincts." Show some moxie, Goldwater exhorted, and express yourselves "boldly."[118]

The book's arguments were preformatted as arrant talking points that could be remembered, repeated, or transposed onto pamphlets. In fact, every aspect of the book's pagination was suited for ease of access and understanding. Even with a large typeface and a full space between each short paragraph, *Conscience* was a brisk read at just over 100 pages. It was also tightly organized with subheadings ("Freedom of Association," "Economic Freedom," and so forth), signposting language establishing an outline for each chapter, and concluding lessons exemplifying the principles guiding Goldwater's case-by-case reasoning (*"The evil to be eliminated is the power of unions to enforce industry-wide bargaining."*).[119] Each political lecture on the necessity of states' rights or the justice of tax cuts was boiled down to a basic pithy proverb. These powerfully worded and plainly stated dictums were often italicized in the text for added ardor.

Goldwater's pointed, brusque writing appeared as an unstylish and authentic recitation of political values. It gained purchase by standing beside elegant, garish rhetorics and seeming candid by comparison. Several libertarian writers used, James Arnt Aune argues, an "antirhetorical rhetoric that favors the plain style and avoids verbal ornament."[120] This "realist style" was so frank that it seemed the opposite of a rhetorical gambit. Realist rhetoricians had no flaw to hide, no failing to decorate. Their language was "indigenous to reality itself."[121] Goldwater's style flaunted what it lacked; it was unadorned, unvarnished, and uncomplicated, plain talk that evinced heartfelt truths. He offered a frank language that seemed interested only in the real and the self-evident, not matters for reflection and speculation. Anti-artifice was a clever form of artifice.

Suspicious of densely composed traditionalist conservatism as little more than an obscure theory for academic backwaters, Goldwater quipped that high-minded conservative intellectuals "couldn't get themselves elected dog-catcher."[122] Goldwater's crack revealed far more than the difference between a vote-conscious politician and academics writing for specialized audiences. Their stylistic differences were, in fact, reflections of their doctrinal differences. In attempting to rescue conservatism from associations with backward reactionaries, traditionalists like Kirk spoke not only differently than the masses, but

about thinkers most people had never heard of. Part of their contribution to the conservative political language was a discourse marked by
its density. Where the traditionalists were suspicious of the masses as
a dangerous, dopey mob, Goldwater considered mass society a collection of venerable individuals, each of whom possessed limitless capacity for achievement. The traditionalists' idealized individual was best
when engaged in reverent reflection rather than bold action; Hayek's
normal individual did not require explicit communal guidance or religious admonitions, but she did need reliable economic information.
Goldwater's individual was a heroic warrior warring against government intervention and unleashing her own grand designs. As Daniel T.
Rodgers observes, "Government was the people's antagonist, the lim-
iter of their limitlessness."[123] In *Conscience* as well as his presidential
campaign, Goldwater addressed these omni-competent warriors with a
war whoop. In one instance, he riled up a California crowd by circling
the warning track in Dodger stadium in a Dodger-blue convertible.[124]

Freedom

The traditionalist dialect was not completely absent from *Conscience*;
the opening rationale for a politics of freedom took some rhetorical cues
from the more religious language of the traditionalists. In the book's
brief foreword and first chapter, Goldwater crafted "Conservatism" as
an "ancient and tested" tradition dedicated to the liberation of individuals.[125] He framed conservatism as "the attempt to apply the wisdom
and experience and the revealed truths of the past to the problems
of today."[126] In these few pages, Goldwater pressed a religious justification for freedom as well. "God" was "the author of freedom," he
wrote.[127] Moreover, Goldwater's assertion of divine and natural laws
without a "dateline" mirrored the traditionalists' discussion of a natural order. Since conservatism was "derived from the nature of man,
and from the truths that God has revealed about His creation," it was
natural, not ideological.[128] Individuals were instinctually equipped
with material, immediate survival needs but also spiritual, incorporeal
needs. Goldwater called this duality the "*whole* man" and claimed that
only conservatism addressed both instincts.[129] To consider one's self an
individual with inviolable possessions was, according to Goldwater, an
instinct, one that conservatives accepted and attended to. Accordingly,

conservatism would never grow outmoded. It was timeless, he assured readers, permanently relevant like "the Golden Rule, or the Ten Commandments or Aristotle's *Politics*."[130]

Although *Conscience* began with a universalist, religious justification for freedom, Goldwater was no hedgehog stylist with a declinist historical narrative, specific division points through history, and overall lamentation of civilizational decay. What also separated Goldwater from the hedgehog style of the traditionalists was that he venerated as timeless a force of social disaggregation rather than cohesion. He understood human nature as infinitely pluralistic; only a philosophy that accounts for, Goldwater wrote, "*the different potentialities of each man can claim to be in accord with Nature*."[131] Conservatives, Goldwater argued, began from the precept that each individual "is a unique creature" whose difference from other humans was "absolute."[132] Riffing on the book's title, Goldwater clarified that "the conscience of the Conservative is pricked by *anyone* who would debase the dignity of the individual human being."[133] His one great truth of human history, that justice was aligned with personal freedom, was hedgehog gloss on an atomized lesson: history was not guided by one great truth if each person was entitled to pursue her own truth, to make her own reality, to chart her own course. Goldwater imported the language of timeless universality in support of a concept that was, as he touted, contingent, personal, and subjective.

After the first few pages of the memorable foreword and first chapter in which Goldwater defined liberty as personal excess and freedom as self-determination consistent with social "order," the rest of *Conscience* did not say much about God or Nature, natural law, or any limitations on individuals.[134] Goldwater noted that order should not be a real priority for conservatives; "order is pretty well taken care of," he surmised.[135] Despite his head fakes in the direction of religion, the Goldwater of *Conscience* "sold himself as a very libertarian figure: anti–farm subsidies, anti–welfare state, anti–New Deal regulations and giveaways."[136] But his libertarianism was not just a matter of policy positions; freedom bestowed public duties on the free. Expanding the range of choices available to individuals required limiting the choices politicians could exercise. Conservatives, Goldwater wrote, should swear public oaths to protect freedom and should only consider candidates who have proclaimed such an oath. He exemplified this commitment to freedom with a succinct oath in *Conscience*: "I have little interest in streamlining government or in making it more efficient, for I mean to reduce its size. I do not undertake to promote welfare, for I propose to extend freedom. My aim is not to pass laws, but to repeal them."[137]

Goldwater's conservatism declared war on government. The legitimate functions of government, he noted briefly, included the "establishment of social order," protection from foreign adversaries, the administration of justice, and ensuring the free exchange of goods. However, since all government carried the inevitable risk of backsliding toward tyrannical rule, Goldwater suggested that government might not be a trustworthy executor of limited goals. *"The conduct of our affairs,"* he emphasized, must be entrusted to politicians who held their first duty as divesting *"themselves of the power they have been given."* The question conservatives should ask of every policy, the question that Goldwater used to organize his analysis of states' rights, labor, taxes, education, and the Cold War, was simple: *"Are we maximizing freedom?"*[138]

In Goldwater's usage, "maximizing freedom" meant empowering individuals to make their own choices and solve their own problems, but he also portrayed freedom as the power to make a historical correction; government, which had grown illegitimately, was ceding power back to individuals. *Conscience* was not about markets or capitalism or federalism as much as it was a celebration of the incredible power of normal individuals. Goldwater did not believe in "the common man" because he did not think of citizens as common; such generic descriptors (like the masses or mass society) were the "ultimate slavery."[139] With freedom defined as individual choice unimpeded by government regulation, the only way to maximize freedom was to limit government. Whereas Hayek defined coercion as any action that resulted in the compulsion of individuals to act against their will or interests, Goldwater's use of the concept suggested that coercion was a power only exercised by national government. Freedom was, by definition, quashed by government culprits. Goldwater imagined a political world of nation-states and citizens, absolute coercion and absolute freedom. For instance, when Goldwater cited Acton's warning about the corrupting force of absolute power, he applied it only to officials of government. Government held regulatory power; government could direct the "lives of other men." As such, only government carried the risk of absolute power. Members of government, he theorized, who hold *"some power"* had a natural instinct to acquire *"more* power" and then dreamed of seizing *"all* power."[140] Political power was a "self-aggrandizing force."[141]

Market behaviors, by contrast, were always reflections of freely made choices. It was as if the market would never limit access to necessary goods or that businesses never colluded to limit supplies or fix prices. Goldwater did not mention the risk that a business's profit motives might contradict public welfare because, to him, there was no risk. It was government that imposed arbitrary limitations on individuals, not businesses. Goldwater did not account for the risk that a behemoth corporation could stifle competition, thwart development, constrain market dynamics, and constitute a threat to freedom for the same reason: he perceived no threat.

Conscience was a paean to the nobility of individuals and the magic of their unfettered initiative; it ended by asserting that all individuals must be willing to fight and die for their country. Goldwater held that every dollar that helped grow the welfare state endangered freedom. Goldwater's only allowance, and this was a tremendous departure from strict libertarianism, was for a substantial national military whose duties included responding to what he cast as an imminent Soviet threat.[142] For all of Goldwater's penny-pinching when it came to farm subsidies, and for all his fears of creeping socialism, he trusted military power implicitly in a necessary war against the Soviets. He simply did not apply his conclusions about the corruption of absolute power, the idleness of government workers, or the ineffectiveness of government programs to the military. Government, which was corrupt and untrustworthy in most endeavors, was capable of organizing the largest fighting force on earth and producing and using instruments of death. Acton's warning was simply irrelevant to the exercise of military power. "Freedom from" was unevenly articulated with "freedom to" in Goldwater's account; independence became joined to collective responsibility. These ideas, while conceptually opposed, cohered within Goldwater's implied meaning that freedom enabled private choices but demanded public expression and dutiful defense. The free person who left the grid for the countryside to live the hermit's life shirked these public duties.

In the book's last chapter, Goldwater assessed the viability of several different theories of how to engage freedom's main foe, the "the Soviet Menace." He found them weak-kneed because each shied away from military confrontation. He dismissed alliances, negotiations, the "exchange" program, arms reductions, the United Nations, and aid to other Communist regimes as the naive belief in U.S.-U.S.S.R. coexistence. As he did with the maxim that all policies should maximize freedom, Goldwater offered a simple formulation for evaluating any foreign policy: "Is it helpful in defeating the enemy?"[143] He listed a host of aggressive options, from encouraging revolt in Communist countries to achieving nuclear superiority, all of which were intended to make sure the nation presented itself internationally the way Goldwater wanted conservatives to present themselves domestically: dominant.

The boldness of Goldwater's rhetoric matched the kind of dramatic military response he desired. Goldwater was sick of the apologies, sick of the excuses, sick of "backing down" from a fight.[144] He tired of critics tacitly endorsing "surrender" when they portrayed nuclear warfare as "unthinkable." A "courageous and honorable and dignified" nation must not only think about conducting a war against the Soviets but actively consider it as the best alternative.[145] Violence was inevitable in his view of the Cold War; the United States would be the aggressor and set the terms of confrontation, or it would grow meek and find itself the victim of a Soviet ambush. Either the nation took an appeasing posture and risked total war, or the nation took "the initiative" and conducted a total war on terms it set.[146] In the book's last line, Goldwater figured that the sacred value Americans fought the Soviets to preserve was worth the biggest sacrifice: "For Americans who cherish their lives, but their freedom more, the choice cannot be difficult."[147] When it came to fighting the Soviets, the free person had no real choice. Individual freedom implied national obligation. Freedom demanded sacrifice.[148] As he avowed several times in *Conscience*, social freedom was more important than individual life.[149]

The idea of individual sacrifice for the collective good left orthodox libertarians aghast. Following precepts similar to those Goldwater opened *Conscience* with, they quickly arrived at far different conclusions about military action. Whereas Goldwater tacitly dissociated the noble armed forces from ignoble government, for doctrinaire antistatists, the military, financed by unjustly collected taxes and populated by government employees not subject to market pressures, was an extension of government largesse. Military power, moreover, was statism at its most coercive, when it posed the greatest threat to individual autonomy. Murray Rothbard was so alarmed by the militarist anti-Communism among conservatives that he supported Adlai Stevenson over

Eisenhower in the 1956 election because he did not think Stevenson itched for a fight. If Eisenhower was unnerving, Goldwater was truly petrifying. Rothbard was genuinely fearful that Goldwater would first-strike the Soviets. Beyond his foreign policy concerns, Rothbard also judged Goldwater a false libertarian because he would not repeal the income tax, make Social Security voluntary, or sell off the Tennessee Valley Authority to private bidders. Framing libertarianism in far more absolute terms than Hayek did, Rothbard concluded, "Goldwater and the Conservative Movement are not only not libertarian, but the pre-eminent enemies of liberty of our time."[150] He made Goldwater conservatives out to be worse than Communists.

Rothbard sensed that Goldwater's freedom had a dual meaning; it was both a hands-off philosophy of self-determination in which a person was solely responsible for her own life, but it was also a sacrosanct obligation that Americans were compelled to export even at the expense of many lives. Freedom was a political goal whose achievement was made possible only by government inaction domestically and assertiveness internationally. If, as Goldwater wrote in *Conscience*, "Conservatism holds the key to national salvation," then the next logical step was to proselytize.[151] So where freedom might legitimize social reclusiveness, empower nonconformists, and justify capitalists, it also required a massive military apparatus both to protect freedom domestically and to, when necessary, use the gun barrel to help other nations dedicate themselves to the cause. Freedom was both liberating and imperious, an individualist mantra that the nation was obliged to promote.

The Public and the Private

Liberty and freedom have been sibling terms, and each was the flagship term of different cases for expanded individual choice and reduced economic regulation. Since their publication, the books that championed these terms and these auspicious and audacious cases, *The Road to Serfdom* and *The Conscience of a Conservative*, have been championed by conservatives as the paradigmatic texts of limited government. For instance, after the 2008 economic crash and the surge of libertarian tea party activism among conservatives, advocates mined these texts for arguments showing a direct tradeoff between federal economic programs and individual choices. Hayek's rejuvenation became so prominent during the downturn that conservative media personalities even jostled with one another over who had been his earliest champion. Rush Limbaugh promised that he had recommended Hayek to listeners "as far back as '88 or '89."[152] Weaving Hayek into a folksy tale about power-grabbing government, Glenn Beck even devoted an entire show on Fox News to Hayek: "We have a government car company, government banks, we're talking about government oil companies, government is hiring all the workers. We are there, gang! And as Hayek so clearly demonstrated, this road only leads to one destination."[153] The tea party movement paid an ideological and rhetorical debt to *Conscience* as well. Various commentators described tea party protests as "Goldwater 2.0," Goldwater's "second coming," and pulling "a Goldwater."[154] Few statements of tea party goals revealed the long reach of Goldwater's rhetorical heritage as clearly as *Tea Party Revival: The Conscience of a Conservative Reborn* (2009).[155]

Whereas Hayek's liberty has been a consistent critique of the size of government, freedom has been a more multidimensional cause used to abjure government expansion at home but also used to justify wars abroad. Although both Hayek and Goldwater were, in the broadest sense, advocates of what Isaiah Berlin called "negative liberty," leaving a person alone "to do or be what he is able to do or be," Goldwater's freedom joined choice with sacrifice; his clarion call for greater individual choices in the marketplace was yoked to a plea for Cold War burden sharing and collective responsibility for the nation's security.[156] Hayek's liberty, moreover, represented a broad set of economic and political arrangements that normal individuals inherited rather passively: the flow of information about the price of goods, the organization of capital markets, and the involvement of government as a market referee. Goldwater's freedom was an asset people took and publicly performed against government. Since Goldwater's freedom encouraged minimizing government domestically while ensuring the spread of individual autonomy abroad through military means, it became the symbolic space where individual prerogatives collided with collective duties. Liberty was a term calling for both personal and federal restraint; it called for a sphere of privacy. Freedom implied both personal and governmental aggression; it beckoned for public action.

Road and *Conscience* have been emblematic of the libertarian dialect of the conservative political language, a dialect that venerates individual choice and denigrates collective management, that cherishes local power and loathes centralized power. In fact, a comparative inventory of these god and devil terms, preferred idioms, and standard lines of argument with those of the traditionalist dialect would reveal near opposites. Whereas libertarians emphasized liberty and freedom, traditionalists emphasized obedience and reverence. Whereas libertarians talked with great suspicion about centralized authority, traditionalists talked with great suspicion about unguided individual choice. Kirk and Weaver inspired a conservative dialect distinct from that of Goldwater and Hayek. "The permanent things," anti-Gnosticism, and antinominalism represented concepts inconsistent with "liberty" and "freedom." At a basic level, the conflict between these rival conservatisms emerged from a disagreement about social authority: the authority of individuals and free markets or the authority of the divine and long-standing traditions. For traditionalist thinkers like Kirk and Weaver, private property was a political good, but the radically individuated libertarian scheme made eternal truths and venerable traditions subservient to fickle market forces. Virtues became market trends. For a group of traditionalists that valued stability, capitalism was notoriously unstable. For a group that rejected "materialism" in all forms, capitalist accumulation was only slightly better than Marxist leveling. In the traditionalists' attacks on individual reason, libertarians heard collectivism with a different accent. In the traditionalists' defense of the eternal over the individual, libertarians heard fascist dogmas. Traditionalists and libertarians were at loggerheads.[157]

These dialects are not, however, perfect opposites. To the consternation of doctrinaire libertarians, both *Road* and *Conscience* preserved some sense of public obligation and collective duty, and each made an extensive case for a sphere of government responsibility. Hayek saw government as protecting markets from forces of monopolization and corruption, and he allowed government a role in protecting individuals from a fickle market. Aside from these practical matters, Hayek's entire approach to midcentury political and economic crises was through the lens of collective experiences, collective suffering, and collective information. He assured the Left that he "shared" their values; he just favored individual solutions to a collective problem.[158] With the exception of calling for individual sacrifice to preserve the nation against Communist enemies, *Conscience* was faithful to libertarian doctrines. But that was a major exception, and it stemmed from Goldwater's sense of an overriding individual duty realized through government action to protect the public from what he viewed as existential threats. As a result, much of *Conscience* fell on the conservative side "of the conservative/libertarian divide" on military matters.[159] Libertarians and traditionalists may have agreed in theory that, in some matters, government should safeguard the public interest; the matters of defining public interest, ascertaining whether the public consisted of disaggregated individuals or an organic society, discerning which matters called for federal intervention, and determining what policies should be pursued were bitterly contested, however.

Although the libertarian dialect to which *Road* and *Conscience* were principal contributors did not nurture lines of antimilitarist or irreligious lines of argument that might threaten the conservative coalition, it remained a source of rupture among conservatives. The key terms of the traditionalist and libertarian dialects did not just mirror a fundamental philosophical divide; these terms constituted and shaped that divide and thereby created durable, persistent, and existential symbolic threats to the conservative coalition. The fusionist project would have to overcome this symbolic fracture. David Frum saw an apt comparison with the genesis of midcentury conservatism in the "nationalist historians" who "manufactured 'Croatia' or 'Czechoslovakia' out of half-forgotten medieval and baroque fragments."[160] Frum's analogy, written in 1996, was telling. Of the two nations he cited, one would break apart, and the other broke off from the larger Yugoslav confederation after a bloody conflict. Hybrid political languages run the risk of Balkanization. So many different concepts are figured in so many different idioms with so many different accepted source texts that secession begins to make sense if each camp agitates for its own political identity.

CHAPTER FOUR

Fusionism as Philosophy and Rhetorical Practice

⌘

N early 100 college students met on the Mexican patio of the Great Elm mansion in Sharon, Connecticut, on September 11, 1960, to define conservatism. For many among the youthful collective gathered there—traditionalists, libertarians, anti-Communists, anti–New Dealers, and Christians—it was the "very first time they felt like they were not alone."[1] Their fledgling cause had profited from the unexpected success of a series of controversial books published since the end of World War II. Friedrich Hayek's *The Road to Serfdom* remade libertarian-conservatism as a humanitarian impulse to protect the public from state violence. Barry Goldwater's *The Conscience of a Conservative* cast the conscience of true conservatives as dedicated to the relentless pursuit of one overriding value: freedom. Richard Weaver's *Ideas Have Consequences*, by contrast, aligned conservatism with permanence, social order, and continuity. Russell Kirk's *The Conservative Mind* Americanized conservatism by linking it to a notable array of domestic thinkers. Both in name and practice, conservatism, the faithful's as yet unheralded political identity, benefited from the creation of magazines like *National Review* as well as formal publishing houses and informal hand-to-hand networks in which these books and articles could be read and distributed widely at low cost.[2] Philosophical conservatism was gaining steam.

Political conservatism was not yet, however, a national force; it had minimal electoral presence. Robert Taft's thwarted 1952 campaign for the presidency and Goldwater's reluctant bid at the 1960 Republican National Convention were the only national efforts bearing the name to date. Conservative electoral victories during the mid-century were, as a whole, "uncoordinated and inconclusive."[3] The faithful hoped to change all that in late 1960 by taking high-minded conservatism to college campuses in order to build a youthful political base. To accomplish this goal and make conservatism meaningful outside of their intellectual enclave, the faithful needed a document that would clarify their beliefs, serve as a catchy constitution to unite cantankerous camps, and become a rallying cry for new converts. They needed a declaration.

These young conservatives—the Young Americans for Freedom (YAF) was the moniker they later adopted—had come to the right place, the palatial mansion of their jet-setting intellectual leader, William F. Buckley. Publicist Marvin Liebman, novelist John Dos Passos, and *National Review* theorist Frank Meyer joined Buckley and the students on the patio. These movement elders listened to the larger group debate the merits of a draft of a declaration written by M. Stanton Evans, the twenty-six-year-old editor of the *Indianapolis News*. Penned quickly on the plane into New York, the declaration that became known as the Sharon Statement mixed traditionalist god terms with libertarian lines of argument.[4] Announcing that an age of "moral and political crises" necessitated the renewal of "eternal truths" and "transcendent values" such as "God-given free will," the document's first lines echoed the canonical texts of traditionalism. The Sharon Statement then proclaimed freedom's indivisibility because, in a loose paraphrase of Hayek as well as Lincoln at Gettysburg, "Political freedom cannot long exist without economic freedom." A limited government could guarantee freedom through its three legitimate functions: the "preservation of internal or-

der, the provision of national defense, and the administration of justice."
The declaration identified "international Communism" as the "greatest
single threat to these liberties" and favored "victory over, rather than
coexistence with this menace." Its conclusion proposed one criterion,
à la Goldwater, to judge U.S. foreign policy: "Does it serve the just
interests of the United States?"[5]

These precepts, along with its proclamation that the market
economy was the "most productive supplier of human needs," made
the Sharon Statement an amalgam of conservatism's dominant poles.[6]
But the Sharon Statement's middle way did not resolve the differences
between conservative rivals; it painted over them. Since the incipient
movement progressed even as it "was constantly threatening to break
apart," the Sharon meeting, in fact, symbolized nascent conservatism
appropriately.[7] For instance, rancorous argument filled the Mexican
patio over the Sharon Statement's invocation of "God" and "eternal
truth." The use of "God" narrowly survived a 44–40 vote.[8] Reflecting an
understandable desire for orthodoxy and unanimity within the movement, one conservative writer thought this discord over the eternal
and the individual, of which the Mexican patio row was a microcosm,
could have doomed the whole conservative enterprise; for him, the
conservative synthesis established in the Sharon Statement brought to
mind the "the Austro-Hungarian Empire in its final agonies, not a very
promising model on which to launch a political movement."[9]

It was not only a promising model but an enduring one as well.
After its codification at Buckley's estate, bourgeoning groups like the
California Republican Assembly adopted Sharon Statement principles
as their own. Their politics "meshed libertarianism and social conservatism—a combination that had constituted diverse segments of
American conservatism in the past and that would propel its future."[10]
In the speeches of conservative politicians, the books of conservative
authors, and its continued reprinting by organizations like the Heritage
Foundation and Young America's Foundation, the document has been
used as its authors hoped: as a concise declaration of conservative
principles worthy of fealty.[11] This synthesized libertarian-traditionalist
conservatism, laissez-faire capitalism tethered to Christianity, became
not just a compromise between philosophical conservatisms but the
dominant expression of political conservatism.[12] The Sharon Statement was undoubtedly the conservatism of the movement's pioneer,
Buckley, but its combination of traditionalist and libertarian doctrines

was indebted to one of conservatism's cardinal theorists, Frank Meyer.[13] Evans, author of the Sharon Statement, was one of Meyer's many acolytes.[14] The definition of alloyed conservatism that Meyer developed came to be called "fusionism" even though the tag was not his and he never liked it.[15]

The wide influence of fusionist conservatism is not evidence that Meyer solved midcentury conservatism's "conceptual chaos."[16] By elevating both personal "freedom" and public "virtue" as coequal conservative values, fusionist conservatism, I argue, combined ideals that excluded one another. Nevertheless, Meyer's influence, especially his seminal 1962 work, *In Defense of Freedom: A Conservative Credo*, is evidence of the generative power of organized internal friction within conservatism. Internal friction within conservatism was not necessarily destructive or politically fractious because it was controlled, directed, and connected to a common canon representing the philosophical core of political identity. Friction, in fact, was productive because it diversified the pool of argumentative resources available to conservatives. Internal debate helped conservatives to adjust their message after political defeats, to recalibrate their stated aims amid economic, political, or global changes. Composite argumentative resources meant that live-and-let-live libertarians, sermonizing Christians, states' rights localists, loyal nationalists, and law-and-order candidates could all call themselves conservative. Friction, in sum, was a political liability if unattended but a rhetorical resource when directed by fusionist rhetoric. In the end, controlled friction produced a dedicated political community that would not let a petty thing like disagreement get in the way of political action under a common symbol.

In the two preceding chapters, I demonstrated that conservatism was remade as a political identity in the decades following World War II by a variety of claimants whose political visions and modes of expression were antithetical to one another. In the next three chapters, I demonstrate how three canonical writers forged a conservatism that became more collaborative than combative. In this chapter, I show how Meyer's midcentury writings afforded conservatives the rhetorical resources to overcome doctrinal disputes. In chapter 5, I argue that Buckley furnished a style of intellectual combat whose force among conservative audiences was that of the gladiator before the eager crowd. In chapter 6, I establish that Whittaker Chambers's *Witness*, his account of his defection from Communism, provided conservatives two vital symbols: a Cold War victim to mourn and a vicious Cold War enemy to rally against. Meyer urged cooperation; Buckley showed how to fight; Chambers showed whom to fight. Together, these three writers forged rhetorical templates by which conservatism could be experienced and expressed similarly by advocates advancing dissimilar doctrines. Attentive conservative audiences appropriated the words, idioms, and narratives of canonical tracts that worked best in their political lives.

Fusionism

In 1954, Whittaker Chambers sensed that young conservatism suffered from a problem of definition. As energizing as anti-Communism was, reactionary anti-Communists were propelled by a jumbled hodgepodge of vaguely rightist doctrines. Common enemies necessitated allies, but a strategic partnership against the Soviets was not a fullfledged political philosophy. "A distaste for Communism and socialism," Chambers lamented in a letter to Buckley, "is not a program." Chambers wrote that the Right "can muster great forces" because it had "all the brains, money, and other resources it needs," but those were not enough. The Right's resources could never cohere because it lacked a theoretical foundation, which Chambers termed "indispensable."[17] Although Buckley shunned conformity among conservatives, he also agreed that the lacuna Chambers identified represented a serious problem for the budding movement. "Up where from liberalism?" he asked in 1959. No "conservative political manifesto" had yet solved conservatism's theoretical quandary by pointing "a sure finger in the direction of the good society."[18]

Anti-Communism presented several programmatic and symbolic dilemmas for early conservatism because it brought the lines between traditionalism and libertarianism into sharp relief. Conservatism, of course, was anti-Communist. But the debate over *why* conservatism was anti-Communist raised the question of guiding principles.[19] In what terms or, more accurately, in whose terms should the conservative coalition be cast? Was Communism detestable because it was atheistic, egalitarian, revolutionary, or state controlled? Some of the movement's principal intellectuals were impervious to such programmatic anxieties. "What is more important by far," Willmoore Kendall wrote dismissively of the prospect of a final definition, "than the meaning we assign to 'conservative,' is: who are the anti-Conservatives, and what are their supreme values?"[20] Buckley was not bent on promoting conservative orthodoxy either. *National Review's* eclectic masthead, assembled by Buckley, symbolized the notion that even if conservatives did not always agree, they could disagree together. He tired of "house theologians" looking for any sign of deviation, believing that "a little creative heresy is good for the system."[21]

Notwithstanding Kendall and Buckley, when faced with such foundational disputes over properly conservative doctrine, many conservatives embarked on a seemingly interminable quest for a philosophical foundation.[22] They engaged in self-definition ad nauseam and made "what is conservatism?" an oft-asked and oft-answered question among conservatives.[23] Meyer would have none of Buckley's devil-may-care insouciance. He inveighed against conservative impostors in a regular *National Review* column tellingly titled "Principles and Heresies." Generally, Meyer found his colleagues' nonchalance toward doctrinal uncertainty naive. The specter of inconsistency and contradiction within conservatism was evidence of an unserious, ill-formed philosophy, Meyer thought. His fellow conservative intellectuals' answers to the conservative conundrum were too partisan, too emasculated to lead the West against the Communists, and, most of all, too philosophically shallow. He had been developing a synthesis between traditionalism and libertarianism, considered impossible by many, in *National Review* and other conservative organs since the mid-1950s. Published two months after the Cold War nearly turned nuclear in Cuba, *In Defense of Freedom* was the culmination of his theory-building efforts, his "clarion call" to conservatives.[24] The book was Meyer's chance to fill a rhetorical void within conservatism; it was his chance to show conservatives that their unity was not dependent on their opposition to Communism; it was his chance to give conservatism philosophical coherence. Meyer, the "former Communist warhorse," aspired to become conservatism's premier theorist.[25]

Instead of clearing the definitional haze by siding with one camp of conservatives, Meyer, employing a dialectical approach he learned studying Marx and personally taught during his stint as a Communist Party organizer, figured conservatism as a duality, a necessary and productive interplay between freedom and virtue. The dialectic, a philosophical approach from antiquity that Hegel and Marx used to interpret history, became, quite ironically, in the hands of a former Communist turned conservative anti-Communist, the chief means of establishing philosophical order among midcentury conservatives. Meyer's dialectic was both a philosophical approach that treated conservatism as complex and a rhetorical framework that oscillated between conservative traditions and thereby showcased their similarities. His dialectical understanding of conservatism became a safe route to navigate between the Scylla of traditionalism and the Charybdis of libertarianism, a method to finesse their opposition, to lessen their enmity, and to highlight their mutual dependence. Meyer's dialectical rhetoric taught conservatives the necessity of tension, the productiveness of dispute, and urged them to live with internal differences among themselves. As the architect of fusion, Meyer became a kind of Marxian figure for conservatives, the Right's praxis philosopher.

I assess fusionism doctrinally and rhetorically; that is, I attend to the logical compatibility of its doctrinal precepts while assessing the symbolic appeal of dialectical fusionism as conservatism transitioned from a new midcentury identity to an established political power in the United States. Doctrinal fusion was a rhetorically deft solution to intraconservative warfare, and, all told, Meyer succeeded, but not if judged by the doctrinal criteria he cared about most. He presided over a marriage between traditionalists and libertarians founded on philosophical necessity that worked over the long term for reasons of political success. Although Meyer's fusion did not resolve the logical incompatibility of traditionalism and libertarianism, it guided the creation of an appealingly broad and nonsectarian conservative political identity; fusionism co-opted the key vocabulary of both dialects and created a common language for less doctrinaire and less combative conservatives. At its best, fusionism established a suitable peace between traditionalism and libertarianism. At its worst, the language of fusion held these conservative opponents together in tension. In the end, Meyer's association of freedom and virtue became conservatism's lingua franca.

Meyer, Marx, and the Dialectic

Few philosophical topics have had the shelf life of the dialectic. Despite its different uses by Socrates, medieval philosophers, rhetori-

cal theorists, and Marxists, dialectic pertains to the core ideas of contradiction and conflict.[26] In the ancient rhetorical tradition, dialectic
referred to the back-and-forth process of claim and refutation typified
by the Socratic dialogues.[27] The Socratic dialectical process was one of
collaborative inquiry that attended to competing claims and multiple
sides of a complex issue in the effort to achieve greater understanding
and wider perspective. For Aristotle, dialectic was, like rhetoric, an intellectual disposition toward a world in flux, composed of probabilities,
particularities, and uncertainties.[28] Dialectical conversations examined
the strengths and weaknesses of a thesis.[29]

Hegel's dialectic also emphasized the productiveness of conflict
but for somewhat different purposes. For Hegel, the historical process
of social change could not be reduced to single propositions about the
natural world or to iron laws of history. The world was too vibrant to be
explained so simply. Historical change, by his interpretation, was never
driven by one factor or another, an eternal truth, a transcendent power,
or God's law, but several "logical categories" operating dialectically and
forming the "Spirit" of an age.[30] As a method to achieve greater knowledge, the dialectician approached a work of art, say Edward Munch's
The Scream, or a historical period, say the Reformation, and showed
how each could be broken "into polarities, contradictions, antitheses,
and oppositions."[31] Hegel, however, was not a deconstructionist; he
held that contradictory forces or ideas can be held together in a complex union. Seemingly opposed forces were often joined in tandem
results, and, as such, dialectical idealism emphasized interdependence
rather than singularity, imbricated mutuality rather than clean lines of
division.[32] Dialectical idealists in the Hegelian tradition did not see
concepts like life and death or production and destruction as locked
in permanent polarity; productive acts could be destructive acts, death
was a part of life, and so on.

The Hegelian dialectic, like dialectic in the ancient world, enabled analyses of relationships rather than essences.[33] Marx famously
transformed Hegel's dialectical idealism into dialectical materialism,
thus "standing Hegel upon his head," but he largely accepted the tenets of dialectical analysis.[34] Both Hegel and Marx were concerned
with finding the "inner connection" between social formations, and
both were guided by the general notion "that phenomena must be understood not separately or distinct but as contradictions in a unity."[35]
Notwithstanding the vast difference between Hegel's idealism and

Marx's materialism, each saw relational conflict, whether conflicts between material classes, between ideological essences, or even within economic and political ideas, as both inevitable and productive. For Marx, contradictions within capitalism produced market shocks, and conflict between classes drove historical change. The dialectic was the chief tool by which each thinker accounted for historical change.

Marx suggested the dialectical unity of categorical pairs like the universal and the particular or theory and practice. Social phenomena like economic classes were misunderstood when considered alone; their social function was best shown relationally in economic interactions with other classes and in reactions to political and technological tumult. Although Marx never used the terms "dialectical materialism" and "historical materialism" or developed a methodological rubric for dialectical analysis, his most famous works employed the dialectic.[36] At the outset of *The Communist Manifesto*, Marx noted how "bourgeois society" eventually "sprouted from the ruins of feudal society" and begat new class conflicts. Here, Marx called attention to the cooperation of inimical economic systems, bourgeois capitalism and feudalism, in the creation, he asserted, of "new forms of oppression."[37] Nearly two decades later, *Capital* opened with a model dialectical analysis.[38] Showing the unity of theory and practice, the ideological and the material, and the abstract and the real, Marx stipulated an abstract concept, commodities, then demonstrated its concrete forms in a society.[39] Friedrich Engels would later expound on the dialectic by applying it to the natural sciences in *Dialectics of Nature* and *Anti-Dühring*, which did as much as any work in the Marxian tradition, save *Capital* and *The Communist Manifesto*, to popularize Marxism.[40]

In sum, two broad themes are evident in the history of dialectical philosophy from Socrates to Marx: First, the dialectic was a philosophical approach and a rhetorical method to expose complications and inconsistencies within and between impermanent phenomena rather than to find single, immutable truths. Second, dialecticians saw conflict between supposed opposites as necessary and generative. These two themes, along with the explicit language of dialectic, are noteworthy features of Meyer's midcentury conception of conservatism. He did not learn these from Socrates, though; he learned them studying Marx as he ascended through the ranks of the British and American Communist parties from 1931 to 1945.

Like Marx, Meyer was a dialectical thinker indebted to Hegel.[41]

Meyer studied Hegel's *Phenomenology of Spirit* and considered it a "'holy book.'"[42] More significant, Meyer came of age in a Communist movement culture in the process of "re-Hegelianization" through the writings of Lenin and Stalin as well as theorists like Georg Lukacs, Karl Korsch, and Antonio Gramsci.[43] Under Stalin, who reigned throughout Meyer's membership in the party, dialectical materialism became Communist policy; it became an "agenda that was to have real, practical effects" in the reorganization of society.[44] Stalin's *Dialectical and Historical Materialism*, essentially required reading that was predictably lauded as "brilliant" among Communists, was intended to update the dialectical ideas of Marx, Engels, and Lenin.[45]

Before his defection, Meyer accumulated substantial experience teaching party philosophy and enforcing the party's line. As a student at Oxford, Meyer read Marx, joined the British Communist Party, and was later expelled from the London School of Economics for distributing a pamphlet called *Student Vanguard*.[46] Following his expulsion, Meyer was transferred to the United States where, in 1938, the year Stalin's book on dialectical materialism was issued, he became the American Communist Party's educational director for the entirety of Indiana and Illinois. He even headed the Chicago Workers' School, one of a few dedicated Communist educational centers in the nation.[47] Although Meyer recruited, organized, and educated for the party, another of his primary tasks was to choke off deviationism. He performed it faithfully until he deviated from Communism in 1945 after Stalin purged Earl Browder and the American Communist Party reverted to a less democratic structure.[48]

Meyer's break with Marxism-Leninism "was fundamental" to the fusionism he developed in *National Review*, *In Defense of Freedom*, and scattered writings in the 1950s and 1960s.[49] He strayed from the party because he saw its totalitarian impulses. By the time he became a conservative, he viewed Communism as threatening the survival of the West.[50] Meyer also feared that Communists threatened his own survival in the West. Deeply troubled by Leon Trotsky's murder by Stalin's henchmen in Mexico and worried that Soviet assassins might take his family by surprise in their rural New York home, Meyer worked only at night in order to keep watch.[51] Nevertheless, his experience as a Communist explains the vestiges of Marxism in his conservative writings and gives insights into the roots of the rhetorical form he employed to settle conservatism. The residual legacy of Marxian and

Hegelian dialectics that Meyer appropriated was the view of ideas not as independent things-in-themselves standing fundamentally opposed to other concepts but as relational and overlapping. Like Marx and Hegel, Meyer began from a philosophical position that emphasized the productivity of ideological conflict and the impossibility that concepts had a singular essence or uncorrupted independence. Meyer wrote explicitly about the value of understanding conservatism dialectically. "Such a dialectic," Meyer wrote, "is in the highest degree necessary today between the libertarians and the traditionalists among conservatives."[52] Specifically, Meyer's dialectical definition of conservatism pragmatically addressed two obstacles to conservatism's midcentury ascendancy: contradiction and movement praxis.

The extent to which conservatism became a viable intellectual endeavor was, in Meyer's estimation, measured by the extent to which it overcame one portentous issue, one that figured largely for both Hegel and Marx: contradiction. Meyer set out to show left and right critics that conservatism fused different but complementary traditions, to prove that a "belief in absolute values *and* in the primacy of the individual was no contradiction."[53] Conservatism was complicated, not contradictory. The opening sentence of *In Defense of Freedom* illustrated the power Meyer afforded the charge of contradiction: "My intention in writing this book is to vindicate the freedom of the person as the central and primary end of political society."[54] By portraying his project as vindication, Meyer framed fusionist conservatism as a doctrine under assault by charges of inconsistency and intellectual slights; critics, he alleged, attacked his intellect based on their mistaken assessment of his beliefs. "Anyone," he paraphrased his critics sardonically, "who insists upon freedom in the political and economic sphere together with 'legitimate' conservative beliefs is really half liberal, half conservative, a sad case of intellectual schizophrenia."[55] "It has to be shown," he urged in response, "that the two aspects" of the conservative position, freedom and virtue, "are fundamentally in accord."[56]

The charge of philosophical inconsistency was a vexing, anxiety-inducing matter requiring decisive action. Contradiction threatened the stability of philosophical conservatism because it implied "manifestly *inconsistent* propositions either *within* a theoretical system or *between* a theoretical system and an observational system, so that holding or asserting one proposition implies the denial or negation of another."[57] But Meyer also feared that conservatism would become a midcentury punch line because it contained mutually negating ideas. To some extent, his fears were well-grounded, especially for a developing movement whose opposition to dominant political mores earned it vocal critics. "To display the inconsistency of a group of propositions," Perelman and Olbrechts-Tyteca point out, "is to expose it to a condemnation without appeal, to require anyone who wants to avoid the charge of absurdity to abandon at least certain elements of the system."[58] In making freedom and virtue the coequal values of conservatism, Meyer attempted to avoid contradiction by beginning a "process of association" that attempted to "establish a unity" between previously "separate elements." This dialectical process of definition, Meyer hoped, would demonstrate that conservatism was the philosophical synthesis of traditionalism and libertarianism.[59] Meyer aimed to build a sturdy philosophical edifice meriting "the prestige of logical thought."[60]

Consistency was a necessary but insufficient ingredient of an influential political philosophy; Meyer wanted more. His tacit goal was to create for conservatives a guidebook useful in developing movement strategy and guiding philosophical introspection. Meyer saw that Marxism, dangerous though he thought it was, had this quality in spades. Marx's writings were communal touchstones, and his method had been sown throughout the movement. Although Meyer rejected Marxism, he wrote admiringly, even wistfully, in some of his postconversion writings of the role Marx and other authoritative Communists' writings held for the rank and file. "I well remember," he explained, "the great sureness which I felt when I began to accept Marxism-Leninism." Marxist dialectics afforded Meyer a "vision of the correlation of all aspects of experience, each with each, the certainty that an answer could be found to every meaningful question and that everything which did not fit could be dismissed as meaningless, unreal."[61] The only variable for the Communist to comprehend was "the form of dialectical interplay."[62] Meyer noted how Marxist doctrine gave the Communist Party "shape and cohesion" and addressed questions both "abstruse" and "practical." The theoretical corpus was "sufficiently flexible" to accommodate "every expediency."[63] For defectors from the Communist Party, losing the ideological security of the dialectic could be "debilitating."[64] In his denunciations of the party, Meyer affirmed canonization as an essential feature of successful movement building; moreover, he thought only serious, thorough, and consistent political theories gained such sway.

When reflecting on conservatives' need for consistent philosophical direction, Meyer turned to another term with Marxist roots: "praxis." From his days as a Communist, he "carried over an intense cultivation both of theory and *praxis*," meaning that his mediation of conservative rivals was not only designed to pave over doctrinal disagreement; Meyer hoped settled philosophical doctrines would spur political activity.[65] Praxis, in short, was only possible when a community's politics were inspired by a revered collection of political thought, a collection *In Defense of Freedom* was designed to lead. Reviewing the book, Kirk offered up a scathing jibe, one particularly injurious to a former Communist writing among staunch anti-Communists. Kirk accused Meyer of trying to "supplant Marx."[66] To Kirk, since conservatism was neither a religion nor a formal ideology, it followed "no Holy Writ," and it did not look to any *"Das Kapital* to provide dogmata."[67] Meyer's attempt at a comprehensive political theory of conservatism was really an attempt at thought control, at immanentizing the conservative eschaton and becoming "the law and all the prophets to young persons marching to Zion."[68] Kirk's charge, though hyperbolic and venomous, was not totally without merit; Meyer wrote as if he were conservatism's preeminent philosopher. He asserted jurisdiction over the matter of conservative theorizing. With his dialectical method, his attention to contradiction, and his focus on praxis, Meyer employed Marxian methods to solve conservative problems. Around the *National Review* office, Meyer even became the living embodiment of conservative praxis. As Garry Wills wrote, "Frank's principles were libertarian, but his sentiments were Anglo-Catholic; so he presented himself as a 'fusion' of the two sides, walking proof that it could be done."[69]

The Philosophy of Fusion

In Defense of Freedom, the summation of Meyer's thinking on fusionism, was a dense tome designed to reform conservatives' thinking about conservatism, not a polemic like *The Conscience of a Conservative* designed to draw flocks toward conservatism. But Meyer did not see himself as negotiating an agreement between conservatives; he was not out to reconceptualize conservatism. To him, purist conservative factions failed to see that the dialectical chemistry within conservatism was akin to the dynamism bound within the Western Judeo-Christian philosophical tradition. Meyer framed his efforts not as a bold redefinition but as a "crystallization" of a tacit "consensus" that already operated within much of the conservative community.[70] *In Defense of Freedom* was written to synthesize what factions saw as antithetical visions of conservatism. As such, his signature book read as an academic treatise on a contested topic. Meyer wrote the book in the muscular philosophical vocabulary of traditionalist and libertarian specialists. Along the way, he name-checked Aquinas, Aristotle, Dewey, Marx, Mill, Plato, and other philosophical luminaries as an illustration of philosophical pedigree. *In Defense of Freedom* had all the makings of a philosophical tour de force.

Skilled in forensics, the structure of Meyer's breakthrough book was logically organized as a debate case. In the first chapter, "Clearing Ground," Meyer defined his basic terms—"freedom," "order," "individuality," and "society"—and stipulated his baseline assumptions about the nature of human autonomy and the limits of "scientism" as an approach to understanding political change. Conservatism had both libertarian and traditionalist philosophical claimants, and Meyer added fusionism as a dialectical synthesis of the two. In the book's next two chapters, "Why Freedom?" and "What Kind of Order?," Meyer attempted to prove the fundamental compatibility of capitalist and Burkean conservatism. The remainder of *In Defense of Freedom* consisted of Meyer's theory of the ideal nation-state. He historicized the ancient philosophical roots of the "Leviathan" that suffocated freedom, attacked the contemporary manifestation of the "liberal-collectivist state," and alleged that traditionalist "New Conservatism" was intellectually intertwined with activist governance that interfered with the moral choices free individuals must make on their own.

Meyer's attempt to frame freedom and virtue as dialectically joined conservative goals rather than diametrically opposed political theories rested on his ability to rebut orthodox traditionalists and libertarians. He employed associative rhetorical tactics that, as Perelman and Olbrechts-Tyteca note, "establish a unity" between "separate elements."[71] Throughout *In Defense of Freedom*, Meyer minimized perceived philosophical differences between traditionalists and libertarians and maximized each camp's shared purposes. He rendered common foes hyperbolically, highlighted shared histories, forecast monumental victories as partners, and portrayed those opposed to cooperation as extremists and radicals. Unlike purists in this and, as Roderick Hart identified, many other political communities, Meyer was interested in a philosophical coalition and diversifying conservative doctrine, not in eliminating the undutiful and the permissive.[72]

Casting doctrinal disagreements among traditionalist and libertarian conservatives as mere "divergences," Meyer promised that each was "simply summarized" as a difference in "emphasis."[73] His language of emphasis connoted matters of priority, attention, accentuation, and tone rather than core matters of substance. Conservatives spoke the same God and markets language; they differed only in their pronunciation and inflection. Conservatism represented "consensus amid divergence," no different than the unifying debates among "those who created the Constitution and the Republic."[74] Meyer's claim was essentially a restatement of Jefferson's: we are all traditionalists; we are all libertarians. Although his acolytes insist that Meyer was a philosopher rather than a coalition builder or peacemaker, his writings, especially *In Defense of Freedom*, were useful salves.[75]

In Defense of Freedom finessed a dalliance between the two key terms of the intraconservative struggle: "freedom" and "virtue." Meyer employed "freedom" to represent libertarian thinking and "virtue" to invoke traditionalism. Meyer's proposal for a dually focused conservatism was emphatic: "Neither virtue nor freedom alone, but the ineluctable combination of virtue *and* freedom is the sign and spirit of the West. . . . The recovery of one demands the recovery of the other; the recovery of both is the mission of conservatism today. *Virtue in freedom*—this is the goal of our endeavor."[76] He was careful to couch the philosophical tradition of individual freedom and public virtue as valuable but incomplete without the other. Freedom and virtue must be conceptualized in a tight binary in which each value moderated the extremes of the other.

Freedom, Meyer claimed, was a natural right, "an essential aspect of man's being." Freedom was the natural state of humanity; a yearning to be free was "inherent in the human mind."[77] Humans were free by nature, not made free by some arrangement of social institutions. Meyer accused the New Conservative traditionalists of accepting tradition uncritically. Traditions existed aplenty, and reason was required "to choose between good and evil in tradition" and to distinguish worthwhile possibilities "which have been open to men since the serpent tempted Eve, and Adam ate of the Tree of the Knowledge of Good and Evil."[78] The celebration of nebulous tradition eviscerated free choice

and assumed that individuals progressed as did social traditions, willingly or unwillingly. For him, freedom depended on choices made independent of the arc of history.

Meyer separated freedom from its social impact, the consequences free agents created. Freedom must not be evaluated by its
use because it was the mechanism of both malicious and altruistic
actions. Just as one hammer might build both flimsy and solid struc-
tures, free individuals could behave both virtuously and viciously. As
a prima facie good, freedom should not be judged by its products; it
should be evaluated by its presence and amount in any society. That
the outcomes of free choices should not be used to evaluate whether
freedom is a worthwhile political goal, Meyer admitted, "is the paradox of the human condition." Elsewhere in the book, he described
this paradox differently. The "contradiction in the condition of man"
was that the freedom to reject the good was necessary to achieve the
good.[79] No moral goal retained its goodness when forced upon others;
people must be free to make choices, both moral and immoral ones.
There was, quite simply, no morality without freedom. As such, Meyer
explicitly distinguished between "freedom *for*," the cant of collectivists
and those New Conservatives Meyer derided, and "freedom *from*," the
proper meaning of the term.[80]

Like the libertarians, Meyer was repulsed by the notion of imposing public goods on individuals. "Society and the state" were made for
individuals, not the reverse.[81] Although Meyer conceded that humans
were social animals, he held that the conceptual error that resulted in
widespread coercion arose when "society" was treated as a real entity
"with a life and with moral duties and rights of its own." Treating society
as an "organism" relegated individuals to constituent "cells" and justified transgressions against individuals for the sake of society. "Society,"
in Meyer's framing, was the linchpin of the "liberal-collectivist orthodoxy." If social rather than individual welfare was the ultimate end
of this orthodoxy, then sound political action required acting on the
whole of society. Massive impersonal organizations, the state most importantly, were figured as the most capable political actors. Liberals,
according to Meyer, saw virtue as the province of groups, not their
constituent individuals, "more in the United Steel Workers of America
than in any individual steel worker."[82]

But when Meyer proposed that individuals should be liberated
from rigid social norms and statist rules, he did not mean that individu-

als should be liberated from any larger conception of morality. Meyer was neither a libertine hedonist nor a permissive relativist. He clarified, "I am not defending blind and frivolous action, irresponsibility, immorality or amorality. I believe there are absolute truths and absolute values towards which men should direct themselves."[83] He imagined a nation comprised only of self-serving individuals each guided by their own moral compass to be a blueprint for moral breakdown. Some clear notion of public virtue should be acknowledged and accepted by individuals. Neither society nor the state, however, could impose virtue on the public. Virtue, quite simply, must not be forced. As Meyer explained, "Acceptance of moral authority derived from transcendent criteria of truth and good must be voluntary if it is to have meaning; if it is coerced by human force, it is meaningless."[84] As Meyer framed it, divine truth was cheapened when enforced, exalted when chosen.

Although Meyer, like Goldwater, grounded his vision of conservatism in the language of freedom, Meyer insisted that his "crystallization" of conservatism was not warmed-over classical liberalism; he was quite critical of the moral limitations of libertarianism and aimed to close this gap by wedding freedom to universal moral goods. With its veneration of the individual, nineteenth-century liberalism got social organization right and morality wrong.[85] Unchecked individual freedom would devolve into an anarchic world of might-makes-right. That is, self-interested individuals indulging their basest instincts were unadulterated classical liberals. To Meyer, this was a false freedom: "Only if there exists a real choice between right and wrong, truth and error, a choice which can be made irrespective of the direction in which history and impersonal Fate move, do men possess true freedom."[86] To put it another way, there was no freedom without the freedom to do wrong, and there was no transcendental wrong without God.

If individualism was potentially nefarious, what, then, was the value of individual freedom in the first place? Why did it matter if individuals could make their own determinations? Meyer, sensitive to the criticisms of Voegelin, Weaver, Kirk, and others that nineteenth-century liberalism was merely God-besmirching relativism, consulted religious traditions. Meyer conceptualized individuality and divinity within a tight dialectic. Individual life was sacred, and so individual choice was too. Although individuals had been sacrificed to the sacred, individualism was only legitimized nihilism without the sacred. Individuality was consecrated through a linkage with the divine. The reverse was also true; the divine was venerated through individuals choosing to be faithful.

Like the traditionalists, Meyer proposed the existence of an objective, transcendent moral order based both on divine authority and the Western Judeo-Christian philosophical tradition. Following the traditionalist line of argument, Meyer decried relativism and based many of his arguments about social morality on the existence of "good and evil." Although he denied a community's authority to impose "duties" on individuals, Meyer grounded public morality in the Bible:

> The Great Commandment, which is the cornerstone of the structure of Western moral thought, reflects this hierarchy of values, ignoring utterly everything but God and individual persons: "Thou shalt love the Lord thy God with all thy heart, and with all thy soul, and with all thy strength, and with all thy mind, and thy neighbour as thyself."[87]

Meyer's combination of "Western moral thought" and Old Testament commandments (Leviticus 19:18) clarified the ultimate source of virtue in his fusionism: fixed notions of good and evil set by God. *In Defense of Freedom* invoked a Christian God sparingly, but the relative absence of biblical arguments did not mean that Christianity held a small place in Meyer's thought. The Christian dialectic presaged the conservative dialectic.

True conservatism, the permutation of the two central ideological traditions of the West, was only possible through a "hard-fought dialectic" in which both libertarians and traditionalists acknowledged "a common enemy" and "a common heritage."[88] Conservatism, Meyer surmised, "is the most effective effort ever made to articulate in political terms the Western understanding of the interrelation of the freedom of the person and the authority of an objective moral order."[89] He identified the moral underpinnings of "Western civilization" as the "Christian understanding of the shimmering tension between freedom and virtue."[90] Western thought was "distinguished by its ability to hold these apparently opposed ends," individual autonomy and virtuous order, "in balance and tension."[91] Christianity afforded Western civilization the core principle that morality was contingent on divinity. Meyer just did not happen to subscribe, either privately or publicly, to any version of the divine. He is best described as an areligious Christian before his deathbed conversion in 1972.[92]

As a political theorist, Meyer assessed religion pragmatically rather than by its truth value; he was attracted to the divine because of its social function, because individuals acquiesced to its moral framework. Christian theology did not intrigue Meyer as individualist philosophy did, but he was willing to accept its moral teachings without too much questioning. In his eyes, Christianity was first among equal religions in terms of teaching individuals how to lead moral lives. Meyer argued that its hoary status as an ancient moral guide made it an indispensable part of Western thought. In fact, Meyer portrayed the Christian dialectic between freedom and virtue as the philosophical basis for the American experiment. The Declaration of Independence and the Constitution, he wrote, "promulgated in uncompromising terms" the "simultaneous belief in objective moral value and in the freedom of the individual person."[93] Among "Washington, Franklin, Jefferson, Hamilton, Adams, Jay, Mason, Madison," Meyer enumerated, existed diverse opinions on governance and citizenship. But they, like midcentury conservatives, practiced a "dialectic" to create a political system that acknowledged "truth and virtue" yet trusted individuals to seek them and not government to enforce them.[94]

As Meyer framed the meaning of freedom and virtue, the dialectic was inescapable. Both freedom and virtue, if defined and practiced without reference to the other, became meaningless, monstrous, or both. Fusionism identified the two major strains of midcentury conservative thought as essentially conservative but held that each was philosophically indefensible without the other, that each value led to politically ruinous programs without the moderating force of dialectical interaction. Extreme revanchist, purist, or revolutionary positions, whether traditionalist or libertarian, "vitiate the value of the dialectic."[95] "To claim exclusive sovereignty" for any single element of the dialectic would be to sully a distinctive feature of Western civilization and to "cripple the potentialities of conservatism in its struggle against the Liberal collectivist Leviathan."[96] Freedom and virtue, to put the matter into Cold War terms, could only battle Communism when operating in tandem.

The fusionist dialectic was a way to acknowledge that no ultimate political goal, like equality, came without risks. The genius of the Western dialectic that Meyer thought conservatism continued was that it joined two political goals that negated the worst elements of the other. He wrote, "But both extremes are self-defeating: truth withers when freedom dies, however righteous the authority that kills it; and free individualism uninformed by moral value rots at its core and soon brings about conditions that pave the way for surrender to tyranny."[97] Public moral virtue established freedom's boiling point, the notion that past a certain threshold, individual freedom spilled over into a disaggregated public atomism where social responsibility, civic engagement, and communal living standards were not only meaningless, but each was a rhetorical ploy to limit individual choice. By the same token, valuing individual freedom counterbalanced potentially autocratic quests for virtue. Freedom stood permanent guard against dogmatic moral policing; a permanent concern for individual sovereignty ameliorated attempts to intern populations or exile dissidents for the sake of social unity.

Meyer's Rocky Marriage

The fusion of libertarian and traditionalist doctrines was a bit like forcing mismatched puzzle pieces together; the pieces joined, but not evenly or without struggle. Adroit though it was, Meyer's dialectic could not circumvent a doctrinal conundrum within fusionism: how to square the libertarian laissez-faire morality with the traditionalist's one-morality-under-God. Meyer refused utilitarian calculation regarding the ends to which freedom was put and asserted that freedom was an inherent good in and of itself. He made the same claims about the intrinsic authority of an objective moral order. Meyer's insistence on two coequal goods was inconsistent. If there was a moral system of absolutes independent of human thought by which our actions might be judged, then which took priority, the freedom of choice or the necessity of moral adherence? Simply, which was the greater good? Meyer was caught between deciding whether the ability to choose or the product of individual choice mattered and, if so, how much it mattered. There was no way out. To be free meant being able to choose; or, as Meyer put it in the most basic language, a person must be able to say "quite simply—and literally: to Hell with it; it is wrong and it is false."[98] No doctrinaire libertarian could have said it better, and that fact illustrated a tension unabated by fusionism. It was one thing to say there was a God; it was quite another to say that there was a God who cared how humans behave.

Drawing on his experiences at *National Review*, Garry Wills explained the fusionist tension in practical terms: "The fact that men can live with contradiction does not remove the contradiction—it just makes the contradiction go philosophically 'underground' and play funny games there. Individualist and Catholic are night and day."[99] Some conservatives would have government minimally involved in economic matters, while others would have government maximally involved in moral matters. Wills was correct about this persistent contradiction; doctrinally speaking, so were many of Meyer's critics, both traditionalist and libertarian.[100] For Kirk, the formation of a "league" between traditionalist and libertarians was akin to joining "ice and fire."[101] Purists in both camps refused fusion as a watered-down, fence-straddling version of their more principled politics.[102] Kirk even refused to be listed on *National Review*'s original masthead to avoid formal association with Meyer.[103]

The persistence of the contradiction Meyer feared is evident when fusionism must resolve competing, yet ostensibly conservative, claims. On the one hand, the fusionist celebrated the individual's ability to freely weigh, for example, the familial costs and personal consequences of marital infidelity. On the other hand, by embracing a politics of right and wrong, sin and redemption, the fusionist was conscious of the fact that the moral status of cheating was unambiguous. The model fusionist, of course, would sidestep the dilemma over which good is more important, individual choice or wholesome behavior, by freely choosing to be faithful and live morally for the moment. However, as E. J. Dionne asks, "If American society was fundamentally conservative, liberty was sufficient to allow Americans to be their traditionalist selves. But what if American society really weren't conservative?"[104] Meyer was clear that those who avoided infidelity only because it was restricted by their community have not become virtuous because their choice was restricted. But when people who were not angels chose to cheat and damned the consequences, did they risk damnation?

Meyer alleged that when governments used force or censorship to restrict individual choices, it was an "outrage upon the freedom of man, and, in that, upon the nature of man."[105] But, by the same rigid logic, the use of individual freedom in pursuit of aims not strictly in keeping with a Christian mission could be construed as an outrage upon God. For Brent Bozell, the establishment of a "Christian civilization," not a free people, should be the ultimate goal of conservative politics. In a notable exchange of essays with Meyer, Bozell held that humans were sinful and required help in achieving virtue.[106] A government that honored God's moral order aided in that quest. After all, governments prohibited theft and murder as measures toward a moral society. Why not go further? The "urge to freedom for its own sake," Bozell scolded, was "the urge to be free from God."[107] Bozell's withering criticism of Meyer raised the crucial question regarding the logical coherence of fusionism: when trying to be moral, which was more important, the process or the result? Bozell, unlike Meyer, was unequivocal; the result, achieving God's vision of public morality, was paramount. The fusionist position could not assess relative moral worth because freedom and virtue could not coexist as goods of equal worth. If, as the libertarians and traditionalist positions showed, one value held supremacy over others, consistency was achievable.

These issues of free will and communal norms, individual goods and collective goods, and objective versus subjective morality were more than intriguing brain teasers for conservatives. Such philosophical disputes influenced the direction of conservative policies. When a state is afforded the authority to declare war and enlist citizens to fight and die in battles deemed vital to the "national interest," a state has acquired power over life and death, power that made libertarians quite nervous. This was not just a martial matter; when governments restrict prostitution, limit immigration, legislate voting rights enforcement, regulate business' employment practices, sanction types of marriage, strip Communists of rights, detain enemy combatants without due process, either the freedoms of some are curtailed for a predetermined social good or governments resist imposing visions of the good on society and permit groups to exercise their freedoms through unfair, dangerous, and even seditious behaviors that limit the free choices other groups of people might make.

Meyer's argument that human actions can only be in virtuous harmony with transcendent moral law if the action results from free choice was a creative attempt at synergy. His attempt to rescue conservatism from excessive doctrinal heterogeneity was, if evaluated on its own terms, unsuccessful. However, Meyer's synthesis buckled under logical tension since he elevated freedom and virtue to the same moral perch. Either freedom was a good subservient to virtue, a means to be evaluated by the products of its use, or free choice was a moral good in and of itself. Meyer had not, as one of his contemporary critics put it, answered the "great question of every political theory: who should rule?"[108]

A Durable Peace

Fusionism was not a soft-lit story of a blissful marriage. After Meyer's fusionist template was fully developed in the early 1960s, the traditionalist-libertarian relationship alternated between a low-intensity conflict and a cautious confederation. The key libertarian and traditionalist books would, among some readers on the ramparts of the intraconservative wars, continue to provide rhetorical ammunition versus fellow conservatives after Meyer's death in 1972. Meyer's more purist critics like Kirk, Bozell, and others had credible points about the consistency of fusionism. As *National Review* editor Jonah Goldberg admitted, "Truth be told, as a coherent philosophy it never really worked as well as Meyer wanted it to." The logical composition and use value of fusionism were separate questions, however. Total consistency should not be confused with rhetorical power. Fusionism, Goldberg continued, "worked just fine" within the movement, especially during the Cold War, "when libertarians and conservatives both saw the Soviet Empire as the apotheosis of everything evil in the world."[109] Meyer certainly helped many conservatives look past their differences during the Cold War.

The success of Meyer's project in forging the breach between rival conservatisms was undeniable. Meyer's work became so influential not because the dialectic satisfied the diehard, but because it showed so many conservatives that picking sides was a profoundly unconservative position to take. For all its flexibility and promiscuity, fusionism was the tie that bound factions together and helped create a loyal opposition in lieu of separatists. Although "no real fusion" between Trads and Rads ever happened, as Meyer's work influenced intellectuals and activists, these more doctrinaire positions became conservatism's philosophical periphery rather than its political core. Dialectical fusionism, which flourished "on the practical level" while being ridiculed in pitched "intellectual battles over political theory," became the conservative standard.[110] Meyer succeeded in creating a language that worked for heterogeneous conservatives, one that reached out to the business community and the religious community, hailed advocates of markets and morals, and spoke to all shades in between. A fusionist could inveigh against progressive taxation and mandatory Social Security contributions as limitations on her individual freedom and attend an evangelical church, favor abortion restrictions, and oppose gay marriage without feeling her politics pulled in separate directions most of the time. One could belong to political communities whose mantra was capitalist Christianity and seldom consider freedom and virtue as anything other than concomitant goods.[111]

Looked at another way, the fusionist dialectic was also an act of closure. As much as Meyer's work made sure that the meaning of conservatism included both traditionalist and libertarian god terms, the broad acceptance of this dual framework closed off other possibilities in the midcentury, other directions the meaning of conservatism could have taken. Between Kirk's and Weaver's war against the modern world, the neomedievalism of Eric Voegelin, libertarians with their relativist radicalism, Whittaker Chambers's oracular melancholia, and more exotic conservatives like Otto von Hapsburg, scion of the Austro-Hungarian ruling family and *National Review* contributor, conservatism had a barefaced wildness about it in the midcentury.[112] Considered as a group, early conservatives were an "eccentric rabble" bordering on an intellectual "freak show."[113] Buckley's moves to cast out the John Birchers, overt racists, and anti-Semites were attempts to erect boundaries around intellectual conservatism. As Buckley tried to control conservatism's borders, Meyer ventured to settle conservatism's interior to develop a coherent set of fusionist talking points.[114] Meyer crafted a language that restrained many conservatives' outlandishness, a language conservatives could take public; he domesticated conservatism, and he created what he called for in one of his last books, a conservative mainstream.[115]

For conservatives who saw no conflict between libertarianism and traditionalism and no point in protracted conflict between the prevailing sides, Meyer helped popularize a core conservative doctrine suited to appeal to an electorate often energized by potentially conflicting impulses like the suspicion of government, the desire for reduced taxes, the fear of moral decay, the need for public services, and a belief in the necessity of robust national defense. Meyer's fusionism became the Right's "fait accompli," not because he purged contradiction permanently but because his dialectic was so workable.[116] Conservatives "*wanted* to believe that they had found a base in principle," as Nash argues. Conservatives had become "increasingly cognizant of the need to avoid either quixotic antistatism or morose authoritarianism if their movement was to capture national power and respect."[117]

Fused conservatism worked best for "more and more intellectuals on the Right" because it encouraged thinkers to find resonant truths in classical liberals like John Stuart Mill, continental traditionalists like Edmund Burke, and religious intellectuals like Joseph de Maistre.[118] Meyer's philosophical lessons were also closest to the "aspirations of the conservative rank-and-file."[119] Conservative activists of the 1960s and 1970s confronted a host of controversial political questions—the Cold War, civil rights, Vietnam, abortion, illegal drugs, and others—for which different conservative positions unfolded depending on whether one adopted individual freedom or public virtue as a first principle. Meyer's dialectic gave activists intellectual authorization to seek balance in their positions rather than doctrinal uniformity. A longtime *National Review* writer and former staffer to Vice President Spiro Agnew credited *In Defense of Freedom* with attracting more in his "generation to conservatism than any other single work."[120] Meyer's rhetoric worked in an age when conservatives needed a consensus about conservatism to maintain a political identity, to take over the Republican Party, to develop viable candidates, to raise money, to develop an organizational infrastructure, and to explain their opposition to Communism.

By Meyer's design, freedom and virtue did not have to be a forced choice. His synthetic vocabulary of freedom and virtue "filtered down" into the wider conservative political language including that of think tanks, advocacy groups, and "virtually every major conservative theorist and politician."[121] The Heritage Foundation's mission statement, for instance, promised the promotion of "conservative public policies" based on Meyer's blend of principles: "free enterprise, limited government, individual freedom, traditional American values, and a strong national defense."[122] As the traditionalist-libertarian flare-ups have shown, each item on this list, all of which have become conventionally conservative values after World War II, could be plucked from the rest, promoted as a first principle, and marshaled against the others. Nevertheless, following Meyer's lead, organizations like the Heritage Foundation or the American Conservative Union articulated these values in concert and accepted them as part of a unified whole.[123] "In a nutshell," Paul Ryan

contended, "the notion of separating the social from the economic issues is a false choice. They stem from the same root."[124]

Unsurprisingly, Ronald Reagan became the "beau ideal" of fusionism.[125] Before a conservative audience, Reagan singled out Meyer
among the founding conservatives for creating a sound basis for a
political partnership. Meyer's "synthesis of traditional and libertarian
thought," Reagan proclaimed, became "recognized by many as modern conservatism." As other conservatives did when praising fusionism,
Reagan turned immediately to the question of internal consistency
and resolutely dismissed the possibility of contradiction. "Our goals
complement each other," Reagan declared before framing the matter
dramatically:

> Because ours is a consistent philosophy of government, we can be very
> clear: We do not have a social agenda, a separate economic agenda, and a
> separate foreign agenda. We have one agenda. Just as surely as we seek to
> put our financial house in order and rebuild our nation's defenses, so too
> we seek to protect the unborn, to end the manipulation of schoolchildren
> by utopian planners, and permit the acknowledgement of a Supreme
> Being in our classrooms just as we allow such acknowledgements in
> other public institutions.[126]

For Reagan, the freedom and virtue amalgam produced not contradiction but equilibrium between free choice and self-direction, on
the one hand, and adherence to law, tradition, and heritage, on the
other. Fusionism directed conservatives to maximize freedom but to
consider the human costs of their political goals. The quest to "reduce
government interference in the marketplace" should be achieved with
an abiding "respect for law, an appreciation for tradition, and regard
for the social consensus."[127] Virtue was a worthy social goal if it was
pursued by free individuals; market innovations were manifestations
of individual liberty, but they must be measured against time-honored
practices that built social order.

The coherence of the fusion project was no small matter to
Reagan; Meyer's writings were praxis documents to the president.
Reagan outlined how he planned to govern from Meyer's theoretical vantage point: lowering taxes and restricting abortions, balancing
the budget while permitting the expression of religious faith in public schools.[128] Whereas Reagan praised fusionism as a philosophy of

government, other conservatives heralded it as good politics. Meyer provided Reagan and the larger movement with a conservative philosophy rhetorically suited to tolerate variation; it was a language for conservatism's big tent. Peggy Noonan put the matter in simple terms: "A great party needs give. It must be expansive and summoning. It needs to say, 'Join me.'"[129] Political groupings, in other words, face a basic choice: grow together inconsistently or idle apart purely. Fusionism made political advance amid philosophical discord possible. "Today," Edwin Feulner noted, "when conservatives are sometimes tempted to go their pluralistic ways, it is salutary to be reminded of the common heritage we share and the common goals we cherish."[130] When any of the conservative camps dedicated to these many sentiments collide, movement peacemakers consistently turn to Meyer as a marriage counselor.[131]

The response to conservative infighting in the 2000s is a telling example of the enduring relevance of Meyer's dialectic. Fearing a split between traditionalists and libertarians during George W. Bush's presidency, conservatives turned back to Meyer's language to preserve what they repeatedly called the historic "marriage" between traditionalism and libertarianism that produced mainstream conservatism. In *The Elephant in the Room* (2006), Ryan Sager sensed boiling conservative bitterness, even at pep rally affairs like the Conservative Political Action Conference. Illegal immigrants were decried as "burglars" and "wage thieves" while libertarians sold T-shirts proclaiming "Capitalists of the world unite."[132] Over immigration, an individual's liberty to form contracts freely competed with a restrictive sense of national identity. In other sensitive political controversies like education standards, the war on terror, or stem cell research, individualism butted against collective obligations to protect the nation from moral decline or threatening enemies.[133]

Stepping back from the fray, Sager hoped to remind sparring conservatives of how Meyer's "formula" created the "alliance at the heart of the party."[134] Concluding that "the conservative marriage can be saved" with a "renewal of vows, a renewal of the fusionism described long ago by Frank Meyer," Sager predicted that fusionism could still persuade hidebound libertarians and traditionalists that each wanted small government and social rectitude.[135] Other prominent conservatives framed conservative infighting during the 2000s as a marital spat, and they sought out Meyer as a marriage counselor. "Marriages tend to dissolve when both parties 'grow apart,'" Jonah Goldberg reminded both libertarians and traditionalists. Goldberg's solution, like Sager's, was a renewal of fusionist vows initially recited in the 1960s and 1970s, a recommitment "to the fusionist project." Before either party does anything rash, Goldberg concluded, "Let's seek counseling."[136] When shut out of the White House, staring down an electoral loss, or celebrating a string of victories, conservatives should think about conservatism as a balancing act rather than a solo act. Social conservatives, economic conservatives, neoconservatives, and others have secured a space within the conservative tent. Following Meyer, tent-building conservatives urge inclusiveness, not exclusiveness, accepting "social conservatives or neoconservatives or any other kind of conservative," in total, "a renewed fusionism that will unite all the branches of the now-divided conservative mainstream."[137]

In all likelihood, traditionalists never needed libertarians to achieve doctrinal purity or philosophical completeness. They needed them so that they did not sound like theocrats. They needed them to be politically successful with a diverse electorate. Libertarians did not need traditionalists to fill in missing premises about markets. They needed them to sound savvier than Scrooge. Meyer's was the language that healed wounds from intraconservative conflicts, the language that convinced frustrated factions to give their partner one more chance. For conservatives keen to answer the "what is conservatism?" question ecumenically and avoid bloody secession movements, fusionism offered a peace agreement negotiated in good faith.[138] What Meyer accomplished was not just the comprehensive assembly of meaningful conservative terms, but the rhetorically induced merger of conservative audiences. The back-and-forth dialectic between freedom and virtue has allowed conservatives to sweep aside questions of doctrine as pedantic and focus on issues of survival and growth. Fusionist conservatism became a single body with two arms, one devoted to lowering taxes and the other devoted to policing morality. When prominent conservatives endorsed God and markets simultaneously, they assembled a rhetorical collage of traditionalist and libertarian idioms, one Meyer created.

CHAPTER FIVE

WFB

⌘

He was WFB to readers and Chairman Bill to admirers. The public knew him as Buckley for short, William F. Buckley Jr. more formally. He was labeled an enfant terrible, a bon vivant with a joie de vivre, a dandy, a dilettante, a theocrat, and a fascist.[1] Buckley labeled himself a conservative, but not all of the time.[2] Buckley was a writer, an editor, a publisher, an orator, a debater, a television host, an interviewer, a one-off politician, and a political adviser from 1951 until his death in 2008. Buckley's career, prolific by any measure, included fifty-five books about politics, sailing, and spies; 800 *National Review* articles; 4.5 million words in 5,600 biweekly newspaper columns; and thirty-three years as host of *Firing Line*, one of the longest-running shows in television history.[3]

A broad survey of conservative writings about Buckley reveals praise only describable as Plutarchian. Many conservative writers thought that Buckley walked on water only to find tall buildings to leap, and both before lunch. Buckley's Yale mentor, Willmoore Kendall, once said Buckley could do as much with his voice as Laurence Olivier.[4] Jeffrey Hart estimated steep odds against a "satisfactory biography" of Buckley. "Gibbon with Henry James" was the only authorial combination capable of the task.[5] *National Review* editor Rich Lowry expressed the kind of reverence typical of those enchanted by an idol: "As we all know, it is impossible to exaggerate Bill Buckley's influence in forging a movement that changed the nation."[6]

Buckley was many things to many conservatives, but it was his rhetorical dynamism that made him an identifiable conservative in the first place. In other words, Buckley was a model conservative to a great extent because he became conservatives' rhetorical model. Michael Gerson, George W. Bush's speechwriter, acknowledged, with a vaguely Buckleyan affectation, a significant rhetorical debt to Buckley: "We [conservatives] also learned that language, in the proper hands, could be employed with the precision and effect of an epee."[7] To make Buckley's stylized musings more accessible, one editor even compiled an alphabetized inventory of Buckley's most salacious formulations in a volume whose title, *Quotations from Chairman Bill*, befitted the man who blended mockery and political commentary.[8] These are only a few examples of the relationship—sometimes awestruck, sometimes mimicking, always inspired—between Buckley's words and generations of conservatives.

Conservatism, as Frank Meyer doggedly argued, is a network of political doctrines, but it is also a political identity, one that Buckley helped create. To understand Buckley's influence on the fusion of libertarian, traditionalist, and various other conservatives, it is necessary to assess the communal force of his rhetoric. Specifically, Buckley afforded conservatives of all stripes a provocative rhetorical style, a gladiatorial style as I term it. The gladiatorial style is a flashy, combative style whose ultimate aim is the creation of inflammatory drama. In fact, I argue that conservatives encountered Buckley's potent arguments about God, government, and markets and the gladiatorial style simultaneously. The theatrical appeal of Buckley's gladiatorial style inspired conservative imitators with disparate beliefs and, over several decades, became one of the principal features of the conservative political language. Buckley "personified the militant conservative 'movement,'" Pat Buchanan wrote when he ran for president in 1988, "and we were the *mujahadeen*."[9]

I demonstrate the features and force of Buckley's gladiatorial style in several sections. Using his canonical books, *God and Man at Yale* (1951) and *Up from Liberalism* (1959), as well as several early *National Review* essays, I analyze three of Buckley's favored devices: stylistic spectacles, reversal tropes, and fierce antagonism. Each performs an essentially dramatic function in the gladiatorial style. Then, I use Buckley's admonitions to improve "the conservative demonstration" to argue that the techniques of the gladiatorial style are governed by a strategic *kairotic* sense designed to maximize dramatic conflict. I conclude by exploring the political repercussions of these stylistic choices, arguing that Buckley inspired conservatives to abjure doctrinal uniformity and to express their identity provocatively and combatively.

The Gladiatorial Style

The brio and bravado of Buckley's prose exhibited the characteristics of the gladiatorial style. He emboldened conservatives to reflect on their stylistic choices, to seek rhetorical creativity, and, most of all, to use their words to create dramatic conflict. Whether in ornamented syntax, odd sentence structure, hyperbole, flamboyant irreverence, forceful tone, or verbal aggressiveness, dramatic action is the hallmark of the gladiatorial style. It conveys a sense of pageantry and interrupts the quotidian world of staid and dry political argument with the fantastic and unusual. It shows off without apology. The gladiatorial style's excessive, self-consciously ostentatious discursive performativity distinguishes it from pedestrian, plain language, scholastic, or even otherwise dramatic styles of address. The gladiatorial style is not tethered to any archetypal role, the glorious hero or preening villain, for instance. The style projects a hyperbolized version of the role adopted by the rhetor. Just as ancient gladiators and modern wrestlers understood, the style can be used to turn heel, to play the savior, to heckle a frenzied crowd, or to whip up support so long as dramatic conflict is the result. In other words, only excessiveness is predictable if the gladiatorial style is wielded capably. The style makes no intrinsic connection between, say, aggressive taunts and lewd insults with enticing rising action, an extended climax, a memorable dénouement, and a mesmeric finale, the ends to which the style is a means. A keen *kairotic* sense separates the theatrical gladiator from the merely passable. *Kairos*, "a *dynamic* principle rather than a static, codified rhetorical technique," governs the situational deployment of gladiatorial techniques such as stylistic spectacle, reversal, and attack.[10]

The gladiatorial style is not merely a name for a set of dramatic tropes. To be clear about my claims, the gladiatorial style is not essentially conservative, and not all conservatives are gladiatorial stylists. Robert Hariman argues that style is a heuristic through which to understand templates for political action. A political style, he explains, "evokes a culture—a coherent 'set of symbols giving meaning to the manifest activities of common living—yet has no *a priori* relation with any issue, event, or outcome."[11] To understand politics, "we can consider how a political action involves acting according to a particular political style."[12] Style concerns a realm of political action beyond the arrangement of words on a page, the "dynamics of our social experience" and the impact of rhetoric on political practices.[13] Politics are stylized, and conservatism is no exception. Buckley's gladiatorial style was not simply a unique expression of conservatism; to many, Buckley's style *was* conservatism. As such, replicating his stylistic conventions, repeating his formulations, and invoking Buckleyesque barbs became a way to perform authentic conservatism.

Stylistic Spectacles

Words are weapons in the gladiatorial style, and Buckley was better armed than most. His lingering stylistic influence among conservatives is as the progenitor of an invigorating style of verbal combat. Dwight MacDonald once distinguished between high-utility words and "zoo" words. The latter could be locked away and admired. Buckley, who revered "the wonderful opportunities of the language," opened the cages.[14] "Zoo" words were essential to his performance of virtuoso intellectualism. As he saw it, no one would dare tell Thelonious Monk to cut unfamiliar chords from his music.[15] Buckley wrote in a rollicking syntax distinguished by its use of obscure, hard-to-pronounce terms. Sam Tanenhaus writes, "His famous prose style, with its ornate syntax and rococo vocabulary, conveys, at times, a subtle hint of 'foreignness,' like that of his friend Vladimir Nabokov."[16] He was, one conservative mimicked, the "prince of polysyllabism," a "hapax legomenon" among conservatives.[17] He garnered so much attention for such usage that he was inclined to pen several essays on language, and his editor even compiled a 100-page "Buckley Lexicon" consisting of odd words like "dreadnought," "dithyrambic," "oleaginous," "tergiversation," and "voluptuarian."[18] Not to be outdone, Buckley also published his own book-length lexicon.[19]

Buckley's notorious vocabulary, a vocabulary that seemed to brag about its own capaciousness, showed in his more complex formulations. Buckley's was always, unmistakably, popular writing, but it also directed its audience to stretch to understand its message. A representative passage about capitalism is instructive:

> The American capitalist whose image reifies in the mind of the young is not even the smug, canny, willful powerbroker of Upton Sinclair. He is the inarticulate, self-conscious, bumbling mechanic of the private sector, struck dumb by the least cliché of socialism, fleeing into the protective arms of government at the last hint of commercial difficulty, delighting secretly in the convenient power of the labor union to negotiate for an entire industry, uniformly successful only in his escapist ambition to grow duller and duller as the years go by, eyes left, beseeching popular favor. Poor Miss Rand sought to give him a massive dose of testosterone, to make him virile and irresistible, leader of a triumphant meritocratic revolt against asphyxiative government . . . but soon it transpired, even as Russell Kirk predicted, that her novels were being read not because of their jackbooted individualism, but because of the fornicating bits.[20]

This passage is one of many in which Buckley employed a dizzying array of difficult words and compound sentences and seemingly thumbed his nose at the brevity and parsimony of a book like *The Conscience of a Conservative*. As Buckley framed the controversy, over ten tropes competed to represent the American capitalist. In the first two sentences, Buckley set three adjectives, "smug," "canny," and "willful" against three more adjectives, "inarticulate," "self-conscious," and "bumbling," all of which signified the capitalist to one audience or another. The multiline, multiclause second sentence included five additional images of the weak, boring capitalist. The controversy had no resolution though; Rand's efforts to give the capitalist an image overhaul, complete with three final images of the capitalist, fell short because audiences enjoyed her novels for their ribaldry, not their ideology.

To simplify Buckley's argument and write "Capitalists had a weak image that Ayn Rand failed to reverse" would, ostensibly, communicate the same idea. The simplest explanation, however, is not grandly performative; in the sense that the single sentence unadorned with curious words is predictable and understandable, the sentence is not gladiatorial. Buckley swaggered rhetorically through protracted prose; such writing attracted attention not just because of its length, which required a patient reader to progress from image to image, line after line, but also because of its density, which required effort to comprehend. It was prose that suggested a powerful rhetor, one who commanded the spotlight and placed demands on audiences.

The polysyllabic word was a novel weapon brandished in battle to achieve effect with conservative audiences. Buckley disavowed the rhetorical combatant whose barebones sword-and-shield style was capable but dull and predictable. Buckley chose words whose meaning few were likely to know in order to amplify the spectacle of rhetorical combat. Just as important, he appeared to take pleasure in doing so. When a *Firing Line* guest asked him why he used "irenic" rather than "peaceful," Buckley replied with a playful guile: "I desired that extra syllable."[21] Audiences may have left puzzled by the choice of "desideratum" when "goal" would have worked in the same way that a peculiar weapon—a trident, for instance—might have looked quixotic in a swordfight. They were more likely to remember the gladiator with the morningstar, or the sesquipedalian rhetorical gladiator.

Buckley's stylistic spectacles were not universally appealing. His critics said he overused "*parcelon*," "the addition of superfluous words."[22] He violated nearly all of George Orwell's rules for unpretentious writers.[23] Some audiences found Buckley's frequent use of technical jargon, foreign phrases, and irregular metaphors mystifying; others found the experience as engaging as listening to a braggart endlessly recount triumphs. Sometimes his "collage" writing technique could be "diffuse and unfocused," and he misused big words—once confusing "mendacity" and "mendicancy," for instance—in his efforts to dazzle.[24] To those who enjoyed the show, however, Buckley's conservatism was to be experienced both emotionally and intellectually as literature. Buckley wrote in anticipation of such a reaction: "There is nothing more amusing," he told Morley Safer, "than theatrical pomposity."[25] The conservatism Buckley modeled was difficult and delectable, serious and sportive, and imagistic and imaginative. Buckley's intellectual exhibitions were also acts of rhetorical enjoinment in which conservative readers sensed that Buckley winked at them collusively as he performed his popular style. Many readers wanted to be let in on the secret and share in the fun.

"Winning arguments required a debater and a performer," Buckley's onetime protégé Richard Brookhiser explained, and building a political movement "required someone who was very cool."[26] Rush Limbaugh was one of many young conservatives who found Buckley cool and tried to imitate him, "to talk like him, dress like him, write like him— and, of course, think like him."[27] Limbaugh's memories of his infatuation with Buckley demonstrate the emotional work done by Buckley's stylistic grandstanding:

> I was reading Buckley when I was 15, 16 years old, and I said, "Boy, I wish I could be that. I wish I could be this. How does he know all these words?" I'd sit there with the dictionary looking up words that he used, and points that he made. . . . If you know what an idol is, multiply it times two or three. I thought him unreachable, untouchable.[28]

In his radio show Limbaugh appropriated a version of the spectacles that mesmerized him in his youth. R. Emmett Tyrell noted the significance of both conservatives' stylistic spectacles: "We [conservatives] need to have people who can dramatize issues. . . . Buckley has it. And, though he is a great talker rather than a great writer, Rush has it too."[29]

Reversal

Buckley energized readers and inspired confidence in the conservative mind through more than vocabulary. One persistent dramatic trope in his prose was reversal. "Reversal" is a master term that denotes other tropes, such as sarcasm and irony, which turn on violations of social power, meaning, and audience expectation.[30] Sarcasm and irony influence audiences because the intended meaning of a statement defies the conventional meaning of its constituent terms. Sarcasm and irony assumed the power to generate humor at the expense of others and to play with conventional meaning.

Irony is a transactional process because it "requires interpretation in order to do its intended work, such that the recipient of the message plays an active role" in its creation.[31] Irony is, as Wayne Booth summarizes, an "astonishing communal achievement."[32] One of the chief effects of irony is "a reversal of expectations," "A" returning as "non-A" as Kenneth Burke noted.[33] As such, irony is a potentially disruptive political tool. The ironist questions the world as it is presented, plays with the justifications of the powerful, and reiterates "ordinary terms from a position outside of their usual discourses or meanings."[34] Irony's powerful subversive capability stems from its stipulation that the opposite of what is commonly believed is true and its solicitation of company in that conclusion.

Irony has the potential to upend tacit social hierarchies and popular assumptions about authority figures. Buckley's *God and Man at Yale* (1951), whose full title includes the subtitle *The Superstitions of "Academic Freedom"*, was not controversial because it criticized an Ivy League institution but because a twenty-five-year-old recent graduate, practically a student, presumed to teach Yale's teachers something about teaching. Academic freedom, Buckley clarified, was not a hallowed value of freethinking; it was a "hoax." "I believe it to be an indisputable fact," he declared, "that most colleges and universities, and certainly Yale, the protests and pretensions of their educators and theorists notwithstanding, do not practice, cannot practice, and cannot even believe what they say about education and academic freedom." They may "utilize the rationale" of academic freedom when advantageous, but their decisions about whom to hire, what to teach, and what to publish were governed by an expedient orthodoxy of acceptable opinion.[35] "Tolerance" for opposing viewpoints was a "sonorous pretension" that was intended either to hide a biased orthodoxy or to resist critics like Buckley who insisted that Yale teach a Christian individualist orthodoxy.[36] Buckley, the student, became the teacher; the teachers needed an education.

As with the upended student/teacher dichotomy, the dramatic movement of Buckley's reversals drew power from their play with several binaries. In *God and Man at Yale*, professors were not the academic elite imparting knowledge to immature students. The students were wise to resist the lecturing professors. An age reversal accompanied this student/teacher move. No enlightenment accompanied the professors' advanced years. The young were wise and the old were naive. Buckley's reversals did not stop there. Liberals and Communists who insisted that they promoted freedom did exactly the opposite. Titans of academia, Yale's professors, were not learned and logical; they were "superstitious." It was not reactionary of Buckley to worry about the fate of Christian individualism at Yale but, instead, reactionary of Yale's professors to reject religion and preach empiricism.

Buckley's next single-authored book, *Up from Liberalism* (1959), began predictably with an ironic reversal. "Fashionable observers," Buckley alleged coyly, posited that the United States "is a non-ideological nation." These "observers," the barely camouflaged liberal consensus historians like Richard Hofstadter, supposed that "American political conflicts are not generally fought on the battleground of ideas." That was for the best, Buckley said with tongue-in-cheek, because "everyone knows that ideological totalism can bring whole societies down, as it did Hitler's, and permanently terrorize others, as Communism has done."[37] Buckley had labeled the intellectual leaders and identified their fixed ideas. The trap was about to spring on a man of straw. To Buckley, there was no liberal consensus; the United States failed "to nourish any orthodoxy at all." As a direct result of the "attenuation of the early principles of this country," the nation was "vulnerable to the most opportunistic ideology of the day, the strange and complex ideology of modern liberalism."[38] The persuasive power of the reversal trope was generated by the device's unmasking function. Liberalism, contrary to popular opinion, was nefarious. Liberals, purportedly defenders of individual liberties, were totalitarians. Buckley portrayed the success of liberal notions like empiricism and welfare statism as functions of trickery rather than the result of their rational force.

Liberals had help in tricking the nation. Leaders tasked with defending the nation in the ideological struggle of the Cold War were, in fact, incapable of such expressions. When President Eisenhower admitted the difficulty of rebutting Communist claims, like those of Red Army commander and Soviet minister of defense Georgy Zhukov, Buckley pounced. The president "clearly did not know what he was defending, how to defend what he defended, or even whether what he defended was defensible."[39] The criticism was unfair; the nation was not at risk because Eisenhower did not recite Friedrich Hayek's free market teachings. Buckley, however, had ideal ammunition with which to complete the reversal of power. Eisenhower had failed in "the distinctive challenge of our time," stopping "the philosophical infiltration of the West by Communism." Buckley thought rhetoric was essential to meeting the challenge. Accomodationist, weak-kneed liberalism "cannot teach Mr. Eisenhower to talk back effectively to Mr.

Khrushchev; but conservatism can, and hence the very urgent need to make the conservative demonstration."[40] Conservatism was powerful; political leaders were impotent. Only the conservative political language could play the savior.

Sarcasm was another reversal trope Buckley used unsparingly. In *National Review's* second year, Buckley devoted six pages, long by the magazine's standards, to the acerbically titled "Reflections on the Failure of 'National Review' to Live Up to Liberal Expectations." The article trounced critics like Dwight Macdonald and *Harper's* editor John Fischer and was typical of the sarcasm Buckley consistently used to deride opponents. *Commentary* and several midcentury journals of opinion, Buckley told his readers, had charged his new magazine with "all manner of offenses against the light and the truth." *National Review* would be a welcome addition to U.S. political discourse, these journals argued, if it were a real conservative magazine. Buckley's sarcasm reversed their reversal. He replied, "Nothing, absolutely nothing, is more urgently needed than a real conservative magazine; but, alas, ours is not such a thing, and they must, accordingly, continue to scan the heavens for it."[41] As this example illustrates, sarcasm is a wounding rhetorical device that removes the social authority of the object of address. Direct insults can also function to remove status. Insults, nevertheless, acknowledge an interlocutor and take aim at his or her authority. Sarcasm finds authority unworthy of such direct aim. Sarcasm is not only more creatively dismissive, it involves its audience in the act as well.

Buckley also deployed a gentler sarcasm that relied more on enthymeme and less on absurdist allegations for its effect. In his answer to Macdonald's assessment of *National Review's* quality, Buckley highlighted the critic's most severe criticisms of the magazine with insincere set-up questions. Buckley wrote: "Well, then, they [*National Review* writers] are surely normal, healthy, well-adjusted folk? *Decidedly not, they are 'anxious, embittered, resentful.'* . . . Editorials any good?—'*as elegant as a poke in the nose, as cultivated as a camp meeting, as witty as a pratfall.*'"[42] Buckley's interrogatives were phrased so innocently, and his wit was usually so injurious, that their sarcasm was plain; his opponents deserved none of the respect presumably afforded the generous, thoughtful, and fair-minded. They were hacks and deserved to be treated as such.

Reversal strategies were a vital characteristic of the gladiatorial style because their use created a doubly dramatic move. Reversal not only signified social power and political authority but also mocked those adhering to outmoded hierarchy. Reversal, in the first place, assumed a power that conservatism, barely a toddler as a political identity when Buckley started *National Review*, had not earned. Reversal presumed the authority to speak, to engage in debate, and to contradict. Moreover, Buckley's rebuttals were armed with all the indignation of the unjustly challenged. Sarcasm and irony moved further than other acts of reversal because each presumed the prestige to evaluate the social and political establishment and to do so flippantly while parading around the arena.

To conservatives, what was so riling about Buckley was that he seized the territory of the secure and castigated elites. This move inspired many imitators. Conservative pundit and polemicist Ann Coulter trades on the reversals of Buckley rhetorical legacy frequently. A clear connection exists between this feature of the gladiatorial style, exemplified in Buckley's 1963 *National Review* cover article, "How to Attack a Liberal," and, to take just one of many possible examples, Ann Coulter's 2004 *How to Talk to a Liberal (If You Must)*.[43] Although Coulter replaced some of his syntactical showiness and argumentative nuance with discourteous bombast, this difference of degree is negligible. When she wrote sneeringly about liberals that "there is some good in everyone," she invoked the sarcasm of Buckley's conservative punditry. Coulter continued by featuring Buckley's usual enemies, Communists and liberals: "Hitler didn't smoke, for example. . . . Even among the staunchest members of the Communist Party, there turned out to be a few good ones. Similarly, the vast majority of liberals are not intentionally sabotaging the nation."[44] Communists' and liberals' peculiar combination of dumb malice that Buckley repeatedly alleged persisted in her scornful commentary.

Spoiling for a Fight

Buckley's books in the 1950s were, as Garry Wills described, "extended dossiers on the Enemy."[45] Beyond their stylistic spectacles and reversal tropes, Buckley's books also provided a unique model by which liberals' policies could be mocked and international Communism could be derided. Buckley, playing the righteous outsider, ridiculed prominent politicians and intellectuals in *God and Man at Yale, McCarthy and His Enemies, Up from Liberalism*, and numerous *National Review* entries. In fact, lampooning, mocking, and jeering enemies composes almost all of *God and Man at Yale*, and Buckley devoted 180 of *Up from Liberalism's* 215 pages to decrying liberalism. In the latter book he lambasted the redistributionism of John Maynard Keynes, the "sophism" of John Kenneth Galbraith, the weakness of Republican senators, the dimwittedness of Dwight Eisenhower, and the villainy of Communists before quickly outlining a "conservative alternative."[46]

The drama of Buckley's writing arose not just from insults of liberals' character or answers to their arguments. The drama was interactional; Buckley needed an oppositional claim to destroy on its own terms. Rebuttal not only answers an opposing view but, in many instances, reverses its symbolic prominence in the argumentative exchange. Buckley's rebuttals frequently blended *antistrephon*, "reasoning from the premises of one's opponent," and reductio ad absurdum, reasoning from self-contradictory conclusions to disprove a proposition. It became difficult to note where his concession of opponents' stated values ended and his exaggeration of the logical consequences of their positions began.[47] Buckley showed the faithful how to fight; he refined a gladiatorial style of rhetorical combat among conservatives distinct from the mere identification and disparagement of enemies.

For all his wit in generating political material, Buckley's most striking maneuver took at face value his opponents' statements and either accused them of hypocrisy, as with "academic freedom," or claimed conservatism to be their proper defender, as with free markets and individual equality. These strategies required that Buckley allocate substantial space to re-create his opponents' arguments. Buckley was willing to dedicate so much space in so many of his important writings to liberals' arguments because they were necessary to the drama he sought; without re-creating a liberal voice in his writing, Buckley had no opponent to reverse, no enemy to use. The rhetorical battle was abstract minus a John Kenneth Galbraith quotation to strike down. The rhetorical gladiator minus an enemy was the matador minus the bull; conflict and animosity were the basics of gladiatorial theater.

Buckley realized the dramatic potential of combat and made sport of it. Liberal pundits' hyperbolic criticisms warning that Buckley's books would make goose-steppers of the masses assisted him immeasurably in attracting new followers who delighted in joining a controversial cause. Put simply, calling Buckley a "fascist" did more to aid his case than to disprove it. In an extended introduction to the fiftieth anniversary edition of *God and Man at Yale*, Buckley still profited from the reviews that greeted his first book. Reviewers commented on his Roman Catholic upbringing and upbraided him for deliberately concealing his religion. These "acidulous" reviews, Buckley wrote, were nothing more than religious persecution.[48] One *New Republic* review likened his proposals for Yale to those "employed in Italy, Germany, and Russia." One *Saturday Review* commentary noted that Buckley wanted Yale's administration to "turn themselves into the politburo."[49] Reproducing these reviews gave Buckley punches to counter. He literally staged the fight for readers to witness. To mark the fiftieth anniversary of the book, Buckley showed that he had a serious fight on his hands, but he, and conservatism, was winning. Combat, not dialogue or reform, held the political fortunes of conservatism.

Beyond *God and Man at Yale* and *Up from Liberalism*, conservatives have celebrated two aspects of Buckley's rhetorical career as exemplars of ideological combat. First, *Firing Line*, his television interview program, featured Buckley and a guest seated in plain office chairs on an unadorned stage. Buckley questioned, cross-examined, and even poked fun at guests as wide ranging as Noam Chomsky, Muhammad Ali, and Ronald Reagan. *Firing Line* entertained because, as one viewer noted, of "all the beating up."[50] More than any particular exchange on the program though, conservatives have recounted Buckley's signature posture, leaning back, eyebrow raised, pencil in hand, clipboard in lap, waiting to pounce. In particular, Buckley's clipboard acquired synecdochic power as the symbol of effective intellectual exchange. George Will's assessment demonstrates this trope: "The fun began when Bill picked up his clipboard, and conservatives' spirits, by bringing his distinctive brio and élan to political skirmishing."[51]

Second, the "Notes & Asides" section of *National Review* also showcased Buckley's combative shrewdness for conservative readers. Buckley designed the section as his "own personal page in the magazine," and it featured well-wishing letters to *National Review* from celebrities and national leaders. Buckley used the section to reprint the less flattering letters followed by his terse, acerbic retort. Hence, "Notes & Asides" became a "polemicist's batting practice," a vehicle for Buckley to deliver laugh lines at his detractors' expense.[52] Ron Kelly, for instance, led with his chin by claiming, "Your syntax is horrible." "Dear Mr. Kelly," Buckley retorted, "If you had my syntax, you'd be rich. Cordially, WFB." Another amateur writer, Earl J. Beck, erred in thinking he could beat Buckley in a word game. "Sedulously avoid all polysyllabical profundity," Beck exhorted. Buckley, parodying a stereotype of Native American patois, teased: "Me Bill. Me no like-um Beck. Bad Beck. WFB."[53] Such exchanges, published scores of times in *National Review*, were even collected and published in a book whose title was taken from another "Notes & Asides" interaction: *Cancel Your Own Goddam Subscription*. When, following Buckley's death, *National Review* convened several prominent conservatives to debate where a conservative aspirant might begin reading the Buckley corpus, one contributor thought his laugh lines from "Notes & Asides" would be a good start.[54]

"Notes & Asides," like *Firing Line*, strategically deployed uneven matches. The section allowed readers to take pleasure in the quick work Buckley made of liberal "pseudo-intellectuals" who dared match wits. Buckley's attacks, when directed at a named critic or public figure, were akin to the body blows that make hometown fight crowds salivate. With "theatrical flair," Richard Viguerie and David Franke praised, Buckley made "mincemeat of liberal totems like Arthur Schlesinger Jr. and John Kenneth Galbraith."[55] His readers could revel in his debates as they might a blood sport. Audiences were invited to imagine the frustrated, sputtering rage that their battling hero created through epigrammatic aptitude.

If his detractors thought that Buckley's conservative style was only pose and pomp, they missed the importance of his strategic agonism in the creation of conservatism. Buckley stirred writers and politicians to practice a conservative language signified by its sharp tones and fierce argumentativeness. Conservatives had taken notice of Buckley's stylistic warnings and followed his stylistic lead. While explaining the reasons for liberal dominance in Washington, D.C., Barry Goldwater opened *The Conscience of a Conservative* with a similarly phrased concern: "I blame Conservatives—ourselves—myself. Our failure, as one Conservative writer has put it, is the failure of the Conservative demonstration."[56] Buckley, of course, was the unnamed writer. The gladiatorial style was not for the unimaginative, the battle weary, or the euphemistic. Ann Coulter, parroting Buckley's baroque syntax, preferred to think of his legacy as primarily combative: "William F. Buckley was the original *enfant terrible*. . . . I prefer to remember the Buckley who scandalized to the *bien-pensant*. . . . I shall revel in the 'terrible' aspects of the *enfant terrible.*"[57] The American Conservative Union Foundation's magazine, the appropriately titled *Conservative Battleline*, exhorted its readers after Buckley's death: "It is now up to us to continue his struggle up from liberalism."[58]

Most emblematic, however, of the kind of praise that Buckley received for his gladiatorial role was an epic tale told by Ronald Reagan in 1985. In addition to anointing Buckley "the most influential journalist and intellectual in our era," Reagan proclaimed that he "changed our country, indeed our century."[59] Grand though that praise was, Reagan offered praise far more illustrative of the gladiatorial relationship between Buckley's rhetoric and conservatives. In mythic terms, the president recalled the time of "the forest primeval," a period "when nightmare and danger reigned" and conservatives lacked a "champion in the critical battle of style and content." Buckley answered the call. Blending generic heroic images and symbols, such as Buckley's notorious clipboard, from the conservative rhetorical environment, Reagan extolled: "He was our clipboard-bearing Galahad: ready to take on any challengers in the critical battle of point and counterpoint." In Reagan's mythic re-creation, Buckley as Galahad taught the techniques of ideological battle in the Cold War. But their conservative knight, who capably "set loose the forces of good," barked no onerous orders at followers. As Reagan concluded, "Bill, thanks too for all the fun."[60]

Teaching Style

Brute force and barbed attack are the standout features of the gladiatorial style, yet *kairos*, meaning both the "right timing and proper measure" of symbol usage, is its fulcrum.[61] The imposing gladiator may discharge a series of kill shots just as the gladiatorial stylist may fire scores of ad hominem attacks at an interlocutor. Neither attacker, however, activates the fullest *kairotic* dimensions of the gladiatorial style that, instead of hastily resorting to decisive blows, uses the novelty of an unexpected technique to squeeze all available surprising drama from a given context. A well-timed personal attack can be even more cutting if it follows an exchange over policy details. In other words, the continued effectiveness of the gladiatorial style rests on its ability to be continually surprising. The style operates by a logic of innovation rather than repetition. For the gladiatorial stylist, the excitement generated by the finishing move wanes as its use becomes repetitive.

Buckley's rhetorical directions were ultimately concerned with inculcating conservatives with the dramatic *kairotic* sense of the gladiatorial style. Buckley's writings throughout the 1950s focused on "the conservative demonstration" almost as much as Communism, Korea, or Eisenhower. As Buckley argued in *Up from Liberalism*, "Conservatives, as a minority, must learn to agonize more meticulously."[62] In high-profile features in *National Review* and most thoroughly in *Up from Liberalism*, Buckley appointed himself the movement's chief rhetorician and dispensed stylistic advice. Shortly after *God and Man at Yale* was published, Buckley's fellow writer at *American Mercury*, Max Eastman, heard of Buckley's plans for a new magazine and cautioned him to be a careful editor. Buckley's reply demonstrated the extent to which cultivating a dramatic style, as well as developing doctrinal topoi, was his chief editorial priority: "All I can say to satisfy you is that I want discretion in the sense that I want intelligence, and no crackpottery. But I want some positively unsettling vigor, a sense of abandon, and joy, and cocksureness that may, indeed, be interpreted by some as indiscretion."[63] Buckley wanted a magazine about political ideas; however, he also sought a magazine that set itself apart from the dull droning of policy wonks and radiated with rhetorical energy.

In *Up from Liberalism*, Buckley isolated several stylistic challenges faced by conservatives. The most pressing challenge was how the dangers of collectivism might be proclaimed without conservatives appearing paranoid. For conservatives to be a political force independent of Republican leadership, moderate liberals, and many others, conservatism needed a distinct mode of political argument. "A libertarian theorist," Buckley lamented, can quickly call up a concise case against the welfare state. Conservatives needed such standardized maneuvers, "highly explicit postulates" as he called them.[64] Additionally, political success required a unique voice, one that broke through the shouting and drew listeners. The difference between, as he put it, "the rightness, *sub specie aeternitatis*, of the conservative position, and the cogency of its appeal to a presumptively right-minded body politic" was pivotal in the creation of conservatism as a political force.[65]

Buckley linked the conservative demonstrative failure to a multitude of factors that concern *kairotic* sensibilities. Its enemies successfully portrayed conservatism as "a crassly materialist position, unconcerned except with the world of getting and spending."[66] Moreover, self-identified conservatives had failed as well. They had "failed to make distinctions," for instance, by forgetting to separate their economic from their philosophical objections to Social Security.[67] Conservatives neglected, he posited, to make the case for "the interconnection between economic freedom and—freedom." Many conservatives, he parodied, rhetorically gambled on impossible predictions: "Our insistence that the economic comeuppance is just around the corner (not *this* corner, *that* one. No, not *that one, that* one over *there* . . .) has lost to conservatism public confidence in its expertise."[68] To make promises about the timing of catastrophe was to risk argumentative credibility. If conservatism became associated with dire economic predictions about government spending, Buckley argued, "we will, like the Seventh Day Adventists who close down the curtain of the world every season or so, lose our credit at the bar of public opinion, or be dismissed as cultists of a terrestrial mystique."[69] Buckley's admonition bordered on disingenuousness. He also employed hyperbole in his pursuit of dramatic results. Timing was the trick, however. Maximum drama was not achieved in a persistent firestorm of ludicrous prophecies and derogatory attacks. Such tactics should not be outlawed, but their repetition diminished expectations and compromised political respectability. Drama did not come instantaneously; it had to be built.

Instead of issuing calamitous prophecies, Buckley encouraged conservatives to become versatile performers schooled in varied modes of critique. He hoped to cultivate showy conservative rhetoricians, but he understood the theatrical and tactical value of capable logicians and nimble debaters who could operate from first principles. In *Up from Liberalism*, Buckley offered conservatives a model logical argument by countering the rationale for Social Security:

> 1. *Blanket social security coverage encourages malingering and abuse.* (Tacit premise: That which encourages sloth is philosophically objectionable.) . . . 2. *Social Security laws are an imposture.* (Tacit premise: They are presented as an "insurance" program. They are not that, in the orthodox sense.) . . . 3. *The social security program is redistributionist in character, since, as we have seen, it implicitly contemplates taking from some in order to give to others.* (Tacit premise: Forcible redistribution is, except in extraordinary situations, ethically indefensible.) . . . 4. *Participation*

in the social security program is compulsory. (Tacit premise: Compulsory participation in any enterprise is wrong, because human freedom is diminished.)[70]

Buckley critiqued the program in four italicized theses and provided readers with parenthetical notes identifying the conservative principles from which each thesis was derived. The Social Security lesson was a demonstration of intellect from an otherwise excessive writer as much as it was debate advice. Conservatives, Buckley feared, had nothing but a small trove of finishing moves about Social Security and "slavery" that they rolled out tirelessly.[71] They needed not only to add nuance but to improve their technical argumentative skill complete with opening arguments, leading arguments, and point-by-point refutation. Conservatives' use of diverse rhetorical figures displayed political competency as well as built anticipation for the more dramatic elements of the conservative demonstration: spectacle, reversal, and attack.

A Community "Athwart History"

Many conservatives have made a similar case (chapter 1), but George Will put it most dramatically: "All great biblical stories begin with Genesis." Before Reagan came Goldwater; before Goldwater came *National Review*, but Buckley, he rhapsodized, came first "with a spark in his mind."[72] With the typical tropes of the gladiatorial style established, it is worth asking how Buckley wielded the gladiatorial style to create conservatism as a political community. I suggest that the political passion generated by the gladiatorial style allowed Buckley to attract a constellation of ostracized midcentury ideologies to conservatism. Moreover, with the gladiatorial style as their most salient rhetorical model, conservatives in the United States contradicted classical conservatism's emphasis on stability and tradition and became provocative and contrarian.

Although Buckley used gladiatorial tactics to cut an ideological image, his role within an expanding post–World War II conservatism was that of a peacekeeper and coalition builder. *National Review*'s first masthead featured an impressive variety of writers. Buckley was the editor and publisher. He was followed by ex-Communist and veteran of *Partisan Review* James Burnham, maverick political theorist Willmoore

Kendall, individualist Suzanne La Follette, and émigré Willi Schlamm. Virtually everyone got a column. One year after its founding, L. Brent Bozell, John Chamberlain, and Whittaker Chambers were added to the masthead.[73] Anti-Communists, traditionalists, and libertarians may not have shared common principles, but they did have common enemies and a weekly venue from which to launch attacks.[74] *National Review*'s early readers could pick up an issue and find a number of different conservative ideas represented. No writer would defend the Soviets or the New Deal. There was a great deal of room to the right of those enemies, and *National Review* writers explored the territory well. As E. J. Dionne concluded, "Absent Buckley's charm and magnetism, conservatism and the *National Review* might well have collapsed somewhere around 1959."[75]

Buckley's own writings contributed to the fusion of traditionalist, libertarian, and anti-Communist perspectives within conservatism. Like Meyer's, Buckley's books and articles were an ideological adhesive for conservative combatants. But more than Meyer's, his writings also reflected the fissures that have divided conservatives since the midcentury. On the one hand, Buckley expressed an "aristocratic conservatism" that was reverent of social tradition, suspicious of political change, and fearful of mass politics.[76] On the other hand, Buckley linked his conservatism to social disruption when he identified as a "revolutionary."[77] He pondered writing an extension of Jose Ortega y Gasset's *Revolt of the Masses* at one turn and, playing the populist the next turn, joked that he would prefer to be governed by the first 2,000 names in the Boston phone book than the Harvard faculty.[78] Buckley embodied, as one analyst put it, "most of the apparent contradictions and incoherence of American conservatism."[79]

The appeal, nevertheless, of Buckley's explicit political commitments insufficiently explains Buckley's rhetorical power among conservatives. Buckley's contemporaries, to illustrate by comparison, are fondly remembered for teaching principled lessons; Kirk emphasized social tradition in *The Conservative Mind*, and Hayek linked economic freedom to political freedom in *The Road to Serfdom*. Neither of these writers, and few other conservative for that matter, has been lionized as grandly as Buckley. Requiems to Buckley demonstrate the passionate, rebellious response of an identity produced by the gladiatorial style; conservatism became something worth fighting for. Reading Buckley, Michael Uhlmann said, was like watching "Henry at Agincourt, in-

structing and inspiring through noble speech and leading by courageous example." The Buckley experience was, Uhlmann confessed,
"utterly intoxicating."[80] Other conservatives have described being "under his spell."[81] What distinguished Buckley from other conservatives
was that he was not just defending a political program, he was crafting
an attractive and strategically flexible outsider identity that invited several alienated groups to call their politics conservative.

Conservatives rallied around Buckley because he equipped them
with a self-consciously formidable style to perform intellectual sophis-
tication during a period in which conservatism was both out of favor
and under attack. Conservatives have argued that the complexity of
Buckley's rhetorical style, far from Hofstadter's "paranoid style," legitimized conservatism as an intellectual enterprise and exposed liberalism as the facile recitation of dogmata.[82] As a result of Buckley's
"prolific pen," "sharp tongue," and "charming wit," one conservative
writer praised in 2008, intellectual display was "the hallmark of the
postwar conservative movement."[83] Buckley's stylistic spectacles gave
conservatives more than a set of beliefs; he afforded membership in an
undaunted community that had a claim to profundity.

When Buckley addressed conservatives in his "Publisher's
Statement" in *National Review*'s first issue in 1955, he cast them
romantically as a righteous band of rebels eschewing cooperation
for gate-crashing. Whereas liberals were censorious, Buckley, using
a dramatic alliteration, called new conservatives "non-licensed nonconformists" in a conformist age. They were "out of place" and under
siege; being conservative was "dangerous business in a liberal world."
As new arrivals to a political scene populated by dogmatic liberals and
the "irresponsible Right," conservatives enjoyed none of the benefits of
entrenched power, but "unattenuated by a thousand vulgar promises
to a thousand different pressure groups," conservatism could be, as he
hoped, "the hottest thing in town."[84] Buckley framed conservatives as
new and brash despite his own leanings toward aristocracy and a stable
social order. *National Review*, he wrote, "stands athwart history, yelling Stop, at a time when no one is inclined to do so, or to have much
patience with those who so urge it."[85] Buckley's consummate conservatives viewed the political world dramatically; to be conservative was to
clear away the dominant political order.

As seemingly contradictory as a band of revolutionary conservatives was, his characterization of the conservative identity also exuded

romantic appeal. He empowered readers to understand their politics not as antiquated or irrelevant, but as conservative ideals under attack *because* of their vital relevance. The community that experienced conservatism through the gladiatorial style was not stodgy or typical; instead, they were righteous, merry warriors and members of a special community. For instance, Buckley's conservatism would broker no partnership with Dwight Eisenhower and the Eastern Establishment Republicans, the decadent, "well-fed Right" as he portrayed them.[86] Buckley's goal of using *National Review* to read "Eisenhower out of the conservative movement" was an audacious dissociation of stalwart conservatives from those he framed as weak New Deal knockoff Republicans.[87]

Conservatism in the midcentury became a kind of exclusive identity politics in which various groups seized and defended the moniker against all enemies. In addition to helping conservatism cohere by popularizing the gladiatorial style as a common pattern of rhetorical expression, Buckley's style also generated an ironic interpretive pattern, an insider hermeneutic, among readers. The style asked readers to understand the ironic reversals that were employed, to decode the sarcasm, to follow Buckley's meandering sentences, to comprehend the big words, and to decipher the slang. Buckley's style offered a corrective to a political order that was upside-down, where what was right was dismissed. The reversal tropes of the gladiatorial style instructed conservatives to reject the political common sense of the day, to speak no-holds-barred truths to New Dealers, socialists, Trotskyists, "enlightened" atheists, and liberal Republicans. The righteousness of the conservative cause was signified not by how many political observers agreed with them but by how many aligned against them. If Hofstadter, Schlesinger, or the *New York Times*'s editorialists were not worried, conservatives must have erred. Buckley, a conservative wrote in 2009, was their source of "psychological armor." Being targeted as "cranks and menaces" was a "badge of honor and a source of great, iconoclastic fun."[88] Buckley encouraged conservatives to view iconoclasm as energizing; the tropes of the gladiatorial style became, in Louis Menand's terms, "badges of identity."[89] To be a part of "the hottest" political group in town, readers, quite simply, had to get it. Decoding particular syntaxes signified specialized knowledge and authoritative status.

Weekly Standard founder William Kristol, for instance, proudly displayed his badge, a political button, in his high school yearbook photo. Its big letters read "Don't let THEM immanentize the Eschaton." The phrase, coined by Eric Voegelin in 1952 and reworked into a combative slogan by Buckley, was cumbersome shorthand for the notion that liberal plans to create heaven on earth actually created hell on earth.[90] Jonah Goldberg, a prominent conservative still fond of the formulation fifty years after Voegelin wrote it, explained its power for conservative readers, many of whom "really want to know what that phrase means."[91] The slogan was a "conservative dork trap," as he put it, a "hard-core conservative insider thing" equivalent to "'TK-421, where are you?' to a *Star Wars* freak." But Kristol, a presumably precocious high-school kid, knew the phrase's meaning and wore the button as a badge of authenticity. Understanding the dense vocabulary of the "dork trap" allowed readers like Kristol a sense of being let in on a conservative secret. Voegelin's prolix locution became vintage Buckley loquacity. As Kristol remembered, Buckley's words, "immanentize," "Eschaton," and otherwise, so thrilled him that he felt compelled to adorn them: "To read Buckley growing up in the 1960s was bracing. Buckley and his colleagues—some merrily, some mordantly—mercilessly eviscerated the idiocies of the New Left."[92] Kristol experienced Buckley's conservatism as many have experienced gladiatorial contests since antiquity, as a witness so taken by the conflict that he sought to learn the means of the gladiator.

Orthodox and Heterodox Conservatism

William F. Buckley crafted a conservatism known for its intellectual, exuberant, and take-no-prisoners gladiatorial style. His influence on conservatism was due as much to his emotional defense of an embattled political identity as it was a logical appeal for traditionalists and libertarians to join forces. The provocative contrarianism enabled by the gladiatorial style had both costs and benefits. The gladiatorial style engendered the expression of an adjustable conservatism, but it constrained its users within the tumultuous framework of opposition politics. As functional as the gladiatorial style was in the creation of the conservative coalition, a community of contrarians was difficult to sustain, both in terms of communal fidelity and doctrinal loyalty. Where Buckley's style engrossed, and thereby fused, conservatives, it also inspired conservatives to be unconventional, thereby stoking the possibility of fracture.

The gladiatorial style aims at drama, and discord is often a means to that end. The rhetorical gladiator is a controversialist for whom doctrinal inconsistency is a tool to be selectively deployed, not a taboo to be avoided. Instead of passing down consistent political principles, Buckley's rhetorical legacy was nearly the opposite; he encouraged heterodoxy, even a joyful defiance, in conservatism. I am not suggesting that all conservatives followed Buckley's ecumenical conservatism. Indeed, many conservatives, contra Buckley, were doctrinally rigid and insisted on closing ranks and protecting "real" conservatism from pretenders. I am suggesting, however, that strict doctrinal adherence is inconsistent with the gladiatorial style. Buckley was a flexible stylist, not a dogmatic catechist, and that difference separated the conservatism he inspired from the conservatism he resisted.

Buckley could be inconveniently doctrinaire when he thought the herd encroached on independent minds. He supported the legalization of drugs, "*hardly* a conservative position."[93] He turned on the war in Iraq, a venture begun and supported by conservatives, with a terse admonishment: "It didn't work."[94] Forty years prior, students "openly wept" when Buckley told their Young Americans for Freedom convention of Barry Goldwater's "impending defeat" just prior to the 1964 election.[95] "We do not believe," Buckley enjoined them characteristically, "in the Platonic affirmation of our own little purities."[96]

Buckley even defended Ronald Reagan against conservative critics for, of all things, *increasing* government spending. When then governor Reagan's first budget proposal did not fulfill his budget-slashing campaign promises, Buckley answered critics as any good student of language would: words are deeds. He argued, "They say that his [Reagan's] accomplishments are few, that it is only the rhetoric that is conservative. But the rhetoric is the principal thing. It precedes all action. All thoughtful action."[97] It may not have made sense to doctrinaire libertarians, but Buckley's rebuttal was strictly in line with the competitive instinct of conservative contrarians and his rhetorical approach to political life. Buckley wanted conservatives to weigh the power of Reagan's performance of limited government conservatism against the delicate choices Reagan made given California's budgetary realities. To Buckley, political principles were vital in defining the broad range of a belief system, but they were not necessarily restrictive. It was far better to engage principles artfully than to encourage principled automatons. Principles need not direct the political actor with exacting specificity; they function best as does a rudder on a large ship, useful for directional steering rather than sharp turns.

The relationship, nevertheless, between the gladiatorial style and the growth of conservatism is somewhat of a paradox. The style, so effective in conservatism's growth from political eccentricity to national prominence, can also be a hindrance. The elasticity of gladiatorial argument can be confused with wanton doctrinal promiscuity. A controversy over the meaning of Buckley's 1955 "Publisher's Statement" is illustrative. In *The Last Best Hope*, conservative pundit Joe Scarborough reached back for Buckley's pragmatic legacy as the antidote to conservative dogmatism. "Like the prophets of old," Scarborough declared, Buckley "understood that there was a season for advancing, a season for holding steady, and a season for taking tactical retreats." Authentic conservatives "align themselves with reality and restraint."[98] Buckley, he praised, knew that "standing athwart history and yelling 'Stop!'" was "a guiding light rather than a rigid ideology."[99] The same "Publisher's Statement" that Scarborough lauded for its flexibility, *National Review* writer Ramesh Ponnuru celebrated for its attacks on "relativism" and its language of "fixed postulates."[100] Both Scarborough and Ponnuru read Buckley accurately, and their disagreement highlights the instability of audience interpretation as a drawback of gladiatorial irony.[101] Buckley's dramatic conservatism provoked passionate, if inconsistent, responses from readers, even among those parsing his words to identify his legacy.

Christopher Buckley, WFB's son, showed himself to be, as one conservative put it, "the swashbuckling heir to his father's defiant spirit" by endorsing Barack Obama for president in 2008.[102] Christopher Buckley became an apostate to some.[103] The apostasy accusation, however, assumed that apostasy was not a normal part of the show; by WFB's design, it had always been. Conservatism, by his blueprint, was revolutionary, not reactionary; offensive, not defensive; and counter- rather than proestablishment. Posthumous praise for WFB's individualism became a chorus as many conservative eulogists lauded his "fearlessness," "his willingness to go against the grain," and his "independence of mind."[104] Rich Lowry, in fact, ignored his own eulogy of WFB—"He spawned so many impersonators because his mannerisms were utterly original"—when he accepted Christopher Buckley's resignation from *National Review*.[105] Lowry once argued that WFB's individualism erased distinctions between conservatives: "We live in a time of sometimes confusing intra-conservative fights. People ask, 'Are you a neoconservative, a paleoconservative?' The appropriate answer . . . is, 'I'm a Bill Buckley conservative.'"[106] Had Lowry taken his own claims further, he may have realized that deadening conformity, whether Communist or conservative, was WFB's bête noire.[107]

The problem of Buckley's consistency suggests a related disadvantage; the gladiatorial style is useful for opposition politics, but its value in governing, carefully negotiating, or settling principles to guide a community is limited. The style is capable of mobilizing diverse coalitions against an extant enemy, and it is a formidable debate tactic to score points against opponents and elicit crowd support. Quick wit and a gift for one-liners generate drama in mass-mediated politics but are not nearly as helpful when laying out a broad governing philosophy or hammering out the details of complex legislation. Latter-day conservative firebrands, authors of popular books like *Liberalism Is a Mental Disorder*, *Godless: The Church of Liberalism*, and *Deliver Us from Evil: Defeating Terrorism, Despotism, and Liberalism*, swing hard with gladiatorial cudgels and make contentious spectacles of political disputes.[108] The style they wield is designed to dramatize, to show off, in short, to gain attention. It is a style, as the gladiatorial metaphor suggests, to best a threatening opponent and to entertain a wanting crowd. Such display may produce dazzling spectacles but does not enjoin an audience in careful deliberation. This opposition style benefits the gadfly who gains much from bold moves in a dramatic political argument and benefits little from finely tuned compromises. The gladiatorial style is great for provoking debates, not for deliberative resolution.

Difficult ideological choices are required of those who seek either consistency in their politics or predictability in their governors. The gladiatorial style affords flexibility, but absent reflective guidance it can stretch conservatism to incoherence. When the chance to define the essence of conservatism came, and it came many thousands of times, Buckley refused, and delighted in doing so. In *Did You Ever See a Dream Walking?*, a collection of excerpts from American conservatism's founding texts, he wrote:

I confess that I know who is a conservative less surely than I know who is a liberal. Blindfold me, spin me about like a top, and I will walk up to the single liberal in the room without zig or zag and find him even if he is hiding behind a flower pot. I am tempted to try to develop an equally sure nose for the conservative, but I am deterred by the knowledge that conservatives, under the stress of our times, have had to invite all kinds of people into their ranks to help with the job at hand.[109]

Buckley claimed that "What is conservatism?" was the question he faced most frequently from lecture audiences. To the most insistent, those who seemed to need a definition or just needed to see Buckley provide one, Buckley obliged by offering Richard Weaver's torturous "the paradigm of essences towards which the phenomenology of the world is in continuing approximation." Weaver's cagey line was delivered best, as Buckley put it, "with a straight face."[110] In the moments when a complex but quotable synthesis would have been welcomed, Buckley delivered the opposite. Buckley did not just evade the definitional query; he announced its impossibility and mocked those who required such certainty.

That conservatism's chief spokesman would refuse to define conservatism was a galling irony, but it also did not provide an answer to a challenge Whittaker Chambers put to Buckley shortly before the founding of *National Review*: "Those who remain in the world, if they will not surrender on its terms, must maneuver within its terms. That is what conservatives must decide: how much to give in order to survive at all; how much to give in order not to give up the basic principles." The gladiatorial style is not useful in providing a method for "dancing along the precipice" separating conservative belief and engaged political activity.[111] Buckley was more, as Wills explains, "a quick responder" than a systematic thinker. His "gifts were facility, flash, and charm, not depth or prolonged wrestling with a problem."[112] Although the gladiatorial style can be reduced to a kind of sophistry in the pejorative sense, I do not mean to suggest that Buckley was only a garish hype man; nonetheless, he was not a theorist who showed where the philosophical bedrock was, the threshold separating conviction and capitulation.

The conservatism Buckley shaped through the gladiatorial style was, in sum, cavalier, not conformist. As entertaining as this conservatism may be, contrarian controversy does not necessarily lend prudence to a political program. Just as the gladiatorial style may popularize conservative principles, it may also attract devotees to the controversial, provocateurs bent on deviance and individuality. Yet even as some conservatives might speak in baser, more Philistinic tones than Buckley did, those with economic, nationalist, or culture war messages still follow Buckley's template. Whether sage or shrill, bloviating or bookish, many conservatives have clearly in mind how Buckley might have made the case. Buckley wanted to win the argument and to entertain the crowd, and he was certain that there was a close relationship between the two.

CHAPTER SIX

Whittaker Chambers's Martyrdom

⌘

W hittaker Chambers began writing his memoirs in 1950, two years after he alleged before the House Un-American Activities Committee (HUAC) that Soviet spy cells, of which he was an integral part, had infiltrated the U.S. government. Both in his trial and subsequent memoirs, Chambers named the names of secret Soviet agents who masqueraded as idealistic New Deal bureaucrats. Most notable among his fellow apparatchiks was Alger Hiss. Hiss was no functionary; he was president of the Carnegie Endowment for International Peace at the time of Chambers's allegation, and, before that, Hiss was prominently positioned in the State Department and Office of Far Eastern Affairs. He directed the Office of Special Affairs, which spearheaded the creation of the United Nations. As a delegate to the Yalta conference in 1945, Hiss even sat mere feet from Stalin, his purported boss. In gripping, televised testimony, Chambers testified that he, Hiss, and others ferreted State Department documents to their Soviet handlers. Hiss was convicted of perjury but pressed the case forward on appeal.[1] The legal case was finally resolved in 1951 as Hiss commenced a forty-four-month prison stint, but public fury on both sides remained deafening long after the cell door shut on Hiss.[2]

Like the Dreyfus Affair in fin de siècle France, the Hiss-Chambers case was a "dervish trial" in which courtroom dramatics wrecked cultural bonds.[3] "Who is lying, Hiss or Chambers?" was a ubiquitous above-the-fold headline.[4] The legal question over whether the dapper Hiss with the sterling résumé and Brahmin background was a Soviet agent exposed massive "ideological fault lines."[5] Chambers, whose slovenly image and tarnished pro-Soviet past won him no favor with wide swaths of the public, was transformed into one of "the most divisively controversial Americans of the twentieth century."[6] Completed sixteen months past due in November 1951, *Witness* cemented that reputation.[7] It was to be his "final brief in the unfinished case," a meticulous exegesis of his and Hiss's clandestine Communism.[8]

The book was an expansive backgrounder on the trial, but Chambers also used it to pursue far bolder literary and philosophical ambitions.[9] His acceptance of Communism as secular egalitarianism and then his subsequent rejection of Communism as atheist materialism personified his notion that the Cold War was a theological rather than ideological conflict. Chambers's double conversion, falling for Communism then accepting Christianity, was a wrenching personal anecdote representing human enfeeblement, a synecdoche for "the tragedy of man in the 20th century."[10] The "compact volume" he planned became a 340,000-word, 800-page tome, and the book Random House pressured Chambers to finish for more than a year debuted as a mustread.[11] When *Witness* was serialized in the *Saturday Evening Post*, an illustration did not grace the magazine's cover for the first time in its fifty-three-year history. Norman Rockwell was supplanted by a stark headline: "One of the Great Books of Our Time: Whittaker Chambers' Own Story of the Hiss Case."[12]

Witness was a genre cocktail; it blended bildungsroman with apologia, autobiography with international intrigue, whistle-blowing with journalism, and penance with political commentary. Sam Tanenhaus, Chambers's biographer, called it "cold war poetry."[13] The book's main generic ingredients, tragedy and a Christian conversion epic, rendered the Cold War in familiar literary molds. Chambers employed what Kenneth Burke and others identified as the hallmark tropes of tragedy:

ultimate conflict between good and evil, cycles of guilt and redemption, and the universalization of personal circumstances.[14] Chambers's message that life was suffering, his palpable dread during his flight from Communism, and his public persecution during the Hiss case called literary analogies like Dante[15] and Dostoevsky[16] to the minds of some reviewers. Chambers's deeply revealing description of his misery invited biblical analogies as well; he was, like Jonah in the Gospel according to Matthew, "cast into the sea in order to save his shipmates" or, like Mark's Jesus, pained, prostrate, and forsaken.[17] Above all, *Witness*, "a book of shadows, urban gloom, and cultural despair," was unrelentingly dark.[18]

It began ominously with Chambers leading his children on a mystical journey to Golgotha, the site of Christ's crucifixion, and ended as Chambers wished for death and predicted the end of the world.[19] The saga that unfolded between these dim poles was peppered with macabre scenes of Communists killing their own and Chambers, like his brother, twice attempting suicide. Chambers survived both attempts; his brother, who put his head in a gas oven, did not. With good cause, William F. Buckley said that *Witness* was soaked in "Spenglerian gloom."[20] One of Chambers's most famous lines, initially uttered during his HUAC testimony and repeated in *Witness*, typified his despondency: "You know," he told his wife when he broke with Communism, "we are leaving the winning world for the losing world."[21]

By one measure, Chambers's memoir was one of many midcentury books promising to show the true face of Soviet Communism, some of which, like *You Can Trust Communists (to Be Communists)*, *Communist America—Must It Be?*, *The Naked Communist*, and books by canonical writers like Frank Meyer and James Burnham, inspired grassroots study groups on the right.[22] These and other books were influential, even essential, to coalitional conservatism because each helped vivify a "common mortal enemy" against whom free-marketers and religious moralists could join forces.[23] Whether opposed to Communism on religious grounds by traditionalists or economic grounds by libertarians, anti-Communism among newly minted midcentury conservatives was, as Garry Wills described, "the operative element in self-definition."[24]

By another measure, *Witness* was not one of many books; it was one of a kind, a "crucial intellectual experience" for conservatives.[25] As John Judis argues, "No book was more important in establishing the new movement's understanding of Communism than Chambers's

Witness."[26] Despite its dark tone and stubborn length, conservatives of every variety lavished praise on *Witness*. "*Witness*," one conservative avowed, "may have enlisted more American anti-communists than almost any other book of the Cold War."[27] Chambers's "gripping account," both "prescient and moving," stirred "generations of conservatives," one of his canonists summarized.[28] More than that of his contemporaries, it was Chambers's language that conservatives would parrot when describing the Cold War or depicting Communists. It was his language that many conservatives, including Ronald Reagan, memorized. It was his farm that conservatives registered as a National Historic Landmark.[29] *Witness* has been regaled in breathless encomiums surpassing every other anti-Communist text and even most canonical books of the era. Robert Novak's was typical; *Witness*, he wrote, "changed my worldview, my philosophical perceptions, and, without exaggeration, my life."[30] The book became, one writer declared bluntly, the movement's Cold War "Ur-text."[31]

But how did such a depressing book written by a doomsaying former Communist turncoat who neither espoused conservatism nor defended the inherent goodness of the West become a movement "bible"?[32] How did its saturnine visions of personal sin and Cold War defeat become "absolutely compelling" to activists, commentators, and key figures in two presidential administrations?[33] Why have conservatives of all stripes used a book about Cold War suffering, a book that predicted a Communist victory, as a rallying point?[34]

What made *Witness* distinct was that Chambers humanized the Cold War by casting it within a tragic drama in which he, and the wider West, failed to find redemption against an insidious foe. The rhetorical power of the book's tragic tale stemmed not just from its depiction of Communism but also from the imbalanced relationship between the protagonist and antagonist. The essence of Chambers's story was Tolkien in reverse: the forces of darkness prevailed over the forces of light.[35] The Cold War was converted into an absorbing tragedy complete with a sacrificial protagonist with a farm and a family battling a groomed, serpentine villain capable of endless deceptions and alluring illusions. I posit that the asymmetric narrative relationship between the doomed hero and calculating enemy in *Witness* became, among conservatives, not just a heuristic to understand the Cold War but a Rosetta stone useful in deciphering the stakes of many other political controversies.[36]

Witness's tragic narrative dynamic captivated conservatives of different philosophical predispositions, and, accordingly, the meanings unlocked by users of Chambers's Rosetta stone varied considerably. For Chambers's traditionalist readers, the Cold War battle between American light and Soviet darkness was the largest in a larger, centuries-long war between religious faith and rationalist atheism. Chambers stood up not just against Communism but against creeping secularism, Enlightenment scientism, and base materialism, and he lost. For Chambers's libertarian readers, the Cold War battle between American light and Soviet darkness was the largest in a larger, centuries-long war between individual autonomy and state power. Chambers stood up not just against the Soviets but against the united powers of collectivism, including Communism, socialism, and liberalism, and he lost. Chambers's more fusionist readers found both; *Witness* pitted religious individualism against secular collectivism.

Among these different meanings and uses of the text, however, existed a common denominator: conservatives of all kinds found in Chambers's martyrdom a tragic rationale to cooperate. When conservatives experienced the Cold War in Chambers's terms, they were shown his travails, not his salvation. Although Chambers died of a heart attack in 1961, it became common sense that the Cold War sent him to his grave, that he was "a martyr who told the truth and was crucified in the left-wing press."[37] Chambers morphed into a "tragic symbol," which, as Kenneth Burke argues, "is the device *par excellence* for *recommending* a cause."[38] I treat Chambers's story as a unique type of conversion narrative, what I term a "twice-born" conversion narrative, a distinctly tragic species of "I once was lost, but now I am found" conversion tales that end not in redemption but mortification.[39] The twice-born narrative is a story of unending guilt, of a cursed life, in which no new beginning can undo a sinful past. As Buckley became the movement's rhetorical Galahad, Chambers became the movement's righteous victim, its martyr, whose symbolic force united traditionalist, libertarian, and fusionist conservatives against "evil" both during and after the Cold War.[40]

Witness became a meeting ground for various conservatives. After an initial discussion of the narrative features of twice-born conversion rhetoric, I explore the tragic, asymmetric narrative relationship between the sacrificial hero and the evil enemy in *Witness*. Specifically, the bulk of this chapter takes shape in two sections, the first on the rhetorical design of Chambers's martyrdom in *Witness* and its reception among varying conservatives, the second on the rhetorical design of his portrait of Communism in *Witness* and its reception among varying conservatives. I conclude by analyzing conservatives' use of his twice-born narrative prism after the Cold War. Conservative readers, including those at the highest reaches of American politics, immortalized Chambers through a politics of sacrificial remembrance. These readers interpreted Chambers's glum conclusions as warnings that if he could become complicit with evil, so could they.[41]

Chambers's Twice-Born Tragedy

Conversion narratives are scattered throughout the print culture of conservatism.[42] In acts befitting conservatives' reverence of their print foundations, two original conservative authors were awarded the Presidential Medal of Freedom in the 1980s by Ronald Reagan, himself a self-proclaimed conservative convert. In 1983, Reagan gave the honor to James Burnham, the former Trotskyist, and, in 1985, bestowed the honor on Sydney Hook, the former Marxist. Chambers, the former Communist, won posthumously in 1984.[43] The multitude of conservative conversion testimonies is not just a curious historical coincidence; these stories provide an argumentative advantage. They provide captivating models of lives rescued from sin for other potential converts, and the converts' zeal can be infectious to members of the flock.[44]

Witness, however, was a conversion story unlike the others. Chambers's agonized account of his break with Communism contained none of the guilt-then-redemption arcs of other conservative Cold War narratives or the flip levity found in books like *Conservatives Are from Mars, Liberals Are from San Francisco: 101 Reasons I'm Happy I Left the Left*.[45] Chambers saw the human condition as hopeless. Showcasing his characteristic despair, Chambers wrote, "For it is not only to the graves of dead brothers that we find ourselves powerless at last to bring anything but prayer. We are equally powerless at the graves of ourselves, once we know that we live in shrouds."[46] Although Chambers's conversion to Christianity was propelled by the desire for redemption, he portrayed himself, and the West by extension, as helpless to achieve salvation.

Conversion rhetoric, or testimony about a conversion experience, is a "widely recognized pattern of religious discourse."[47] The act of conversion is typically conceived as a straightening of a wayward life, the clarification of life's priorities, and a wholesale acceptance of a new theory of the world's workings. Constantine famously converted after being confronted by a cross of light in the sky and visited by Jesus in a dream.[48] Almost seventy years later, Augustine heard a divine voice in a Milanese garden, read Paul's epistle to the Romans, and "all the darkness of doubt vanished away."[49] The plot of conversion narratives proceeds in discrete stages, beginning with a "transgression phase" in which an individual runs afoul of hallowed communal conventions, continuing in a "transformation phase" in which the life of the individual is revolutionized, and concluding with a "commissioning phase" in which the convert enumerates how the conversion experience has altered life's course.[50] If, as "Amazing Grace" tells, those who are blind may see, the enormity of that experience seems also to require an evangelical response. Those with sight must speak so that those who are blind may be told of their chance to see.[51]

The standard conversion account is broad and rhetorically influential, but it proceeds solely from narratives that William James called "once-born" in *The Varieties of Religious Experience*. Following James, I call a second type of conversion, a martyr's tale, the "twice-born" narrative. Renouncing a personal history of sin, once-born converts dedicated themselves to the divine and inherited the Kingdom of Heaven as a result. In twice-born narratives, converts must abandon a misguided faith and martyr themselves for a just, lost cause. In short, the once-born convert is saved and victorious; the twice-born convert is brave and condemned.

By "once-born," James referred to a single ideological rebirth; "twice-born" denoted an ideological rebirth followed by disenchantment then a second ideological birth in a new faith that still did not address the convert's guilt. James treated differences between the two converts as indicative of the "healthy minded" and the "sick souled."[52] For optimistic once-born converts, "a new heaven seems to shine up on a new earth." For twice-born "melancholiacs," "the world now looks," James juxtaposed, "remote, strange, sinister, uncanny."[53] Pleasure inevitably leads to pain; love results in grief; life ends in death.[54] Life, as Leo Tolstoy's case illustrated to James, was miserable. The novelist wrote that he developed a "thirst for God" while he debated whether to "end the business . . . by the rope or by the bullet."[55]

The major alteration twice-born narratives make to the conversion template is to tweak the narrative dynamic between hero and villain by significantly amplifying the authority of evil and significantly minimizing the influence of good. Once-born tales promise the convert personal power; by accepting a new faith, the convert gains strength to fight enemies and overcome temptation. Twice-born tragedies, however, assure an inevitably dreadful conclusion because the protagonists' good intentions seldom overwhelm their complicity or overcome their devilish opposition. The twice-born conversion story eschews visions of unfaltering heroes in large part because "natural evil" plays a foundational role in the narrative. Evil is not a far-off prospect; it is close and draws closer by the second, producing a "grisly blood-freezing heart-palsying sensation of it close upon one."[56]

With so much evil and pain in the world, tragic deaths of all types, the twice-born convert expresses her personal responsibility within the interconnected web of human relationships. The convert knows that she has sacrificed for an idol and become a false prophet for a false God. The tragic twice-born convert's task is Sisyphean; he seeks forgiveness for the unforgivable. The twice-born believes that "there is an element of real wrongness which is neither to be ignored nor evaded, but which must be squarely met and overcome by an appeal to the soul's heroic resources, and neutralized and cleansed away by suffering."[57] Condemned to be self-reflective sinners in a sinful world, the convert embarks, unheeded by knowledge of sure defeat, on a single-minded quest against sin.

The tragedy of the twice-born conversion narrative builds not just from its portrayal of evil over good but also evil within good; that is, an irreducible wickedness has burrowed deeply into the convert's soul. The twice-born narrative is, by extension, a powerful rhetorical template by which one becomes a blameworthy vector of a larger political malady. One performs the conversion ritual, acknowledges the permanence of shame, and, plagued by self-loathing, begins a kamikaze mission. In so doing, the twice-born narrative inevitably achieves what Burke called "mortification." He theorized, "Martyrdom is the idea of total voluntary self-sacrifice enacted in a grave cause before a perfect (absolute) witness. It is the fulfillment of the principle of mortification, suicidally directed, with the self as scapegoat (in contrast with homicidal use of an external scapegoat as purificatory victim)."[58] Mortification was the "deliberate slaying of appetites and ambitions," thorough acts of self-denial.[59] Burke linked such rhetorics of redemptive sacrifice to the maintenance of social order. In Burke's system, "mortification is a symbolic attempt to purify or atone for pollution or guilt through confession or self-sacrifice for the sake of forgiveness."[60] Burke argues that after political controversy or public tragedy, social order is reestablished through the "victimage" of a scapegoat or the mortifying acknowledgment of blame by guilty parties.[61] Collective guilt and anxiety are transferred onto a sacrificial vessel and feature a "*substitution*" of the sufferer for a larger community.[62] Standard conversion narratives give readers a victorious model, a person who bested her foes and erased her past; twice-born tales give readers a sentimental victim matched against overwhelming evil.

The Mortification of Whittaker Chambers

Witness was the only first-person narrative that conservatives' canonized, the only book with a richly rendered plot, dynamic reoccurring characters, and a vivid protagonist with whose motivations and circumstances readers were invited to sympathize. It may have been "the most important non-fiction work of its time," former Indiana governor Mitch Daniels estimated, but "*Witness*, if invented, would have made a splendid novel."[63] "Beloved Children," Chambers wrote in the powerful "Foreword in the Form of a Letter to My Children," "I am writing a book. In it I am speaking to you. But I am also speaking to the world. To both I owe an accounting."[64] Even more than a first-person account, *Witness* was a revealing confessional in which the enumeration of personal detail produced what David Foster Wallace once labeled "a feeling of intimacy between the writer and the reader."[65] Deeply personal and mercilessly disclosive, *Witness* was a book on which to "lose" one's "heart."[66] Chambers held little back. He was a Communist courier; he was a contact point for Soviet sleeper cells in the United States; he led a secret Communist outfit in Washington, D.C.; he was a traitor.

Chambers's conversion to and defection from Communism gave *Witness* a coherent narrative arc. Chambers detailed his youthful fascination with Communism as the solution to the twentieth-century "crisis of history" and explained his role within the complex and secretive structure of the Communist Party before arriving at "The Division Point" halfway through the book. "Until 1937," he explained in this interstitial chapter, "I had been . . . a typical modern man, living without God except for tremors of intuition."[67] Chambers enveloped his traumatic conversions and the Hiss case as well as his childhood, his farm, his wife, his brother, and his grandmother in biblical tropes. Appropriately, he began *Witness* by casting himself as a resurrected figure from the Gospel according to John. "In 1937," Chambers proclaimed, "I began, like Lazarus, the impossible return."[68] Chambers's use of Lazarus as an opening allegory to explore his conversion revealed his deep pessimism, rather than his burning hope, about salvation. In John, Jesus raised Lazarus from his tomb to show that believers were rewarded.[69] Chambers subtly figured his Communist years as a death tomb; his essential humanity had been destroyed. Chambers, however, was not rewarded with a new physical life or an eternal afterlife. Instead, Chambers called his rebirth an "impossible return" to grace. His Communism, his entombment, was permanent.

Chambers framed his initial conversion to Communism as an individual solution to a global problem. As a collegian, Chambers sat on Columbia's campus facing a statue of Alexander Hamilton, his "old political hero," after World War I and pondered two questions: "Can a man go on living in a world that is dying? If he can, what should he do in the crisis of the twentieth century?" Communism provided the only answer to the "crisis," grand economic and political tribulations requiring drastic solutions.[70]

Although the faith he chose provided ideological security about the global "crisis," Chambers eventually recognized the grisly reality hidden behind Communism's egalitarian and progressive public facade. At some point during his tenure in the party, Chambers surmised that Communism relied on terror to solve the "crisis." Communists created a horrific network of "execution cellars," "torture chambers," "citadels of terror," and "freight cars" with human cargo. Communists justified brutal conditions in which workers starved and guards beat slaves who labored "in the freezing filth of sub-arctic labor camps."[71] To protect the collective, Communists sacrificed individuals, especially deviationists and detractors. "What Communist has not heard those screams?" Chambers asked. They rang out during "midnight arrests" and echoed from basement cells in "the Lubianka."[72]

By accepting an ideology that compromised the sanctity of an individual's soul and the inviolability of the individual's body, Communists separated themselves from their senses, from their empathy, from their basic humanity. Over time, hearing screams wore down some Communists' ideological rationalizations. The daughter of a pro-Soviet German diplomat told Chambers that her father discarded Communism after the screams he heard one Moscow night shook him.[73] This beginning of the diplomat's conversion experience was startling because it unearthed his natural senses, a standard feature of the generic conversion narrative. Years of Communist lies were cleared away for the diplomat in a moment, and he heard screaming as if "for the first time."[74]

When Chambers broke from Communism, "slowly, reluctantly, in agony," he, too, recovered his humanity by encountering, through the raw corporeality of his daughter, evidence that all humans had been designed by a knowing maker. His separation from Communism began during a typical household routine:

> I do not know how far back it began. Avalanches gather force and crash, unheard, in men as in the mountains. But I date my break from a very casual happening. I was sitting in our apartment on St. Paul Street in Baltimore. It was shortly before we moved to Alger Hiss's apartment in Washington. My daughter was in her high chair. I was watching her eat. She was the most miraculous thing that had ever happened in my life. I liked to watch her even when she smeared porridge on her face or dropped it meditatively on the floor. My eye came to rest on the delicate convolutions of her ear—those intricate, perfect ears. The thought passed through my mind: "No, those ears were not created by any chance coming together of atoms in nature (the Communist view). They could have been created only by immense design." The thought was involuntary and unwanted. I crowded it out of my mind. But I never wholly forgot it or the occasion. I had to crowd it out of my mind. If I had completed it, I should have had to say: Design presupposes God. I did not then know that, at that moment, the finger of God was first laid upon my forehead.[75]

When Communists began to hear screaming and considered the source of such anguish, they tacitly acknowledged the existence of a soul. Admitting that screams were evidence of injustice meant admitting "that there is something greater than Reason, greater than the logic of mind, of politics, of history, of economics, which alone justifies the vision."[76] Chambers's conversion moment was similar; God became immediately apparent in his life. Chambers's sense that his daughter had been created by design arose on its own almost as if it awaited the right moment to manifest. Its power, in other words, existed apart from his mind; he was accosted by the thought, hailed by truth to become its servant. Chambers even tried to rid himself of the idea that his daughter's ear was testament to intelligent design because it was anathema to the faithful Communist.[77] Similar to Paul's experience on the road to Damascus, Chambers's transformative moment was signified by a physical sensation that accompanied the spiritual change.[78] Paul's vision was taken and restored; the diplomat could hear; God, Chambers recalled, touched his forehead and he could see.

A "religious experience" though it was, Chambers's conversion offered little freedom and less deliverance.[79] The twice-born convert was not triumphalist because the convert's doubt and anguish were not palliated. Although he described himself with another term from the Christian lexicon—"witness"—Chambers depicted himself as a martyr. The words were interchangeable in his usage. The book's title, in fact, was a play on the legal and religious meanings of witness. Legally, Chambers bore witness against Alger Hiss. Religiously, Chambers bore witness on God's behalf to a doubting nation.[80] In a book teeming with religious imagery, the link to the witness's role as described in Isaiah was plain. "You are my witnesses," God said in Isaiah 43:10, "and my servant whom I have chosen, so that you may know and believe me and understand that I am he." In his performance as one of God's chosen servants, Chambers emphasized that self-destruction before an audience was vital to convince others of God's glory. There could be no act of witnessing without mortification, without Chambers sacrificing his life to achieve "God's purpose."[81] The witness defended religious principles steadfastly and owned up to his mistakes accountably; the witness faced down evil regardless of personal consequences; the witness essentially embarked on a slow suicide mission.

Living up to the standard of this pure sacrifice without even a realistic hope of salvation was a nearly impossible task, and Chambers came close to divesting himself of the burden. Friendless; fearful of the impact of the case on his children; paranoid about a covert, Soviet-led, Trotsky-style attempt on his life; and convinced of the futility of his political choices, Chambers slipped out to the barn on his Maryland farm to do what Tolstoy did not and end his life.[82] Concealed in the darkness, contemplating his suffering, Chambers suddenly became aware that his young son was searching for him. Knowing that he was making "the most terrible surrender," Chambers hugged his son and gave him a "promise not to kill myself."[83] He nearly took his own life, but Chambers was conscious of the public necessity of his pain: "I must continue to bear a living witness, which would only mean my destruction by slower means."[84]

After the ruminating on the "crisis," after his acceptance of Communism, after admitting his powerlessness before God, Chambers realized that everyone faced a final judgment in the same place: Golgotha. "If I have led you aright," he addressed his children directly, "you will make out three crosses, from two of which hang thieves." What was tragically false about the hope Communism provided was that it committed the unthinkable and promised the impossible; it denied God and promised an end to misery. What Chambers wanted his children to know was that God and misery were inseparable; it took one to know the other. Chambers hoped they found Golgotha. The most infamous site in Christianity, the "place of the skulls," should teach them that "life is pain" and that "each of us hangs always upon the cross of himself."[85] James understood these dark dictums half a century earlier. Golgotha was the world the twice-born convert inhabited, a place where sinners and believers were sacrificed before God. James might as well have been writing about Chambers when he noted, "When disillusionment has gone as far as this, there is seldom a *restitutio ad integrum*. One has tasted of the fruit of the tree, and the happiness of Eden never comes again."[86]

Remembering Chambers's Martyrdom

Witness, Buckley reflected, had an "emotional" impact on legions of conservative readers.[87] Ralph de Toledano, for instance, reported sobbing when he first read its opening scenes.[88] Conservatives found a sacrificial hero in Chambers, and his symbolic martyrdom attracted libertarians, traditionalists, and fusionists alike, each for different reasons.[89] To libertarian readers, especially those who stopped short of outright hostility toward religion, Chambers's conversion held both dramatic and doctrinal appeal. Chambers's depressive manner may not have signified the exuberant individual of Goldwater's libertarian vision, but there were definitive libertarian themes in the book, all stemming from Chambers's adamant display of individuality: his courageous testimony, his daring departure from Communism, his one-on-many battle against Hiss and his backers, even his productivity as both a farmer and a writer. In fact, beneath the book's religious imagery, beneath all the wrenching stories of people feeling trapped by uncontrollable historical circumstances, its main theme affirmed what individualists within and beyond the confines of the conservative political identity had long believed: choice mattered. *Witness* was, at base, a story about a man taking responsibility for his choices. Sensing that history had reached a momentous point, the young Chambers chose to become a Communist; realizing that Communism's initial appeal, the empowerment of humankind, was a fiction, he chose a different course; wracked by guilt, he chose to come forward and take accountability for committing the "characteristic crimes" of the twentieth century.[90] Whether Chambers felt redeemed or not, his story affirmed the libertarian maxim that individuals, not collectives, not governments, not historical circumstances, were responsible for their actions.

Libertarian readers seized on *Witness's* demonstration of individual responsibility. Reviewing *Witness* in 1952, noted libertarian John Chamberlain viewed Chambers's life as "symbolic" of every individual capable of recognizing and fighting the "overwhelming evil" of Communism. Chamberlain recognized Chambers's distinctiveness but made no distinction between the witness's guilt and the guilt he thought many Americans should feel for their failure to fight Communism. He wrote, "Not many of us have been spies, not many of us have ever joined the Communist Party, either openly or secretly. But that has not been because of our superior virtue. For the truth is that most of us who came off the college campuses of America in the twenties and the thirties succumbed to the evil of collectivist thinking in little, comfortable ways."[91] Although Chamberlain's move to an individualist political position from the left had been inspired by more doctrinaire libertarian writers like Rose Wilder Lane, Isabel Paterson, and Ayn Rand, all of whom rebuffed midcentury conservatism, he still found in the tome's more religious lines a renewal of his own beliefs.[92] Chamberlain was averse to any metaphysical discussions of souls, but he saw in Chambers's yearning to free his guilt-wracked soul and his own desire to see free people exercise their own free will a certain synergy. "Whittaker Chambers," he concluded, "feels the presence of God where I feel the need for a certain view of the free man possessed of free will and an innate moral sense."[93] Looking past its religiosity, Chamberlain read *Witness* as classical liberalism rendered tragically.

Some traditionalists, conversely, interpreted *Witness* as an anti-libertarian text. Chambers's suspicion of the Enlightenment legacy, including individual reason and materialism, was "anathema to laissez-faire individualists."[94] Whether they read intraconservative divisiveness in Chambers's book or not, however, most traditionalist readers of *Witness* cherished Chambers not as a free thinker but as a believer. They relished his depiction of Communism as a false religion as well as his religious conversion, which had "the grandeur of a religious pilgrimage."[95] "Witness" and "martyr" are just two of the religious monikers traditionalists have used when discussing Chambers's resonance; traditionalists also found a prophet in Chambers.[96] "*Witness*," former Heritage Foundation president Edwin Feulner concluded, "is the work of a prophet in the ancient sense: one who gives what he believes is a divinely inspired explanation of man's plight and warns what will happen if society does not change radically."[97] Chambers saw the nation's Cold War plight as a "transcendent crisis" of faith, an interpretation that attracted "many conservative intellectuals, so many of whom were religious."[98] The success of true religion against the Communists' false religion was, Chambers prophesied, a matter of personal and national faith. Success in the Cold War required not greater freedom from an oppressive state but greater devotion to God. With an impact on traditionalists that surpassed that of other like-minded writers, Chambers "persuaded his contemporaries that religious belief was central to the tradition they proposed to defend."[99]

Witness's Cold War eschatology enchanted traditionalists; its affirmation of the inviolability and worth of individuals enchanted libertarians. Fusionist conservatives appreciated Chambers's rehearsal of both. Chambers was not a fusionist conservative as Meyer was, and *Witness* did not theorize conservatism of any kind. After *Witness* became seminal to early conservatives, Chambers, who had grown close to Buckley and worked briefly at *National Review*, broke with conservatism. Chambers argued that he defended, unlike Buckley and other conservatives, no religious or political "orthodoxy."[100] Chambers stated flatly, "I am not a conservative."[101] His conversion was, nevertheless, susceptible to a fusionist reading because Chambers saw, as Meyer did, political freedom and religious faith as intertwined. In one of the book's resonant scenes, the moment of his break with Communism when he attends closely to his daughter's ear, the connection between individuality and religion was intimate; his daughter's ear represented the unique constitution of every individual, not just in body but in soul. In some of the book's more terrifying passages, Chambers drew the same connection between the significance of every individual's life and the divine. Chambers both heard God's design and sensed an unmistakable singularity in individual screams. Human beings, Chambers came to believe, were not undifferentiated members of a class; they were individuals, vastly different from one another, equally important in God's eyes, all striving for greater meaning.

Some of Chambers's most poetic lines welcomed this fusionist reading of *Witness* by invoking the key terms of the traditionalist and libertarian dialects as coequal values. The few brave enough to become "ex-Communists" hoped for the same condition that libertarians did: personal freedom.[102] Freedom, however, did not mean unfettered independence; it meant a personal relationship with God. "Religion and freedom are indivisible" as values to Chambers; by contrast, so were atheism and totalitarianism. The individual soul only exists and matters because of God. Chambers wrote, "God alone is the inciter and guarantor of freedom."[103]

Although he did not develop the case as Meyer did, Chambers channeled the fusionist dialectic of his ex-Communist colleague: "Political freedom, as the Western world has known it, is only a political reading of the Bible. . . . Without freedom the soul dies. Without the soul there is no justification for freedom."[104] Philosophical fusionists saw in Chambers a "Cold War hero" around whom to assemble, and, spurred on by these lines, they saw in *Witness* a synthesized conservative case against Communism.[105] *Witness*, William Rusher concluded, "demonstrated that philosophical anti-Communism was a full and worthy partner of classical liberalism in the arsenal of the American right."[106] It was, another conservative concluded, Chambers's personal courage, words, and revelations about Soviet Communism that drew together "the fragmentary pieces of the American Right." His "negative witness" against Hiss, the New Deal, and Communists and his "positive witness for liberty and truth" unified "previously disparate conservatism."[107]

Libertarians, traditionalists, and fusionists were drawn to various features of Chambers's philosophical anti-Communism, but they were all drawn to his sacrifice, his persecution. Chambers was, one scholar assessed, both a "spokesman and a martyr" for conservatives.[108] Chambers was not in a fair fight; he was scourged through the bulk of *Witness*. For conservatives like Heritage Foundation president Edwin Feulner, it was Chambers's pain that made his story poignant, and his immense anguish should be the standard by which other conservatives measured their dedication."[109] To Feulner, Chambers wrote *Witness* as a passion play "so others may profit from his sacrifice and suffering, so that some lasting victory may be won as a result of them, so that from his passion some resurrection will be wrought—for himself, for his children, and for the West."[110] Given his treasonous transgressions, Chambers was not, however, a prototypical Christ figure. Chambers's unremitting sense of personal guilt was certainly un-Christ-like, but his agony was not.[111] The book was his Cold War passion play, an explicit, methodical public rehearsal of an unjust trial and intense suffering through which audiences experienced torment by identifying with the tormented. Conservatives were invited to connect intimately with Chambers and thus suffer alongside him against the "venomous calumnies of the Hiss forces" and the "cunning" Communists.[112]

Regardless of their doctrinal differences, conservatives felt an intimate bond with Chambers's suffering at the hands of Communists, his ridicule by the domestic Left both during and after the Hiss case, and what they felt was his mistreatment by the press. Conservatives identified with Chambers's distress and were enraged by the unfairness of the "anti-Chambers whispering campaign."[113] His victimage, in fact, has been a significant part of his legacy among conservatives. Chambers's departure from Communism in 1939 came at great personal risk, and his later testimony "that an entire network of malefactors had metastasized within the Franklin Roosevelt administration came at great personal cost." He was vilified and threatened by "every segment of liberal society."[114] Conservatives remember Chambers's "desire to immolate himself" before his critics.[115] Chambers, one of his devotees told a Heritage Foundation conference in 1984, "put his life on the line at a time when the press was full of vituperative attacks—attacks on his wife, on his children—and only once did he falter."[116] Whether he was a traditionalist holy warrior, a libertarian prototype, or a fusionist trailblazer, conservatives saw him as an embattled exemplar of their fledgling community, belittled, disparaged, outnumbered, and brave.

Although Buckley galvanized the early movement and Meyer and others began to synthesize a philosophy, to most Americans, conservative was an untested political identity, and conservatism was a foreign concept. Lionel Trilling's survey of the political landscape in 1950 was harsh: "In the United States at this time liberalism is not only the dominant but even the sole intellectual tradition." Those "conservative or reactionary ideas" dotting the intellectual landscape were "irritable mental gestures."[117] In 1954, Richard Hofstadter even described these new rumblings on the right as "pseudo-conservatism," a label that divided conservatism as a thoughtful tradition from knee-jerk, anti-New Deal imitators.[118] Prominent commentators of the era saw conservatives as anxious, absolutist, insecure, and resentful; conservatism was the "province of cranks and fanatics."[119]

Chambers, waging an asymmetrical battle against his blue-blooded detractors, came to embody early conservatism's asymmetrical battle against conservatives' own detractors. His outcast cause was theirs; his enemies were theirs; his suffering was theirs. The "personal connection," one journalist wrote, between Chambers and decades of conservatives was "visceral." Conservatives "could have stepped into the shoes of this 'little fat man,' with his unfashionable anti-Communism, conducting a brave but lonely struggle against an elite 'conspiracy of gentlemen.'"[120] Chambers, like upstart conservatism, was brave enough to fight a lost cause. In sum, Chambers's martyrdom was far more than the tragic story of someone whose politics conservatives shared. Chambers "offered young people on the Right a powerful paradigm explaining their own underdog standing in modern America."[121] Chambers's story was a prism through which conservatives made sense of themselves as righteous victims of unjust persecution in the struggle for political power.

"The Focus of Concentrated Evil"

Chambers's martyrdom was amplified by its asymmetry with the enemy's evil. The more dangerous Communists became, the more appealing Chambers's combination of meekness and self-sacrificing bravery became. Since once-born converts find their path to salvation or a sign under which to conquer, as in Constantine's case, the once-born narrative stages a power dynamic between hero and villain that favors the former. Sure, setbacks and backsliding may interfere, but the once-born convert has ultimately found a true north, and the believer is rewarded with community, a sense of purpose, and, likely, a heavenly hereafter. Since twice-born conversions career toward the tragic, the protagonist-antagonist power ratio tilts toward the latter, sometimes dramatically. No righteous toil alters the inevitable for the twice-born; the beast is at the door, and, eventually, it will find a way in.

When Chambers became a double agent, he lived on a knife's edge: an arbitrary decree could jeopardize his relationship with the party; a wrong word here or a revealing comment there could reveal his treasonous secret. But it was not, of course, the desire for Soviet persecution or American prosecution that drove Chambers to Communism. Chambers was charmed by the illusion of control over his destiny. Communism was not a sinister plot hatched by devious people, and its essence was not found in Soviet Gulags. Those were manifestations of a deeper philosophical commitment. Its blasphemous intellectual core gave rise to its labyrinthine underground and its population of nauseating functionaries. Communism's beating heart was "a simple statement of Karl Marx, further simplified for handy use: 'Philosophers have explained the world; it is necessary to change the world.'"[122] Chambers found in this slightly altered version of Marx's eleventh thesis on Feuerbach a cipher that helped solve the mystery of Communist evil. What Chambers saw in Marx's line was that humans could understand the world as oracles and change the world as gods.

Protagoras was the first to call man the measure of all things. The basic idea, nevertheless, that Marx and Protagoras advanced was older than either's gloss. The vainglorious notion that humans created, understood, and governed the realm of possibility was "man's second oldest faith" in Chambers's estimation. Illustrating his personal twentieth-century struggle as the last battle of an eternal war between good and evil, Chambers located the roots of sinful pride in Genesis: "Its promise was whispered in the first days of the Creation under the Tree of Knowledge and Good and Evil: 'Ye shall be as gods.'"[123] Evil, Chambers left unsaid, was allowed into the world because Eve made a choice to control her destiny. Chambers used this epic story to pin the origin of sin to any human attempt to control the environment, to plan scientifically, or to reason through public controversy. The Enlightenment was the fully formed version of the promise under the Tree, and Communism was the Enlightenment at the end of the rationalist line. Communism, he famously declared, was "the focus of the concentrated evil of our time."[124]

Witness's many subplots reduced, through the synecdochic experiences of one person, the teeming ideological and material struggles
of the twentieth century to one choice: *"God or Man?"*[125] Chambers
chose both—Man first, then God—and endured two conversions in
the process. In his usage, "God" and "Man" were two great rhetorical whirlpools drawing in all variations of culture, politics, and human
relationships.[126] There was no way out of the binary; one was invari-
ably assigned to the camp of God or Man. Chambers wrote, "At every
point, religion and politics interlace, and must do so more acutely as
the conflict between the two great camps of men—those who reject
and those who worship God—becomes irrepressible."[127] Every political controversy was a religious crossroads, every political decision a
purity test. The instruments of Man were science, reason, and state
planning; Man's ostensible goals were egalitarianism and technological
progress. As Meyer argued a decade later, Chambers claimed that the
world of Man was a moral wasteland of might-makes-right where altru-
ism, good-naturedness, and community were used only as cloaks for
the will to power, hedonism, and megalomania. Without divine truth
and transcendental ethics, human beings were only restricted by their
abilities. There was no resistance to tyranny within the world of Man;
there was no moral argument against slavery without God. Chambers's
closed system mapped neatly onto the Cold War. The conflict between
East and West was the apex of a perennial conflict between the faith-
less and the faithful.

All political differences grew from the basic difference between
the politics of God and the politics of Man. Portraying himself as a
doomed Cold War David, Chambers wrote, "The simple fact is that
when I took up my little sling and aimed at Communism, I also hit
something else. What I hit was the forces of that great socialist revolution, which, in the name of liberalism, spasmodically, incompletely,
somewhat formlessly, but always in the same direction, has been inching its ice cap over the nation for two decades."[128] Secularism and the
desire to guide political relationships through rational planning rendered moot any doctrinal, historical, contextual, or cultural differences
among those on the left.[129] Derivatives of evil were, whether latent or
disguised, still evil.

It was not just that Chambers ignored political distinctions among
the Left, but that he repudiated distinction as a sign of weakness, of
muddled thinking, of shirking a hard choice between God or Man.

Political questions were moral questions; moral questions were meta-physical questions. As Irving Howe put it, "If you believe that the two great camps of the world prepare for battle under the banners, Faith in Man and Faith in God, what is the point of close study and fine distinctions? You only need sound the trumpets."[130] The apostates, Chambers prophesied, were winning, and they would inevitably triumph over the armies of faith.

This evil, moreover, was not an external threat to the West; through liberalism, evil lurked within the West. Chambers reported that the New Deal bureaucrats he met were largely Communists and ex-Communists.[131] When he alleged that Washington brimmed with Soviet spies, Chambers was also making a larger allegation about liberals. Whether they worked on behalf of the Soviets or not, liberals paved the way for Communism. The New Deal itself was a form of espionage. It proceeded under the guise of a reform movement, but it was, in fact, a "genuine revolution, whose deepest purpose was not simply reform within existing traditions, but a basic change in the social, and, above all, the power relationships within the nation."[132] Although Chambers avoided becoming one of the "slaves of the Communist mill," there was no gleeful retreat into the warm folds of the West. The West would lose the Cold War; Chambers was sure of that much. Conversion, Chambers wrote, "is not a matter of leaving one house and occupying another—especially when the second is manifestly in collapse and the caretakers largely witless."[133] Communists and liberals were members of the same political species, and it was no accident to Chambers that both flourished during and after the New Deal.

Interpreting the Evils of Communism

The twice-born enemy functions as a nefarious God-head, both omnipotent and omniscient. The enemy lurks behind every corner, hides in every shadow. This is an enemy that, within the logic of the twice-born narrative, must be faced but cannot be beaten.[134] Many of Chambers's eager conservative readers—traditionalist, libertarian, and fusionist—found in *Witness* the most compelling, the most resonant, the most chilling version of Communism. Conservative factionalism was "always subordinated to the larger anti-Communist, anti-liberal consensus that Chambers had first sketched out."[135] Chambers, one conservative speaker clarified, "taught many of us, maybe most of us, what we were fighting."[136] *Witness*, William Rusher attested, represented the "Alpha and Omega" of his conception of about Communism.[137] Chambers's enemy occupied a central role within early conservatism because his narrative vivified its power; Chambers himself was flesh-and-blood evidence of its reach, a homegrown example of the seduction of decent Americans.

Communism, for libertarians, was the epitome of revolutionary statism. Chambers's portrait of international Communism was the realization of libertarians' fears about government power: the centralization of power in an unaccountable government entity, the inevitable destruction of private property by a greedy government, the mobilization of a vast network of spies to protect the state's interests, and the sacrifice of individuals at the altar of the collective. Chambers's account of state power run amok was "life-shaping" for readers fearful of government overreach. Grover Norquist, chairman of Americans for Tax Reform and the architect of the influential American Taxpayer Pledge, even joined an organization during the 1980s dedicated to rearticulating Chambers's version of Communism. The Pumpkin Paper Irregulars, in fact, preserved the memory of a hollow pumpkin where Chambers hid crucial evidence against Hiss with pumpkin decorations, pumpkin refreshments, and cannonades against Reagan-era Soviet apologists.[138]

Communism, for traditionalists, was the epitome of revolutionary atheism. Chambers's portrait of international Communism was the realization of traditionalists' most basic fears about the Enlightenment legacy: the institutionalization of atheism, the deification of humankind, the destruction of long-settled traditions to achieve a more "rational" organization of society, and the persecution of religious believers. The modern, "rational mind," in Chambers's estimation, sought to end the "bloody meaninglessness of man's history—by giving it purpose and a plan." The modern fascination with "science and technology" excluded "all supernatural factors in solving problems."[139] Following Chambers's line of argument, one conservative professor explained that the witness's final struggle was against a "radical modernity" that excused atheism and materialism.[140] Reading *Witness* compelled even the most battle-hardened anti-Communists toward a less strategic and more transcendent interpretation of the Cold War. Even those on the right who had organized against Communism for years, wrote de

Toledano, never realized that "this struggle was not one of police files and espionage." The Cold War "was a struggle, as Whittaker Chambers said, between God and man."[141]

To libertarian readers of *Witness*, the state was an executioner, torturer, and slaver. As the creator of millions of screams, the Communist state was the state at its worst. To traditionalists, *Witness* showed that statism was symptomatic of an organized, rational attempt by individuals to impose their own designs on the world and deny God. The horrors of Communism flowed naturally from faithlessness, "the vision of Almighty Mind."[142] In each case, Chambers, the hero of this twice-born narrative, was the doomed advocate for his audiences' sacred ideals, freedom and faith. Communism, the devil figure of the narrative, perfectly opposed freedom with maximum state power and perfectly opposed religion with institutional atheism. For fusionist conservatives, *Witness* developed a conservative case because of its defense of both freedom and faith, and it developed an anti-Communist case because of its attack on both atheism and materialism.[143]

Either way, Chambers's portrayal of the Soviet Union "provided a kind of negative rallying point." Upstart "conservatives of all stripes could agree about the hideousness of the Communist system."[144] Conservative factions found various Communist attributes odious, but after reading *Witness*, they agreed on one thing: the Communist threat was immediate. Chambers exposed how fully Communists had infiltrated and subverted the federal government, but the exposure of spy networks was only part of a larger goal. Chambers redefined the Communist threat as imminent because of American liberalism.

Witness arrived as Americans audiences were riveted by Cold War newspaper headlines attesting to a global ideological struggle that occasionally, as in the *Amerasia* affair and the trial of Julius and Ethel Rosenberg, touched home. Soviet agents threw Jan Masaryk from a Prague window, and Czechoslovakia was enclosed behind the Iron Curtain just a few months before Chambers first appeared before HUAC in 1948.[145] Mao consolidated power in 1949, and the North Korean army crossed the thirty-eighth parallel in 1950.[146] But *Witness*, upon publication, became some of the first "American testimony" confirming the growth of Communism within America. What Chambers had seen "first hand," that "Stalin's spy network" snaked through the entirety of Washington, countered the notion that Stalin was "far away" or that his European encroachment was "not really our problem."[147] As

Jeffrey Hart notes, "*Witness* in 1952 literally hit home—hit the United
States. Communism was not something that went on in Prague or
some such place."[148] Conservatism was not yet a self-aware political
movement when Chambers testified or when *Witness* was published,
but many protoconservatives and other remnants of the disorganized
Right came to believe that defeating Communism at home and abroad
should be the most pressing national concern. As Chamberlain wrote,
"Even the most recalcitrant reviewer, however, can hardly fail to be
shaken by the massed weight of Whittaker Chambers's evidence that
there *was* a Communist apparatus, or series of apparatuses, working
in Washington from 1933 to 1941."[149] Conservatives' concerns about
Communist agents, Rusher concluded after reading *Witness*, "were not
imaginary."[150]

    Most of Chambers's domestic critics, however, were not
Communists. When Chambers stepped forward with his Davidian
"sling" to confront Hiss and Communism, an expansive network of liberals, socialists, and Communist supporters counterattacked. Tellingly,
Chambers's sling line, in which he styled himself as David to the
Left Goliath, became his most quoted line among conservatives.[151]
Chambers's depiction of the enemy as "establishment" power rounded
out early conservatives' sense of themselves as outcasts "on the defensive."[152] In response to the personal attacks on Chambers, the weak rebuttals to his allegations of spy activity, and the exaggerated defenses of
Hiss, conservatives began to frame their cause as anti-Communist and
antiestablishment; indeed, the two were nearly synonymous. Although
Chambers's allegations were correct and Hiss was a spy who had lied
under oath, the witness, conservatives remember, had been "brushed
aside by virtually the entire liberal establishment."[153] One *Human Events*
writer even framed Hiss and the midcentury "liberal establishment"
in terms of an ancient Jewish sect, "New Deal Sadducees," aligned
with the ruling elite.[154] If conservatives were to follow Chambers, they
would wage a lonely battle against Hiss replicas: deeply engrained,
spotlessly credentialed, vigorously defended, and intrinsically suspicious. With *Witness*'s twice-born narrative as their interpretive prism,
conservatives portrayed themselves as up against a multiheaded hydra
including the liberal establishment, the prestige press, the Ivy League,
and international Communism. They depicted their "ideological opponents" as iterations of "the elegant Alger Hiss, with his impeccable
Ivy League credentials, his position as a pillar of an entrenched liberal

establishment, and his ultimate duplicity."[155] They adopted, in short, an indomitable us-against-the-world rhetoric.

Witness helped conservatives of every variety see both strategic and philosophical linkages between Hiss, his liberal defenders in the government and media, and international Communism. Liberals, as one scholar paraphrased Chambers, "were pushing a Trojan horse toward the gates of Western civilization."[156] Consistent with Communism, liberalism was antimarket, anti–private property, and expansionist.[157] Liberalism was a Communist way station; the New Deal was an incomplete revolution.[158] Chambers offered early conservatives a powerful reinterpretation of the dominant philosophical and political realities of the midcentury: liberalism and New Dealism.[159] By showing that the New Deal nurtured a comfortable environment for Communists and sympathizers, Chambers also demonstrated that the nation-state, whether the United States or the Soviet Union, was deceitful. These revelations about the subversion of Roosevelt's government created a "moment of acute uncertainty" for American liberals and, like other canonical texts such as *The Road to Serfdom* and *Ideas Have Consequences*, stirred conservatives.[160] When midcentury liberalism seemed untouchable to the Right, Chambers landed "a punch in the gut to the New Deal coalition's main philosophical pillar, that the American people should place more trust in Washington bureaucracy than any other institution."[161] In a pitched battle between, as Chambers put it, "irreconcilable" faiths, liberals had, both unwittingly and maliciously, made peace with evil.

Chambers's vision of imminent, permanent, and total conflict with the interconnected Left shaped the politics of Cold War conservatives. Ronald Reagan was one of them; *Witness* sped his conversion from a New Deal Democrat to a conservative Republican.[162] Calling Communism "the most dangerous enemy that has ever faced mankind in his long climb from the swamp to the stars," Reagan spoke in stark, Chambersian terms as early as his 1964 "A Time for Choosing" speech.[163] *Witness* also figured influentially during Reagan's presidency. Meetings with the president could sound like book club proceedings. Reagan even quizzed his staff, which included *Witness* enthusiasts like Anthony Dolan, about the event that inspired Chambers to reject "communist metaphysics."[164] When he posthumously awarded Chambers the Presidential Medal of Freedom in 1984, Reagan invoked a lonely martyr's anguished battle. The award's language corresponded exactly

with the asymmetric twice-born narrative. It read that "the solitary figure of Whittaker Chambers personified the mystery of human redemption in the face of evil and suffering."[165]

Reagan exalted Chambers in numerous speeches during his
presidency, particularly his 1983 speech to the National Association
of Evangelicals (the "evil empire" speech).[166] Before Reagan called the
Soviet Union an "evil empire," he described Communism as "the focus of evil in the modern world," a line lifted directly from *Witness*.[167]
Reagan urged his audience to recognize that Communism was unal-
terable. "But if history teaches anything," he argued, "it teaches that
simpleminded appeasement of wishful thinking about our adversaries
is folly."[168] The existence of such an implacable enemy necessitated
a religious war, what he called "a test of moral will and faith."[169] To
compel his listeners to see their moral status as inextricably bound to
the Cold War, to see their complicity in its outcome, Reagan called
upon Chambers's example: "Whittaker Chambers, the man whose own
religious conversion made him witness to one of the terrible traumas of
our time, the Hiss-Chambers case, wrote that the crisis of the Western
world exists to the degree in which the West is indifferent to God, the
degree to which it collaborates in Communism's attempt to make man
stand alone without God."[170] The Cold War was an internal personal
conflict as well as an international political battle.

Reagan was moved by and moved audiences with Chambers's tale
of woe; he adopted Chambers's vision of Communism as evil wholesale; he did not, however, replicate Chambers's despair. Reagan adjusted Chambers's twice-born narrative dynamic between the protagonist
and antagonist. He imagined a more symmetrical melee between a
"perfect" hero and a "perfect" villain.[171] He presented a more balanced
narrative ratio between hero and villain in which each exactly opposed
the military strength, will, and ideological dedication of the other.[172]
Reagan concluded his "evil empire" speech on a triumphant note:
"Yes, change your world. One of our Founding Fathers, Thomas Paine,
said, 'We have it within our power to begin the world over again.'"[173] In
Reagan's telling, Chambers's legacy was not a gloomy prophecy but an
individual and national challenge to pay any price against evil. Reagan
turned Chambers's weak, rotting West into "a special people placed
between two great oceans for God's purpose."[174] Yet *Witness* was always
a "sobering reality" for him, a reminder of the nation's permanent vul-

nerability, of the chance that Soviet darkness might never give way to Reagan's American dawn. One conservative writer even thought that Reagan and Chambers "held to the same faith" but "differed in their predictions of the future of freedom."[175] That is, Chambers and Reagan differed in their assessment of Communism's strength and the West's weakness. Victory over Communism required the kind of total dedication Reagan saw in Chambers, and Reagan's public tributes told audiences of freedom's price.[176] Chambers was a continual caution that the president's otherwise exceptionalist visions of American conquest were conditional.[177] As John Patrick Diggins concluded, "Chambers spoke to our fears, Reagan to our desires."[178]

In Remembrance of Chambers

Witness became a Cold War meeting ground for different kinds of conservatives in large part because the book reaffirmed each group's different beliefs. But *Witness* also became an "epochal step" for Cold War–era conservatism as a whole because this compelling, twice-born tragedy introduced a narrative so compelling to conservatives that it became an interpretative template by which many made sense of conservatism, its political prospects, its obligations, and its enemies.[179] That is, *Witness* was conservatives' dossier on evil and on their corresponding obligations. That traditionalists, libertarians, and fusionists gathered around *Witness* well after the fall of Soviet Communism suggests the adaptability of his twice-born narrative. In closing, I argue that when many conservatives think about threats—threats to the nation, threats to religion, threats to civilization, threats to markets, and beyond—they think about Chambers's Cold War drama, and, more important, they think through Chambers's sacrifice. As the Hiss-Chambers affair faded in the public's memory, *Witness* remained a bibliographic reminder to conservatives that his sacrifice required theirs.[180]

Chambers's narrative imagined a horrible enemy, amplified its strengths, and depicted its overarching purpose, pursued with relish, as the destruction of the nation. To allow its continued existence, in any form, was tantamount to tolerating, even welcoming evil. The existence of evil was a moral summons for which there was no escape. As Reagan argued during the Cold War, the failure to challenge evil stained the consciences of those who collaborated and even those mistakenly hoping to hew to a neutral position.[181] George W. Bush's case for a global war on terror after the tragedy of September 11, 2001, followed a similar logic. The connection between the two conservative presidents' approach and language was not accidental; Chambers's language influenced the Bush administration considerably; officials in the Bush White House proudly announced even before 9/11 that *Witness* "permeates our philosophy in a broader sense."[182]

When, after 9/11, Michael Gerson and David Frum, two of Bush's top speechwriters, needed a formulation to recommend an expansive assault on international terrorist networks, they famously chose "axis of evil" and, Tanenhaus notes, "settled on an immovably absolutist course, inspired by the dark vision projected in *Witness*."[183] Bush's depiction of terrorism as a political evil was closely yoked to Reagan's not just in terminology. Bush described terrorists with terrifying qualities similar to those Reagan attributed to Communists; they were abhorrent, unpredictable, and immediately threatening: "Thousands of dangerous killers, schooled in the methods of murder, often supported by outlaw regimes, are now spread throughout the world like ticking timebombs, set to go off without warning."[184] Bush then framed the existence of evil as a tacit demand on any moral nation; the world faced a dire choice between what Robert Ivie calls "redemptive violence" and guilty complicity.[185] Repeating both the word and sentiment that Reagan attributed to Chambers, Bush argued, "In any of these cases, the price of indifference would be catastrophic."[186] In a world divided by good and evil, there was no moral refuge in indifference. He summarized this global binary succinctly during an exchange with reporters: "You are either with us or you are against us in the fight against terror."[187] The United States had been drafted to serve a larger cause that required national sacrifice. "History" beckoned, and it was the nation's "responsibility and our privilege to fight freedom's fight."[188]

Conservatives outside presidential politics have also, in regular intervals, updated Chambers's lessons on Cold War combat to post–Cold War political realities. One writer lamented a 1992 Environmental Protection Agency rule as evidence that, quoting Chambers, "the statist revolution that began in the thirties continues 'inching its ice cap over the nation.'"[189] Other conservative foreign policy specialists have used *Witness* to shed light on Chinese Communism and "Jihadist extremism."[190] Traditionalist and libertarian conservatives have also found Chambers useful in describing a less specific cast of enemies, including Enlightenment modernity, self-deification, and "the constant mothering of government."[191]

But *Witness* did not instruct post–Cold War conservatives to identify evil; the book taught them that evil anywhere was a threat everywhere. Chambers's twice-born testimonial was predicated on evil's proximity and its advantage. Although many conservative intellectuals and politicians did not, like Reagan and Bush, "share Chambers's despair," the witness's dark prophecies were always "in the background."[192] *Witness* was a permanent warning against political complacency, against underestimating conservatism's opponents, against a lazy American exceptionalism. His alarming representation of an ascendant, malleable enemy and the impossible standard of his sacrifice have led conservatives to question whether they, too, resided in "the losing world."[193] In a telling example, Mitch Daniels invoked Chambers's "martyrdom" and "pessimism" when noting conservatives' disappointment after the 2012 presidential election.[194] He even struggled to imagine how he might rebut Chambers's hypothetical claim "that Western civilization was still terminally ill." "I suppose I could just tell him: Credo quia impossibile," he concluded.[195]

As much as Chambers's martyrdom inspired conservatives, conservatives also feared that his dark prophecies had come true, that they had given in to evil. As Richard Reinsch noted, "His witness still haunts our hollow condition." Conservatives advised one another that forgetting Chambers meant forgetting the power of political evil.[196] Evil, for Chambers, went hand-in-hand with self-examination. Evil implied an obligation that could only be satisfied through sacrifice. Chambers had, after all, mortified himself as he exposed Communists, detailing how he aided evil, how he had become evil. As one Heritage Foundation writer showed, there was always cause to honor Chambers's sacrifice through greater vigilance against liberalism: "Whittaker Chambers' birthday seems an appropriate time to remember his witness, and redouble our efforts."[197]

Conservatives' martial resolve was goaded by Chambers's ghost. Incited by Chambers, conservatives fretted about the nation's "standing," questioned its "special virtue," and identified a sinister enemy to annihilate to restore the symbolic order.[198] At a conservative conference on *Witness* one month after the second war in Iraq began, Terry Teachout claimed that the basic question that tortured Chambers should also torture contemporary conservatives: Does the West deserve to be saved? [199] National vindication, he felt, was earned, not granted. As he watched "citizens of Bagdad pulling over the statues of Saddam," Teachout said he knew that America had earned temporary absolution. By "marching through Iraq," the West "justified its existence, for now." But, reciting Dostoevsky's line that godlessness permitted all conduct, including cannibalism, Teachout moved far beyond the Iraq War to depict postmodern secularism as a permanent, global enemy against which only an endless battle would save the West and satisfy the supervising martyr. The West faced down these enemies "at Auschwitz," battled them "in Iraq," and would see them again in "North Korea and other places that know not truth." The key question for the West, the question on which the West's deliverance hinged, "the question Chambers still asks us is what can a secular culture do to stop them?"[200] Like boxers who clamored ceaselessly for more bouts to prove themselves and silence doubters, Chambers must be continually honored in purifying deeds in which the nation was willing to go down fighting. The West was redeemed by delivering tough justice in which warriors risked it all. Teachout considered Chambers as both a sacrificial and a watchful figure, one who gave everything for conservatism and looked back to see if others would do the same.

Chambers's martyrdom set a high bar for his avenging legatees. Chambers risked his life when he left Communism; he risked his reputation on the witness stand against Hiss; he accepted these risks knowing that he joined the "losing side," but he was willing to die for his faith. Strength and faith were proven in dutiful acts of mortification. It was both a severe standard and a versatile prism. Science, school prayers, abortion, taxation, and foreign affairs could all become national battlegrounds between truth and relativism and tests of every conservative's bravery or complicity no matter their differing first principles. Unless conservative warriors would "cheerfully commit" to their "duty for the duration, fully expecting to die on the losing side," they were not worth saving.[201] Chambers thought that as complicated as our political choices may seem, we all head to Golgotha for the ultimate judgment.

CHAPTER SEVEN

Conservatism and Canonicity

⌘

onservatives' quarrel over conservatism is evinced by the manifold
modifying terms they employ to distinguish between conservative
camps. The most popular augmentations—libertarian
conservatism, fiscal conservatism, traditionalist conservatism, social
conservatism, paleoconservatism, and neoconservatism—have been
generated since the 1950s in response to fundamental disagreements
over what counted as an authentic conservative belief. Such modifiers
proliferated further in the ensuing decades. Between "crunchy
conservatism," "reformist conservatism," "Bull Moose conservatism,"
"progressive conservatism," "big government conservatism," "Costco
conservatism," "Sam's Club conservatism," "Wal-Mart conservatism,"
"patio man conservatism," "heroic conservatism," and "comeback
conservatism," the only common denominator is the oft-repeated root
word.[1] This denominator, moreover, is common in name alone because
each prefix injects tremendous variety into the root suffix.

Two questions about this awkward confederation have occupied a host of scholars, pundits, and commentators, especially since the 1990s.[2] First, how has conservatism cohered amid such internal rancor? Second, how has conservatism succeeded in winning elections and currying favor with the American public? *Creating Conservatism*, a book about conservative books, has been, for the most part, an attempt to answer the first question. I have argued that the canonization of roughly ten books written between World War II and 1964 exerted a powerful influence on the development of conservatism's robust political language, its dialects, standard idioms, repeated tropes, god and devil terms, and common narratives. I began by cataloging how conservatives have commemorated canonical books through persistent citation and quotation, historiographic origin stories, the distribution of "must read" syllabi, founding study groups, hosting conferences, and organizing lecture programs about these tomes. The second section of *Creating Conservatism* analyzed the potential for symbolic fracture within the fragile conservative partnership. I inventoried two dialects of the conservative political language, traditionalism and libertarianism, whose speakers not only used different key words and lines of argument in their performances of conservatism but traced these rhetorical preferences to different canonical texts as well. The third section of *Creating Conservatism* examined how canonical authors fused different conservatives together through a dialectical philosophical platform (Frank Meyer), a rousing gladiatorial style (William F. Buckley), and a tragic Cold War narrative (Whittaker Chambers).

This book, in sum, has examined conservatives' sense of conservatism—its meaning, its core ideas, its historical origins, its boundaries, its political possibilities—by attending to the books that conservatives have considered iconic for over five decades. This book has not analyzed other sources of conservatism's rapid postwar growth, its organizations, its demographics, its campaign strategies, its responses to specific political and social controversies. While distinct, these two topics are interrelated because conservatism, as I argue in closing, benefited from internal debate. Specifically, I note two intertwined advantages the conservative movement has enjoyed as a result of its shared relationship with common texts. These are advantages that aided both the growth of the conservative coalition during the mid-century and its maintenance through myriad intramovement disputes. In conservatism's case, and more speculatively in other movements as well, canonicity has been a vital factor in movement-making because common texts and celebratory discourses about these texts established a ballast point among conservatives and afforded the conservative political language flexible rhetorical resources.

Ballast

Considered as a whole, these canonical texts contain a kaleidoscope of conservative doctrines on individual freedom and social order, capitalism and local traditions, the role of religion in public life, the value of mass democracy, and the legitimate role of government. The canon's prismatic doctrinal contents were matched only by the diversity of its rhetorical styles: the guileless moxie of Goldwater, the careful claims of Hayek, the hoary mysticism of Kirk, the bold sweep of Weaver, the dense philosophizing of Meyer, the combative fireworks of Buckley, and the morose eloquence of Chambers. Conservatives canonized the polemic and the phrenic, the dense and the readable. Plain language polemics existed side by side with complex intellectual histories in the print culture. Although each book has been a hallowed gateway to conservatism, these gateways have not led readers to the same place.

Canonical texts became meaningful not just for their individual contents or patterns in readers' interpretations but because each has been conserved alongside other select books as the textual heritage of American coalitional conservatism. Some traditionalists and libertarians, of course, would have surely dissolved their partnership and gone their separate ways. Yet in a movement culture fond of capacious formulations trumpeting "seminal works like Russell Kirk's *The Conservative Mind* and Whittaker Chambers's *Witness* and Richard Weaver's *Ideas Have Consequences* and F. A. Hayek's *The Road to Serfdom*" as a seminal group, the conservative canon possessed rhetorical force greater than the sum of its parts.[3] Christopher Buckley, for example, relied on the aggregate force of canonical authors when he sounded the alarm bell on behalf of "true" conservatism in 2006: "My fellow Republicans, it is time, as Madison said in *Federalist* 76, to 'Hand over the tiller of governance, that others may fuck things up for a change.' (Or was it *Federalist* 78?)"[4] Buckley developed no thorough philosophical alternative to the Bush administration; instead, he noted perfunctorily that conservatives had strayed from both *The Road to*

Serfdom and *The Conservative Mind.*[5] Buckley's summoning of Hayek and Kirk in tandem illustrated the pliability of the canon. He and others treated canonical writers, some inspired by Burke, some inspired by capitalism, as a univocal authority.[6]

Common texts, especially texts modeling such different conservatisms, afforded a combative and cantankerous community, one conservative testified, "a center of gravity, some focal point, that addressed them as members of a movement and taught them, in Lenin's words, 'what is to be done.'"[7] Whether addressed directly by movement-centered books like *The Conservative Mind, Up from Liberalism,* or *The Conscience of a Conservative* or addressed indirectly in reverential discourses about adopted books like *The Road to Serfdom* or *Witness,* conservatives became coreligionists with common saints. The diverse canon allowed discordant intellectuals to occupy the masthead of the movement and, in so doing, promoted debate as a central tradition within conservatism. To debate the definition of conservatism was to engage in a long-standing conservative ritual.[8] Diversity within traditionalist and libertarian canonical doctrine became so expected, tolerated, and even celebrated as "thought provoking paradoxes" that the risk of total ideological fracture was forestalled without being eliminated.[9] The canon, in sum, provided a relatively stable framework for conservatives to engage in self-reflexive examination.

The canon was a versatile instrument to build the conservative coalition, close ranks, and cut ties. Internally, canonical rhetorics have highlighted conservatives' common heritage and kept their rows at a simmer. Moreover, the ideological and stylistic variety of the canon mollified competing conservatives. So long as conservative conferences and book clubs featured an ecumenical collection of founding texts, so long as rattling off familiar postwar books by Buckley, Kirk, Chambers, Hayek, Goldwater, and a smattering of other writers was a staple feature of conservative discourse, then its factions could link their politics to conservatism's founders and sense that conservatism could be molded to fit their particular designs. To some extent, the diverse canon haunted those stalwart conservatives who could not cotton to conservatives of different minds. One faction's concerns about the prominence of social conservatives or another's fears of the base morality of capitalists did not disappear entirely. Nevertheless, since a coalition of conservatives revered founding texts, at least one of which all factions rallied around, calls for secession were muted.[10] The diversity of the canon reflected a tacit recognition that conservatives profited from internal disagreements.[11] The canon made stakeholders out of potential separatists and helped conservatives become, as H. L. Mencken once said of Democrats, a gang of "natural enemies in a state of perpetual symbiosis."[12]

To tell the story of conservatism's emergence relying almost exclusively on how conservatives after World War II have talked about their most revered texts is to tell a story that risks removing some of postwar conservatism's "baroque strangeness," cropping members of the John Birch Society and segregationists from the picture.[13] But if this book has shown anything, it is the centrality of this book-centered narrative in conservatives' impression of their movement. The horizon of these rhetorical and doctrinal traditions authorized by this bookish narrative was wide, but it was not infinite. It is mistaken to conclude that conservatives canonized the most influential works of the founding era. Ideological disputes, especially those of the postwar period, taught conservatives to compromise on intractable doctrinal questions as well as "the art of discipline—of being able to purge elements from the movement that might hinder it, yet continuing to forge ahead."[14] To that end, if canonical texts are conservatives' argumentative ideals, their rhetorical epitomes, what has been excluded is just as telling as what has been included.

Beginning with their opposition to *Brown v. Board of Education* and continuing with fears that civil rights advocates were agents of Communism, there is no doubt that race was a key motivator among conservative intellectuals of the midcentury.[15] A shared opposition to federally enforced desegregation helped many libertarians and traditionalists look past their other differences.[16] Prominent conservatives made public arguments grounded in notions of inherent racial difference.[17] Although he later disavowed his anti–civil rights stance, in a 1957 *National Review* editorial Buckley partly based his opposition to federal enforcement of integration on the alleged superiority of white culture.[18] Buckley's was far from the only such editorial *National Review* published.[19] Buckley, moreover, was far from the only influential midcentury conservative whose views on race and civil rights the later movement would abandon. In books like the Regnery-published *The Sovereign States* (1957), James Jackson Kilpatrick, the widely read columnist and *National Review*'s civil rights specialist, developed a philosophical and legal "vernacular to serve the culture of massive resistance" and "provided an intellectual shield for nearly every racist action and reaction in the coming years."[20] Other noteworthy conservative authors like Felix Morley followed suit with vehement anti–civil rights, pro-interposition books.[21] Finally, some postwar conservatives celebrated southern culture without taking up the segregation question directly or theorizing Tenth Amendment jurisprudence. Richard Weaver and others romanticized the segregated South, even the antebellum South, as a feudal holdout to the modern trend toward industrialism and humanism.[22]

For the most part, however, conservative intellectuals during the midcentury and afterward attempted to purge racists from the growing conservative coalition and purge explicit racial appeals (and "extremist" appeals generally) from their argumentative repertoire.[23] As conservatism grew into a national political power, these moves were motivated both by principle and public relations. Buckley and other conservatives, Hart notes, recognized that the Southern Agrarian position was outmoded.[24] Moreover, the least mainstream anti-Communist, states' rights, and antifluoridation voices of the Right, Robert Welch, H. L. Hunt, Dan Smoot, Carl McIntire, and Billy James Hargis, were "ostracized by the early 1970s."[25] In the 1960s, especially after the passage of the Civil Rights Act of 1964 and the Voting Rights Act of 1965, *National Review* conservatives couched their positions on civil rights issues in a color-blind "rights-based" language rather than a race-based language.[26] Discrimination, segregation, and inequality, they insisted, were sins best combated locally.[27] As early as Buckley's *Up from Liberalism* in 1959 and Goldwater's *The Conscience of a Conservative* in 1960, conservatives began making the distinction between conservatism and racism forcefully and rebuking any public association with old-guard white supremacists.[28] In *The Conscience of a Conservative*, Goldwater detested both segregation and prejudice but still held that there was no constitutional mandate for forced integration.[29] Conservatives of the 1960s even cited the high-minded writings of founders like Buckley as rebuttals to those who conflated conservatism and racism.[30]

The postwar books of the conservative canon and the movement culture of the ensuing decades that organized around these texts were both reflective and constitutive of conservatism's mainstreaming efforts. As diverse as their doctrinal contents were, conservatism's canonical books were overwhelmingly books of ideas whose doctrines were developed by examining first principles and core assumptions.

Aside from Goldwater's, these were not books featuring timely political commentary or applications of conservative ideas about freedom or virtue to raging political controversies. That was what *National Review* was for. Some canonical texts said more about medieval Europe than midcentury America. Even *The Conservative Mind*, which "included antebellum apologists for slavery and defenders of states' rights within the conservative tradition," said very little about slavery, states' rights, or the South while extolling the virtues of social tradition and small-property holders.[31] Richard Weaver's *Visions of Order* featured an extended eulogy for antebellum southern culture, but the much-lauded *Ideas Have Consequences* was relatively silent on the South.[32]

This exclusion of arguments about race and traditional southern culture does not mean that canonical books were not used to justify the preservation of de facto racial hierarchies.[33] It does, however, mean that of all the influential midcentury conservative texts, with their myriad doctrines and argumentative styles, the canonical texts moved away from race-based claims, fears of "race-mixing," threats of violence, or calls for sedition.[34] Canonical books, especially in comparison with other conservative texts of the era, did not directly signal, legitimize, or encourage de jure racism. As a whole, several canonical books opposed federal intervention on civil rights and favored individual, local, and traditional solutions, but their justifications were philosophical rather than racial. Milton Friedman, for example, despised "the prejudice and narrowness of outlook" of employers practicing racial discrimination, but he thought "the appropriate recourse" was to convince them "that their tastes are bad and that they should change their views and their behavior."[35]

As was the case with Rand's atheist materialism in *Atlas Shrugged*, Robert Welch's unreasonable anti-Communist positions in *The Politician*, and a variety of overheated defenses of states' rights, the antebellum South, or cultural or racial hierarchies, conservative intellectuals pivoted away from groups whose politics they partly shared if those groups threatened to splinter the conservative coalition or overshadow the beliefs of mainstream conservatives. The canon, like *National Review*, was an instrument in the management of the conservative political identity's rhetorical borders; the canon sanctioned both doctrines and modes of argument as quintessentially conservative.[36] Books with anachronistic racial claims seldom appeared on the ubiquitous best conservative books lists; such books, while influential during the midcentury, have not been taught at Intercollegiate Studies Institute seminars alongside *The Road to Serfdom* or *Witness*; they have not been the subjects of dozens of commemorative Heritage Foundation lectures; they have not been cited frequently and reverentially by conservative politicians; and they do not hold prominent places in conservatives' memories of the origins of conservatism.[37] Conservatives' emblematic books were chief indicators of the rhetorical models conservative leaders and conservative organizations wanted to associate with their political identity.

An Adaptable Political Language

One of the advantages enabled by a diverse canon was that the conservative political identity encompassed more than a single doctrine, political posture, or rhetorical style. American conservatism, more an alloy than an essence, has been the performance of a range of doctrinal and rhetorical positions under a single term of identity. The conservative canon has enabled a second and related benefit as well. These texts, and the movement culture that canonized them, afforded conservatism a shape-shifting quality and allowed conservatives to reform how conservatism should be enacted without departing from self-evidently authoritative sources of wisdom. The keystone words of the political language like "freedom," with its suggestion of low taxes, unregulated economic markets, and personal choice, and "tradition," which cultivated suspicion toward political and social change, were far-flung boundaries on a wide trail that most conservatives slalomed between. Such oscillations have been countenanced by widely appealing canonical writers who supported both freedom and tradition and who fused unlike conservatives together under a common sign of identity with attractive modes of expression.

A telling example of conservatism's dynamic language becomes evident not by examining the meaning of conservatism in a single historical moment but, rather, the recalibration of conservatism in different ones.[38] A snapshot comparison of conservatism just six years apart, in 2004 and 2010, demonstrates how the dominant expressions of conservatism can be prudently adjusted to historical circumstances. In 2004, conservatives, both explicitly and implicitly, favored increasing government power on a host of issues. Prosecuting wars in Afghanistan and Iraq, both begun by George W. Bush, a self-identified conservative, required not only massive increases in federal defense spending but also an array of incursions on individual freedoms in the name of national security.[39] Utilizing a host of novel legal arguments, including the theory of the "unitary executive," a notion generated in conservative legal circles, the Bush White House concentrated unprecedented governmental authority in the executive branch.[40] As illustrated by the 2003 expansion of Medicare, Bush showed his "compassionate conservatism" by pushing Congress to increase the scope of federal entitlement programs.[41] Aside from issues of economics and security, Bush and many other conservatives also sought to use government to legislate on social issues by supporting a constitutional amendment to ban gay marriage.[42] Congressional social conservatives, backed by a host of influential religious organizations campaigning for a national "culture of life," spearheaded an effort to involve the federal government in whether Terri Schiavo, an incapacitated Florida woman, should remain on a feeding tube.[43] Reflecting on the political climate after 9/11, one conservative commented that conservatism showed its "statist side" by "building new bureaucracies, empowering central authorities, and invoking the mystical bonds of the national community, so long as national security is deemed to be at stake."[44]

The public face of conservatism transformed after the 2008 economic meltdown. In 2010, Bush's "big-government conservatism" had been repudiated by many conservatives and, after suffering a dramatic electoral defeat in 2008, a revamped small-government message reigned victorious, historically so, in the 2010 midterm elections.[45] Whereas Vice President Dick Cheney had dismissed financial deficits as a political nonissue in the early 2000s, insurgent libertarian tea party groups were deficit hawks for whom the nation's debt was perilous.[46] Ron Paul's insurgent presidential campaigns in 2008 and 2012 aided this libertarian comeback. His candidacy was premised on the reduction of government across the board, including social programs, defense spending, and moral policing.[47] Although some tea partiers supported an active international role for the U.S. military, the 2004 preoccupation with international security had been, in a period of economic insecurity, sidelined in 2010 for domestic fiscal conservatism.[48] The same was true of issues that motivated social and religious conservatives. Noting that the patriots in Boston harbor "weren't arguing about who was gay or who was having an abortion," influential tea party organizations urged the GOP to avoid mentioning social issues and to focus exclusively on economic concerns.[49]

There were, of course, political positions common to Bush's compassionate conservatism and the tea party's more libertarian leanings. Neither was irreligious; both favored tax cuts; neither was keen on "activist judges," and so on.[50] I am not suggesting that conservatives are motivated only by political success. If that were true, they would not have begun their crusade by fuming at Eisenhower and the midcentury Republican establishment.[51] Finally, I am also not suggesting that such shifts in conservatives' emphasis are not hard won. Conservatism does not change willy-nilly or without some bloodletting; it is, however, capable of undergoing such internal strife and ending up with potent language firmly at home with doctrinal and performative traditions the movement has nurtured since World War II. As Steven Hayward argues, "The fractiousness of the Right, rooted in conflicting intellectual principles in its different camps, is nothing new, and has always been a source of conservatism's dynamism in ways few liberals perceive."[52] The communal value of debate among oppositional factions loyal to a common political identity is quite different than rancor among potential separatists and splinter factions. One generates the vital rhetorical resources for invention; the other generates the resources of implosion. Conservatism can veer toward neoconservatism, jerk back to libertarianism, bear to traditional morality, and flirt with permutations of these and other conservatisms without dying, disintegrating, killing off a segment of the coalition, or losing electoral sway. Conservatisms recede and advance as conservatives, compelled by the need for a resonant message and the desire to adjust their politics to historical realities, perform their varied political traditions.

The conservative political language is gladiatorial, bombastic, resourceful, polarizing, pragmatic, innovative, imperialistic, and opportunistic. The political language is, to offer a summary judgment, flexible. When political languages become stale, hackneyed, or overly formal, they risk becoming incapable of expressing a multitude of political positions, of responding to historical exigencies, of reaching a shifting electorate.[53] When the language becomes tame, drab, and unvaried, its appeal may shrink. These limited languages can become the vernacular of factions or temporary partnerships, not long-term coalitions. The pragmatic language whose usage culture encourages but guides innovation is capable of growth, expansion, and partnership. In the case of conservatism, the fusion of divergent traditionalist, libertarian, and anti-Communist political expressions created a political language whose adaptability ensured variegated political action.

Constraining Conservatism

There are, however, both persistent and recent threats to conservatism's ballast and adaptability. First, although some conservatives see conservatism as a grand bargain between somewhat incompatible camps and figure conservatism inclusively, others hope to close ranks, enforce "purity" tests, and demand eternal fealty to a "checklist" of "core principles" like cutting taxes and opposing abortion.[54] These and similar proposals might rein conservatism in as their advocates hope, but the cost could be fossilization.

Second, although debate has been a hallmark of postwar conservatism, corralling conservative debaters has never been a simple matter. Even when conservatives praised their diverse philosophical foundations, the risk of a "crack-up" was subtly implied.[55] Conservatives worried that as conservatisms proliferated, a central conservatism, one bedrock idea to unite the others, would dissolve. Contemporary conservatives have been at odds with one another over defense policy, market regulations, individual morality, health insurance, global warming, campaign finance reform, trade agreements, immigration, and education. Each of these is a potentially explosive flash point, but recurring disagreements among conservatives spring from a fundamental fissure, the same one that sent Trads and Rads at one another's throats in the 1960s: freedom and order cannot be woven together without leaving a few threads exposed.

Finally, since midcentury, political pundits have, in regular and predictable intervals, failed to find conservatism's pulse.[56] Although conservatives have regularly proven such overeager gravediggers wrong, other pathologists, both within and beyond the ranks of conservatives, did not think that conservatives had argued themselves to death; rather, they had gone brain-dead. The trailblazing conservative thinkers of the midcentury gave way to revanchist, polemical, self-promoters.[57] As E. J. Dionne opined, "The cause of Edmund Burke, Leo Strauss, Robert Nisbet and William F. Buckley Jr. is now in the hands of Rush Limbaugh, Sean Hannity—and Sarah Palin. Reason has been overwhelmed by propaganda, ideas by slogans, learned manifestoes by direct-mail hit pieces."[58]

Conservatives also feared a slow intellectual death, that the best conservative ideas were exhausted in the frenetic theoretical disputes of the midcentury. Worried that conservatism "lost its mind," these anxious stalwarts were vexed by an "epistemic closure" within conservatism; talking points, catering to the GOP base, and playing politics all supplanted serious political and philosophical thought.[59] Influential conservatives repeated doltish canards about matters of science, like stem cell research, global warming, and evolution, as well as economics, like favoring tax cuts as the solution to every financial problem.[60] Pedantic conservative authors dismissed the "vast" expanses of conservative literature written by "talk-radio personages" as "rubbish" and found comedic relief in comparisons of cerebral post–World War II books with the "Happy Meal conservatism" of recent vintage.[61]

This kind of densely philosophical conservatism obsessed with defining first principles did not disappear as conservatism grew in popularity. Indeed, it never left. "We may," one conservative writer stressed in 2005, "on the contrary, be living through the high summer of conservative ideas in America."[62] Moreover, this kind of antagonistic conservative rhetoric was not invented by Limbaugh in the late 1980s. Although Buckley, quite the antagonist in his own right, excluded what he called "crackpottery" from *National Review*, he also said he wanted his new magazine to be unnervingly brash.[63] Within ascendant conservatism, there are simply far more of each of the four types of advocates that, in Heritage Foundation historian Lee Edwards's view, contributed to the growth of the movement: "philosophers, popularizers, politicians, and philanthropists."[64] Coulter and Limbaugh, popularizers in Edwards's schema, have been promoters of an influential political identity whose political power has long been established, one whose precepts were developed decades hence when Buckley and company competed with few others to define conservatism.

Although some mistake midcentury conservatism for a philosophers' workshop and confuse contemporary conservatism with a shouting contest, they are correct to note that Limbaugh and Coulter are different public faces of conservatism than Buckley and Kirk. Limbaugh's and other polemicists' durable popularity above contemporaneous conservative writers and philosophers does not, nevertheless, denote the regression of conservative thought. It only denotes different exigent historical circumstances; what was lost was not an eloquent era but an exigency. The philosophical disputes of the midcentury, esoteric back-and-forths over whether John Stuart Mill was a conservative, were in demand when the fledgling movement was precariously unstable, when all conservatives were newly conservative. These converts needed core beliefs; they needed answers to basic political questions about how a new, American conservative should think about government. Conservatives needed to develop and debate intense, "soul searching" tracts because of the novelty of their endeavor.[65] These definitive discourses were in demand as the midcentury American Right gave their new political identity an old name. For the first time, the historically diffuse political communities of the American Right excavated a European name, adopted select books as vanguard expressions of their adaptable political identity, and amassed their rhetorical and ideological traditions into a coherent political language.

Notes

⌘

Prologue. The Old Argument Comes Full Circle

1. Biographical information from Tom Reiss, "The First Conservative: How Peter Viereck Inspired—and Lost—a Movement," New Yorker, October 24, 2005.

2. Quoted in Suzanne Fields, "More Than Peace in Our Time," Washington Times, November 19, 2006.

3. Peter Viereck, "Conservatism under the Elms," New York Times, November 4, 1951, 39.

4. John Judis, William F. Buckley, Jr.: Patron Saint of the Conservatives (New York: Touchstone Books, 1988), 104. When Buckley was asked about the book proposal, he replied that "Viereck represented 'a sort of pre-neoconservatism none of us had any use for.'" Riess, "First Conservative."

5. Linda Kintz, Between Jesus and the Market: The Emotions That Matter in Right-Wing America (Durham, N.C.: Duke University Press, 1997). See also William E. Connolly, Capitalism and Christianity, American Style (Durham, N.C.: Duke University Press, 2008).

6. Peter Viereck, "But—I'm a Conservative!" Atlantic Monthly, April 1940.

7. George Nash, *The Conservative Intellectual Movement in America since 1945* (New York: Basic Books, 1976), 67.

8. Cited in Paul Johnson, "George Sylvester: Poet and Propagandist," *Books at Iowa* 9 (1968).

9. Reiss, "First Conservative."

10. Nash, *Conservative Intellectual Movement in America*, 60.

11. Whatever conservatism meant, one methodologically dubious 1936 study found that 33 percent of high school students had a favorable perception of the term, a far cry from liberalism at 84 percent, but still ahead of Communism, fascism, and radicalism. Selden S. Menefree, "The Effect of Stereotyped Words on Political Judgments," *American Sociological Review* 1 (1936): 614–621. See also Patrick Allitt, *The Conservatives: Ideas and Personalities throughout American History* (New Haven, Conn.: Yale University Press, 2009), 2; David Green, *The Language of Politics in America: Shaping Political Consciousness from McKinley to Reagan* (Ithaca, N.Y.: Cornell University Press, 1987), 1.

12. Rick Perlstein, *Before the Storm: Barry Goldwater and the Unmaking of the American Consensus* (New York: Hill & Wang, 2001), 74.

13. Henry Regnery, *Perfect Sowing: Reflections of a Bookman* (Wilmington, Del.: ISI Books, 1999), 383–384.

14. William F. Buckley, Jr., *God and Man at Yale: The Superstitions of "Academic Freedom"*, 50th anniv. ed. (Washington, D.C.: Regnery, 2002). For some anti–New Deal advocates, conservatism represented an antistatist philosophy of individualism. See Allan J. Lichtman, *White Protestant Nation* (New York: Atlantic Monthly Press, 2008), 10; John Robert Moore, "Senator Josiah W. Bailey and the 'Conservative Manifesto' of 1937," *Journal of Southern History* 31 (1965): 21–39. For others, conservatism represented a robber baron philosophy of wealth. Richard Hofstadter, *The American Political Tradition and the Men Who Made It* (New York: Vintage, 1989), 283–289.

15. A. James Reichley, "The Conservative Roots of the Nixon, Ford, and Reagan Administrations," *Political Science Quarterly* 4 (1981–1982): 537.

16. Viereck noted in the 1949 edition of *Conservatism Revisited*, "I hope the reader will consider this conservative credo on its own merits and demerits. I hope he will not consider it on the basis of popular conditioned reflexes against a word that deserves to be scrubbed clean again, being the historic, traditional name for an outlook needed today." Peter Viereck, *Conservatism Revisited: The Revolt against Ideology* (New York: Transaction, 2009), 63. See also Francis O. Wilson, "A Theory of Conservatism," *American Political Science Review* 35 (1941).

17. Nash, *Conservative Intellectual Movement in America*, 67–68.

18. John J. Miller, "Veering Off Course," *National Review*, October 26, 2005.

19. Viereck won the Pulitzer Prize for poetry in 1949 for his collection *Terror and Decorum*. See Brian Marqaurd, "Peter Viereck, 89; Writings Helped Inspire Conservatism," *Boston Globe*, May 19, 2006.

20. In the end, only an inexact irony remains in the fact that it is the distant progeny of Louis Viereck, the man who kept company with Marx and Engels, whose "conservative" ideas would make such an impact.

21. Riess, "First Conservative."

22. Dan LeRoy, "The Conservative Lion in Winter," *New York Times*, October 9, 2005.

23. James Roberts, *The Conservative Decade: Emerging Leaders of the 1980s* (Westport, Conn.: Arlington House, 1980), 27.

24. Jay Nordlinger, "Only a Few Notes . . . ," *National Review*, March 3, 2008.

25. See the cover of *Time*, November 3, 1967.

26. Cited in Perlstein, *Before the Storm*, 108.

27. Ibid., 74.

28. William F. Buckley, Jr., "Publisher's Statement," *National Review*, November 19, 1955.

29. Arthur Schlesinger Jr.'s comment from 1955 is illustrative of the term's growing force: "No intellectual phenomenon has been more surprising in recent years than the revival in the United States of conservatism as a respectable social philosophy." See Arthur Schlesinger Jr., *The Politics of Hope and the Bitter Heritage: American Liberalism in the 1960s* (Princeton, N.J.: Princeton University Press, 2008), 94.

30. Jerome Himmelstein, *To the Right: The Transformation of American Conservatism* (Berkeley: University of California Press, 1990), 13. See also Ryan Sager, *The Elephant in the Room: Evangelicals, Libertarians, and the Battle to Control the Republican Party* (Hoboken, N.J.: John Wiley & Sons, 2006), 25.

31. Jonah Goldberg, "The Future of Conservatism," panel sponsored by the *National Review Institute*, November 18, 2008, video available via http://nrinstitute.org/futureofconservatismvideo.php.

32. Kevin Mattson, *Rebels All! A Short History of the Conservative Mind in Postwar America* (New Brunswick, N.J.: Rutgers University Press, 2008); Sean Wilentz, *The Age of Reagan: A History, 1974–2008* (New York: HarperCollins, 2008); Mark A. Smith, *The Right Talk: How Conservatives Transformed the Great Society into the Economic Society* (Princeton, N.J.: Princeton University Press, 2007); Peter Berkowitz, ed., *Varieties of Conservatism in America* (Stanford, Calif.: Hoover Institution Press, 2004).

33. Richard Weaver, *The Ethics of Rhetoric* (Chicago: Henry Regnery, 1953), 212–214, 222.

34. Donald Devine, "Revitalizing Conservatism," American Conservative Union, May 13, 2003, available via http://www.conservative.org/pressroom/revitalizingconservatism.asp.

35. For studies of influential conservative thinkers, see Carl T. Bogus, *Buckley: William F. Buckley Jr. and the Rise of American Conservatism* (New York:

Bloomsbury Press, 2011); Michael Kimmage, *The Conservative Turn: Lionel Trilling, Whittaker Chambers, and the Lessons of Anti-Communism* (Cambridge, Mass.: Harvard University Press, 2009); Jacob Heilbrunn, *They Knew They Were Right: The Rise of the Neocons* (New York: Doubleday, 2008); Gerald J. Russello, *The Postmodern Imagination of Russell Kirk* (Columbia: University of Missouri Press, 2007); Nicholas Xenos, *Cloaked in Virtue: Leo Strauss and the Rhetoric of American Foreign Policy* (New York: Routledge, 2007); W. Wesley McDonald, *Russell Kirk in an Age of Ideology* (Columbia: University of Missouri Press, 2004); Anne Norton, *Leo Strauss and the Politics of American Empire* (New Haven, Conn.: Yale University Press, 2004); Bruce Caldwell, *Hayek's Challenge: An Intellectual Biography of F. A. Hayek* (Chicago: University of Chicago Press, 2004); Shadia B. Drury, *Leo Strauss and the American Right* (New York: Palgrave Macmillan, 1999); Ted V. McAllister, *Revolt against Modernity: Leo Strauss, Eric Voegelin, and the Search for a Postliberal Order* (Lawrence: University Press of Kansas, 1996). For recent studies of the influence of conservative leaders, see Wilentz, *Age of Reagan*; Rick Perlstein, *Nixonland: The Rise of a President and the Fracturing of America* (New York: Simon & Schuster, 2008); Judis, *William F. Buckley, Jr.* For studies of grassroots conservatism, see Sean P. Cunningham, *Cowboy Conservatism: Texas and the Rise of the Modern Right* (Lexington: University Press of Kentucky, 2010); Bruce J. Schulman and Julian Zelizer, eds., *Rightward Bound: Making America Conservative in the 1970s* (Boston: Harvard University Press, 2008); Michael Schaller, *Right Turn: American Life in the Reagan-Bush Era, 1980–1992* (New York: Oxford University Press, 2006); David Farber and Jeff Roche, eds., *The Conservative Sixties* (New York: Peter Lang, 2003); Lisa McGirr, *Suburban Warriors: The Origins of the New American Right* (Princeton, N.J.: Princeton University Press, 2002); Mary C. Brennan, *Turning Right in the Sixties: The Conservative Capture of the GOP* (Chapel Hill: University of North Carolina Press, 1995); Jerome Himmelstein, *To the Right: The Transformation of American Conservatism* (Berkeley: University of California Press, 1990).

36. For studies of individual conservative organizations, see Kim Phillips-Fein, *Invisible Hands: The Making of the Conservative Movement from the New Deal to Reagan* (New York: W. W. Norton, 2010); Ann Southworth, *Lawyers of the Right: Professionalizing the Conservative Coalition* (Chicago: University of Chicago Press, 2008); Steven M. Teles, *The Rise of the Conservative Legal Movement: The Battle for Control of the Law* (Princeton, N.J.: Princeton University Press, 2008); Gregory L. Schneider, *Cadres for Conservatism: Young Americans for Freedom and the Rise of the Contemporary Right* (New York: New York University Press, 1999); John A. Andrew, *The Other Side of the Sixties: Young Americans for Freedom and the Rise of Conservative Politics* (New Brunswick, N.J.: Rutgers University Press, 1997). For studies of conservative electioneering, see Andrew E. Busch, *Reagan's Victory: The Presidential Election of 1980 and the Rise of the Right* (Lawrence: University Press of Kansas, 2005); Matthew Dallek, *The Right Moment: Ronald Reagan's First Victory and the Decisive Turning Point in American Politics* (New York: Oxford University Press, 2004); Perlstein, *Before the Storm*. For studies on conservatism and race, see Joseph E. Lowndes, *From the New Deal to the New Right: Race and the Southern Origins of Modern Conservatism* (New Haven,

Conn.: Yale University Press, 2008); Kevin M. Kruse, *White Flight: Atlanta and the Making of Modern Conservatism* (Princeton, N.J.: Princeton University Press, 2005); Dan T. Carter, *The Politics of Rage: George Wallace, the Origins of the New Conservatism, and the Transformation of American Politics* (Baton Rouge: Louisiana State University Press, 2000); Dan T. Carter, *From George Wallace to Newt Gingrich: Race in the Conservative Counterrevolution, 1963–1994* (Baton Rouge: Louisiana State University Press, 1999).

37. Donald T. Critchlow, *Phyllis Schlafly and Grassroots Conservatism: A Woman's Crusade* (Princeton, N.J.: Princeton University Press, 2007), 40. See also Allitt, *Conservatives*, 159. George Nash's *The Conservative Intellectual Movement in America since 1945* is the most thorough treatment of the key books by midcentury conservative intellectuals but does conceptualize these books as rhetorical resources for cooperation and disagreement within the conservative movement. See Nash, *Conservative Intellectual Movement in America*.

38. A broad survey of scholarship on conservatism reveals that only one scholarly study has examined conservative literature in detail, but its approach was debatable; it included neo-Nazi literature as conservative. See Chip Berlet, "The Write Stuff: U.S. Serial Print Culture from Conservatives Out to Neo-Nazis," *Library Trends* 56 (2008): 570–600.

39. For analyses of various forms of conservatism in the United States that attend to conservative rhetoric, see Morgan Marietta, *The Politics of Sacred Rhetoric: Absolutist Appeals and Political Persuasion* (Waco, Tex.: Baylor University Press, 2012); David M. Ricci, *Why Conservatives Tell Stories and Liberals Don't* (Boulder, Colo.: Paradigm, 2011); Christina R. Foust, "Aesthetics as Weapons in the 'War of Ideas': Exploring the Digital and Typographic in American Conservative Websites," *Southern Communication Journal* 73 (2008): 122–142; Kenneth M. Cosgrove, *Branded Conservatives: How the Brand Brought the Right from the Fringes to the Center of American Politics* (New York: Peter Lang, 2007); Smith, *Right Talk*; Kevin Coe and David Domke, "Petitioners or Prophets?: Presidential Discourse, God, and the Ascendancy of Religious Conservatives," *Journal of Communication* 56 (2006): 309–330; Sharon Jarvis, *The Talk of the Party: Political Labels, Symbolic Capital, and American Life* (Lanham, Md.: Rowman & Littlefield, 2005); George Lakoff, *Don't Think of an Elephant: Know Your Values and Frame the Debate—The Essential Guide for Progressives* (New York: Chelsea Green, 2004); James Arnt Aune, "The Argument from Evil in the Rhetoric of Reaction," *Rhetoric & Public Affairs* 6 (2003): 518–522; Robert Rowland and John Jones, "Entelechial and Reformative Symbolic Trajectories in Contemporary Conservatism: A Case Study of Reagan and Buchanan in Houston and Beyond," *Rhetoric & Public Affairs* 4 (2001): 55–84; Lloyd Rohler, "Conservative Appeals to the People: George Wallace's Populist Rhetoric," *Southern Communication Journal* 64 (1999): 316–322; Kurt Ritter, "Ronald Reagan's 1960s Southern Rhetoric: Courting Conservatives for the GOP," *Southern Communication Journal* 64 (1999): 333–345; Edward C. Appel, "Burlesque Drama as a Rhetorical Genre: The Hudibrastic Ridicule of William F. Buckley, Jr.," *Western Journal of Communication* 60 (1996): 269–284; Kenneth Zagacki, "The Rhetoric of American Decline: Paul Kennedy, Conservatives, and

the Solvency Debate," *Western Journal of Communication* 56 (1992): 372–393; Albert O. Hirschman, *The Rhetoric of Reaction: Perversity, Futility, Jeopardy* (Cambridge, Mass.: Harvard University Press, 1991); Martin J. Medhurst, "Resistance, Conservatism, and Theory Building: A Cautionary Note," *Western Journal of Speech Communication* 49 (1985): 103–115; Bernard K. Duffy, "The Anti-humanist Rhetoric of the New Religious Right," *Southern Speech Communication Journal* 49 (1984): 339–360; Charles Conrad, "The Rhetoric of the Moral Majority: An Analysis of Romantic Form," *Quarterly Journal of Speech* 69 (1983): 159–170; Barbara Warnick, "Conservative Resistance Revisited: A Reply to Medhurst," *Western Journal of Speech Communication* 46 (1982): 373–378; G. Thomas Goodnight, "The Liberal and the Conservative Presumptions: On Political Philosophy and the Foundation of Public Argument," *Proceedings of the Alta Conference on Argumentation* (1980): 304–337; Thomas J. Hynes Jr., "Liberal and Conservative Presumptions in Public Argument: A Critique," *Proceedings of the Alta Conference on Argumentation* (1980): 338–347; Thomas D. Clark, "An Analysis of Recurrent Features of Contemporary American Radical, Liberal, and Conservative Political Discourse," *Southern Speech Communication Journal* 44 (1979): 399–422; Barbara Warnick, "The Rhetoric of Conservative Resistance," *Southern Speech Communication Journal* 42 (1977): 256–273.

40. William F. Buckley, Jr., *Up from Liberalism* (New York: Stein and Day, 1985), 195.

41. Marietta, *Politics of Sacred Rhetoric*, 214. See also Drew Westen, *The Political Brain: The Role of Emotion in Deciding the Fate of the Nation* (New York: PublicAffairs, 2008), 85, 146.

42. Rick Perlstein, "Gone Astray," *Washington Post*, May 4, 2008.

43. Nash, *Conservative Intellectual Movement in America*, xiii. Since the 1950s, notable studies have popularized several enduring misconceptions about conservatism, each of which was premised on a single, once-and-for-all definition of conservatism. Conservatism has been treated as a fixed political force: reactionary politics, nationalism, capitalism, racism, cultural imperialism, religious fundamentalism, and fascism. Paul Krugman, *The Conscience of a Liberal* (New York: W. W. Norton, 2009); Lichtman, *White Protestant Nation*; Thomas Frank, *What's the Matter with Kansas?* (New York: Metropolitan Books, 2004). See also Edwin J. Feulner and Doug Wilson, *Getting America Right: The True Conservative Values Our Nation Needs Today* (New York: Crown Forum, 2006). Some social science even operates from a rigid conception of conservatism. See Jack Block, "Millennial Contrarianism," *Journal of Research in Personality* 35 (2001): 98; Fred Kerlinger, *Liberalism and Conservatism: The Nature and Structure of Social Attitudes* (Hillsdale, N.J.: Erblaum, 1984), 14. For more on the errors of this approach to defining political ideologies, see Quentin Skinner, "Meaning and Understanding in the History of Ideas," *History and Theory* 8 (1969): 37.

44. The impact of scholarly categorization choices is substantial because choosing an organizational scheme often coincides with choosing a vocabulary to describe, taxonimize, and judge conservatism. Jonathan Schoenwald, for

instance, accepts Nash's categorization and adds practical distinctions between Republican Party activists ("mainstream or electoral conservatism") and those anti-eastern establishment activists ambivalent toward the Republican Party as a political vehicle ("extremist conservatives"). Jonathan M. Schoenwald, *A Time for Choosing: The Rise of Modern American Conservatism* (Oxford: Oxford University Press, 2001), 6. The prominence of these dyadic or tripartite schemes can be seen in recent scholarly histories of the movement. See Berkowitz, *Varieties of Conservatism in America*; John Micklethwait and Adrian Wooldridge, *The Right Nation: Conservative Power in America* (New York: Penguin Books, 2004), 19; Charles W. Dunn and J. David Woodard, *The Conservative Tradition in America* (New York: Rowman & Littlefield, 1996), 41; Paul Gottfried, *The Conservative Movement*, rev. ed. (New York: Twayne, 1993); William R. Harbour, *The Foundations of Conservative Thought* (Notre Dame, Ind.: Notre Dame University Press, 1982), 103.

45. Sam Tanenhaus sees two basic brands: "those who have upheld the Burkean ideal of replenishing civil society by adjusting to changing conditions" and "those committed to a revanchist counterrevolution, the restoration of America's pre–welfare state *ancien regime*." Sam Tanenhaus, "Conservatism Is Dead: An Intellectual Autopsy of a Movement," *New Republic*, February 18, 2009, 13. John Micklethwait and Adrian Wooldridge identify "at least three competing forms of conservatism," including "laissez-faire individualism," "Christian moralism," and "militaristic nationalism." Micklethwait and Wooldridge, *Right Nation*, 19. James W. Ceasar spots additional particulars, a conservative hydra with "four heads," including "religious conservatives, economic or libertarian-minded conservatives, natural-rights or neoconservatives, and traditionalists or paleoconservatives." James W. Ceasar, "Creed versus Culture: Alternative Foundations of American Conservatism," *The Lehrman Lectures on Restoring America's Identity*, Heritage Foundation, March 10, 2006, available via http://www.heritage.org/research/politicalphilosophy/hl926.cfm.

46. For more on the power of definitions to exclude, see Edward Schiappa, *Defining Reality: Definitions and the Politics of Meaning* (Carbondale: Southern Illinois University Press, 2003).

47. Micklethwait and Wooldridge, *Right Nation*, 19. For additional explanation of the contradictory impulses within conservatism, see Donald T. Critchlow, *The Conservative Ascendancy: How the GOP Right Made Political History* (Cambridge, Mass.: Harvard University Press, 2007), 3.

48. J. G. A. Pocock, "Texts as Events: Reflections on the History of Political Thought," in *Politics of Discourse: The Literature and History of Seventeenth-Century England*, ed. Kevin Sharp and Steven N. Zwicker (Berkeley: University of California Press, 1987); J. G. A. Pocock, "The Reconstruction of Discourse: Towards the Historiography of Political Thought," *MLN* 96 (1981): 959–980; J. G. A. Pocock, "Verbalizing a Political Act: Toward a Politics of Speech," *Political Theory* 1 (1973): 27–45; J. G. A. Pocock, *Politics, Language, and Time: The Transformation of the Study of Political Thought* (New York: Atheneum, 1971), 28. See also Richard Weaver, *The Ethics of Rhetoric* (Chicago: Henry Regnery, 1953), 212–214.

49. I am distinguishing between, in essence, big political language and smaller political languages. To be sure, *the* political language of an age is the discursive context in which *a* political language functions. In reverse, *a* political language may be an essential element in *the* whole political language. For more on approaches to the political language of an era, ethnicity, or nation as opposed to specific political languages tied to political identities, see Terrence Ball, James Farr, and Russell L. Hanson, "Introduction," in *Political Innovation and Conceptual Change*, ed. Terence Ball, James Farr, and Russell L. Hanson (Cambridge: Cambridge University Press, 1989), 1; David Green, *The Language of Politics in America: Shaping Political Consciousness from McKinley to Reagan* (Ithaca, N.Y.: Cornell University Press, 1987); Murray Edelman, *The Symbolic Uses of Politics* (Urbana: University of Illinois Press, 1985); James Boyd White, *When Words Lose Their Meaning* (Chicago: University of Chicago Press, 1984), 192; Murray Edelman, *Political Language: Words That Succeed and Policies That Fail* (New York: Academic Press, 1977). J. G. A. Pocock, *The Machiavellian Moment: Florentine Political Thought and the Atlantic Republican Tradition* (Princeton, N.J.: Princeton University Press, 1975). For more on the link between key words and political concepts, see J. G. A. Pocock, "Concepts and Discourses: A Difference in Culture? Comment on a Paper by Melvin Richter," in *The Meaning of Historical Terms and Concepts: New Studies on Begriffsgeschichte*, ed. Hartmut Lehmann and Melvin Richter (Washington, D.C.: German Historical Institute, 1996), 53; Melvin Richter, "Appreciating a Contemporary Classic," in Lehmann and Richter, *Meaning of Historical Terms and Concepts*, 10; Terence Ball, *Transforming Political Discourse: Political Theory and Critical Conceptual History* (Oxford: Basil Blackwell, 1988), 9; Otto Brunner, Werner Conze, and Reinhart Koselleck, eds., *Geschichtliche Grundbegriffe:. Historishces Lexikon zur politisch-sozialen Sprache in Deutschland (Basic Concepts in History: A Dictionary on Historical Principles of Political and Social Language in Germany)*, 8 vols. (Stuttgart: Klett-Cotta, 1972–1973). For more on ideology and individual political terms, see Celeste Michelle Condit and John Louis Lucaites, *Crafting Equality: America's Anglo-African Word* (Chicago: University of Chicago Press, 1993); Michael C. McGee, "The Ideograph: A Link between Rhetoric and Ideology," *Quarterly Journal of Speech* 66 (1980): 1–16. For more on the study of particular terms in the larger political vocabulary, see Roderick P. Hart, Sharon E. Jarvis, William P. Jennings, and Deborah Smith-Howell, *Political Keywords: Using Language That Uses Us* (New York: Oxford University Press, 2005), 252; Raymond Williams, *Keywords: A Vocabulary of Culture and Society* (New York: Oxford University Press, 1983), 15.

50. Pocock, "Concepts and Discourses,", 47. For similar approaches to the performance of political languages and rhetorical traditions, see James Jasinski, "Instrumentalism, Contextualism, and Interpretation in Rhetorical Criticism," in *Rhetorical Hermeneutics: Invention and Interpretation in the Age of Science*, ed. Alan G. Gross and William M. Keith (Albany: State University of New York Press, 1997), 195–224; John Murphy, "Inventing Authority: Bill Clinton, Martin Luther King, and the Orchestration of Rhetorical Traditions," *Quarterly Journal of Speech* 83 (1997): 71–89. Other scholars have examined similar rhetorical phenomena under the broader heading "public vocabulary." See

Paul J. Achter, "TV, Technology, and McCarthyism: Crafting the Democratic Renaissance in an Age of Fear," *Quarterly Journal of Speech* 90 (2004): 313; Celeste Michelle Condit, *Decoding Abortion Rhetoric: Communicating Social Change* (Champaign: University of Illinois Press, 1994), 4–6; John M. Murphy, "Domesticating Dissent: The Kennedys and the Freedom Rides," *Communication Monographs* 59 (1992): 62–63; John Louis Lucaites and Celeste Michelle Condit, "Reconstructing <Equality>: Culturetypal and Counter-Cultural Rhetorics in the Martyred Black Vision," *Communication Monographs* 57 (1990): 8; Stephen E. Lucas, "The Renaissance of American Public Address: Text and Context in Rhetorical Criticism," *Quarterly Journal of Speech* 74 (1988): 249.

51. Pocock, "Verbalizing a Political Act," 33.

52. Pocock, "Reconstruction of Discourse," 969.

53. Pocock, "Texts as Events," 28.

54. See Jarvis, *Talk of the Party*, 11–12.

55. See, for example, Celeste Michelle Condit, "Hegemony in a Mass-Mediated Society: Concordance about Reproductive Technologies," *Critical Studies in Mass Communication* 11 (1994): 205–230.

56. Large language communities are a heterogeneous lot. As heterogeneity increases, so does linguistic innovation. Some purist language-users "agonize" about threats to the mother tongue, fearing that linguistic change signals the demise of basic standards and foreshadows a community on the skids. See Robert McCrum, *Globish: How the English Language Became the World's Language* (New York: W. W. Norton, 2010), 8.

57. Zdenek Salzmann, *Language, Culture, and Society*, 4th ed. (Boulder, Colo.: Westview Press, 2007), 175.

58. McCrum, *Globish*, 283.

59. Barbie Zelizer, "Journalists as Interpretive Communities," *Critical Studies in Media Communication* 10 (1993): 223.

60. Ronald Reagan, *Speaking My Mind: Selected Speeches* (New York: Simon & Schuster, 1989), 95.

61. When Republican presidential candidates dropped the names of canonical authors on the campaign trail, like Michelle Bachmann's half-joking claim in 2011 that Ludwig von Mises was her beach reading, Fred Thompson endearing himself to Goldwater's *The Conscience of a Conservative* in 2007, or Pat Buchanan's breathless elegy to virtually the whole group in 1988, it signaled both like-mindedness and communal status to potential constituencies. See Ariel Sabar, "Fred Thompson: A Maverick Conservative Who Loves the Law," *Christian Science Monitor*, December 13, 2007; Steven Moore, "'On the Beach, I Bring von Mises,'" *Wall Street Journal*, June 11, 2011; Patrick J. Buchanan, *Right from the Beginning* (Boston: Little, Brown, 1988), 218–245.

62. The rhetorical force of canons within political communities has generated scarce interest from scholars interested, cast broadly, in the relationship between texts,

audiences, and the development of collective mentalities. For more on print culture, see David Reinking, "Valuing Reading, Writing, and Books in a Post-Typographic World," in *A History of the Book in America*, vol. 5, ed. David P. Nord, Joan S. Rubin, and Michael Schudson (Chapel Hill: University of North Carolina Press, 2009), 491; Cathy Davidson, *Revolution and the Word* (Oxford: Oxford University Press, 2004); Wayne A. Wiegand, "Introduction: Theoretical Foundations for Analyzing Print Culture as Agency and Practice in a Diverse Modern America," in *Print Culture in a Diverse America*, ed. James P. Dansky and Wayne A. Wiegand (Urbana: University of Illinois Press, 1998), 4; Jurgen Habermas, *The Structural Transformation of the Public Sphere* (Cambridge, Mass.: MIT Press, 1994); Elizabeth Eisenstein, *The Printing Press as an Agent of Change: Communications and Cultural Transformation in Early-Modern Europe*, 2 vols. (Cambridge, Mass.: Cambridge University Press, 1982), xii; Jennifer Tebbe, "Print and American Culture," *American Quarterly* 32 (1980): 260. For more on interpretive communities, see Thomas R. Lindlof, "Interpretive Community: An Approach to Media and Religion," *Journal of Media and Religion* 1 (2002): 62; Stanley Fish, *Is There a Text in This Class? The Authority of Interpretive Communities* (Cambridge, Mass.: Harvard University Press, 1980). For more on reading formations, see Tony Bennett, "Texts in History: The Determination of Readings and Their Texts," in *Reception Study: From Literary Theory to Cultural Studies*, ed. James L. Machor and Philip Goldstein (New York: Routledge, 2001); Nancy Glazener, *Reading for Realism: The History of a U.S. Literary Institution, 1850–1910* (Durham, N.C.: Duke University Press, 1997); Tony Bennett, "Texts, Readers, Reading Formations," *Bulletin of the Midwest Modern Language Association* 16 (1983): 3–17.

63. Frank Kermode, *History and Value: The Clarendon Lectures and the Northcliffe Lectures* (New York: Oxford University Press, 1989), 115.

64. Moshe Halbertal, *People of the Book: Canon, Meaning, and Authority* (Cambridge, Mass.: Harvard University Press, 1997), 1–2.

65. Robert Alter, *Canon and Creativity: Modern Writing and the Authority of Scripture* (New Haven, Conn.: Yale University Press, 2000), 5.

66. Kathleen Hall Jamieson and Joseph Capella, *Echo Chamber: Rush Limbaugh and the Conservative Media Establishment* (New York: Oxford University Press, 2008).

67. Numerous publications validate my selection of canonical texts. *National Review*'s list of the "100 Best Books of the Century" included the works of Buckley, Chambers, Friedman, Hayek, Kirk, Nisbet, and Weaver. See "The 100 Best Non-Fiction Books of the Century," *National Review*, available via http:// old.nationalreview.com/100best/100_books.html. The Intercollegiate Studies Institute's similar list deviated only slightly by including Leo Strauss and Eric Voegelin and excluding books by Buckley. See M. C. Henrie, W. J. C. Myers, et al., "The Fifty Worst (and Best) Books of the Century," *Intercollegiate Review* (Fall 1999). Jeffrey Nelson's list included Hayek, Mises, Nock, Chambers, Voegelin, Meyer, Kirk, Weaver, Nisbet, and Kristol. See Jeffrey O. Nelson, *Ten Books That Shaped America's Conservative Renaissance*, Intercollegiate Studies

Institute, n.d., available via http://www.isi.org/conservative_tho/PDF/tenbooks. pdf. Lee Edwards's *Reading the Right Books* featured largely the same works but added *In Defense of Freedom* by Frank Meyer, *The Conscience of a Conservative* by Barry Goldwater, *Memoirs of a Superfluous Man* by Albert Jay Nock, and *Atlas Shrugged* by Ayn Rand. See Lee Edwards, ed., *Reading the Right Books: A Guide for the Intelligent Conservative* (Washington, D.C.: Heritage Foundation, 2007). For other examples of authors affirming similar lists, see Bogus, *Buckley*, 118; Benjamin Wiker, *Ten Books Every Conservative Must Read: Plus Four Not to Miss and One Impostor* (Washington, D.C.: Regnery, 2010), 3–4; Richard Viguerie, *Conservatives Betrayed: How George W. Bush and Other Big Government Republicans Hijacked the Conservative Cause* (Los Angeles: Bonus Books, 2006), 229–230; Edwin Feulner, ed., *The March of Freedom: Modern Classics of Conservative Thought* (Dallas: Spence, 2004); Dunn and Woodard, *Conservative Tradition in America*, 16–17; John P. East, *The American Conservative Movement: Its Philosophical Founders* (Chicago: Regnery, 1986).

68. Lee Edwards, "Introduction," in Edwards, *Reading the Right Books*, 6. Five second-order canonical books appeared often on such lists and encomiums but not with the same consistency as the first-order texts: *Bureaucracy* (Ludwig von Mises, 1944), *The New Science of Politics* (Eric Voegelin, 1951), *Natural Right and History* (Leo Strauss, 1953), *The Conservative Affirmation* (Willmoore Kendall, 1963), and *The Suicide of the West* (James Burnham, 1964). One author mentioned often in conservative retrospectives whose work fell slightly outside the postwar period I examine is Albert Jay Nock, whose *Memoirs of a Superfluous Man* (1943) and *Our Enemy, The State* (1935) remain influential.

69. Critchlow, *Phyllis Schlafly*, 40–41.

70. One conservative historian called *The Road to Serfdom, Ideas Have Consequences, Witness,* and *The Conservative Mind* "four essentials of the modern conservative canon." See Lee Edwards, *Educating for Liberty: The First Half-Century of the Intercollegiate Studies Institute* (Washington, D.C.: Regnery, 2003), 165–166. See also Perlstein, *Before the Storm*, 65. In 1967, Henry Regnery acquired the paperback rights to Whittaker Chambers's *Witness* and "built partnerships with conservative student organizations in order to distribute thousands of copies of the book." See Nicole Hoplin and Ron Robinson, *Funding Fathers: The Unsung Heroes of the Conservative Movement* (Washington, D.C.: Regnery, 2008), 49–50. For more on the Intercollegiate Society of Individualists, see Brian Doherty, *Radicals for Capitalism: A Freewheeling History of the Modern American Libertarian Movement* (New York: Public Affairs, 2007), 202; Perlstein, *Before the Storm*, 72–73; Schneider, *Cadres for Conservatism*, 16; George Nash, "The Influence of *Ideas Have Consequences* on the Conservative Intellectual Movement in America," in *Steps toward Restoration: The Consequences of Richard Weaver's Ideas,* ed. Ted J. Smith III (Wilmington, Del.: ISI Books, 1998), 103. For more on the Foundation for Economic Freedom, see Doherty, *Radicals for Capitalism*, 157–158, 166; Perlstein, *Before the Storm*, 115; Nash, *Conservative Intellectual Movement in America*, 18–19. See also Lisa McGirr, *Suburban Warriors: The Origins of the New American Right* (Princeton, N.J.: Princeton University Press, 2002), 13, 95, 135–136.

71. Michelle Nickerson, "Moral Mothers and Goldwater Girls," in Farber and Roche, *Conservative Sixties*, 61.

72. Perlstein, *Before the Storm*, 478.

73. McGirr writes, "Orange County conservatives were, for example, avid readers of magazines like *National Review* and *Human Events*." See McGirr, *Suburban Warriors*, 95.

74. For an example of a different approach to exploring conservatism, one that emphasizes ordinary individuals, see David Farber and Jeff Roche, "Introduction," in Farber and Roche, *Conservative Sixties*, 4.

75. Other prominent conservatives testify to the broader importance of these texts. For instance, David Keene, president of both the ACU and the NRA, told a group of Citadel students in 2012 that his "conversion" to conservatism began when he read Hayek and "devoured" issues of *National Review* "like thousands of other young conservatives." David Keene, "William F. Buckley, Jr., Fusionism, and the Three-Legged Stool of Conservatism," lecture at The Citadel sponsored by the Intercollegiate Studies Institute, March 7, 2012, video available via http://www.isi.org/lectures/lectures.aspx?SBy=search&SSub=title&SFor=fusion.

76. Purely in terms of method, arguing for the existence of a canon and then tracking the influence of that canon on a specific political community is, on a smaller scale, like assessing the influence of a historic author, say Shakespeare, on modern literary culture. To begin, the critic must amass considerable and wide-ranging instances of the community celebrating specific texts. Generally, the critic must account for various uses of canonical language in the service of numerous goals: direct invocations of tracts in the corpus, appropriations of the Bard's language without explicit attribution to *King Lear* or *Hamlet*, subtle similarities in sentence-level formulations between modern books and *Macbeth*, familiar narrative arcs between recent novels and *Romeo and Juliet*, and simple praise for a literary idol. Then, the critic must integrate and explain the testimonials of readers inspired by different plays for different reasons, or, even better, the same play for different reasons. Finally, the critic should identify patterns in the relationship between the community and these texts.

In order to organize a survey of more than four decades of conservative discourse about their founding texts, I systematically collected, indexed, and analyzed three kinds of conservative texts since 1964: books by conservative authors, speeches and lectures by conservatives, and magazine and journal articles written by or for conservative audiences. Where possible, I included other forms of evidence, including newspaper editorials and conservative talk radio and/or television programs. In addition to recording and analyzing how conservatives discuss canonical authors and their benchmark texts, I have followed the term "conservative" in relation to these canonical books because my interest lies in charting how conservatives have created and given meaning to conservatism, not in imposing a particular conception of conservatism on self-identified conservatives.

77. Allitt, *Conservatives*, 188.

78. Mattson, *Rebels All!* 134–135.

79. Richard Viguerie and David Franke, *America's Right Turn: How Conservatives Used New and Alternative Media to Take Power* (Chicago: Bonus Books, 2004), 54. M. Stanton Evans captured the conservative ambivalence about Rand perfectly in the *National Review*. Rand's sense of the inner-workings of capitalism, efficient markets, and the importance of private property was "excellent." She rebuked, however, "the Christian culture which has given birth to all our freedoms." Cited in Jonathan Chait, "Ayn Rand and the Invincible Cult of Selfishness on the American Right," *New Republic*, September 14, 2009. To be clear, some prominent conservatives, even those like Viguerie who consider her work a bridge too far, still consider Rand part of their heritage. See Viguerie, *Conservatives Betrayed*, 230. Rand has also influenced more libertarian-minded Republican politicians. See Ryan Lizza, "Fussbudget: How Paul Ryan Captured the G.O.P.," *New Yorker*, August 6, 2012.

80. Rand's books are seldom mentioned in conservatives' frequently published encomiums to their founding texts. Moreover, short courses and leadership programs, like the New Centurion Program, that teach conservatism to students consistently cover Buckley, Kirk, Goldwater, Hayek, and Chambers without mentioning Rand. The New Centurion's curriculum is available via http://newcenturionprogram.org/.

81. Whittaker Chambers, "Big Sister Is Watching You," *National Review*, December 28, 1957, 595. Buckley's biographer, John Judis, explains the incident and its aftermath: "Rand and her followers were stung by Chambers's attack. Rand's young disciple, economist Alan Greenspan, who later became President Gerald Ford's chief economist [and later chair of the Federal Reserve], wrote Buckley, 'This man is beneath contempt and I would not honor his "review" of Ayn Rand's magnificent masterpiece by even commenting on it.'" Rand herself complained aloud, "What would you expect from an ex-Communist writing in Buckley's Catholic magazine?" She never talked to Buckley again and refused to enter any room in which he was present. See Judis, *William F. Buckley*, 161. When a student told Rand in 1965 that he could understand why Buckley was an attractive mayoral candidate, Rand responded, "If you never want to speak to me again, go ahead and consider voting for him." Quoted in Doherty, *Radicals for Capitalism*, 238. See also Jennifer Burns, *Goddess of the Market: Ayn Rand and the American Right* (New York: Oxford University Press, 2009), 279; Anne Heller, *Ayn Rand and the World She Made* (New York: Doubleday, 2009), 285.

82. William F. Buckley, Jr., "Did You Ever See a Dream Walking," in *Keeping the Tablets*, ed. William F. Buckley, Jr., and Charles R. Kesler (New York: Harper & Row, 1988), 22.

83. Burns, *Goddess of the Market*, 4. See also Nash, *Conservative Intellectual Movement in America*, 144–145.

Chapter One. The Conservative Canon and Its Uses

1. Patrick J. Buchanan, "Introduction: The Voice in the Desert," in Barry Goldwater, *The Conscience of a Conservative*, 30th anniv. ed. (Washington, D.C.: Regnery Gateway, 1990), vii–xxv.

2. William F. Buckley, Jr., *Flying High: Remembering Barry Goldwater* (New York: Basic Books, 2008), 24.

3. Milton Friedman, "Introduction," in Friedrich A. Hayek, *The Road to Serfdom*, 50th anniv. ed. (Chicago: University of Chicago Press, 1994), ix.

4. Paul Kengor, "The Intellectual Origins of Ronald Reagan's Faith," *Heritage Foundation Lectures*, April 30, 2004; Lee Edwards, "Whittaker Chambers: Man of Courage, Man of Faith," *Heritage Foundation Lectures*, April 2, 2001. Anthony Dolan, the Reagan aide who wrote the "evil empire" speech, was also a *Witness* devotee. See John Patrick Diggins, *Ronald Reagan: Fate, Freedom, and the Making of History* (New York: W. W. Norton, 2007), 8. See also Martin J. Medhurst, "Writing Speeches for Ronald Reagan: An Interview with Tony Dolan," *Rhetoric & Public Affairs* 1 (1998): 245–256.

5. Sam Tanenhaus, "The End of the Journey: From Whittaker Chambers to George W. Bush," *New Republic*, July 2, 2007, 46.

6. Jeffrey Hart, *The Making of the American Conservative Mind: National Review and Its Times* (Wilmington, Del.: ISI Books, 2007), 18–19.

7. George Nash, *The Conservative Intellectual Movement in America since 1945* (New York: Basic Books, 1976), 139–140. See also Michael Uhlmann, "The Right Stuff," *Claremont Review of Books*, July 5, 2005.

8. Rich Lowry, "I Was a Teenage Conservative," in *Why I Turned Right: Leading Baby Boom Conservatives Chronicle Their Political Journeys*, ed. Mary Eberstadt (New York: Threshold Editions, 2007), 280.

9. See also Kathleen Hall Jamieson and Joseph Capella, *Echo Chamber: Rush Limbaugh and the Conservative Media Establishment* (New York: Oxford University Press, 2008), 57.

10. John Micklethwait and Adrian Wooldridge, *The Right Nation: Conservative Power in America* (New York: Penguin Books, 2004), 19. See also William F. Buckley, Jr., "Introduction," in *Did You Ever See a Dream Walking? American Conservative Thought in the Twentieth Century*, ed. William F. Buckley, Jr. (Indianapolis: Bobbs-Merrill, 1970), xvii; Frank S. Meyer, ed., *What Is Conservatism?* (New York: Holt, Rinehart, & Winston, 1964), 4.

11. Gregory L. Schneider, *The Conservative Century: From Reaction to Revolution* (New York: Rowman & Littlefield, 2009). See also Paul Gottfried, *Conservatism in America: Making Sense of the American Right* (New York: Palgrave Macmillan, 2007), xi.

12. Jan Gorak, *The Making of the Modern Canon: Genesis and Crisis of a Literary Idea* (London: Athlone, 1991), ix.

13. Conservatism's constitutive phrases were circulated through a dedicated print culture receiving and debating ideas from *National Review* but also through a lecture circuit dedicated to advancing canonical ideas. For example, one such lecture series, recounted in *National Review* in 1975, featured Friedrich Hayek, Eric Voegelin, and others. See M. J. Sobran Jr., "Hayek and the Angels," *National Review*, May 9, 1975, 506. *National Review* also covered regularly held conferences, like those held by the Mont Pelerin Society, that celebrated the work of conservative heroes. For example, one Mont Pelerin Society meeting in 1985 began with a symposium titled "*The Road to Serfdom*: Forty Years Later" before moving forward to 1980s-era inflation. See John Chamberlain, "Hayek Returns to Cambridge," *National Review*, January 11, 1985, 38.

14. American Enterprise Institute and National Review Institute, "On the Ropes: What William F. Buckley Jr. Can Teach Today's Conservatives," March 3, 2009, video available via http://app2.capitalreach.com/esp1204/servlet/tc?cn=aei&c =10162&s=20271&e=10720&&espmt=2. The Conservative Political Action Conference regularly features panels with titles like "God and Man at CPAC: The Enduring Legacy of William F. Buckley Jr." See the 2012 conference schedule at http://www.washingtonpost.com/r/2010–2019/WashingtonPost/2012/02/09/ National-Politics/Graphics/cpac.pdf; watch the full 2009 panel on *God and Man at Yale* at http://www.isi.org/lectures/lectures.aspx?SBy=search&SSub=title&SF or=god%20and%20man%20at%20cpac.

15. Charles Kesler, speech at "On the Ropes: What William F. Buckley Jr. Can Teach Today's Conservatives," hosted by the American Enterprise Institute and the National Review Institute, March 3, 2009, video available via http://app2. capitalreach.com/esp1204/servlet/tc?cn=aei&c=10162&s=20271&e=10720& &espmt=2.

16. Buckley, *Did You Ever See a Dream Walking?*; William F. Buckley, Jr., and Charles R. Kesler, eds., *Keeping the Tablets* (New York: Harper & Row, 1988); Chilton Williamson, *The Conservative Bookshelf: Essential Works That Impact Today's Conservative Thinkers* (New York: Citadel Press, 2005); Edwin J. Feulner, ed. *The March of Freedom: Modern Classics in Conservative Thought* (Dallas: Spence, 2004).

17. See David Frum, *Comeback: Conservatism That Can Win Again* (New York: Doubleday, 2008), 177; David Frum, *Dead Right* (New York: Basic Books, 1994), 1, 4–5.

18. John Stossel, "Hurtling Down the Road to Serfdom," *Townhall*, February 10, 2010; Edward John Craig, "Speeding Down the Road to Serfdom," *National Review Online*, December 18, 2010; Roger Kimball, "Traveling Down the Road to Serfdom," *Pajamas Media*, March 7, 2009. See also Edwin J. Feulner and Doug Wilson, *Getting America Right: The True Conservative Values Our Nation Needs Today* (New York: Crown Forum, 2006), 27.

19. Robert Stacy McCain, "God and Man at Columbia," *American Spectator*, December 13, 2010; Daniel McCarthy, "GOP and Man at Yale," *American Conservative*, November 6, 2006; Ernest W. Lefever, "God, Man, and Green

at Yale," *Weekly Standard*, July 25, 2007; Joe Carter, "God and Man in the Conservative Movement," *First Things*, August 25, 2010.

20. James Roberts, *The Conservative Decade: Emerging Leaders of the 1980s* (Westport, Conn.: Arlington House, 1980), 27, 29.

21. Alfred S. Regnery, *Upstream: The Ascendance of American Conservatism* (New York: Threshold Editions, 2008), 53. From the nationally recognized to the scholarly to the niche, several publishers invested in postwar conservative books, especially Regnery Publishing, founded by Alfred's Regnery's father, Henry. See Henry Regnery, *Perfect Sowing: Reflections of a Bookman* (Wilmington, Del.: ISI Books, 1999).

22. John J. Miller, "The Ghosts of Kirk," *National Review*, January 23, 2003; Kathryn Jean Lopez, "Michelle Bachmann and WFB," *National Review*, March 25, 2011; David Franke, *Quotations from Chairman Bill* (New Rochelle, N.Y.: Arlington House, 1970).

23. Mori Dinauer, "American Exceptionalism Is How Conservatives Immanentize the Eschaton," *American Prospect*, March 1, 2010; William Kristol, "The Indispensable Man," *New York Times*, March 3, 2008; William F. Buckley, *Cancel Your Own Goddam Subscription: Notes & Asides from* National Review (New York: Basic Books, 2007), 21–24; Jonah Goldberg, "Immanent Corrections: Getting Gays Straight and Other Odd Things," *National Review*, January 16, 2002.

24. Jonah Goldberg, "Goldberg's Conservative Canon," *National Review*, February 9, 2001.

25. Ann Coulter, "Snuggle Up with Ann Coulter's Top 10 Favorite Books," *Human Events*, November 11, 2005.

26. "The 100 Best Non-Fiction Books of the Century," *National Review*, available via http://old.nationalreview.com/100best/100_books.html; M. C. Henrie, W. J. C. Myers, et al., "The Fifty Worst (and Best) Books of the Century," *Intercollegiate Review* (Fall 1999).

27. "Top 10 Books Liberals Want to Burn," *Human Events*, May 23, 2006; "Top 10 Books Every Republican Congressman Should Read," *Human Events*, November 21, 2006.

28. John Guillory, "Canonical and Noncanonical," in *Debating the Canon: A Reader from Addison to Nafisi*, ed. Lee Morrissey (New York: Palgrave Macmillan, 2005), 209.

29. Lisa McGirr, "Piety and Property: Conservatism and Right-Wing Movements in the Twentieth Century," in *Perspectives on Modern America: Making Sense of the Twentieth Century*, ed. Harvard Sitkoff (New York: Oxford University Press, 2000), 38. See also Donald T. Critchlow, "Rethinking American Conservatism: Toward a New Narrative," *Journal of American History* 98 (2011): 753–754.

30. Martin Medhurst, "Resistance, Conservatism, and Theory Building: A Cautionary Note," *Western Journal of Communication* 49 (1985): 107. As Jerome Himmelstein argues, "American conservatism had certainly existed before

the 1950s, but during that decade conservatives substantially transformed themselves. They reconstructed their ideology, discarding some themes, adding new themes, and modifying still others. . . . They even for the first time agreed on *conservative* as the name for their new ideology and their fledgling movement—a symbolic expression of a new political beginning." Jerome Himmelstein, *To the Right: The Transformation of American Conservatism* (Berkeley: University of California Press, 1990), 13.

31. For more on rhetorical traditions as inventional resources, see John Murphy, "Inventing Authority: Bill Clinton, Martin Luther King, and the Orchestration of Rhetorical Traditions," *Quarterly Journal of Speech* 83 (1997): 74.

32. Lisa McGirr, "Now That Historians Know So Much about the Right, How Should We Best Approach the Study of Conservatism?" *Journal of American History* 98 (2011): 770.

33. See Allitt, *Conservatives*, 109–111.

34. Jonathan M. Schoenwald, *A Time for Choosing: The Rise of Modern American Conservatism* (Oxford: Oxford University Press, 2001), 21.

35. Frank Meyer, "Richard M. Weaver: An Appreciation," *Modern Age* 14 (1970): 243.

36. Richard Viguerie and David Franke, *America's Right Turn: How Conservatives Used New and Alternative Media to Take Power* (Chicago: Bonus Books, 2004), 265.

37. Nash, *Conservative Intellectual Movement in America*, 11, 18. See also Brian Doherty, *Radicals for Capitalism: A Freewheeling History of the Modern American Libertarian Movement* (New York: Public Affairs, 2007), 157; Frank Chodorov, *Out of Step: The Autobiography of an Individualist* (New York: Devin-Adair, 1962), 252; Frank Chodorov, "A Fifty-Year Project to Combat Socialism on the Campus," *analysis* 6 (1950): 1–2.

38. Jason DeParle, "Passing Down the Legacy of Conservatism," *New York Times*, July 31, 2006, 13.

39. Ibid.

40. ISI has organized conferences and lectures series on Buckley, Chambers, Friedman, Hayek, Kirk, Nisbet, and Weaver. For a list of such programs, see ISI's online records. ISI sponsored an "annual fellowship retreat" to Piety Hill, Russell Kirk's Michigan home. See Lee Edwards, *Educating for Liberty: The First Half-Century of the Intercollegiate Studies Institute* (Washington, D.C.: Regnery, 2003), 304. The Heritage Foundation regularly convened encomiums to conservatism's Great Books. For example, see Richard M. Reinsch II, "Still Witnessing: The Enduring Relevance of Whittaker Chambers," Heritage Foundation's *First Principles Series Report*, 38, April 1, 2011.

41. "Order and Liberty in the American Tradition at Oxford University," July 28–August 10, 2005, ISI Honors Fellowship Program, Oxford, description available via http://www.isi.org/programs/conferences/2004–2005_conference.html.

42. Young America's Foundation, "Recommended Reading," n.d., available via http://www.yaf.org/InnerPageTemplate.aspx?id=84&terms=reading.

43. Lee Edwards, "Great Books to Read in College," panel at the National Conservative Student Conference, August 7, 2009, video available via http://www.yaf.org/videogallery.aspx?id=189.

44. Alex Beam, *A Great Idea at the Time: The Rise, Fall, and Curious Afterlife of the Great Books* (New York: Public Affairs, 2009), 1.

45. Ibid., 20–21.

46. Lee Morrissey, "The Canon Brawl: Arguments over the Canon," in *Debating the Canon: A Reader from Addison to Nafisi*, ed. Lee Morrissey (New York: Palgrave Macmillan, 2005), 3; Mortimer J. Adler and Charles Van Doren, *How to Read a Book*, rev. ed. (New York: Touchstone, 1972), 343.

47. Harold Bloom, *How to Read and Why* (New York: Scribner, 2001), 142. See also Harold Bloom, *The Western Canon: The Books and School of the Ages* (New York: Riverhead Trade, 1995), 27.

48. Ted Striphas, *The Late Age of Print: Everyday Book Culture from Consumerism to Control* (New York: Columbia University Press, 2009), 17.

49. Dinesh D'Souza, *Letters to a Young Conservative* (New York: Basic Books, 2002), 225.

50. Ibid.

51. Edwards, "Introduction," 2.

52. Wells Tower, "The Kids Are Far Right: Hippie Hunting, Bunny Bashing, and the New Conservatism," *Harper's*, November 2006, 43.

53. Quoted in DeParle, "Passing Down."

54. Stanley Fish, "Yet Once More," in *Reception Study: From Literary Theory to Cultural Studies*, ed. James L. Machor and Philip Goldstein (New York: Routledge, 2001), 37.

55. F. Clifton White and William J. Gill, *Suite 3505: The Story of the Draft Goldwater Movement* (Ashland, Ohio: Ashbrook Press, 1992); Nicole Hoplin and Ron Robinson, *Funding Fathers: The Unsung Heroes of the Conservative Movement* (Washington, D.C.: Regnery, 2008).

56. See William A. Rusher, *The Rise of the Right* (New York: William Morrow, 1984), 33; Lee Edwards, *The Conservative Revolution: The Movement That Remade America* (New York: Free Press, 1999), 293; Lee Edwards, *The Power of Ideas: The Heritage Foundation at 25 Years* (Ottawa, Ill.: Jameson Books, 1997), 225; F. Clifton White and William J. Gill, *Why Reagan Won: A Narrative History of the Conservative Movement 1964–1981* (Chicago: Regnery Gateway, 1981), 34–35; Roberts, *Conservative Decade*, 20; Viguerie and Franke, *America's Right Turn*, 55.

57. Bruce Frohnen, Jeremy Beer, and Jeffrey O. Nelson, "Editors' Introduction," in *American Conservatism: An Encyclopedia*, ed. Bruce Frohnen, Jeremy Beer, and Jeffrey O. Nelson (Wilmington, Del.: ISI Books, 2006), ix. ISI's online journal,

First Principles, posited that the canon built the conservative coalition. Its "short course" on "conservative thought" included three recommended reading lists featuring the canonical texts and secondary literature about postwar authors. See "Conservative Thought," *First Principles: ISI Web Journal*, March 10, 2008.

58. Regnery, *Upstream*, 73. Other conservative arguments about particular canonical texts took a similar form. As Lee Edwards, once a secretary in Young Americans for Freedom, argued, "The '60s began not with a bang but with a book, *The Conscience of a Conservative*." Cited in Andrew, *Other Side of the Sixties*, 17.

59. Viguerie and Franke, *America's Right Turn*, 262–263.

60. Mircea Eliade, *Myth and Reality* (New York: Harper Colophon Books, 1975), 5.

61. Ibid., 6.

62. Ibid., 18.

63. Regnery, *Upstream*, xiv.

64. Viguerie and Franke, *America's Right Turn*, 52.

65. Rusher, *Rise of the Right*, 13.

66. Regnery, *Upstream*, xiv.

67. Jeffrey O. Nelson, *Ten Books That Shaped America's Conservative Renaissance*, Intercollegiate Studies Institute, n.d., available via http://www.isi.org/conservative_tho/PDF/tenbooks.pdf, 7.

68. Edwards, *Educating for Liberty*, 30.

69. Ibid., 29–30.

70. Regnery, *Upstream*, xiv.

71. Edwards, *Educating for Liberty*, 30.

72. John Engler, "First Principles in the Public Arena," lecture at the Heritage Foundation, September 26, 1995, available via http://www.heritage.org/research/lecture/first-principles-in-the-public-arena.

73. Cited in Edwards, *Conservative Revolution*, 82.

74. Ralph de Toledano, "I Witness," *American Conservative Magazine*, February 14, 2005; Hart, *Making of the American Conservative Mind*, 48.

75. Patrick Buchanan, *Right from the Beginning* (Boston: Little Brown, 1988), 218.

76. To one of Buckley's eulogists, a "chance encounter" with *National Review* "caused the scales to fall" from his eyes. Jack Dunphy, "That Buckley Guy Was Right," *National Review*, March 4, 2008. Similarly, Peggy Noonan, Reagan's speechwriter, recalled her reaction when she first read *National Review* as a young liberal: "It sang to me," she said, "I was moved, and more." In Smant, *Principles and Heresies*, 346.

77. Ronald Reagan, *Speaking My Mind: Selected Speeches* (New York: Simon & Schuster, 1989), 95.

78. Ronald Reagan, "Remarks to the Conservative Political Action Conference Dinner," March 20, 1981, available via http://www.presidency.ucsb.edu/ws/index.php?pid=43580&st=conservative&st1=.

79. Ibid.

80. Rusher, *Rise of the Right*, 48.

81. Ibid., 21–22.

82. Ibid., 25.

83. Ibid., 28.

84. Ibid., 31.

85. Ibid.

86. George Nash's account is most influential. See Nash, *Making of the Conservative Intellectual Movement*, 1–117. See also Edwards, *Conservatism Revolution*, 16–17; Regnery, *Upstream*, 20–86.

87. Many writers, including a few conservatives, have disputed some conservatives' claims to a consistent philosophy. See Ryan Sager, *The Elephant in the Room: Evangelicals, Libertarians, and the Battle to Control the Republican Party* (Hoboken, N.J.: John Wiley & Sons, 2006), 20; Michael Lind, *Up from Conservatism: Why the Right Is Wrong for America* (New York: Free Press Paperbacks, 1997), 54–55. For a history of arguments against fusionist conservatism, see Niels Bjerre-Poulsen, *Right Face: Organizing the American Conservative Movement 1945–1965* (Copenhagen: Museum Tusculanum Press, 2002), 39–54.

88. Reagan, *Speaking My Mind*, 95.

89. McCarthy, "GOP and Man at Yale," 7.

90. Richard Bishirjian, "Reinventing Conservatism: Read All About It—Or Lose It," *Washington Times*, October 7, 2009, 4.

91. Canonical sources were, of course, not the only respected voices on conservative philosophy. The difference between Mickey Edwards's *Reclaiming Conservatism* and Andrew Sullivan's *The Conservative Soul* is illustrative. Both considered conservatism a lost political movement during the 2000s, yet the former cited nearly every canonical writer, in many cases at length, in defense of an ideal conservatism whereas the latter cited different source material, mostly European writers like Edmund Burke and Michael Oakeshott. The operative distinction here is between "movement conservatives" invested in canonical texts, conservative organizations, and, largely, Republican politics, and conservatives in the broadest international sense of the term. See Mickey Edwards, *Reclaiming Conservatism: How a Great American Political Movement Got Lost—and How It Can Find Its Way Back* (New York: Oxford University Press, 2008); Andrew Sullivan, *The Conservative Soul: Fundamentalism, Freedom, and the Future of the Right* (New York: Harper Perennial, 2007).

92. Murphy, "'Time of Shame and Sorrow,'" 403. See also John M. Jones and Robert C. Rowland, "A Covenant-Affirming Jeremiad: The Post-presidential Ideological

Appeals of Ronald Wilson Reagan," *Communication Studies* 56 (2005): 157–174; Sacvan Bercovitch, *The American Jeremiad* (Madison: University of Wisconsin Press, 1978).

93. John Derbyshire, "How Radio Wrecks the Right," *American Conservative*, February 23, 2009; John Batchelor, "Rahm's Historic Stupidity," *Daily Beast*, September 23, 2009; Christopher Buckley, "My Brush with Rush," *Daily Beast*, October 27, 2008.

94. Nash, *Conservative Intellectual Movement in America*, 145.

95. George A. Panichas, "Restoring the Meaning of Conservatism," *Modern Age* 47 (2005): 195.

96. Ibid., 197.

97. George A. Panichas, "Restoring the Meaning of Conservatism (Part Two)," *Modern Age* 48 (2006): 4.

98. Ibid., 4–5.

99. Panichas, "Restoring," 196.

100. Ibid., 198.

101. Edwards, *Reclaiming Conservatism*; Victor Gold, *Invasion of the Party Snatchers: How the Holy-Rollers and Neo-Cons Destroyed the GOP* (Naperville, Ill.: Sourcebooks, 2007); Bruce Bartlett, *Impostor: How George W. Bush Bankrupted America and Betrayed the Reagan Legacy* (New York: Doubleday, 2006); Viguerie, *Conservatives Betrayed*; Philip Gold, *Take Back the Right: How the Neocons and the Religious Right Have Hijacked the Conservative Movement* (New York: Basic Books, 2004).

102. Michael Tanner, *Leviathan on the Right: How Big-Government Conservatism Brought Down the Republican Revolution* (Washington, D.C.: Cato Institute, 2007), vii.

103. Ibid., 217.

104. Ibid., 8–9.

105. Ibid., 23.

106. Murphy, "'Time of Shame and Sorrow,'" 411.

107. Bercovitch, *American Jeremiad*, 180.

108. Nash, *Conservative Intellectual Movement in America*, 141.

109. Robert Nisbet, *Conservatism: Dream and Reality* (New Brunswick, N.J.: Transaction, 2008), 42. Other figures associated with this eighteenth- and nineteenth-century tradition of English conservatism are Walter Bagehot, Benjamin Disraeli, and G. K. Chesterton.

110. Nash, *Conservative Intellectual Movement in America*, 173. *The Conscience of a Conservative, The Road to Serfdom,* and *Capitalism and Freedom* are exceptions. Richard Weaver, *The Ethics of Rhetoric* (Chicago: Henry Regnery, 1953), 76–77.

111. Kirk, *Conservative Mind*, 4. Kirk interpreted Burke as indicting the French Revolution was based on timeless, transhistorical principles as opposed to pragmatic ones. Hart notes, "Kirk's Burke was not the historian's Burke, or the biographer's, or the Burke of the political theorists. . . . Kirk's Burke was a bit of an antiquarian, a lover of 'old things,' and more mysterious than he actually was." Hart, *Making of the American Conservative Mind*, 355.

112. Bloom, *Western Canon*, 39.

113. Hart, *Making of the American Conservative Mind*, 369.

Chapter Two. The Traditionalist Dialect

1. William L. O'Neill, *Max Eastman: The Last Romantic* (Oxford: Oxford University Press, 1991), 45, 244.

2. Max Eastman, "Am I Conservative?" *National Review*, January 28, 1964, 57.

3. Ibid., 58.

4. Ibid.

5. George Nash, *The Conservative Intellectual Movement in America since 1945* (New York: Basic Books, 1976), 70–71. Erik von Kuehnelt-Leddihn, Thomas Molnar, Francis Wilson, Frederick Wilhelmsen, and William F. Buckley Jr. were Catholics, and Russell Kirk was becoming a Catholic by the time he wrote *The Conservative Mind*. See also Patrick Allitt, *Catholic Intellectuals and Conservative Politics in America: 1950–1985* (Ithaca, N.Y.: Cornell University Press, 1995).

6. Whittaker Chambers, *Witness* (New York: Random House, 1952), 191.

7. Eastman had even written a fairly charitable favorable review of Buckley's first book, although he found it "ridiculous" to see "little, two-legged fanatics running around the earth fighting and arguing on behalf of a deity they profess to be omnipotent." Quoted in John Judis, *William F. Buckley Jr.: Patron Saint of the Conservatives* (New York: Simon & Schuster, 1988), 92.

8. Eastman, "Am I Conservative?" 58. William F. Buckley, Jr., "Did You Ever See a Dream Walking?" in *Keeping the Tablets*, ed. William F. Buckley, Jr., and Charles R. Kesler (New York: Harper & Row, 1988), 29.

9. Buckley, "Did You Ever See a Dream Walking?" 29. See also John Patrick Diggins, *Up from Communism: Conservative Odysseys in American Intellectual History* (New York: Harper & Row, 1975), 346. Diggins notes, "In the light of his intense animus against religion, it is surprising that Eastman stayed with the *National Review* as long as he did." Eastman wrote for the *National Review* for nearly ten years.

10. Diggins, *Up from Communism*, 350.

11. Jeffrey Hart, *The Making of the American Conservative Mind: National Review and Its Times* (Wilmington, Del.: ISI Books, 2007), 116–117.

12. Even in the Eastman case, Buckley did not think that he was removing Eastman from conservatism. See Buckley, "Did You Ever See a Dream Walking?" 28.

13. Cited in Hart, *Making of the American Conservative Mind*, 117.

14. Buckley, "Did You Ever See a Dream Walking?" 31.

15. Robert C. Rowland and John M. Jones, "Entelechial and Reformative Symbolic Trajectories in Contemporary Conservatism: A Case Study of Reagan and Buchanan in Houston and Beyond," *Rhetoric & Public Affairs* 4 (2001): 55–84

16. Richard Weaver, *The Ethics of Rhetoric* (Chicago: Henry Regnery, 1953), 212–214, 222.

17. Isaiah Berlin, *The Hedgehog and the Fox: An Essay on Tolstoy's View of History* (New York: Simon & Schuster, 1986), 1.

18. Ibid.

19. Austin Bramwell, "Defining Conservatism Down," *American Conservative*, August 29, 2005.

20. Chilton Williamson Jr., *The Conservative Bookshelf: Essential Works That Impact Today's Conservative Thinkers* (New York: Citadel Press, 2004), 4.

21. Nash, *Conservative Intellectual Movement in America*, 73.

22. Russell Kirk, "Libertarians: The Chirping Sectaries," *Modern Age* 25 (1981): 349.

23. Nash, *Conservative Intellectual Movement in America*, 180.

24. Edwin J. Feulner, "Introduction," in *The March of Freedom: Modern Classics in Conservative Thought*, ed. Edwin J. Feulner (Dallas: Spence), ix.

25. Robert Nisbet, *The Quest for Community* (New York: Oxford University Press, 1970), 25.

26. Ibid.

27. Quoted in Williamson, *Conservative Bookshelf*, 3.

28. John Micklethwait and Adrian Wooldridge, *The Right Nation: Conservative Power in America* (New York: Penguin Press, 2004), 47.

29. Berlin, *Hedgehog and the Fox*, 63.

30. See G. K. Chesterton, *The Collected Works of G .K. Chesterton* (San Francisco: Ignatius Press, 2005), 12:356.

31. Nisbet, *Quest for Community*, 32.

32. Ibid., 32, 33.

33. Quoted in Russell Kirk, *Enemies of the Permanent Things*, rev. ed. (Peru, Ill.: Sherwood, Sugden, 1988), 57.

34. Berlin, *Hedgehog and the Fox*, 63.

35. With few exceptions, the traditionalists continued what Albert Hirschman identified as three consistent tropes of reactionary rhetoric. The "perversity thesis" held that collective action makes social problems worse. The "futility

thesis" argued that collective action fails. The "jeopardy thesis" posited that political reforms come at the cost of previous gains. See Albert O. Hirschman, *The Rhetoric of Reaction: Perversity, Futility, Jeopardy* (Cambridge, Mass.: Harvard University Press, 1991), 7.

36. See Max Horkheimer, *The Eclipse of Reason* (New York: Continuum, 2004).

37. See Arthur Herman, *The Idea of Decline in Western History* (New York: Free Press, 1997).

38. Berlin, *Hedgehog and the Fox*, 58.

39. Russell Kirk, *The Conservative Mind: From Burke to Eliot*, 6th rev. ed. (South Bend, Ind.: Gateway Editions, 1978).

40. See Bramwell, "Defining Conservatism Down."

41. Leo Strauss, *Natural Right and History* (Chicago: University of Chicago Press, 1953).

42. Richard Weaver, *Ideas Have Consequences* (Chicago: University of Chicago Press, 1984), 3.

43. Eric Voegelin, *The New Science of Politics* (Chicago: University of Chicago Press, 1952), 126. For other examples of assertions of historical division points, see Paul Boyer, "The Evangelical Resurgence in 1970s American Protestantism," in *Rightward Bound: Making America Conservative in the 1970s*, ed. Bruce J. Schulman and Julian E. Zelizer (Cambridge, Mass.: Harvard University Press, 2008), 36.

44. Arthur M. Schlesinger Jr., *The Politics of Hope and the Bitter Heritage: American Liberalism in the 1960s* (Princeton, N.J.: Princeton University Press, 2008), 104, 95–96.

45. In Harold Holzer, *Lincoln at Cooper Union: The Speech That Made Abraham Lincoln President* (New York: Simon & Schuster, 2004), 269.

46. Bruce Frohnen, Jeremy Beer and Jeffery O. Nelson, eds., *American Conservatism: An Encyclopedia* (Wilmington, Del.: ISI Books, 2006), 872.

47. Nisbet, *Quest for Community*, vii, 30.

48. Ibid., 28–29.

49. Nisbet, it is only fair to note, disagreed. If it were possible, he wrote in a new preface to *The Quest for Community* in 1970, he would "preclude any possible supposition on the reader's part that there is in this book any lament for the old, any nostalgia for village, parish, or other type of now largely erased form of social community of the past. . . . It is not the revival of old communities that the book in a sense pleads for; *it is the establishment of new forms*: forms which are relevant to contemporary life and thought." Nisbet, *Quest for Community*, viii. See also John East, *The American Conservative Movement: Its Philosophical Founders* (Chicago: Regnery, 1986), 205.

50. Berlin, *Hedgehog and the Fox*, 73.

51. Weaver concluded that the South was *"the last non-materialist civilization in the Western world."* Quoted in Nash, *Conservative Intellectual Movement in America*, 32. Kirk wrote similarly of the South: "Despite its faults of head and heart, the South—alone among the civilized communities of the nineteenth century—had hardihood sufficient for an appeal to arms against the iron new order which, a vague instinct whispered to Southerners, was inimical to the sort of humanity they knew." Kirk, *Conservative Mind*, 160. See also Richard Weaver, *Visions of Order: The Cultural Crisis of Our Time* (Baton Rouge: Louisiana State University Press, 1964); Russell Kirk, *John Randolph of Roanoke: A Study in American Politics* (Indianapolis: Liberty Fund, 1997). For more on the importance of the South in Kirk's and Weaver's political theory, see Hart, *Making of the Conservative Mind*, 53; East, *American Conservative Movement*, 41.

52. Jonah Goldberg, "Immanent Corrections: Getting Gays Straight and Other Odd Things," *National Review*, January 16, 2002.

53. Kevin J. Smant, *Principles and Heresies: Frank S. Meyer and the Shaping of the American Conservative Movement* (Wilmington, Del.: ISI Books, 2002), 334; William F. Buckley, Jr., *Cancel Your Own Goddam Subscription: Notes & Asides from* National Review (New York: Basic Books, 2007), 21–24.

54. Goldberg, "Immanent Corrections." "Immanentizing the eschaton" has a long history in the pages of *National Review*. For examples, see John Miller, "The Good 'Dr.,'" *National Review*, November 21, 2003; Kevin M. Cherry, "It's a Very Un-Merry, Un-Muppet Christmas Movie," *National Review*, November 27, 2002; Jonah Goldberg, "We Can See Clearly Now," *National Review*, January 2, 2002.

55. William F. Buckley, Jr., *The Unmaking of a Mayor* (New York: Viking Press, 1966), 316. Buckley's biographer, John Judis, notes that Buckley was fond of repeating the phrase in other venues. See Judis, *William F. Buckley, Jr.*, 316.

56. Goldberg, "Immanent Corrections."

57. Paul Gottfried, *The Conservative Movement*, rev. ed. (New York: Twayne, 1993), 20. Buckley was so taken by Voegelin's intellect that he invited him to write a monthly column for *National Review*. Voegelin refused but occasionally published his work in other conservative organs like *Modern Age* and *Intercollegiate Review*. Voegelin also refused any official connection with political conservatism in America, even though his writings were popular among conservatives. See James L. Wiser, "Eric Voegelin and American Conservatism," in *The Dilemmas of American Conservatism*, ed. Kenneth L. Deutsch and Ethan Fishman (Lexington: University Press of Kentucky, 2010), 29, 40.

58. Mark Lilla, "Mr. Casaubon in America," *New York Review of Books*, June 28, 2007, 29.

59. Nash, *Conservative Intellectual Movement in America*, 51–52.

60. Ibid., 54.

61. Voegelin, *New Science of Politics*, 121.

62. Wiser, "Eric Voegelin," 32.

63. Voegelin was a prolific writer but, like Whittaker Chambers, not because he amassed publications. The historian Mark Lilla describes his eclectic hedgehog writings this way: "He brings to mind George Eliot's Mr. Casaubon, the obsessive polymath whose search for the 'keys to all mythologies' left him only torsos of unfinished works." Lilla, "Mr. Casaubon," 29.

64. Karen L. King, *What Is Gnosticism?* (Cambridge, Mass.: Harvard University Press, 2003), 1.

65. Lilla, "Mr. Casaubon," 30.

66. Elaine Pagels, *Beyond Belief: The Secret Gospel of Thomas* (New York: Random House, 2005), 25.

67. Ibid., 33. Gnosticism is hard to define because the term was never adopted by an ancient religious movement. As King explains, "There was and is no such thing as Gnosticism, if we mean by that some kind of ancient religious entity with a single origin and a distinct set of characteristics. Gnosticism is, rather, a term invented in the early modern period to aid in defining the boundaries of normative Christianity." See King, *What Is Gnosticism?* 2.

68. Elaine Pagels and Karen L. King, *Reading Judas: The Gospel of Judas and the Shaping of Christianity* (New York: Viking, 2007), 6.

69. Ibid.

70. Ibid., 9.

71. Voegelin, *New Science of Politics*, 126.

72. Ibid., 124.

73. Pagels and King, *Reading Judas*, 7–8.

74. Voegelin, *New Science of Politics*, 124.

75. Ibid., 184. Thomas Hobbes, in particular, is credited with creating a symbolic order comparable in destructiveness to Joachim's. For instance, Voegelin charges Hobbes with replacing Augustus's *amor Dei* (love of God) with *amor sui* (self-conceit or pride of the individual) as "the organizing volitional centers of the soul."

76. Ibid., 127, 188–189. To Voegelin, not all Gnosticism is manifested in its extreme forms. He juxtaposed varying degrees of Gnosticism in the American and French revolutions and found that both paled to the amount in the Nazis' overthrow of the Weimar Republic.

77. Ibid., 110. For midcentury Catholics' reaction to *The New Science of Politics*, see Wiser, "Eric Voegelin," 30.

78. Voegelin, *New Science of Politics*, 114.

79. Lilla, "Mr. Casaubon," 30.

80. Voegelin, *New Science of Politics*, 131.

81. Nash, *Conservative Intellectual Movement in America*, 70–71.

82. Voegelin, *New Science of Politics*, 166.

83. Ibid., 119.

84. William F. Buckley, Jr., *God and Man at Yale: The Superstitions of "Academic Freedom"*, 50th anniv. ed. (Washington, D.C.: Regnery, 2002), xxxii.

85. Ibid.

86. See Steven D. Ealy and Gordon Lloyd, "The Eric Voegelin–Willmoore Kendall Correspondence," *Political Science Reviewer* 33 (2004): 357–412.

87. East, *American Conservative Movement*, 172, 195.

88. Hart, *Making of the American Conservative Mind*, 39, 40.

89. Buckley, *God and Man at Yale*, xxiii.

90. William F. Buckley, Jr., *Miles Gone By: A Literary Autobiography* (Washington, D.C.: Regnery, 2004), 285, 286. Buckley wrote that he had seen "provocative prose" before, but "The Liberal Line," Kendall's regular *National Review* column, was outright inflammatory.

91. Hart, *Making of the American Conservative Mind*, 170. Saul Bellow wrote a resemblance of him in *Mosby's Memoirs*. Sidney Zion based a character on him. Buckley's novel *Redhunters* featured a character of Kendall's makeup as well.

92. Wilmoore Kendall, *The Conservative Affirmation* (Chicago: Henry Regnery, 1963), 244.

93. Ibid., 242.

94. Ibid., 108. See also Richard Weaver, "Language Is Sermonic," in *Language Is Sermonic: Richard Weaver on the Nature of Rhetoric*, ed. Richard L. Johannesen, Rennard Strickland, and Ralph T. Eubanks (Baton Rouge: Louisiana State University Press, 1985), 160.

95. Quoted in Hart, *Making of the American Conservative Mind*, 176.

96. Kendall, *Conservative Affirmation*, 244.

97. Ibid., 116.

98. Wiser, "Eric Voegelin," 41.

99. Kendall, *Conservative Affirmation*, 113.

100. Richard Weaver, "Up from Liberalism," *Modern Age* 3 (1958–1959): 24.

101. Weaver, "Up from Liberalism, 22. For a similar story, see Henry Regnery, *Memoirs of a Dissident Publisher* (New York: Harcourt Brace Jovanovich, 1979), 17.

102. Weaver, "Up from Liberalism, 23.

103. M. Stanton Evans, "The Legacy of Richard Weaver," in *Steps toward Restoration: The Consequences of Richard Weaver's Ideas*, ed. Ted J. Smith III (Wilmington, Del.: ISI Books, 1998), 293.

104. Ted J. Smith III, "How *Ideas Have Consequences* Came to Be Written," in Smith, *Steps toward Restoration*, 25–26.

105. Ibid., 1.

106. George Nash, "The Influence of *Ideas Have Consequences* on the Conservative Intellectual Movement in America," in Smith, *Steps toward Restoration*, 86–87.

107. Ibid., 84.

108. Ibid., 86.

109. Evans, "Legacy of Richard Weaver," 287.

110. Nash, "Influence of *Ideas Have Consequences*," 92.

111. Smith, "How *Ideas Have Consequences* Came to Be Written," 23–27.

112. Richard Weaver, *Ideas Have Consequences* (Chicago: University of Chicago Press, 1984), 16.

113. Ibid., 113.

114. Ibid., 2.

115. Ibid., 3.

116. Ibid.

117. Ibid.

118. Smith, "How *Ideas Have Consequences* Came to Be Written," 22.

119. Evans, "Legacy of Richard Weaver," 294.

120. Weaver, *Ideas Have Consequences*, 2.

121. Ibid., 130–131.

122. Ibid., 53.

123. Ibid., 59, 60, 62, 65, 108.

124. Ibid., 4.

125. Evans, "Legacy of Richard Weaver," 294.

126. Robert A. Preston, "The Relation of Intellect and Will in the Thought of Richard Weaver," in *The Dilemmas of American Conservatism*, ed. Kenneth L. Deutsch and Ethan Fishman (Lexington: University Press of Kentucky, 2010), 69.

127. Smith, "How *Ideas Have Consequences* Came to Be Written," 22–23.

128. East, *American Conservative Movement*, 41. Nash wrote that the book "made its mark on American conservative intellectuals, not a few of whom eventually converted to the Roman Catholic faith." Nash, "Influence of *Ideas Have Consequences*," 95–96.

129. Weaver, *Visions of Order*, 117.

130. Ibid., 122.

131. Ibid., 121.

132. Ibid., 121–122.

133. Ibid., 133.

134. Quoted in Gerald J. Russello, *The Postmodern Imagination of Russell Kirk* (Columbia: University of Missouri Press, 2007), 13.

135. Quoted in Micklethwait and Wooldridge, *Right Nation*, 47. Kirk hoped to move completely off of the industrial modernist grid. He even talked about becoming a wandering poet in Michigan. Nash, *Conservative Intellectual Movement in America*, 63.

136. George Nash, "The Life and Legacy of Russell Kirk," *Heritage Foundation Lecture #1035*, June 10, 2007, available via http://www.heritage.org/research/lecture/the-life-and-legacy-of-russell-kirk.

137. Patrick Allitt, *The Conservatives: Ideas and Personalities throughout American History* (New Haven, Conn.: Yale University Press, 2009), 170.

138. Weaver's antipathy for the automobile did not quite match Kirk's, but it came close. Driving in Chicago made him nervous, so he simply stopped. His technophobia was no "pose." Evans, "Legacy of Richard Weaver," 290. Along with the automobile, he counted the airplane, the radio, the television, and the newspaper among those modern inventions he disliked. His personal quarrel with technological mass society necessitated a regular getaway. Every summer, Weaver boarded a train and left the whir of city life behind for Weaverville, North Carolina, and, it is rumored, tended his land with a horse-drawn plow. Nash, "Influence of *Ideas Have Consequences*," 85.

139. Russello, *Postmodern Imagination of Russell Kirk*, 2.

140. James E. Person Jr., *Russell Kirk: A Critical Biography of a Conservative Mind* (Lanham, Md.: Madison Books, 1999), 51.

141. Kirk, *Enemies of the Permanent Things*, 52.

142. Hart, *Making of the American Conservative Mind*, 5.

143. Kirk, *Conservative Mind*, 423. See also W. Wesley McDonald, *Russell Kirk and the Age of Ideology* (Columbia: University of Missouri Press, 2004), 9.

144. Kirk, *Conservative Mind*, 483–484.

145. Kirk, *Enemies of the Permanent Things*, 60–61.

146. Ronald Reagan, "The Defense of Freedom and the Metaphysics of Fun," in *Tear Down This Wall: The Reagan Revolution—a* National Review *History*, ed. *National Review* (New York: Continuum, 2004), 75.

147. See Hart, *Making of the American Conservative Mind*, 352.

148. Gleaves Whitney, "Recovering Rhetoric: How Ideas, Language, and Leadership Can Triumph in Post-Modern Politics," *Heritage Foundation Lecture*, January 14, 2000. See also George A. Panichas, "Restoring the Meaning of Conservatism," *Modern Age* 47 (2005): 195; Jonah Goldberg, "Crunchy Conservatism, Reconsidered," *National Review*, October 8, 2002.

149. Alfred S. Regnery, *Upstream: The Ascendance of American Conservatism* (New York: Threshold Editions, 2008), 73.

150. Russell Kirk, *The Conservative Mind: From Burke to Santayana* (Chicago: Henry Regnery, 1953).

151. Russell Kirk, *The Sword of Imagination: Memoirs of a Half-Century of Literary Conflict* (Grand Rapids, Mich.: William B. Eerdsmans, 1995), 213.

152. Henry Regnery, *A Few Reasonable Words: Selected Writings* (Wilmington, Del.: ISI Books, 1996), 100.

153. George Panichas, ed., *The Collected Works of Russell Kirk* (Wilmington, Del.: ISI Books, 2007), xxxii–xxxiii.

154. Quoted in Richard Viguerie and David Franke, *America's Right Turn: How Conservatives Used New and Alternative Media to Take Power* (Chicago: Bonus Books, 2004), 55. See also Hart, *Making of the American Conservative Mind*, 370; David Frum, *What's Right: The New Conservative Majority and the Remaking of America* (New York: Basic Books, 1996), 168.

155. Nash, *Conservative Intellectual Movement in America*, 66.

156. Schlesinger, *Politics of Hope*, 96–97.

157. Kirk, *Conservative Mind*, 9; Allitt, *Conservatives*, 168.

158. Nash, *Conservative Intellectual Movement in America*, 177.

159. Schlesinger, *Politics of Hope*, 104.

160. See Richard Hofstadter, *The Age of Reform: From Bryan to F.D.R.* (New York: Vintage, 1960); Louis Hartz, *The Liberal Tradition in America* (New York: Harcourt Brace Jovanovich, 1955), 151–155, 174–175, 264–265.

161. Quoted in John East, "The Conservatism of Frank Straus Meyer," *Modern Age* 18 (1974): 242.

162. Hart, *Making of the American Conservative Mind*, 355.

163. Nash, *Conservative Intellectual Movement in America*, 64.

164. Kirk, *Conservative Mind*, 3.

165. Hartz, *Liberal Tradition in America*, 177.

166. Kirk, *Conservative Mind*, 5. John Miller notes, "By granting an intellectual pedigree to the American Right, *The Conservative Mind* made it impossible— or at least irresponsible—for liberals to recycle John Stuart Mill's hackneyed comment about conservatives being 'the stupid party.'" See John J. Miller, *A Gift of Freedom: How the John M. Olin Foundation Changed America* (San Francisco: Encounter Books, 2006), 28–29.

167. Russello, *Postmodern Imagination of Russell Kirk*, 1.

168. Kirk, *Conservative Mind*, 8.

169. Ibid.

170. Ibid., 421.

171. Ibid., 427.

172. Ibid., iii.

173. Ibid., 473.

174. Ibid., 399.

175. See also Nash, "Influence of *Ideas Have Consequences*," 100.

176. Schlesinger, *Politics of Hope*, 101.

177. Nisbet, *Quest for Community*, 53–54.

178. Ibid., 4.

179. Weaver, *Ideas Have Consequences*, 132.

180. Robert A. Preston, "*Ideas Have Consequences* Fifty Years Later," in Smith, *Steps toward Restoration*, 56.

181. Eugene Genovese, *The Southern Tradition: The Achievement and Limitations of American Conservatism* (Cambridge, Mass.: Harvard University Press, 1994), 35.

182. Weaver, *Ideas Have Consequences*, 132.

183. Ibid., 133.

184. Ibid.

185. Kirk, *Conservative Mind*, 426.

186. Ibid.

187. Ibid., 421.

188. Malcolm Barber, *The Two Cities: Medieval Europe 1050–1320*, 2nd ed. (New York: Routledge, 2004), 52–53.

189. Nash, "Influence of *Ideas Have Consequences*," 105.

190. Kirk, "Libertarians," 349.

191. Ibid., 350–351.

192. Ibid., 350.

193. Ibid.

194. Ibid., 348.

Chapter Three. The Libertarian Dialect

1. Brian Doherty, *Radicals for Capitalism: A Freewheeling History of the Modern American Libertarian Movement* (New York: Public Affairs, 2007), 585.

2. Ibid.; Jennifer Burns, *Goddess of the Market: Ayn Rand and the American Right* (New York: Oxford University Press, 2009), 254–255.

3. Doherty, *Radicals for Capitalism*, 16.

4. Burns, *Goddess of the Market*, 254–255. See also Murray Rothbard, *For a New Liberty: The Libertarian Manifesto* (New York: MacMillan, 1973), 5–7; Gregory L. Schneider, *Cadres for Conservatism: Young Americans for Freedom and the Rise of the Contemporary Right* (New York: New York University Press, 1999), 134–137.

5. Doherty, *Radicals for Capitalism*, 357.

6. Amy Sullivan, "Frosty Fusion," *DLC Blueprint Magazine*, October 16, 2006. After the melee, 300 libertarian members of YAF were kicked out of the organization. See Ryan Sager, *The Elephant in the Room: Evangelicals, Libertarians, and the Battle to Control the Republican Party* (Hoboken, N.J.: John Wiley & Sons, 2006), 8.

7. Burns explains, "The largest and most influential organization to emerge from the libertarian secession, the Society for Individual Liberty (SIL), grew out of objectivist roots. The group was formed by a merger between YAF's Libertarian Caucus and the Society for Rational Individualism, publisher of *The Rational Individualist*." See Burns, *Goddess of the Market*, 257.

8. Ibid., 202–203.

9. Doherty, *Radicals for Capitalism*, 60–61.

10. Quoted in ibid., 133–134.

11. Randal Hamowy and William F. Buckley, Jr., "'*National Review*': Criticism and Reply," *New Individualist Review*, November 1961, 7. Ready with a rebuttal quip, Buckley cast Russell Kirk sardonically as "Contributing Torturer Kirk" in his response. Buckley thought libertarians could not tell the difference between first- and second-order threats; he basically thought conservatives were libertarians who could prioritize.

12. Doherty, *Radicals for Capitalism*, 260.

13. True libertarians, Doherty writes, would "tell you you were wrong, and very sharply, if you called them conservative." Ibid., 8.

14. Quoted in ibid., 204. Chodorov was radical indeed. *The Road to Serfdom* gave him a "let-down." Serfdom was caused by planning, and Hayek, he thought, "offers 'planning for competition' as a way out. How silly!" Quoted in George Nash, *The Conservative Intellectual Movement in America since 1945* (New York: Basic Books, 1976), 14.

15. J. G. A. Pocock, "Verbalizing a Political Act: Toward a Politics of Speech," *Political Theory* 1 (1973): 33.

16. See Mark A. Smith, *The Right Talk: How Conservatives Transformed the Great Society into the Economic Society* (Princeton, N.J.: Princeton University Press, 2007).

17. Brink Lindsay, "Right Is Wrong," *Reason*, August 2010.

18. Jonah Goldberg, "A Lib-Lib Romance," *National Review*, December 31, 2006, 19.

19. Jonah Goldberg, "Libertarians Under My Skin: Grow Up Already," *National Review*, March 2, 2001.

20. Murray N. Rothbard, *The Betrayal of the American Right* (Auburn, Ala.: Ludwig von Mises Institute, 2007), 92–93, 137–139. See also Justin Raimondo, *Reclaiming the American Right: The Lost Legacy of the Conservative Movement* (Wilmington, Del.: ISI Books, 2008).

21. Doherty, *Radicals for Capitalism*, 560.

22. Buckley risked irritating many financial contributors, ostracizing writers, creating internal dissension at *National Review*, and offending readers by ending the association between intellectual conservatism and the Birchers. Both conservatives and Birchers were virulent anti-Communists. But the border had to be drawn, Buckley thought, to ensure that conservatism remained free from association with extreme ideas, like the notion that Eisenhower was the Communists' Manchurian candidate. His ecumenicalism reached its limit. Buckley lampooned the Birchers and Robert Welch in an "excommunicating editorial" in *National Review*. Never a philosophical pragmatist, he was pragmatic about the public image of conservatism. See Linda Bridges and John R. Coyne Jr., *Strictly Right: William F. Buckley Jr. and the American Conservative Movement* (Hoboken, N.J.: John Wiley & Sons, 2007), 75.

23. See also James Jasinski, "The Forms and Limits of Prudence in Henry Clay's (1850) Defense of the Compromise Measures," *Quarterly Journal of Speech* 81 (1995): 465.

24. Robert McCrum, *Globish: How the English Language Became the World's Language* (New York: W. W. Norton, 2010), 50.

25. I am not arguing that Hayek never employed "freedom" and Goldwater never employed "liberty." Both used both "liberty" and "freedom," sometimes as synonyms, sometimes as closely related terms. I am arguing, however, that Hayek clearly preferred "liberty" to "freedom" as Goldwater clearly preferred "freedom" to "liberty." I am also arguing that we can gain a glimpse of a varied dialect through these representative terms.

26. Barry Goldwater, *The Conscience of a Conservative*, 30th anniv. ed. (Washington, D.C.: Regnery Gateway, 1990), 8.

27. Quoted in Anne C. Heller, *Ayn Rand and the World She Made* (New York: Doubleday, 2009), 1.

28. Rand was quite taken with Goldwater and volunteered to assist his presidential campaign. She did, however, have one serious objection: she disliked Goldwater's religious justification for libertarianism. Burns, *Goddess of the Market*, 190, 205.

29. Hayek's *The Constitution of Liberty* placed ninth. "The 100 Best Non-Fiction Books of the Century," *National Review*, available at http://www.nationalreview.com/100best/100_books.html. The *National Review* list stipulates that making the list is more important than any specific ranking. In 2006, *Human Events* published a list of the "Top 10 Books Liberals Want to Burn." Hayek's *The Road to Serfdom* placed second; *Witness* came in third; the Bible won. See

"Top 10 Books Liberals Want to Burn," *Human Events*, May 23, 2006. Also in 2006, *Human Events* published a top ten list of books "every Republican Congressman" should read. Nearly all of the major libertarian tracts made the list: *The Constitution of Liberty* (#9), *The Conscience of a Conservative* (#7), and *The Road to Serfdom* (#1). See "Top 10 Books Every Republican Congressman Should Read," *Human Events*, November 21, 2006.

30. John Patrick Diggins, *Ronald Reagan: Fate, Freedom, and the Making of History* (New York: W. W. Norton, 2007), 268.

31. Friedrich A. Hayek, *The Road to Serfdom*, 50th anniv. ed. (Chicago: University of Chicago Press, 1984), xxxv–xxxvi.

32. Ibid., xxxvi.

33. Hayek was not the only prominent thinker who was drafted by conservatives to make such a declaration. Author John Dos Passos said in a 1959 interview (the same year he praised conservatives in the foreword to Buckley's *Up from Liberalism*), "I am not a conservative. . . . The conservatives must first discover what they have to conserve." See John Patrick Diggins, *Up from Communism: Conservative Odysseys in American Intellectual History* (New York: Harper & Row, 1975), 350.

34. In a 2001 *National Review* entry discussing the conservative-libertarian war over Hayek as an intellectual commodity, Goldberg wrote, "I said that Friedrich Hayek's *The Road to Serfdom* contributed to the core of modern conservative philosophy. I am about the 5,316th person to make this flatly factual assertion, and yet for every 5,316 times someone says this some libertarian somewhere kicks a cat. Every serious telling of the modern conservative story says the same thing." See Goldberg, "Libertarians Under My Skin." Conservatives have also minimized the difference between Hayek and his conservative devotees. See Henry Regnery, *A Few Reasonable Words: Selected Writings* (Wilmington, Del.: Intercollegiate Studies Institute, 1996), 105; John Gray, "The Road from Serfdom," *National Review*, April 27, 1992, 35.

35. Hayek suffered the same fate as had Milton Friedman. Friedman intermittently fought being appropriated as a conservative as well. See Doherty, *Radicals for Capitalism*, 297.

36. Appropriately, Mises is claimed by many conservatives as an earlier forerunner. Ibid., 10. Murray Rothbard attempted to reclaim Mises, noting his profoundly unconservative, at least to *National Review* conservatives, admiration of the French Revolution and criticism of Christianity. See Murray Rothbard, "The Laissez-Faire Radical: A Quest for the Historical Mises," *Journal of Libertarian Studies* (Summer 1981): 237–253.

37. Doherty, *Radicals for Capitalism*, 67–72. Hayek abandoned the technical aspects of his neoclassical economic work to write *The Road to Serfdom*. Hayek was a professional economist whose most famous book was a political tract. He followed that up with a dense treatment of theoretical psychology in *The Sensory Order*. Political theory was his next frontier. His voluminous *The Constitution of Liberty* (1960) would expand on his ideas in *The Road to Serfdom*. From

there he would publish other wide-ranging tracts on social science and political philosophy, such as *Studies in Philosophy, Politics and Economics* (1967), and the trilogy *Law* (1973), *Legislation* (1976), and *Liberty* (1979). None would reach the heights of *Road* and *Constitution*.

38. Milton Friedman, "Introduction," in Hayek, *Road to Serfdom*, xvii. As Hayek wrote in the preface to the 1956 U.S. paperback edition, "Contrary to my experience in England, in America the kind of people to whom this book was mainly addressed seemed to have rejected it out of hand as a malicious and disingenuous attack on their finest ideals." He called the level of adversity "extraordinary." Hayek, *Road to Serfdom*, xxxi. Herman Finer's *The Road to Serfdom to Reaction*, another book-length response, is illustrative of the larger body of invective leveled at Hayek. Finer's first sentence is harsh, but not the harshest: "Friedrich A. Hayek's *The Road to Serfdom* constitutes the most sinister offensive against democracy to emerge from a democratic country for many decades." Hayek considered, but resisted, a libel suit. See Bruce Caldwell, *Hayek's Challenge: An Intellectual Biography of F. A. Hayek* (Chicago: University of Chicago Press, 2004), 148.

39. Donald T. Critchlow, *The Conservative Ascendancy: How the GOP Right Made Political History* (Cambridge, Mass.: Harvard University Press, 2007), 15.

40. Bruce Caldwell, "Introduction," in *The Road to Serfdom: Texts and Documents*, ed. Bruce Caldwell (Chicago: University of Chicago Press, 2007), 1.

41. See Daniel Yergin and Joseph Stanislaw, *The Commanding Heights: The Battle for the World Economy* (New York: Free Press, 2002), xiv.

42. Caldwell, *Hayek's Challenge*, 2.

43. Some conservatives even squared Hayek's lesson with biblical tenets; Edwin Feulner, Heritage Foundation president, summarized, "Hayek's stunningly simple insight was that the biblical warning, 'pride goeth before a fall,' applies to societies as well as individuals, and that hubris is a tragic flaw not only of ancient Greek heroes, but also for modern nation states." Edwin J. Feulner Jr., "F. A. Hayek," in *The March of Freedom: Modern Classics in Conservative Thought*, ed. Edwin Feulner Jr. (Dallas: Spence, 1998), 55.

44. Hayek's classical liberalism, accordingly, was a not a "stationary creed," as he put it but, rather, a flexible system of reasoning that refused "hard-and-fast rules." Any economic dogma continued of such ignorance because, by definition, it opposed values Hayek held dear: accounting for and adjusting to local economic conditions. Pat rules about government spending during a recession or eternal laws about taxation presumed the same omniscience about future economic conditions that socialism did, and dynamic economies inevitably stumped those who presumed themselves omniscient. Hayek, *Road to Serfdom*, 17.

45. Ibid., 45.

46. Caldwell, *Hayek's Challenge*, 289.

47. Quoted in Burns, *Goddess of the Market*, 104.

48. Norman P. Barry, "The Road to Freedom: Hayek's Social and Economic Philosophy," in *Hayek, Co-Ordination and Evolution: His Legacy in Philosophy,*

Politics, Economics and the History of Ideas, ed. Jack Birner and Rudy Van Zijp (New York: Routledge, 1994), 142.

49. Caldwell, *Hayek's Challenge,* 338.

50. Barry, "Road to Freedom," 143–144.

51. Ibid.

52. Hayek, *Road to Serfdom,* 156–157.

53. Ibid., 66, emphasis added.

54. "Liberty" was not just a term Hayek favored; it has been widespread in libertarian literature. *Liberty,* in fact, was an individualist journal in the late nineteenth century. The American icons the Liberty Bell and the Statue of Liberty were appropriated by libertarians. An Old Right anti–New Deal organization in the 1930s, the Liberty League was the brainchild of J. Howard Pew of Sun Oil and Alfred Sloan of General Motors, two of Foundation for Economic Education's most prominent contributors in the 1950s. The Liberty League folded in the late 1930s because of its "plutocratic makeup during times of mass privation" and because General Smedley Butler alleged it had a role in a coup plot against Roosevelt. See Doherty, *Radicals for Capitalism,* 61. The Liberty Fund is a contemporary libertarian foundation. The largest libertarian think tank, the Cato Institute, with its $22 million annual budget, has a fitting slogan: "Individual liberty, limited government, free markets and peace." See http://www.cato.org/about.

55. Hayek, *Constitution of Liberty,* 133.

56. Hayek, *Road to Serfdom,* 17.

57. Caldwell, *Hayek's Challenge,* 289.

58. Hayek, *Road to Serfdom,* 91.

59. Hayek, *Constitution of Liberty,* 205.

60. Caldwell, *Hayek's Challenge,* 289.

61. Hayek, *Road to Serfdom,* 81.

62. Ibid., 90–91.

63. Weaver blamed the midcentury tragedies in Germany on individualism. Richard Weaver, *Ideas Have Consequences* (Chicago: University of Chicago Press, 1984), 14.

64. Hayek, *Road to Serfdom,* 29.

65. Ibid., 17.

66. Ibid., 3–4.

67. Charles Fried, *Modern Liberty and the Limits of Government* (New York: W. W. Norton, 2007), 17.

68. Hayek, *Road to Serfdom,* 148.

69. Ibid., 35.

70. Kenneth Burke, "The Rhetoric of Hitler's Battle," in *Readings in Rhetorical Criticism*, ed. Carl R. Burgchardt (State College, Pa.: Strata, 2000), 210.

71. Hayek, *Road to Serfdom*, 25.

72. Ibid., 106.

73. Doherty, *Radicals for Capitalism*, 108.

74. Friedman, "Introduction," ix.

75. In his 2002 preface to this edition, he used the same rhetorical template to praise trends in global deregulation: "But it took the drama of the Berlin Wall and the collapse of the Soviet Union to make it part of conventional wisdom, so that it is now taken for granted that central planning is indeed *The Road to Serfdom*, as Friedrich A. Hayek titled his brilliant 1944 polemic." See Milton Friedman, *Capitalism and Freedom*, 40th anniv. ed. (Chicago: University of Chicago Press, 2002), viii. Friedman was an early member of an organization founded by Hayek, the Mont Pelerin Society, which collected the finest libertarian minds to discuss economics.

76. Reagan delivered Americanized versions of Hayekian themes in his early speeches as well. In 1962, he told a North Dakota audience that the Founding Fathers sought to minimize government: "They knew that governments don't control things. A government can't control the economy without controlling the people." He offered virtually the same argument in his first inaugural eighteen years later. Reagan had accepted Hayek's argument "completely." See Diggins, *Ronald Reagan*, 268, 270.

77. "The Commanding Heights," William Cran producer, *PBS*, InVision Productions (2002).

78. Nash, *Conservative Intellectual Movement in America*, 5–6.

79. Alfred S. Regnery, *Upstream: The Ascendance of American Conservatism* (New York: Threshold Editions, 2008), 26–29.

80. Rick Perlstein, *Before the Storm: Barry Goldwater and the Unmaking of the American Consensus* (New York: Hill & Wang, 2001), 392.

81. Mary C. Brennan, *Turning Right in the Sixties: The Conservative Capture of the GOP* (Chapel Hill: University of North Carolina Press, 1995), 78.

82. The line seemed suicidal to other observers as well. Shocked by Goldwater's stalwart rhetoric, one on-site reporter blurted to Theodore White, "My God, he is going to run as Barry Goldwater." Quoted in Lee Edwards, "The Unforgettable Candidate," *National Review*, July 6, 1998, 36

83. See Brennan, *Turning Right*, 78. For the most part, the Goldwater campaign had done its best to distance its candidate from extremism as an idea and extremists in the form of virulent racists or John Birch conspiracy theorists. In fact, one of Goldwater's managers later conceded, somewhat ironically, that "he had agreed to exclude Buckley and *National Review* because they were believed by many to

be on the far right fringe of politics, and he did not want any of this to rub off on Goldwater." See Lee Edwards, *The Conservative Revolution: The Movement That Remade America* (New York: Free Press, 1997), 185.

84. Sean P. Cunningham, *Cowboy Conservatism: Texas and the Rise of the Modern Right* (Lexington: University Press of Kentucky, 2010), 57.

85. A five-minute standing ovation shook the Cow Palace when he finished. Perlstein, *Before the Storm*, 391.

86. Ibid., 106.

87. Matthew Dallek, "The Conservative 1960s," *Atlantic Monthly*, December 1995, 132. Many prominent conservatives agree with Dallek's claim. Unsurprisingly, Buchanan credits the book with sparking conservatism: "Without the man who wrote *The Conscience of a Conservative* and the movement it inspired, there would have been no Conservative Decade." See Patrick Buchanan, "Introduction: The Voice in the Desert," in Goldwater, *Conscience of a Conservative*, xviii.

88. Cited Perlstein, *Before the Storm*, 108.

89. The influence of Goldwater's campaign on young conservatives was remarkable. William F. Buckley, Jr., "Barry Goldwater, RIP," *National Review*, June 22, 1998.

90. Goldwater used the word "freedom" twenty-four times during the speech, "liberty" in only six instances. If one read the speech without knowledge of the enduring fame of the "extremism" line, one would be hard-pressed to find a clearer summation of his goals as the leader of the Republican Party: "And this party, with its every action, every word, every breath, and every heartbeat, has but as single resolve, and that is freedom made orderly for this Nation by our constitutional government." Barry Goldwater, "Extremism in the Defense of Liberty Is No Vice," in *Landmark Speeches of the American Conservative Movement*, ed. Peter Schweizer and Wynton C. Hall (College Station: Texas A&M University Press, 2007), 32.

91. Nash, *Conservative Intellectual Movement in America*, 192–193.

92. George Will quoted in *Mr. Conservative: Goldwater on Goldwater*, directed by Julie Anderson, HBO Documentary Films (2007).

93. Nash, *Conservative Intellectual Movement in America*, 273.

94. Jonathan M. Schoenwald, *A Time for Choosing: The Rise of Modern American Conservatism* (Oxford: Oxford University Press, 2001), 126.

95. Edwards, *Conservative Revolution*, 466.

96. Buchanan, "Introduction," ix.

97. The first parody of Goldwater's path-breaking effort, in book form at least, came in Donald Lambro's *The Conscience of a Young Conservative*, a slender volume with such telling chapter titles as "Government: The Money Hungry Bureaucracy," "Taxes: Is There a Limit?," and "Crime: Lock Them Up!"

98. Perlstein, *Before the Storm*, 64.

99. John A. Andrew, *The Other Side of the Sixties: Young Americans for Freedom and the Rise of Conservative Politics* (New Brunswick, N.J.: Rutgers University Press, 1997), 24–25.

100. Perlstein, *Before the Storm*, 64.

101. Richard Brookhiser, "Youth Movement," *National Review*, July 6, 1998, 31.

102. Cited in Andrew, *Other Side of the Sixties*, 28.

103. YAF members were socialized into an environment where print culture devotion and political activity went hand in hand. Members, one conservative boasted, "read twice as much as anyone else, the enemy's ideas and their own, delighting in dangling bait before unsuspecting peers who didn't know their assumptions *required* arguments, then slaughtering them in debate." Perlstein, *Before the Storm*, 107–108.

104. Richard Viguerie, like Pat Buchanan, committed sections of the book to memory. See Edwards, "Unforgettable Candidate," 38.

105. Karl Rove, *Courage and Consequence: My Life as a Conservative in the Fight* (New York: Threshold Editions, 2010), 7.

106. Robert Alan Goldberg, *Barry Goldwater* (New Haven, Conn.: Yale University Press, 1995), 139.

107. William F. Buckley, Jr., "Mr. Conservative," *National Review*, July 6, 1998, 38.

108. Goldberg, *Barry Goldwater*, 138.

109. After a series of debates about Catholicism, conservatism, and birth control in the mid-1960s with Garry Wills, Frank Meyer, and Buckley, Bozell left *National Review* to found *Triumph*, a doctrinaire Catholic magazine. The split was initially amicable, but Bozell later became hostile to *National Review*–style conservatism. See Patrick Allitt, *Catholic Intellectuals and Conservative Politics in America, 1950–1985* (Ithaca, N.Y.: Cornell University Press, 1993), 141–142, 155–156. In the words of *National Review* writer Jeffrey Hart, Bozell was "theocratic" and "anti-American." Bozell, for instance, alienated conservatives by endorsing race riots as revolts against "materialism." Jeffrey Hart, *The Making of the American Conservative Mind:* National Review *and Its Times* (Wilmington, Del.: ISI Books, 2007), 7.

110. Goldberg, *Barry Goldwater*, 138. See also Mary C. Brennan, "Winning the War/Losing the Battle: The Goldwater Presidential Campaign and Its Effects on the Evolution of Modern Conservatism," in *The Conservative Sixties*, ed. David Farber and Jeff Roche (New York: Peter Lang, 2003), 66.

111. Quoted in Lee Edwards, *Goldwater: The Man Who Made a Revolution* (Washington, D.C.: Regnery, 1995), 112.

112. Perlstein, *Before the Storm*, 64.

113. Edwards, *Goldwater*, 112. See also John W. Dean and Barry M. Goldwater Jr., *Pure Goldwater* (New York: Palgrave Macmillan, 2008), 106–109. There is some disagreement among historians about Goldwater's involvement. Some,

such as Perlstein, depict him as completely absent. Others, such as Edwards, clearly attempt to rebut the charge of noninvolvement. Bozell's subsequent commentary contributed to the disagreement. He implied that Goldwater did not have much to do with the book when he charged, "Goldwater didn't know much about conservatism until he read that book." Quoted in Allitt, *Catholic Intellectual*, 142.

114. Quoted in Schneider, *Cadres for Conservatism*, 26.

115. Perlstein, *Before the Storm*, 53.

116. Manion pioneered pricing schemes to ensure that these conservative works could be passed cheaply from neighbor to neighbor. Manion marketed books with strategic price points that mirrored his "nonprofit" distribution of radio broadcasts a decade earlier. For instance, Goldwater's *The Conscience of a Conservative* was cheap at $3, but cheapest if purchased in bulk: 10 copies for $5, 100 copies for $30, and so on. This pricing structure encouraged buyers to share books liberally with friends and acquaintances. Perlstein, *Before the Storm*, 478.

117. Goldwater, *Conscience*, xxiii.

118. Ibid., xv.

119. Ibid., 50.

120. James Arnt Aune, *Selling the Free Market: The Rhetoric of Economic Correctness* (New York: Guilford Press, 2001), 41.

121. Robert Hariman, *Political Style: The Artistry of Power* (Chicago: University of Chicago Press, 1995), 19.

122. John W. Dean, *Conservatives without Conscience* (New York: Viking Press, 2006), 18.

123. Daniel T. Rodgers, *The Age of Fracture* (Cambridge, Mass.: Harvard University Press, 2011), 35.

124. Perlstein, *Before the Storm*, 423.

125. Goldwater, *Conscience*, xxiii.

126. Ibid., xxv.

127. Goldwater, "Extremism in the Defense," 32.

128. Goldwater, *Conscience*, xxv.

129. Ibid., 5.

130. Ibid., xxv.

131. Ibid., 5–6.

132. Ibid., 5.

133. Ibid., 7.

134. Ibid., 7; see also Goldwater, "Extremism in the Defense," 32.

135. Goldwater, *Conscience*, 8.

136. Doherty, *Radicals for Capitalism*, 307.

137. Goldwater, *Conscience*, 17.

138. Ibid., 8.

139. Ibid., 6.

140. Ibid., 11.

141. Ibid., 7.

142. See Doherty, *Radicals for Capitalism*, 309.

143. Goldwater, *Conscience*, 111.

144. Ibid., 117.

145. Ibid., 84–85.

146. Ibid., 117.

147. Ibid.

148. Ronald Reagan echoed this theme both during and after his presidency; more than a rehearsal of first principles, he also recounted the heroic sacrifices of ordinary individuals. See John M. Jones and Robert C. Rowland, "A Covenant-Affirming Jeremiad: The Post-presidential Ideological Appeals of Ronald Wilson Reagan," *Communication Studies* 56 (2005): 163.

149. For more on self-sacrifice for sacred values, see Morgan Marietta, *The Politics of Sacred Rhetoric: Absolutist Appeals and Political Persuasion* (Waco, Tex.: Baylor University Press, 2012), 1.

150. Murray N. Rothbard, "Repartee," *Innovator*, August 1964, 1–27. See also Donald T. Critchlow, *The Conservative Ascendancy: How the GOP Right Made Political History* (Cambridge, Mass.: Harvard University Press, 2007), 25–26.

151. Goldwater, *Conscience*, xxiv.

152. Quoted in Ron Rosenbaum, "Late for the Tea Party," *Slate*, November 1, 2010.

153. Glenn Beck, "The Road to Serfdom," *Glenn Beck*, aired June 9, 2010, available via http://www.foxnews.com/story/0,2933,594203,00.html. *Road*, which averaged 2,000 sales per year, soared up national sales rankings after Beck's approbation and charted a pace for over 100,000 sales in 2010. Jennifer Scheussler, "Hayek: The Back Story," *New York Times*, July 9, 2010; Stephen Foley, "Darling of the Right Is Reborn in the USA," *Independent*, July 10, 2010, 38.

154. Bill Schneider, "The Tea Party: Goldwater 2.0," *National Journal*, April 24, 2010; Michael Gerson, "Signs of Sanity from the Tea Party," *Washington Post*, July 21, 2010, A19; David Kuhn, "GOP Dark Horse Dreams: Can Someone Pull a Goldwater?" *Real Clear Politics*, April 26, 2010.

155. B. Leland Baker, *Tea Party Revival: The Conscience of a Conservative Reborn* (Denver: Outskirts Press, 2009), ix.

156. Isaiah Berlin, *Four Essays on Liberty* (New York: Oxford University Press, 1970), 121–122.

157. See Sager, *Elephant in the Room*, 21.

158. Doherty, *Radicals for Capitalism*, 110.

159. Ibid., 309.

160. David Frum, *What's Right: The New Conservative Majority and the Remaking of America* (New York: Basic Books, 1996), 168.

Chapter Four. Fusionism as Philosophy and Rhetorical Practice

1. Rick Perlstein, *Before the Storm: Barry Goldwater and the Unmaking of the American Consensus* (New York: Hill & Wang, 2001), 105.

2. Ibid., 53.

3. Cited in Lee Edwards, "The Origins of the Modern American Conservative Movement," *Heritage Foundation Lecture #8311*, November 21, 2003.

4. Perlstein, *Before the Storm*, 106.

5. See "The Sharon Statement," September 11, 1960, available via http://www.heritage.org/initiatives/first-principles/primary-sources/the-sharon-statement.

6. Matthew Kuchem, "The Sharon Statement and the Growth of Conservatism," *Foundry*, September 15, 2010.

7. Ryan Sager, *The Elephant in the Room: Evangelicals, Libertarians, and the Battle to Control the Republican Party* (Hoboken, N.J.: John Wiley & Sons, 2006), 35.

8. Perlstein, *Before the Storm*, 106.

9. Sager, *Elephant in the Room*, 35.

10. Lisa McGirr, *Suburban Warriors: The Origins of the New American Right* (Princeton, N.J.: Princeton University Press, 2002), 129. Six months after YAF was founded, over 21,000 members paid dues, and YAF was active on more than 100 campuses. See Matthew Dallek, "The Conservative 1960s," *Atlantic Monthly*, December 1995. See also Gregory L. Schneider, *Cadres for Conservatism: Young Americans for Freedom and the Rise of the Contemporary Right* (New York: New York University Press, 1999), 31–32.

11. The Young America's Foundation reprints the Sharon Statement prominently on its website: http://www.yaf.org/sharon_statement.aspx. Additionally, the Sharon Statement was renewed as "The Mount Vernon Statement" by a gathering of prominent conservatives in 2010. See http://www.themountvernonstatement.com/.

12. Lee Edwards, "The Conservative Consensus: Frank Meyer, Barry Goldwater, and the Politics of Fusionism," *Heritage Foundation First Principles Series*

Report #8, January 22, 2007, available via http://www.heritage.org/Research/ Reports/2007/01/The-Conservative-Consensus-Frank-Meyer-Barry-Goldwater- and-the-Politics-of-Fusionism. See also Matthew Spalding, "A New American Fusionism: Recovering Principles in Our Politics," *Heritage Foundation Lecture #1114*, March 17, 2009.

13. Perlstein, *Before the Storm*, 106; Kevin J. Smant, *Principles and Heresies: Frank S. Meyer and the Shaping of the American Conservative Movement* (Wilmington, Del.: ISI Books, 2002), 91.

14. George Nash, *The Conservative Intellectual Movement in America since 1945* (New York: Basic Books, 1976), 161.

15. L. Brent Bozell coined the term "fusion." The word did not appear in Meyer's *In Defense of Freedom*. Meyer's initial response to Bozell's use of the term was tepid. He wrote in *National Review* in 1962, "I should like to plead innocent to his friendly indictment that I have 'labored earnestly in recent years to promote and justify modern American conservatism as a "fusion" of the libertarian and traditionalist points of view.' Rather I . . . have been attempting something very different from an ideological—and eclectic—effort to create a position abstractly 'fusing' two other positions. What I have been attempting to do is to help articulate in theoretical and practical terms the instinctive consensus of the contemporary American conservative movement—a movement which is inspired by no ideological construct, but by devotion to the fundamental understanding of the men who made Western civilization and the American republic." Frank Meyer, "Why Freedom?," in *In Defense of Freedom and Related Essays*, ed. Frank Meyer (Indianapolis: Liberty Fund Press, 1996), 155.

16. Murray Rothbard, "Frank S. Meyer: The Fusionist as Libertarian Manque," *Modern Age* 25 (1981): 352. As Frank Chodorov asked, "Sometimes as I read these anti-communist manuscripts, the unkind suspicion comes upon me: are these writers *for freedom* or only *against communism?*" Quoted in Brian Doherty, *Radicals for Capitalism: A Freewheeling History of the Modern American Libertarian Movement* (New York: Public Affairs, 2007), 203.

17. Quoted in Smant, *Principles and Heresies*, 94. Chambers wrote to Ralph de Toledano in 1954: "Is it really too much to ask that 20 (or even 10) conservative intellectuals should meet and see, at the very least, whether there would be any point in their ever meeting again." Ralph de Toledano, ed., *Notes from the Underground: The Whittaker Chambers—Ralph de Toledano Letters: 1949–1960* (Washington, D.C.: Regnery, 1997), 177.

18. William F. Buckley, Jr., *Up from Liberalism* (New York: Stein and Day, 1985), 218–219, 229.

19. Rothbard claimed the only programmatic goal that united libertarians and traditionalists was each side's rejection of state-enforced economic leveling. See Rothbard, "Frank S. Meyer," 353.

20. Willmoore Kendall, *The Conservative Affirmation* (Chicago: Henry Regnery, 1963), 142.

21. Quoted in Smant, *Principles and Heresies*, 335.

22. Nash, *Conservative Intellectual Movement in America*, 141.

23. William F. Buckley, Jr., "Introduction," in *Did You Ever See a Dream Walking? American Conservative Thought in the Twentieth Century*, ed. William F. Buckley, Jr. (Indianapolis: Bobbs-Merrill, 1970), xvii.

24. Smant, *Principles and Heresies*, 104.

25. Nash, *Conservative Intellectual Movement in America*, 146.

26. William Desmond, "Hegel, Dialectic, and Deconstruction," *Philosophy & Rhetoric* 18 (1985): 253.

27. Richard Weaver, "Language Is Sermonic," in *Language Is Sermonic: Richard Weaver on the Nature of Rhetoric*, ed. Richard L. Johannesen, Rennard Strickland, and Ralph T. Eubanks (Baton Rouge: Louisiana State University Press, 1985), 165.

28. Thomas Farrell, *Norms of Rhetorical Culture* (New Haven, Conn.: Yale University Press, 1993), 33. See also James Jasinski, *Sourcebook on Rhetoric: Key Concepts in Contemporary Rhetorical Studies* (Thousand Oaks, Calif.: Sage, 2001), 165.

29. Michael Kochin, "Rhetoric, Dialectic, and Public Discourse," in *Rhetoric: Concord and Controversy*, ed. Antonio de Velasco and Melody Lehn (Long Grove, Ill.: Waveland Press, 2012), 52.

30. Z. A. Jordan, *The Evolution of Dialectical Materialism: A Philosophical and Sociological Analysis* (New York: St. Martin's Press, 1967), 74.

31. Desmond, "Hegel, Dialectic, and Deconstruction," 255.

32. Jordan, *Evolution of Dialectical Materialism*, 87.

33. James Russell, "Dialectics and Class Analysis," *Science & Society* 44 (1980/1981): 474.

34. Much of the Marxian corpus, especially his later works, embraced explicitly dialectical principles, including "the law of contradiction, the negation of negations, and the unity of opposites." Karl Marx, *Capital* (Harmondsworth: Penguin, 1988), 1:103. The famous line about "standing Hegel upon his head" was Engels's. See Friedrich Engels, *Ludwig Feuerbach and the Outcome of Classical German Philosophy* (New York: International Publishers, 1935), 54. For Marx's view of Hegel, see James Farr, "Engels, Dewey, and the Reception of Marxism in America," in *Engels After Marx*, ed. Manfred B. Steger and Terrell Carver (University Park: Pennsylvania State University Press, 1999), 279. The dialectical method was rehabilitated by Marx in the late 1850s despite his earlier denunciations. Henri Lefebvre, *Dialectical Materialism* (London: Jonathan Cape, 1968), 82–83.

35. Ian Fraser, "Two of a Kind: Hegel, Marx, Dialectic and Form," *Capital & Class* 61 (1997): 96. See also Jordan, *Evolution of Dialectical Materialism*, 87.

36. See Joan Huber Rytina and Charles P. Loomis, "Marxist Dialectic and Pragmatism: Power as Knowledge," *American Sociological Review* 35 (1970):

310; Jordan, *Evolution of Dialectical Materialism*, 97.

37. Karl Marx, *Manifesto of the Communist Party*, in *The Marx-Engels Reader*, 2nd ed., ed. Robert C. Tucker (New York: W. W. Norton, 1978), 474.

38. Between the *1844 Manuscripts*, the *German Ideology*, the *Grundrisse*, and *Capital*, Marx established methods that some scholars have identified as different, if not contradictory. See Philip J. Kain, "Marx's Dialectic Method," *History and Theory* 19 (1980): 297.

39. Distinguishing between Marx's and Hegel's use of the dialectic, Kain writes, "The process which begins with abstract categories and moves toward the concrete is simply, for Marx, a method, the way in which thought comes to grasp the concrete. It is not to be identified, as it was for Hegel, with the actual historical genesis of the concrete." See ibid.

40. Jordan, *Evolution of Dialectical Materialism*, 4–5. Engels bears much of the responsibility for the application of dialectical materialism to natural science, especially after Marx's death. See Terrell Carver, "The Engels-Marx Question: Interpretation, Identity/ies, Partnership, Politics," in Steger and Carver, *Engels After Marx*; Peter T. Manicas, "Engels's Philosophy of Science," in Steger and Carver, *Engels After Marx*.

41. Lefebvre, *Dialectical Materialism*, 61; Norman Levine, *Dialogue within the Dialectic* (London: George Allen & Unwin, 1984), 144.

42. Quoted in Hart, *Making of the American Conservative Mind*, 47.

43. Levine, *Dialogue within the Dialectic*, 257.

44. Paul Thomas, *Marxism and Scientific Socialism: From Engels to Althusser* (New York: Routledge, 2008), 97.

45. Quoted in Leszek Kolakowski, *Main Currents of Marxism* (New York: W. W. Norton, 2005), 906. See also Thomas, *Marxism and Scientific Socialism*, 98; Robert T. De George, *Patterns in Soviet Thought* (Ann Arbor: University of Michigan Press, 1970), 3.

46. Just like conservative anti-Communist and *National Review* writer James Burnham, Meyer had been drawn to Marx at Balliol in England. See Hart, *Making of the American Conservative Mind*, 49.

47. Smant, *Principles and Heresies*, 7.

48. Ibid., 9.

49. Hart, *Making of the American Conservative Mind*, 50. Meyer founded the American Conservative Union and the New York Conservative Party, lectured frequently before gatherings of the Intercollegiate Society of Individualists, and was deeply involved in Goldwater's campaign against Lyndon Johnson.

50. Frank Meyer, *The Moulding of Communists: The Training of the Communist Cadre* (New York: Harcourt, 1961).

51. Hart, *Making of the American Conservative Mind*, 44.

52. Frank Meyer, "Freedom, Tradition, Conservatism," in *What Is Conservatism?*, ed. Frank. S. Meyer (New York: Holt, Rinehart, & Winston, 1964), 9–10; Meyer, *Moulding of Communists*, 16, 75.

53. Smant, *Principles and Heresies*, 101.

54. Frank Meyer, *In Defense of Freedom: A Conservative Credo* (Chicago: Henry Regnery, 1962), 1.

55. Ibid., 6. When Edwin Feulner, president of the Heritage Foundation, recounted his preferred conservative thinkers, Russell Kirk, Friedrich Hayek, and Milton Friedman, he immediately acknowledged the heated disagreements that would erupt if they occupied the same room. He continued: "But I don't believe my respect for them is schizophrenic. All shared a revulsion against 'gnosticism' and 'social engineering.'" Edwin J. Feulner, "Introduction," in *The March of Freedom: Modern Classics in Conservative Thought*, ed. Edwin J. Feulner (Dallas: Spence, 1998), xix.

56. Meyer, *Defense of Freedom*, 1.

57. James Farr, "Conceptual Change and Constitutional Innovation," in *Conceptual Change and the Constitution*, ed. Terence Ball and J. G. A. Pocock (Lawrence: University Press of Kansas, 1988), 24.

58. Chaim Perelman and Lucie Olbrechts-Tyteca, *The New Rhetoric: A Treatise on Argumentation* (Notre Dame, Ind.: University of Notre Dame Press, 1969), 195. Perelman and Olbrechts-Tyteca, it should be noted, distinguish between contradiction and inconsistency. Both concepts are useful here in that both imply the kind of philosophical deficiency Meyer feared.

59. Ibid., 190.

60. Ibid., 194.

61. Meyer, *Moulding of Communists*, 53.

62. Ibid., 58.

63. Ibid., 50.

64. Ibid., 53.

65. Hart, *Making of the American Conservative Mind*, 48.

66. Russell Kirk, "An Ideologue of Liberty," *Sewanee Review* 72 (April–June 1964): 349. For a similar accusation about Meyer's work, see Rothbard, "Frank S. Meyer," 362.

67. Quoted in Feulner, *March of Freedom*, x.

68. Kirk, "Ideologue of Liberty," 350.

69. Garry Wills, *Confessions of a Conservative* (Garden City, N.Y.: Doubleday, 1979), 55.

70. Quoted in Smant, *Principles and Heresies*, 100–101.

71. Perelman and Olbrechts-Tyteca, *New Rhetoric*, 190.

72. Roderick P. Hart, "The Rhetoric of the True Believer," *Speech Monographs* 38 (1971): 260.

73. Frank Meyer, "Consensus and Divergence," in Meyer, *What Is Conservatism?* 232.

74. Meyer, "Consensus and Divergence," 232.

75. M. Stanton Evans rejected the notion that Meyer was a coalition builder first and a serious theorist second. "From the record, and from innumerable talks with Frank . . . , I think nothing could be further from the truth than these invidious descriptions." Quoted in Smant, *Principles and Heresies*, xvi. See also East, *American Conservative Movement*, 102.

76. Meyer, "Why Freedom?" 163.

77. Hart, *Making of the American Conservative Mind*, 48.

78. Meyer, *In Defense of Freedom*, 44.

79. Ibid., 6.

80. Ibid., 60.

81. Ibid., 27.

82. Ibid., 36.

83. Ibid., 53.

84. Ibid., 3.

85. Many disagree with Meyer's equation of libertarianism and selfishness. See Sheldon Richman, "The Ubiquity of Economic Phenomena," *Freeman*, March 23, 2012; Rothbard, "Frank S. Meyer," 354–355.

86. Meyer, *In Defense of Freedom*, 49.

87. Ibid., 71.

88. Meyer, "Freedom, Tradition, Conservatism," 18.

89. Meyer, *In Defense of Freedom*, 8.

90. Meyer, "Why Freedom?" 158–159.

91. Meyer, "Freedom, Tradition, Conservatism," 8–9.

92. Hart, *Making of the American Conservative Mind*, 109–110. Meyer was raised Jewish but abandoned the faith as a Communist in the 1930s. Smant, *Principles and Heresies*, 339. See also Garry Wills, "The Teacher," *National Review*, April 28, 1972, 473.

93. Meyer, *In Defense of Freedom*, 5.

94. Meyer, "Freedom, Tradition, Conservatism," 19.

95. Ibid., 11.

96. Ibid.

97. Ibid., 9.

98. Quoted in Smant, *Principles and Heresies*, 101.

99. Wills, *Confessions of a Conservative*, 55. See also Lisa McGirr, "Piety and Property: Conservatism and Right-wing Movements in the Twentieth Century," in *Perspectives on Modern America: Making Sense of the Twentieth Century*, ed. Harvard Sitkoff (New York: Oxford University Press, 2000), 34.

100. Meyer's libertarian critics were just as dismissive if not as vitriolic. See Murray Rothbard, "Conservatism and Freedom: A Libertarian Comment," *Modern Age* 5 (1961): 217–220; Justin Raimondo, *Reclaiming the American Right: The Lost Legacy of the Conservative Movement* (Wilmington, Del.: ISI Books, 2008). Other ex-conservatives have been no more charitable toward Meyer. Michael Lind claimed, "The glaring contradiction between social conservatism and radical, destabilizing capitalism had not been resolved, but conservatives pretended it had been." Michael Lind, *Up from Conservatism: Why the Right Is Wrong for America* (New York: Free Press Paperbacks, 1997), 54–55.

101. Russell Kirk, "Libertarians: The Chirping Sectaries," *Modern Age* 25 (1981): 345. As George F. Will noted in 2006, "The tension between Kirk and Meyer prefigured today's tensions between 'social conservatives,' who take their bearings from European and religious thinkers, and minimal government conservatives, whose formative influences were Friedrich Hayek's and Milton Friedman's writings on political economy and Barry Goldwater's sunny Southwestern libertarianism." George F. Will, "The Conservative Imagination," *New York Times*, February 26, 2006.

102. Smant, *Principles and Heresies*, 105.

103. Hart, *Making of the American Conservative Mind*, 45. Kirk's attacks on Mill's *On Liberty* in various outlets were read as attacks on Meyer's approach. See their debate in *National Review* on Mill between January 26 and March 28, 1956. The opening salvo in their dispute had been Meyer's harsh review (titled "Collectivism Rebaptized") of Kirk's *The Conservative Mind* in *Freeman* years earlier. See Meyer, *In Defense of Freedom and Related Essays*, 3.

104. E. J. Dionne, "The Right in the Rearview Mirror," *American Prospect*, September 2, 2008.

105. Frank S. Meyer, "In Defense of John Stuart Mill," *National Review*, March 28, 1956, 24.

106. Smant, *Principles and Heresies*, 100.

107. L. Brent Bozell, "Freedom or Virtue?," *National Review*, September 11, 1962, 181.

108. Stanley Parry, "The Faces of Freedom," *Modern Age* 8 (Spring 1964): 208.

109. Jonah Goldberg, "Libertarians Under My Skin: Grow Up Already," *National Review*, March 2, 2001. Goldberg continued, "Generally speaking, traditionalist conservatives and free-market libertarians agree on about 85% of all public-policy issues."

110. Niels Bjerre-Poulsen, *Right Face: Organizing the American Conservative Movement 1945–1965* (Copenhagen: Museum Tusculanum Press, 2002), 54.

111. Nash, *Conservative Intellectual Movement in America*, 166.

112. Ibid., 161.

113. John Micklethwait and Adrian Wooldridge, *The Right Nation: Conservative Power in America* (New York: Penguin Books, 2004), 47–48.

114. Richard Brookhiser, *Right Place, Right Time: Coming of Age with William F. Buckley Jr. and the Conservative Movement* (New York: Basic Books, 2011), 80.

115. Frank Meyer, *The Conservative Mainstream* (New Rochelle, N.Y.: Arlington House, 1969).

116. Nash, *Conservative Intellectual Movement in America*, 164.

117. Ibid., 165.

118. Smant, *Principles and Heresies*, 107

119. Peter Witonski, ed., *The Wisdom of Conservatism* (New Rochelle, N.Y.: Arlington House, 1971), 1:37.

120. Smant, *Principles and Heresies*, 347.

121. Witonski, "Political Philosopher," 468.

122. See the Heritage Foundation's mission statement available via http://www.heritage.org/about.

123. See the American Conservative Union's mission statement available via http://www.conservative.org/about-acu/principles/.

124. Paul Ryan, "How Will Conservatism Become Credible Again," *New Ledger*, June 3, 2009.

125. Steven F. Hayward, "How Reagan Became Reagan," *Claremont Review of Books*, August 30, 2004.

126. Ronald Reagan, "Remarks at the Conservative Political Action Conference Dinner," March 20, 1981, available via http://www.presidency.ucsb.edu/ws/index.php?pid=43580&st=conservative&st1=.

127. Ibid.

128. Ibid.

129. Peggy Noonan, "'Shrink to Win' Isn't Much of a Strategy," *Wall Street Journal*, May 1, 2009.

130. Feulner, *March of Freedom*, 142–143.

131. Lee Edwards, "The End of Conservatism?" *Heritage Foundation Lectures*, April 27, 2009, available via http://www.heritage.org/Research/Lecture/The-End-of-Conservatism.

132. Sager, *Elephant in the Room*, 6.

133. Ibid., 207. When pollsters have asked conservative respondents to choose whether promoting individual freedom or traditional values was more important, the results have split down the middle.

134. Ibid., 21–22.

135. Ibid., 195.

136. Jonah Goldberg, "A Lib-Lib Romance," *National Review*, December 31, 2006.

137. Edwards, "End of Conservatism?"

138. Perlstein, *Before the Storm*, 65.

Chapter Five. WFB

1. Ann Coulter's obituary exemplifies the persistence of these labels of Buckley. See Ann Coulter, "William F. Buckley: R.I.P., *Enfant Terrible*," *Human Events*, February 27, 2008.

2. Buckley first identified as an "individualist" in *God and Man at Yale*. Much later, he published *Happy Days Are Here Again: Reflections of a Libertarian Journalist*.

3. Bob Colacello, "Mr. and Mrs. Right," *Vanity Fair*, January 2009, 115; Douglas Martin, "William F. Buckley Jr. Is Dead at 82," *New York Times*, February 27, 2008.

4. Jeffrey Hart, *The Making of the American Conservative Mind: National Review and Its Times* (Wilmington, Del.: ISI Books, 2007), 3.

5. Ibid., 2–3. In a more personal testimony, *National Review* writer Jay Nordlinger disclosed that he "just loved being out" with Buckley. "You were the recipient of reflected glory," he explained. "I'd take him to a restaurant, and the maitre d' would be wide-eyed. He would never look at me the same way again." Jay Nordlinger, "Only a Few Notes . . . ," *National Review*, March 3, 2008.

6. Rich Lowry, "A Personal Retrospective: *NR* and Its Founder," *National Review*, November 17, 2005. See also Lee Edwards, *William F. Buckley Jr.: The Maker of a Movement* (Wilmington, Del.: ISI Books, 2010).

7. Michael Gerson, "Buckley Loved Conservatism Enough to Transform It Utterly," *Newsweek*, March 10, 2008.

8. David Franke, *Quotations from Chairman Bill* (New Rochelle, N.Y.: Arlington House, 1970).

9. Patrick J. Buchanan, *Right from the Beginning* (Boston: Little, Brown, 1988), 245.

10. Phillip Sipiora, "Introduction," in *Rhetoric and Kairos: Essays in History, Theory, and Praxis*, ed. Phillip Sipiora and James S. Baumlin (Albany: State University of New York Press, 2002), 10.

11. Robert Hariman, *Political Style: The Artistry of Power* (Chicago: University of Chicago Press, 1995), 11.

12. Ibid., 9.

13. Robert Hariman, "Decorum, Power, and the Courtly Style," *Quarterly Journal of Speech* 78 (1992): 149.

14. William F. Buckley, Jr., *Miles Gone By: A Literary Autobiography* (Washington, D.C.: Regnery, 2004), 397.

15. Ibid., 399.

16. Sam Tanenhaus, "Athwart History," *New Republic*, March 19, 2007, 32.

17. Jonah Goldberg, "Prince of Polysyllabism: He Was a Hapax Legomenon in the Book of Life," *National Review*, February 29, 2008.

18. Samuel S. Vaughn, "Lexicon," in *The Right Word*, ed. Samuel S. Vaughn (New York: Random House, 1996), 407–507. See also Roger Kimball and Linda Bridges, eds., *Athwart History: Half a Century of Polemics, Animadversions, and Illuminations: A William F. Buckley Jr. Omnibus* (New York: Encounter Books, 2010).

19. William F. Buckley, Jr., *The Lexicon: A Cornucopia of Wonderful Words for the Inquisitive Word Lover* (New York: Harvest Books, 1998).

20. William F. Buckley, Jr., "The Intellectuals and Socialism," in *Essays on Hayek*, ed. Fritz Machlup (New York: New York University Press, 1976), 102–103.

21. Quoted in Gerson, "Buckley Loved Conservatism."

22. Richard A. Lanham, *A Handlist of Rhetorical Terms*, 2nd ed. (Berkeley: University of California Press, 1991), 142.

23. George Orwell, "Politics and the English Language," in *Why I Write* (New York: Penguin, 2005), 119.

24. Richard Brookhiser, *Right Time, Right Place: Coming of Age with William F. Buckley Jr. and the Conservative Movement* (New York: Basic Books, 2009), 171. For several instances in which Buckley misused big words, see Garry Wills, "Daredevil," *Atlantic*, July/August 2009.

25. *60 Minutes*, William F. Buckley, Jr., interview with Morley Safer, first broadcast January 19, 1981, by CBS.

26. Brookhiser, *Right Time*, 15.

27. Rick Perlstein, *Before the Storm: Barry Goldwater and the Unmaking of the American Consensus* (New York: Hill & Wang, 2001), 70.

28. Quoted in Lowry, "A Personal Retrospective." Limbaugh summarized Buckley's importance in his development to a reporter in 2008: "I grew up on *National Review* and Mr. Buckley. . . . Aside from my father, he's the most influential man in my life." Quoted in Zev Chafets, "Late Period Limbaugh," *New York Times*, July 6, 2008.

29. Quoted in James Bowman, "The Leader of the Opposition," *National Review*, September 6, 1993, 93.

30. Lanham, *Handlist of Rhetorical Terms*, 92, 135.

31. Elizabeth Galewski, "The Strange Case for Women's Capacity to Reason: Judith Sargent Murray's Use of Irony in 'On the Equality of the Sexes' (1790)," *Quarterly Journal of Speech* 93 (2007): 87.

32. Wayne C. Booth, *A Rhetoric of Irony* (Chicago: University of Chicago Press, 1974), 13. See also Kathryn M. Olson and Clark D. Olson, "Beyond Strategy: A Reader-Centered Analysis of Irony's Dual Persuasive Uses," *Quarterly Journal of Speech* 90 (2004): 24–52.

33. Galewski, "Strange Case," 87; Kenneth Burke, *A Grammar of Motives* (Berkeley: University of California Press, 1969), 514.

34. Galewski, "Strange Case," 87. See also Robert E. Terrill, "Irony, Silence, and Time: Frederick Douglass on the Fifth of July," *Quarterly Journal of Speech* 89 (2003): 216–234.

35. William F. Buckley, Jr., *God and Man at Yale: The Superstitions of "Academic Freedom"*, 50th anniv. ed. (Washington, D.C.: Regnery, 2002), 131.

36. Ibid., 136.

37. William F. Buckley, Jr., *Up from Liberalism* (New York: Stein and Day, 1985), xxi.

38. Ibid., xxii.

39. Ibid., 192–193.

40. Ibid., 195–196.

41. William F. Buckley, Jr., "Reflections on the Failure of 'National Review' to Live Up to Liberal Expectations," *National Review*, August 1, 1956, 7.

42. Ibid., 10.

43. See William F. Buckley, Jr., "How to Attack a Liberal," *National Review*, February 26, 1963.

44. Ann Coulter, *How to Talk to a Liberal (If You Must)* (New York: Three Rivers Press, 2004), 20.

45. Garry Wills, *Confessions of a Conservative* (Garden City, N.Y.: Doubleday, 1979), 33.

46. Buckley, *Up from Liberalism*, 207.

47. Lanham, *Handlist of Rhetorical Terms*, 192, 195.

48. Buckley, *God and Man*, xxxv.

49. Ibid., xlii–xliii.

50. Brookhiser, *Right Time*, 11.

51. George F. Will, *One Man's America: The Pleasures and Provocations of Our Singular America* (New York: Crown Forum, 2008), 12.

52. Brookhiser, *Right Time*, 14.

53. William F. Buckley, Jr., *Cancel Your Own Goddam Subscription: Notes & Asides from* National Review (New York: Basic Books, 2007), 25, 33.

54. "Where Does One Start: A Guide to Reading WFB," *National Review*, February 29, 2008.

55. Richard Viguerie and David Franke, *America's Right Turn: How Conservatives Used New and Alternative Media to Take Power* (Chicago: Bonus Books, 2004), 62.

56. Barry Goldwater, *The Conscience of a Conservative*, 30th anniv. ed. (Washington, D.C.: Regnery Gateway, 1988), xxiv.

57. Coulter, "William F. Buckley."

58. Donald Devine, "Buckley's Program," *Conservative Battleline*, March 12, 2008.

59. Ronald Reagan, "The Defense of Freedom and the Metaphysics of Fun," in *Tear Down This Wall: The Reagan Revolution—a* National Review *History*, ed. *National Review* (New York: Continuum, 2004), 75.

60. Ibid., 76.

61. See Dale L. Sullivan, "*Kairos* and the Rhetoric of Belief," *Quarterly Journal of Speech* 78 (1992): 318. See also James L. Kinneavy, "*Kairos* in Classical and Modern Rhetorical Theory," in *Rhetoric and Kairos: Essays in History, Theory, and Praxis*, ed. Phillip Sipiora and James S. Baumlin (Albany: State University of New York Press, 2002), 60.

62. Buckley, *Up from Liberalism*, 188.

63. Quoted in John Judis, *William F. Buckley, Jr.: Patron Saint of the Conservatives* (New York: Simon & Schuster, 1988), 133.

64. Buckley, *Up from Liberalism*, 205–206.

65. Ibid., 205.

66. Ibid., 188.

67. Ibid., 196.

68. Ibid., 209.

69. Ibid., 189.

70. Ibid., 202–204.

71. Ibid., 211.

72. Quoted in Linda Bridges and John R. Coyne Jr., *Strictly Right: William F. Buckley Jr. and the American Conservative Movement* (Hoboken, N.J.: John Wiley & Sons, 2007), 3.

73. Hart, *Making of the American Conservative Mind*, 18.

74. *National Review* would later change to a biweekly format.

75. E. J. Dionne, "The Right in the Rearview Mirror," *American Prospect*, September 2, 2008.

76. Hart, *Making of the American Conservative Mind*, 5.

77. Quoted in Kevin Mattson, "Remembering Buckley for the Right Reasons," *American Prospect*, March 8, 2008.

78. Hart, *Making of the American Conservative Mind*, 5. See also Evan Thomas, "He Knew He Was Right," *Newsweek*, March 10, 2008.

79. Niels Bjerre-Poulsen, *Right Face: Organizing the American Conservative Movement 1945–1965* (Copenhagen: Museum Tusculanum Press, 2002), 116.

80. Michael Uhlmann, "The Right Stuff," *Claremont Review of Books*, July 5, 2005.

81. Quoted in Judis, *William F. Buckley*, 189.

82. Richard Hofstadter, *The Paranoid Style in American Politics: And Other Essays* (Boston: Harvard University Press, 1996).

83. Alfred S. Regnery, *Upstream: The Ascendance of American Conservatism* (New York: Threshold Editions, 2008), 53.

84. William F. Buckley, Jr., "Publisher's Statement," *National Review*, November 19, 1955.

85. Ibid.

86. Ibid.

87. Quoted in John Patrick Diggins, *Up from Communism: Conservative Odysseys in American Intellectual History* (New York: Harper & Row, 1975), 343.

88. William Voegeli, "The Wilderness Years Begin," *Claremont Review of Books*, June 5, 2009.

89. Louis Menand, "Notable Quotables," *New Yorker*, February 19, 2007.

90. See Eric Voegelin, *The New Science of Politics* (Chicago: University of Chicago Press, 1952).

91. Jonah Goldberg, "Immanent Corrections: Getting Gays Straight and Other Odd Things," *National Review*, January 16, 2002.

92. William Kristol, "The Indispensable Man," *New York Times*, March 3, 2008.

93. Christopher Buckley, "Buckley Bows Out of *National Review*," *Daily Beast*, October 14, 2008.

94. *National Review*'s Ramesh Ponnuru noted that when the Iraq War began, "almost everyone who considers himself a conservative did support it." Ramesh Ponnuru, "Getting to the Bottom of the 'Neo' Nonsense: Before You Talk about Conservatives Know What You're Doing," *National Review*, June 16, 2003, 29; William F. Buckley, Jr., "It Didn't Work," *National Review*, February 24, 2006.

95. Lee Edwards, "The Unforgettable Candidate," *National Review*, July 6, 1998, 37; Perlstein, *Before the Storm*, 473.

96. Quoted in Perlstein, *Before the Storm*, 472.

97. William F. Buckley, Jr., "A Relaxing View: On the Pros and Cons of a Would-be President," *National Review*, November 28, 1967.

98. Joe Scarborough, The *Last Best Hope: Restoring Conservatism and America's Promise* (New York: Crown Forum, 2009), 21.

99. Ibid., 7, 21.

100. Ramesh Ponnuru, speech at "On the Ropes: What William F. Buckley Jr. Can Teach Today's Conservatives," March 3, 2009, American Enterprise Institute and National Review Institute, available via http://app2.capitalreach.com/esp1204/servlet/tc?cn=aei&c=10162&s=20271& e=10720&&espmt=2.

101. For more on unstable irony, see Booth, *Rhetoric of Irony*, 250.

102. Kathleen Parker, "The Buckley Son Rises and Runs," *National Review*, October 17, 2008.

103. Buckley, "Buckley Bows."

104. See brief eulogies in "Where Does One Start: A Guide to Reading WFB."

105. Rich Lowry, "Gratitude: WFB, R.I.P." *National Review*, February 29, 2008.

106. Ibid.

107. R. Emmett Tyrell explained Buckley's celebrity in conservative circles: "Bill's exploits fascinated most members of the conservative movement, though jealous murmurs did emit from some who, weighted down by the conservative temperament, disapproved of Bill's proclivity for glamour and—worst of all—his proclivity for going it alone, independent of the movement." R. Emmett Tyrell, *The Conservative Crack-Up* (New York: Simon & Schuster, 1992), 264.

108. Michael Savage, *Liberalism Is a Mental Disorder* (Nashville, Tenn.: Thomas Nelson, 2006); Ann Coulter, *Godless: The Church of Liberalism* (New York: Three Rivers Press, 2007); Sean Hannity, *Deliver Us from Evil: Defeating Terrorism, Despotism, and Liberalism* (New York: HarperCollins, 2004).

109. William F. Buckley, Jr., "Introduction," in *Did You Ever See a Dream Walking? American Conservative Thought in the Twentieth Century*, ed. William F. Buckley, Jr. (Indianapolis: Bobbs-Merrill, 1970), xvii.

110. Ibid.

111. Whittaker Chambers, *Odyssey of a Friend: Whittaker Chambers' Letters to William F. Buckley Jr.: 1954–1961*, ed. William F. Buckley, Jr. (New York: G. P. Putnam's Sons, 1969), 83.

112. Wills, "Daredevil."

Chapter Six. Whittaker Chambers's Martyrdom

1. Sam Tanenhaus, *Whittaker Chambers* (New York: Random House, 1997), 461.

2. David Cort, "Of Guilt and Resurrection," in *Alger Hiss, Whittaker Chambers,*

and the Schism in the American Soul, ed. Patrick A. Swan (Wilmington, Del.: ISI Books, 2003), 142. See also George Nash, *Reappraising the Right: The Past and Future of American Conservatism* (Wilmington, Del.: ISI Books, 2009), 43.

3. Rebecca West, "Whittaker Chambers," in Swan, *Alger Hiss*, 108. See also Michael Kimmage, *The Conservative Turn: Lionel Trilling, Whittaker Chambers, and the Lessons of Anti-Communism* (Cambridge, Mass.: Harvard University Press, 2009), 204.

4. Ralph de Toledano, "A Tribute to Whittaker Chambers," *Heritage Foundation Lectures*, March 23, 1984, 10.

5. Susan Jacoby, *Alger Hiss and the Battle for History* (New Haven, Conn.: Yale University Press, 2009), 29.

6. John V. Fleming, *The Anti-Communist Manifestos: Four Books That Shaped the Cold War* (New York: W. W. Norton, 2009), 12.

7. Quoted in Tanenhaus, *Whittaker Chambers*, 461.

8. Kimmage, *Conservative Turn*, 216.

9. Ibid., 218.

10. Quoted in Tanenhaus, *Whittaker Chambers*, 446. Robert Kenny writes that rhetorical tragedy *"takes particular people and events in the play of our lives and dresses them up with the characteristics of universals."* Robert Wade Kenny, "The Phenomenology of the Disaster: Toward a Rhetoric of Tragedy," *Philosophy & Rhetoric* 39 (2006): 97.

11. Tanenhaus, *Whittaker Chambers*, 446.

12. Ibid., 462–463. *Witness* occupied the top spot on the *New York Times* nonfiction list for the entire summer of 1952 and was reviewed by the era's most influential intellectuals. Hannah Arendt, John Dos Passos, Irving Howe, Sidney Hook, and Arthur Schlesinger Jr., among others, reviewed *Witness*. More copies of *Witness* were sold in 1952 than all but eight other books.

13. Sam Tanenhaus, "The End of the Journey: From Whittaker Chambers to George W. Bush," *New Republic*, July 2, 2007, 46.

14. Kenneth Burke, *Permanence and Change: An Anatomy of Purpose*, 2nd ed. (Indianapolis: Bobbs-Merrill, 1954), 195–196; Michael L. Butterworth, "The Passion of the Tebow: Media and Heroic Language in the Tragic Frame," *Critical Studies in Media Communication* 30 (2013): 20; Edward C. Appel, "'Tragedy-lite' or 'Melodrama'? In Search of a Standard Generic Tag," *Southern Communication Journal* 73 (2008): 182–183; Kenny, "Phenomenology of the Disaster," 97. See also Kenneth Burke, *A Grammar of Motives* (Berkeley: University of California Press, 1969), 406–408.

15. Fleming, *Anti-Communist Manifestos*, 271.

16. Hilton Kramer, "Thinking About *Witness*," in Swan, *Alger Hiss*, 308; Jeffrey Hart, *The Making of the American Conservative Mind: National Review and Its Times* (Wilmington, Del.: ISI Books, 2007), 12. Chambers, in fact, studied both

Dante and Dostoevsky when composing *Witness*, along with the touchstones of Western autobiography by Augustine, Rousseau, and Henry Adams. Tanenhaus, *Whittaker Chambers*, 452.

17. For the Jonah reference, see Chambers, *Witness*, 770. See also Fleming, *Anti-Communist Manifestos*, 216. For the similarity between Chambers and Mark's Jesus, see Whittaker Chambers, *Witness* (New York: Random House, 1952), 764–769.

18. Kimmage, *Conservative Turn*, 205.

19. Chambers, *Witness*, 799.

20. Lee Edwards, "Whittaker Chambers: Man of Courage, Man of Faith," *Heritage Foundation Lectures*, April 2, 2001. Other reviewers likened its dismal sentimentality to a "Sophoclean tragedy in slow motion." Cited in William F. Buckley Jr., "The End of Whittaker Chambers," in Swan, *Alger Hiss*, 143.

21. Chambers, *Witness*, 25. For the influence of the line, see, among others, William Voegeli, "The Wilderness Years Begin," *Claremont Review of Books*, June 5, 2009.

22. Paul Boyer, "The Evangelical Resurgence in 1970s American Protestantism," in *Rightward Bound: Making America Conservative in the 1970s*, ed. Bruce J. Schulman and Julian E. Zelizer (Cambridge, Mass.: Harvard University Press, 2008), 33. See also Donald T. Critchlow, *Phyllis Schlafly and Grassroots Conservatism: A Woman's Crusade* (Princeton, N.J.: Princeton University Press, 2007), 40. James Burnham, in particular, exerted a powerful force on the Right's Cold War consciousness. Burnham's books, such as *The Suicide of the West*, were widely read among conservatives as dossiers on the disguised intentions and secret military capabilities of the Soviets. He refused to call a war that killed millions "cold"; instead, he consistently dubbed the Cold War the "Third World War" in a frequent *National Review* column. As a writer and as an adviser to Buckley, "Burnham was absolutely central to *National Review*." See Hart, *Making of the American Conservative Mind*, 18.

23. As Charles Kesler noted, "the protean ideological attractiveness" of Communism, one conservative explained, "forced conservatives to look past their myriad disagreements and focus on a common threat." See Charles Kesler, speech at the American Enterprise Institute and National Review Institute, "On the Ropes: What William F. Buckley Jr. Can Teach Today's Conservatives," March 3, 2009, available via http://app2.capitalreach.com/esp1204/servlet/tc?cn=aei&c=1016 2&s=20271&e=10720&&espmt=2. For more evidence that anti-Communism united disparate strands of the Right, see Alfred Regnery, speech at Buckley Program's Conference on *Witness*'s 60th Anniversary, Yale University, November 30, 2012, available via http://www.c-spanvideo.org/program/309872-3; Sean P. Cunningham, *Cowboy Conservatism: Texas and the Rise of the Modern Right* (Lexington: University Press of Kentucky, 2010), 4; Andrew E. Busch, *Reagan's Victory: The Presidential Election of 1980 and the Rise of the Right* (Lawrence: University Press of Kansas, 2005), 21; Richard Viguerie and David Franke, *America's Right Turn: How Conservatives Used New and Alternative Media to Take Power* (Chicago: Bonus Books, 2004), 63.

24. Garry Wills, *Confessions of a Conservative* (Garden City, N.Y.: Doubleday, 1979), 59.

25. George Nash, *The Conservative Intellectual Movement in America since 1945* (New York: Basic Books, 1976), 94. Conservative anti-Communist and, later, anti-ERA activist Phyllis Schlafly published *A Reading List for Americans* in 1957 as a guide to notable anti-Communist books. *Witness* was the most widely read book on the list. Critchlow, *Phyllis Schlafly*, 40.

26. John Judis, "The End of Conservatism," *New Republic*, August 31, 1992.

27. Edwards, "Whittaker Chambers." See also Terry Teachout, "Introduction," in *Notes from the Underground: The Whittaker Chambers—Ralph de Toledano Letters: 1949–1960*, ed. Ralph de Toledano (Washington, D.C.: Regnery, 1997), x.

28. Jeffrey O. Nelson, *Ten Books That Shaped America's Conservative Renaissance*, Intercollegiate Studies Institute, n.d., available via http://www.isi.org/conservative_tho/PDF/tenbooks.pdf.

29. Jon Weiner, *How We Forgot the Cold War: A Historical Journey across America* (Berkeley: University of California Press, 2012), 55–59.

30. Quoted in Robert Novak, *The Prince of Darkness* (New York: Crown Forum, 2007), 20. He continued: "From time to time in after dinner conversation with politicians on the campaign circuit over the years, I find a common bond with other people—some a generation younger—who have been alarmed, entranced, and always inspired by *Witness*." This defeatist element in Chambers's rhetoric, an element deeply opposed to the triumphalist, exceptionalist version of America's history and national destiny so popular among many conservatives, led a few to describe Chambers as "un-American." Nash, *Conservative Intellectual Movement in America*, 368. See also R. Emmett Tyrell, *The Conservative Crack-Up* (New York: Simon & Schuster, 1992), 35.

31. Michael M. Uhlmann, "The Right Stuff," *Claremont Review of Books*, September 5, 2005. One conservative depicted Chambers as a historical "fork in the road" in which "nothing was ever the same in the West in terms of its perception of the rise of Communism and the meaning of Communism." Frank Shakespeare, "A Tribute to Whittaker Chambers," *Heritage Foundation Lectures*, March 23, 1984.

32. Ralph de Toledano, "I Witness," *American Conservative Magazine*, February 14, 2005.

33. Chilton Williamson, *The Conservative Bookshelf: Essential Works That Impact Today's Conservative Thinkers* (New York: Citadel Press, 2004), 105.

34. The book did not become so salient because it provided conservatives specific advice on policy or tactics either. "It gives," Irving Howe remarked, "the opponents of the totalitarian state no strategy, no program with which to remake the world." *Witness* was an absorbing autobiography and did not take up doctrinal questions. Irving Howe, "God, Man and Stalin," in Swan, *Alger Hiss*, 89.

35. See also Carl T. Bogus, *Buckley: William F. Buckley Jr. and the Rise of American Conservatism* (New York: Bloomsbury Press, 2011), 97.

36. Nina J. Easton, *Gang of Five: Leaders at the Center of the Conservative Crusade* (New York: Simon & Schuster, 2000), 79.

37. John Patrick Diggins, *Ronald Reagan: Fate, Freedom, and the Making of History* (New York: W. W. Norton, 2007), 10. See also Buckley, "End of Whittaker Chambers," 163.

38. Burke, *Permanence and Change*, 196.

39. See also Tanenhaus, *Whittaker Chambers*, 465. Daniel Bell also made the connection between Communist converts and James's notion of the twice-born. Remarking on the relative lack of "optimism" and reduced "faith in the rationality or common sense of men" possessed by midcentury intellectuals, Bell concluded in *The End of Ideology* that "ours, a 'twice-born' generation, finds its wisdom in pessimism, evil, tragedy, and despair." Daniel Bell, *The End of Ideology: On the Exhaustion of Political Ideas in the Fifties* (New York: Free Press, 1962), 300.

40. Tragedy, Burke argues, can dignify those in trying circumstances. Kenneth Burke, *Counter-Statement*, 2nd ed. (Berkeley: University of California Press, 1968), 154. See also Philip Wander, "The Rhetoric of American Foreign Policy," *Quarterly Journal of Speech* 70 (1984): 342–347.

41. For more on conservatives' rhetoric of "evil," see James Arnt Aune, "The Argument from Evil in the Rhetoric of Reaction," *Rhetoric & Public Affairs* 6 (2003): 518–522.

42. Rick Perlstein, *Before the Storm: Barry Goldwater and the Unmaking of the American Consensus* (New York: Hill & Wang, 2001), 104.

43. Never a prodigal son, Buckley did not stray from Catholicism or individualism and secured the medal in 1992. Whereas Buckley's lifelong conservatism represented, as John Patrick Diggins writes, a conservative "virgin birth unsoiled by the sins of the Left," many other prominent conservatives in the 1950s and 1960s, especially *National Review* writers, were "haunted ideologues, ex-radicals with stained pasts." See John Patrick Diggins, *Up from Communism: Conservative Odysseys in American Intellectual History* (New York: Harper & Row, 1975), 404.

44. Robert James Branham, "The Role of the Convert in *Eclipse of Reason* and *The Silent Scream*," *Quarterly Journal of Speech* 77 (1991): 407–426.

45. See also Mary Eberstadt, ed., *Why I Turned Right: Leading Baby Boom Conservatives Chronicle Their Political Journeys* (New York: Threshold Editions, 2007); Michael K. Deaver, ed., *Why I Am a Reagan Conservative* (New York: Harper Collins, 2005).

46. Chambers, *Witness*, 446.

47. David C. Bailey, "Enacting Transformation: George W. Bush and the Pauline Conversion Narrative in *A Charge to Keep*," *Rhetoric & Public Affairs* 11 (2008): 216.

48. This is the historian Eusebius's account of Constantine's conversion. Imagery differs in other accounts.

49. Augustine, *The Confessions of Saint Augustine*, trans. E. B. Pusey (New York: Modern Library, 1999), 167.

50. Bailey, "Enacting Transformation," 218–220. Converts' proselytizing features "rhetorical indicators," including the adoption of a master attribution scheme, biographical reconstruction, the suspension of analogical reasoning, and the embracement of a master role in a new life. See also Clifford L. Staples and Armand L. Mauss, "Conversion or Commitment? A Reassessment of the Snow and Machalek Approach to the Study of Conversion," *Journal for the Scientific Struggle of Religion* 26 (1987): 122–147; David Snow and Richard Machalek, "The Sociology of Conversion," *Annual Review of Sociology* 10 (1984): 167–190.

51. Peter G. Stromberg, *Language and Self-transformation: A Study of the Christian Conversion Narrative* (Cambridge: Cambridge University Press, 1993), 3.

52. James defines conversion: "To be converted, to be regenerated, to receive grace, to experience religion, to gain an assurance, are so many phrases which denote the process, gradual or sudden, by which a self hitherto divided, an consciously wrong inferior and unhappy, becomes unified and consciously right superior and happy, in consequence of its firmer hold upon religious realities. This at least is what conversion signifies in general terms, whether or not we believe that a direct divine operation is needed to bring such a moral change about." William James, *The Varieties of Religious Experience: A Study in Human Nature* (New York: Penguin Books, 1982), 189.

53. Ibid., 151.

54. Ibid., 166.

55. Quoted in ibid., 157.

56. Ibid., 162.

57. Ibid., 362.

58. Kenneth Burke, *The Rhetoric of Religion: Studies in Logology* (Berkeley: University of California Press, 1970), 135.

59. Ibid.

60. Mark P. Moore, "To Execute Capital Punishment: The Mortification and Scapegoating of Illinois Governor George Ryan," *Western Journal of Communication* 70 (2006): 312.

61. Brian L. Ott and Eric Aoki, "The Politics of Negotiating Public Tragedy: Media Framing of the Matthew Sheppard Murder," *Rhetoric & Public Affairs* 5 (2002): 490.

62. Burke, *Rhetoric of Religion*, 223.

63. Mitch Daniels, Keynote Address at Buckley Program's Conference on *Witness*'s 60th Anniversary, Yale University, December 1, 2012, available via http://

buckleyprogram.com/media/release/2012/12/01/governor-mitch-daniels-delivers-keynote-address-buckley-program%E2%80%99s-november.

64. Chambers, *Witness*, 4.

65. Quoted in David Lipsky, *Although of Course You End Up Becoming Yourself: A Roadtrip with David Foster Wallace* (New York: Broadway, 2010), 72.

66. Michael Dirda, "James Lees-Milne," *Barnes and Noble Review*, August 10, 2010. For analyses of confession rhetoric, see Dave Tell, "Stanton's 'Solitude of Self' as Public Confession," *Communication Studies* 61 (2010): 172–183; Dave Tell, "The 'Shocking Story' of Emmett Till and the Politics of Public Confession," *Quarterly Journal of Speech* 94 (2008): 156–178.

67. Chambers, *Witness*, 450.

68. Ibid., 25. In Linda Bridges and William F. Rickenbacker's short tome, *The Art of Persuasion*, a style guide for conservatives with chapter titles like "Grab Your Reader!" and "A Pleasing Style," the authors begin by isolating the first task of the writer: to "entice" the reader to keep reading. They consider how several of the "masters" have handled the task, but the first one considered is Chambers's portrayal of himself as Lazarus. Linda Bridges and William F. Rickenbacker, *The Art of Persuasion: A National Review Rhetoric for Writers* (New York: Continuum, 1993), 5.

69. See John 11:40.

70. Chambers, *Witness*, 195–196.

71. Ibid., 14.

72. Ibid.

73. Ibid.

74. Ibid.

75. Ibid., 16.

76. Ibid., 15.

77. Ibid.

78. Acts 9:1–9:22. Paul's conversion, Krister Stendahl argues, diverged from other powerful "born again" narratives of Christian conversion in which a sinner's torment was alleviated through contact with the divine. The Pauline converted figure, like the twice-born convert, suffers for God. This convert's quest for redemption is made impossible by the haunting legacy of his tainted past. See Krister Stendahl, "The Apostle Paul and the Introspective Conscience of the West," in *Paul among the Jews and Gentiles and Other Essays*, ed. Krister Stendahl (London: SCM Press, 1976), 78–96.

79. Chambers, *Witness*, 16.

80. Ibid., 5. See also Fleming, *Anti-Communist Manifestos*, 270.

81. Chambers, *Witness*, 769.

82. Ibid., 204. Chambers had been in hiding avoiding regular work, steady hours, and normal mailing methods since his disappearance from underground Soviet contacts in 1939. He wrote that he did not want to end up like "Juliet Stuart Poyntz, a Midwestern American and Barnard graduate whose murder by the Russian secret police . . . made a deep impression on me about the time of my break with the Soviet underground."

83. Ibid., 21.

84. Ibid., 747.

85. Ibid., 22.

86. James, *Varieties*, 156–157.

87. Cited in Nash, *Conservative Intellectual Movement in America*, 105.

88. de Toledano, "I Witness."

89. Kimmage, *Conservative Turn*, 215. See also Mary C. Brennan, *Turning Right in the Sixties: The Conservative Capture of the GOP* (Chapel Hill: University of North Carolina Press, 1995), 10–11.

90. Chambers, *Witness*, 2, 450.

91. John Chamberlain, "Whittaker Chambers: Witness," *Freeman*, June 2, 1952, 579.

92. Brian Doherty, *Radicals for Capitalism: A Freewheeling History of the Modern American Libertarian Movement* (New York: Public Affairs, 2007), 123.

93. Chamberlain, "Whittaker Chambers," 581.

94. Terry Teachout, "Does Chambers Still Matter?" Speech at the Intercollegiate Studies Institute, April 26, 2003, video available via http://www.isi.org/lectures/lectures.aspx?SBy=lecture&Sfor=8C880C0B-9761-4219-8EF4-. See also Dan Mahoney, Speech at Whittaker Chambers Conference, Intercollegiate Studies Institute, April 26, 2003, available via http://www.c-spanvideo.org/program/177826-1.

95. Nash, *Reappraising the Right*, 42.

96. For analyses of similar rhetorics, see James Darsey, *The Prophetic Tradition and Radical Rhetoric in America* (New York: New York University Press, 1997).

97. Edwin Feulner, *The March of Freedom: Modern Classics of Conservative Thought* (Dallas: Spence, 2004), 217. Others have called him a "man of faith" and a model of "moral courage." See Edwards, "Whittaker Chambers"; Thomas Sowell, "Quotes on Trial," *Townhall*, June 8, 2003.

98. Nash, *Conservative Intellectual Movement in America*, 92. See also K. Alan Snyder, "Was Whittaker Chambers Wrong?" *First Principles*, January 22, 2008.

99. Teachout, "Does Chambers Still Matter?" See also Novak, *Prince of Darkness*, 20.

100. Whittaker Chambers, *Odyssey of a Friend: Whittaker Chambers' Letters to*

William F. Buckley, Jr.: 1954–1961, ed. William F. Buckley, Jr. (New York: G. P. Putnam's Sons, 1969), 227.

101. Ibid., 228. Chambers admitted that he had only tepidly accepted "conservative" when first asked to identify himself politically after the Hiss fracas. He later offered Buckley a different, oblique descriptor; Chambers considered himself a "man of the Right." Repeating Louis Hartz's argument, Chambers contended that true conservatism looked back fondly to a stable, hierarchal, and feudal past. Chambers said the United States had no such past. Chambers, *Odyssey of a Friend*, 247. Nash even argued that Chambers became an "ambivalent godfather of postwar conservatism" because he departed from Buckley's more aggressive political identity. Nash, *Reappraising the Right*, 41–42. See also Sam Tanenhaus, "Conservatism Is Dead: An Intellectual Autopsy of a Movement," *New Republic*, February 18, 2009.

102. Chambers, *Witness*, 12. See also Hart, *Making of the American Conservative Mind*, 11.

103. Chambers, *Witness*, 16.

104. Ibid. For an example of this line's impact, see Lowry, *Why I Turned Right*, 283–284.

105. Alfred S. Regnery, *Upstream: The Ascendance of American Conservatism* (New York: Threshold Editions, 2008), 42.

106. William A. Rusher, *The Rise of the Right* (New York: William Morrow, 1984), 26.

107. Richard M. Reinsch II, "Still Witnessing: The Enduring Relevance of Whittaker Chambers," Heritage Foundation's *First Principles Series Report* 38, April 1, 2011.

108. Kimmage, *Conservative Turn*, 215.

109. Feulner, *March of Freedom*, 215–216, 217. See also Kimmage, *Conservative Turn*, 215.

110. Feulner, *March of Freedom*, 217.

111. See Christian Lundberg, "Enjoying God's Death: *The Passion of the Christ* and the Practices of an Evangelical Public," *Quarterly Journal of Speech* 95 (2009): 396.

112. Easton, *Gang of Five*, 79.

113. Kimmage, *Conservative Turn*, 215.

114. Stephen Smoot, "Exposing Evil: 'Witness' Has Its 60th Anniversary," *Human Events*, July 21, 2012. See also Ann Coulter, *Treason: Liberal Treachery from the Cold War to the War on Terrorism* (New York: Crown Forum, 2003), 8–34.

115. Reinsch, "Still Witnessing." The Right remembers Chambers "as an extraordinarily sensitive and gifted man who was willingly destroying himself in order to awaken the nation to the Communist peril symbolized by the unrepentant traitor Alger Hiss." See Nash, *Conservative Intellectual Movement in America*, 100.

116. de Toledano, "Tribute to Whittaker Chambers."

117. Lionel Trilling, *The Liberal Imagination* (Boston: Harvard University Press, 1950), i. The line has subsequently been used by conservatives for contradictory purposes, as a yardstick of conservative progress since then as well as evidence of liberal dismissiveness. For example, see Rusher, *Rise of the Right*, 11. See also Ryan Sager, *The Elephant in the Room: Evangelicals, Libertarians, and the Battle to Control the Republican Party* (Hoboken, N.J.: John Wiley & Sons, 2006), 26.

118. Richard Hofstadter, "The Pseudo-Conservative Revolt—1954," in *The Paranoid Style in American Politics and Other Essays* (New York: Alfred A. Knopf, 1966), 44. Goldwater illustrated in his 1960 Republican National Convention speech that conservatives were also outsiders in their own party. See Regnery, *Upstream*, 90.

119. Kim Phillips-Fein, "Conservatism: A State of the Field," *Journal of American History* 98 (2011): 725.

120. Easton, *Gang of Five*, 81.

121. Ibid., 79.

122. Chambers, *Witness*, 9.

123. Ibid.

124. Ibid., 8.

125. Ibid., 191.

126. See also Wander, "Rhetoric of American Foreign Policy," 347.

127. Chambers, *Witness*, 449.

128. Ibid., 741.

129. In a review of *Witness*, the one-time Marxist theorist Sydney Hook argued, "He [Chambers] recklessly lumps Socialists, progressives, liberals, and men of good will together with the Communists. All are bound according to him by the same faith; but only Communists have the gumption and guts to live by it and pay the price." Sidney Hook, "The Faiths of Whittaker Chambers," in Swan, *Alger Hiss*, 75.

130. Howe, "God, Man and Stalin," 85.

131. Chambers, *Witness*, 471.

132. Ibid., 472.

133. Ibid., 444.

134. Calling Joseph McCarthy a "raven of disaster for the Right" and fearing that unchecked anti-Communist fervor risked creating an Orwellian police state, Chambers later resisted taking these assumptions about Communist enemies to the end of the line. Quoted in Tanenhaus, *Whittaker Chambers*, 492, 507.

135. Judis, "End of Conservatism."

136. Teachout, "Does Chambers Still Matter?"

137. Quoted in Nash, *Conservative Intellectual Movement in America*, 94. See also Rusher, *Rise of the Right*, 24–25.

138. Easton, *Gang of Five*, 81–82.

139. Chambers, *Witness*, 10.

140. Mahoney, Speech at Whittaker Chambers Conference.

141. de Toledano, "Tribute to Whittaker Chambers." See also Kevin Mattson, *Rebels All! A Short History of the Conservative Mind in Postwar America* (New Brunswick, N.J.: Rutgers University Press, 2008), 27–28.

142. Chambers, *Witness*, 15.

143. See Rusher, *Rise of the Right*, 24.

144. Roger Kimball, speech at Buckley Program's Conference on *Witness*'s 60th Anniversary, Yale University, November 30, 2012. See also Alfred Regnery, speech at Buckley Program's Conference on *Witness*'s 60th Anniversary, Yale University, November 30, 2012. Both speeches are available via http://www.c-spanvideo.org/program/WhatDef.

145. Like the Chambers case, the *Amerasia* affair concerned the security of classified government documents and the loyalty of government employees. The case began when an OSS officer noticed that an article in the journal *Amerasia* bore resemblance to a memo he had written. Although a subsequent FBI probe found classified documents from the Navy, the State Department, and the OSS in *Amerasia*'s offices, no link to foreign espionage was ever proven.

146. Ben Hart, "A Tribute to Whittaker Chambers," *Heritage Foundation Lectures*, March 23, 1984.

147. Ibid.

148. Jeffrey Hart, "A Tribute to Whittaker Chambers," *Heritage Foundation Lectures*, March 23, 1984, 8.

149. Chamberlain, "Whittaker Chambers," 580.

150. Rusher, *Rise of the Right*, 24.

151. Bogus, *Buckley*, 85.

152. Phillips-Fein, "Conservatism," 739.

153. Lee Edwards, *The Conservative Revolution: The Movement That Remade America* (New York: Free Press, 1997), 41.

154. Smoot, "Exposing Evil."

155. Easton, *Gang of Five*, 81.

156. Bogus, *Buckley*, 96.

157. Charles Kesler, "Statesmanship for America's Future," *Claremont Review of Books*, May 28, 1998.

158. Nash, *Conservative Intellectual Movement in America*, 93.

159. Regnery, *Upstream*, 44.

160. Nash, *Conservative Intellectual Movement in America*, 94.

161. Smoot, "Exposing Evil."

162. As Diggins writes, "The nature of Reagan's religious beliefs is baffling. He seemed to offer a Christianity without Christ and the crucifixion, a religion without reference to sin, evil, suffering, or sacrifice. Reagan's sense of religion was opposite that of Whittaker Chambers, who condemned America to purgatory." Diggins, *Ronald Reagan*, 7–8, 14.

163. Reagan, "Time for Choosing," 53–54.

164. Anthony Dolan, "Where a Masterpiece Was Written," *Washington Post*, May 22, 1988, C8. See also Martin J. Medhurst, "Writing Speeches for Ronald Reagan: An Interview with Tony Dolan," *Rhetoric & Public Affairs* 1 (1998): 245–256.

165. Lou Cannon, "Reagan Honors Whittaker Chambers," *Washington Post*, March 27, 1984, A7.

166. John Judis, "The Two Faces of Whittaker Chambers," in Swan, *Alger Hiss*, 236. See also Paul Kengor, *God and Ronald Reagan: A Spiritual Life* (New York: HarperCollins, 2004), 77–88.

167. Ronald Reagan, "Remarks to the National Association of Evangelicals," in *Tear Down This Wall: The Reagan Revolution—A* National Review *History*, ed. *National Review* (New York: Continuum, 2004), 35. For the link between Reagan's and Chambers's rhetoric, see Tanenhaus, "End of the Journey," 46; Diggins, *Ronald Reagan*, 8; Paul Kengor, "The Intellectual Origins of Ronald Reagan's Faith," *Heritage Foundation Lectures*, April 30, 2004.

168. Reagan, "Remarks to the National Association of Evangelicals," 36.

169. Ibid.

170. Ibid.

171. Kenneth Burke, "The Rhetoric of Hitler's Battle," in *Readings in Rhetorical Criticism*, ed. Carl R. Burgchardt (State College, Pa.: Strata, 2000), 210.

172. Ibid.

173. Reagan, "Remarks to the National Association of Evangelicals," 37. George Will called this conclusion the "least conservative sentiment conceivable." Quoted in Steven F. Hayward, "Reagan Reclaimed," *National Review*, February 4, 2011.

174. Quoted in John M. Murphy, "Power and Authority in a Postmodern Presidency," in *The Prospect of Presidential Rhetoric*, ed. James Arnt Aune and Martin J. Medhurst (College Station: Texas A&M Press, 2008), 36. See also Steven F. Hayward, *The Age of Reagan: The Conservative Counterrevolution: 1980–1989* (New York: Random House, 2009), 13.

175. Snyder, "Was Whittaker Chambers Wrong?"

176. Ronald Reagan, "The Defense of Freedom and the Metaphysics of Fun," in *National Review, Tear Down this Wall*, 87–88.

177. For more on Reagan's belief in American exceptionalism, see Hayward, *Age of Reagan*, 13.

178. Diggins, *Ronald Reagan*, 14.

179. Rusher, *Rise of the Right*, 24.

180. Chambers, *Witness*, 20, 21.

181. When Reagan relaxed his position on the Soviet Union later in his presidency, he drew some conservatives' ire. See Jane Matlock, *Reagan and Gorbachev: How the Cold War Ended* (New York: Random House, 2004); Beth A. Fischer, *The Reagan Reversal* (Columbia: University of Missouri Press, 1997).

182. Quoted in Elaine Sciolino, "G.O.P. Devotees Pay Honor to Whittaker Chambers," *New York Times*, July 10, 2001.

183. Tanenhaus, "End of the Journey," 47.

184. George W. Bush, "Address Before a Joint Session of Congress on the State of the Union," January 29, 2002, available via http://www.presidency.ucsb.edu/ws/index.php?pid=29644#ixzz1kgVCyzfB.

185. Robert Ivie, "Fighting Terror by Rite of Redemption and Reconciliation," *Rhetoric & Public Affairs* 10 (2007): 243.

186. Bush, "Address Before a Joint Session of Congress."

187. George W. Bush, "Remarks Following Discussions with President Jacques Chirac of France and an Exchange with Reporters," November 6, 2001, available via http://www.presidency.ucsb.edu/ws/index.php?pid=62940&st=&st1=#ixzz1kgvBpPeG.

188. Bush, "Address Before a Joint Session of Congress."

189. K. L. Billingsley, "The Food Police Are Watching You," *Freeman*, December 1, 1992.

190. Elliot Abrams, speech at Buckley Program's Conference on *Witness*'s 60th Anniversary, Yale University, November 30, 2012, available via http://www.c-spanvideo.org/program/309872-2; Max Boot, speech at Buckley Program's Conference on *Witness*'s 60th Anniversary, Yale University, November 30, 2012, available via http://www.c-spanvideo.org/program/309872-2.

191. For traditionalist uses of Chambers after the Cold War, see Richard Reinsch II, "Two Faiths: The Witness of Whittaker Chambers," *Religion & Liberty* 22 (2012): 5; Reinsch, "Still Witnessing." For libertarian uses of Chambers after the Cold War, see Smoot, "Exposing Evil."

192. Nash, *Conservative Intellectual Movement in America*, 117. For more on the reception of apocalyptic rhetoric, see Darsey, *Prophetic Tradition*, 117.

193. Some conservatives have adopted Chambers's tragic view wholesale. See Susan P. Jacobse, "Why I Am a Conservative," *Handmaiden*, August 2004; Pat Buchanan, "The Assisted Suicide of the West," *Townhall.com*, April 22, 2002, available via http://townhall.com/columnists/PatBuchanan/2002/04/22/the_

assisted_suicide_of_the_west. Other conservatives have excised the dark tropes from *Witness* and reframed Chambers's story as a standard redemption story. See Sarah Palin, *American by Heart: Reflections on Family, Faith, and Flag* (New York: Harper, 2010), 107.

194. Daniels, Keynote Address.

195. Ibid.

196. Reinsch, "Still Witnessing."

197. Anna Leutheuser, "The Relevance of the Pumpkin Patch: Whittaker Chambers' Enduring Legacy," *Foundry*, April 1, 2011.

198. Ivie, "Fighting Terror," 233.

199. Teachout, "Does Chambers Still Matter?"

200. Ibid.

201. Voegeli, "Wilderness Years Begin."

Chapter Seven. Conservatism and Canonicity

1. For the use of these terms in context, see Rod Dreher, *Crunchy Cons: The New Conservative Counterculture and Its Return to Roots* (New York: Three Rivers Press, 2006); Gene Healy, "The Future of Conservatism," panel sponsored by the *National Review Institute*, November 18, 2008, available via http://www.nrinstitute.org/events/whitherconservatism111908.php; Michael Gerson, *Heroic Conservatism* (New York: HarperCollins, 2007); David Frum, *Comeback: Conservatism That Can Win Again* (New York: Doubleday, 2008); Ross Douthat and Reihan Salam, "The Party of Sam's Club," *Weekly Standard*, November 14, 2005.

2. Julian E. Zelizer, "Reflections: Rethinking the History of American Conservatism," *Reviews in American History* 38 (2010): 367.

3. Lee Edwards, *The Conservative Revolution: The Movement That Remade America* (New York: Free Press, 1999), 293.

4. Christopher Buckley, "Let's Quit While We Are Behind," *Washington Monthly*, October 2006.

5. Ibid.

6. See also Lee Edwards, "Roaring Along Conservatism's Rocky Road," *Washington Times*, April 1, 2013.

7. Richard Viguerie and David Franke, *America's Right Turn: How Conservatives Used New and Alternative Media to Take Power* (Chicago: Bonus Books, 2004), 64.

8. Gregory L. Schneider, *The Conservative Century: From Reaction to Revolution* (New York: Rowman & Littlefield, 2009), xii.

9. John Derbyshire, "How Radio Wrecks the Right," *American Conservative*, February 23, 2009.

10. Donald Devine, "Libertarian Divorce?" American Conservative Union Foundation, n.d., available via http://www.conservative.org/wp-content/themes/ Conservative/bl-archive/Issues/issue32/050319news.php.

11. See Jonah Goldberg, "Introduction," in *Proud to Be Right: Voices of the Next Conservative Generation*, ed. Jonah Goldberg (New York: Harper, 2010), xvii–xx; Jeffrey Hart, *The Making of the American Conservative Mind: National Review and Its Times* (Wilmington, Del.: ISI Books, 2007), 376–378.

12. Quoted in Rick Perlstein, *Before the Storm: Barry Goldwater and the Unmaking of the American Consensus* (New York: Hill & Wang, 2001), 12.

13. Kim Phillips-Fein, "Right On," *Nation*, September 9, 2009.

14. Viguerie and Franke, *America's Right Turn*, 72.

15. Heather Hendershot, *What's Fair on the Air?: Cold War Right-Wing Broadcasting and the Public Interest* (Chicago: University of Chicago Press, 2011), 14; Joseph Crespino, *In Search of Another Country: Mississippi and the Conservative Counterrevolution* (Princeton, N.J.: Princeton University Press, 2006), 10.

16. Joseph E. Lowndes, *From the New Deal to the New Right: Race and the Southern Origins of Modern Conservatism* (New Haven, Conn.: Yale University Press, 2008), 49.

17. Hendershot, *What's Fair on the Air?* 79.

18. William F. Buckley, Jr., "Why the South Must Prevail," *National Review*, August 24, 1957, 149.

19. Lowndes, *From the New Deal to the New Right*, 49–51. See Carl T. Bogus, *Buckley: William F. Buckley Jr. and the Rise of American Conservatism* (New York: Bloomsbury Press, 2011), 162. See, for example, Donald Davidson, "The New South and the Conservative Tradition," *National Review*, September 10, 1960, 141–146; Richard Russell, "Voice of the South," *National Review*, July 27, 1957, 105–106.

20. Gene Roberts and Hank Kilbanoff, *The Race Beat: The Press, the Civil Rights Struggle, and the Awakening of a Nation* (New York: Vintage Books, 2007), 118–119.

21. See George Nash, *The Conservative Intellectual Movement in America since 1945* (New York: Basic Books, 1976), 187.

22. Ibid., 189–190. See also Nancy MacLean, "Neo-Confederacy versus the New Deal: The Regional Utopia of the Modern American Right," in *The Myth of Southern Exceptionalism*, ed. Matthew D. Lassister and Joseph Crespino (New York: Oxford University Press, 2010), 309, 316.

23. See Nancy MacLean, *Freedom Is Not Enough: The Opening of the American Workplace* (Boston: Harvard University Press, 2006), 226; MacLean, "Neo-Confederacy versus the New Deal," 320.

24. Hart, *Making of the American Conservative Mind*, 108.

25. Hendershot, *What's Fair on the Air?* 7, 15.

26. Kim Phillips-Fein, "Conservatism: A State of the Field," *Journal of American History* 98 (2011): 731.

27. Donald T. Critchlow, *The Conservative Ascendancy* (Cambridge, Mass.: Harvard University Press, 2007), 73.

28. William F. Buckley, Jr., *Up from Liberalism* (New York: Stein and Day, 1985), 65–66. See also M. Stanton Evans, *The Future of Conservatism: From Taft to Reagan and Beyond* (New York: Holt, Rinehart & Winston, 1968), 173–174. Conservatives continued to forcefully reproach those who implied a connection between opposing civil rights laws and racism. Paul Weyrich argued in 1984 that the New Right leadership "bears no resemblance to the reactionary Southern icons of the past." Quoted in Crespino, *In Search of Another Country*, 10. See also Gerard Alexander, "The Myth of Republican Racism," *Claremont Review of Books*, Spring 2004.

29. Robert Alan Goldberg, *Barry Goldwater* (New Haven, Conn.: Yale University Press, 1995), 140.

30. Jeffrey Hart, *The American Dissent: A Decade of Modern Conservatism* (Garden City, N.Y.: Doubleday, 1966), 112–125.

31. Donald Critchlow, "Rethinking American Conservatism: Toward a New Narrative," *Journal of American History* 98 (2011): 752. See also Kirk, *Conservative Mind*, 160.

32. See also Richard Weaver, *The Southern Tradition at Bay* (New Rochelle, N.Y.: Arlington House, 1968).

33. Robert Goldberg explains how some southerners interpreted *The Conscience of a Conservative*: "Southerners were particularly interested in Goldwater's chapter on civil rights. It offered them a defense of states' rights and a narrow interpretation of federal responsibilities. Differentiating civil rights from human or natural rights, the Arizona senator determined that the Constitution afforded blacks protection only in voting, contractual relations, and property holding. . . . Racists would blink Goldwater's abhorrence of prejudice to embrace him as an ally." See Goldberg, *Barry Goldwater*, 140.

34. Several examples of such arguments are noted in Kevin Mattson, *Rebels All! A Short History of the Conservative Mind in Postwar America* (New Brunswick, N.J.: Rutgers University Press, 2008), 54. Of all the first- and second-tier canonical books, *The Conservative Affirmation*, which reprinted Willmoore Kendall's review of Nathaniel Weyl's *The Negro in American Civilization* (1960), most resembled archaic racial claims. See Willmoore Kendall, *The Conservative Affirmation* (Chicago: Henry Regnery, 1963), 215.

35. Milton Friedman, *Capitalism and Freedom*, 40th anniv. ed. (Chicago: University of Chicago Press, 2002), 111.

36. Martin Durham, "On American Conservatism and Kim Phillips-Fein's Survey of the Field," *Journal of American History* 98 (2011): 758.

37. See Alfred S. Regnery, *Upstream: The Ascendance of American Conservatism* (New York: Threshold Editions, 2008); Edwards, *Conservative Revolution*; William A. Rusher, *The Rise of the Right* (New York: William Morrow, 1984).

38. Some conservatives have even bragged about conservatism's adjustability. A 2004 edition of the *American Conservative Magazine*, for instance, framed conservatism as remarkably flexible as it commissioned different writers to support each of that year's presidential candidates, including George Bush and John Kerry, but also every also-ran, including Ralph Nader. This diversity of these cases tacitly suggested that, depending on the conservative principle from which one began, a conservative case could be made for just about any political course. See *American Conservative Magazine*, November 8, 2004.

39. See Eric Lichtblau and James Risen, "Bank Data Is Sifted by U.S. in Secret to Block Terror," *New York Times*, June 23, 2006; James Risen and Eric Lichtblau, "Bush Lets U.S. Spy on Callers without Courts," *New York Times*, December 16, 2005; Dana Priest, "Memo Lets CIA Take Detainees Out of Iraq," *Washington Post*, October 24, 2004.

40. Elizabeth Drew, "Power Grab," *New York Review of Books*, May 24, 2006. See also Steven G. Calabresi and Christopher Yoo, *The Unitary Executive: Presidential Power from Washington to Bush* (New Haven, Conn.: Yale University Press, 2008); James Pfiffner, *Power Play: The Bush Presidency and the Constitution* (Washington, D.C.: Brookings Institution Press, 2008).

41. "Bush Signs Landmark Medicare Bill into Law," *CNN*, December 8, 2003.

42. Jim Rutenberg, "Bush to Press for U.S. Ban on Same-Sex Marriage," *New York Times*, June 3, 2006.

43. Sheryl Gay Stolberg, "Schiavo Case May Reshape American Law," *New York Times*, April 1, 2005.

44. Ross Douthat, "Introduction," in Robert Nisbet, *The Quest for Community* (Wilmington, Del: ISI Books, 2010), xv.

45. Michael Tanner, *Leviathan on the Right: How Big-Government Conservatism Brought Down the Republican Revolution* (Washington, D.C.: Cato Institute, 2007).

46. For Cheney's quotation, see Jonathan Weisman, "Reagan Policies Gave Green Light to Red Ink," *Washington Post*, June 9, 2004. For a discussion of the tea party's libertarian thrust, see Mark Lilla, "The Tea Party Jacobins," *New York Review of Books*, May 27, 2010.

47. Peter Beinart, "How Ron Paul Will Change the GOP in 2012," *Daily Beast*, December 27, 2011; Tucker Carlson, "Pimp My Ride," *New Republic*, December 31, 2007.

48. See Kate Zernike, "Tea Party Avoids Divisive Social Issues," *New York Times*, March 12, 2010; see also Walter Russell Mead, "The Tea Party and U.S. Foreign Policy," *New York Times*, February 11, 2011.

49. Ben Smith and Byron Tau, "GOP Is Urged to Avoid Social Issues," *Politico*, November 14, 2010. Even Rick Santorum, a steadfast social conservative of early 2000s vintage, toned down his moral messaging during his 2012 presidential bid. For his mid-2000s views on religion, feminism, personal privacy, and the like, see Rick Santorum, *It Takes a Family: Conservatism and the Common Good* (Wilmington, Del.: Intercollegiate Studies Institute, 2006). For his later de-emphasizing of these views, see Walter Shapiro, "Rich Santorum's Mysterious, Paradoxical Manifesto, 'It Takes a Family': Character Sketch," *Ticket*, February 17, 2012; David Weigel, "A Kinder, Gentler Rick Santorum," *Slate*, February 15, 2012.

50. See Allison Aubrey, "Conservatives Rail Against Bush Domestic Spending," *National Public Radio*, July 13, 2003; Amanda Terkel, "Tea Party Movement Rift," *Huffington Post*, September 17, 2010.

51. Rusher, *Rise of the Right*, 63–66.

52. Steven F. Hayward, "Reading Up on the Right," *Claremont Review of Books*, March 29, 2010. See also Grover Norquist, "Tea Timing Republicans," *American Spectator*, November 2010.

53. See also Robert McCrum, *Globish: How the English Language Became the World's Language* (New York: W. W. Norton, 2010), 45–46, 149, 283.

54. Jim Rutenberg and Adam Nagourney, "Conservatives Make a List to Measure Candidates' Commitment," *New York Times*, November 23, 2009.

55. Paul Waldman, "The Coming Conservative Crack Up," *American Prospect*, September 30, 2008; W. James Antle III, "Conservative Crack Up," *American Conservative*, November 17, 2003; R. Emmett Tyrell, *The Conservative Crack-Up* (New York: Simon & Schuster, 1992).

56. For dismissals in the 1950s, see Arthur M. Schlesinger Jr., *The Politics of Hope and the Bitter Heritage: American Liberalism in the 1960s* (Princeton, N.J.: Princeton University Press, 2008), 103. For examples of pundits assuming conservatism died with the Goldwater campaign, see Gary Donaldson, *Liberalism's Last Hurrah: The Presidential Campaign of 1964* (Armonk, N.Y.: M. E. Sharpe, 2003), 293. See also Perlstein, *Before the Storm*, ix. For examples after Reagan and George W. Bush, see John Judis, "The End of Conservatism," *New Republic*, August 31, 1992; Jacob Heilbrunn, "The Great Conservative Crack-Up," *Washington Monthly*, May 2006; John Heilemann, "The Right's Class War," *New York Magazine*, October 17, 2008.

57. Sam Tanenhaus, *The Death of Conservatism* (New York: Random House, 2009), 5.

58. E. J. Dionne, "Civil War on the Right," *Washington Post*, October 24, 2008.

59. Bruce Frohnen, "Has Conservatism Lost Its Mind," *Policy Review* 67 (1994): 62–67.

60. Patricia Cohen, "'Epistemic Closure?' Those Are Fighting Words," *New York Times*, April 27, 2010.

61. Daniel McCarthy, "Five Conservative Classics," *American Conservative*, September 16, 2009; Derbyshire, "How Radio Wrecks the Right." See also Austin Bramwell, "Goodbye to All That," *American Conservative*, November 20, 2006.

62. Austin Bramwell, "Defining Conservatism Down," *American Conservative*, August 29, 2005.

63. Quoted in John Judis, *William F. Buckley, Jr.: Patron Saint of the Conservatives* (New York: Simon & Schuster, 1988), 133.

64. Lee Edwards, "The End of Conservatism?" *Heritage Foundation Lectures*, April 27, 2009, available via http://www.heritage.org/Research/Lecture/The-End-of-Conservatism.

65. Lisa McGirr, "Now That Historians Know So Much about the Right, How Should We Best Approach the Study of Conservatism?" *Journal of American History* 98 (2011): 770.

Selected Bibliography

⌘

Adler, Mortimer J., and Charles Van Doren. *How to Read a Book*. Rev. ed. New York: Touchstone, 1972.

Allitt, Patrick. *Catholic Intellectuals and Conservative Politics in America: 1950–1985*. Ithaca, N.Y.: Cornell University Press, 1993.

———. *The Conservatives: Ideas and Personalities throughout American History*. New Haven, Conn.: Yale University Press, 2009.

Alter, Robert. *Canon and Creativity: Modern Writing and the Authority of Scripture*. New Haven, Conn.: Yale University Press, 2000.

Andrew, John A. *The Other Side of the Sixties: Young Americans for Freedom and the Rise of Conservative Politics*. New Brunswick, N.J.: Rutgers University Press, 1997.

Appel, Edward C. "Burlesque Drama as a Rhetorical Genre: The Hudibrastic Ridicule of William F. Buckley, Jr." *Western Journal of Communication* 60 (1996): 269–284.

Aune, James Arnt. "The Argument from Evil in the Rhetoric of Reaction." *Rhetoric & Public Affairs* 6 (2003): 518–522.

———. *Selling the Free Market: The Rhetoric of Economic Correctness*. New York: Guilford Press, 2001.

Bailey, David C. "Enacting Transformation: George W. Bush and the Pauline Conversion Narrative in *A Charge to Keep*." *Rhetoric & Public Affairs* 11 (2008): 215–241.

Baker, B. Leland. *Tea Party Revival: The Conscience of a Conservative Reborn.* Denver: Outskirts Press, 2009.

Ball, Terence. *Transforming Political Discourse: Political Theory and Critical Conceptual History.* Oxford: Basil Blackwell Press, 1988.

Ball, Terrence, and J. G. A Pocock, eds. *Conceptual Change and the Constitution.* Lawrence: University Press of Kansas, 1988.

Ball, Terrence, James Farr, and Russell L. Hanson, eds. *Political Innovation and Conceptual Change.* Cambridge: Cambridge University Press, 1989.

Bartlett, Bruce. *Impostor: How George W. Bush Bankrupted America and Betrayed the Reagan Legacy.* New York: Doubleday, 2006.

Beam, Alex. *A Great Idea at the Time: The Rise, Fall, and Curious Afterlife of the Great Books.* New York: Public Affairs, 2009.

Bell, Daniel. *The End of Ideology: On the Exhaustion of Political Ideas in the Fifties.* New York: Free Press, 1962.

Bercovitch, Sacvan. *The American Jeremiad.* Madison: University of Wisconsin Press, 1978.

Berkowitz, Peter, ed. *Varieties of Conservatism in America.* Stanford, Calif.: Hoover Institution Press, 2004.

Berlin, Isaiah. *Four Essays on Liberty.* New York: Oxford University Press, 1970.

———. *The Hedgehog and the Fox: An Essay on Tolstoy's View of History.* New York: Simon & Schuster, 1986.

Birner, Jack, and Rudy Van Zijp, eds. *Hayek, Co-Ordination and Evolution: His Legacy in Philosophy, Politics, Economics and the History of Ideas.* New York: Routledge, 1994.

Bjerre-Poulsen, Niels. *Right Face: Organizing the American Conservative Movement 1945—1965.* Copenhagen: Museum Tusculanum Press, 2002.

Bloom, Harold. *How to Read and Why.* New York: Scribner, 2001.

———. *The Western Canon: The Books and School of the Ages.* New York: Riverhead Trade, 1995.

Bogus, Carl T. *Buckley: William F. Buckley Jr. and the Rise of American Conservatism.* New York: Bloomsbury Press, 2011.

Booth, Wayne C. *A Rhetoric of Irony.* Chicago: University of Chicago Press, 1974.

Branham, Robert James. "The Role of the Convert in *Eclipse of Reason* and *The Silent Scream*." *Quarterly Journal of Speech* 77 (1991): 407–426.

Brennan, Mary C. *Turning Right in the Sixties: The Conservative Capture of the GOP.* Chapel Hill: University of North Carolina Press, 1995.

Bridges, Linda, and John R. Coyne Jr. *Strictly Right: William F. Buckley Jr. and the American Conservative Movement.* Hoboken, N.J.: John Wiley & Sons, 2007.

Brookhiser, Richard. *Right Time Right Place: Coming of Age with William F. Buckley and the Conservative Movement.* New York: Basic Books, 2009.

Brunner, Otto, Werner Conze, and Reinhart Koselleck, eds. *Geschichtliche Grundbegriffe: Historishces Lexikon zur Politisch-sozialen Sprache in Deutschland (Basic Concepts in History: A Dictionary on Historical Principles of Political and Social Language in Germany).* 8 vols. Stuttgart: Klett-Cotta, 1972–1973.

Buchanan, Patrick J. *Right from the Beginning.* Boston: Little, Brown, 1988.

Buckley, William F., Jr. *Cancel Your Own Goddam Subscription: Notes & Asides from* National Review. New York: Basic Books, 2007.

———, ed. *Did You Ever See a Dream Walking? American Conservative Thought in the Twentieth Century.* Indianapolis: Bobbs-Merrill, 1970.

———. *Flying High: Remembering Barry Goldwater.* New York: Basic Books, 2008.

———. *God and Man at Yale: The Superstitions of "Academic Freedom".* 50th anniv. ed. Washington, D.C.: Regnery, 2002.

———. *The Lexicon: A Cornucopia of Wonderful Words for the Inquisitive Word Lover.* New York: Harvest Books, 1998.

———. *Miles Gone By: A Literary Autobiography.* Washington, D.C.: Regnery, 2004.

———, ed. *Odyssey of a Friend: Whittaker Chambers' Letters to William F. Buckley, Jr.: 1954–1961.* New York: G. P. Putnam's Sons, 1969.

———. *The Unmaking of a Mayor.* New York: Viking Press, 1966.

———. *Up from Liberalism.* New York: Stein and Day, 1985.

Buckley, William F., Jr., and Charles R. Kesler, eds. *Keeping the Tablets.* New York: Harper & Row, 1988.

Burke, Kenneth. *Counter-Statement.* 2nd ed. Berkeley: University of California Press, 1968.

———. *A Grammar of Motives.* Berkeley: University of California Press, 1969.

———. *Permanence and Change: An Anatomy of Purpose.* 2nd ed. Indianapolis: Bobbs-Merrill, 1954.

———. "The Rhetoric of Hitler's Battle." In *Readings in Rhetorical Criticism,* edited by Carl R. Burgchardt, 206–221. State College, Pa.: Strata, 2000.

———. *The Rhetoric of Religion: Studies in Logology.* Berkeley: University of California Press, 1970.

Burns, Jennifer. *Goddess of the Market: Ayn Rand and the American Right.* New York: Oxford University Press, 2009.

Busch, Andrew E. *Reagan's Victory: The Presidential Election of 1980 and the Rise of the Right.* Lawrence: University Press of Kansas, 2005.

Caldwell, Bruce. *Hayek's Challenge: An Intellectual Biography of F. A. Hayek.* Chicago: University of Chicago Press, 2004.

————, ed. *The Road to Serfdom: Texts and Documents.* Chicago: University of Chicago Press, 2007.

Carter, Dan T. *From George Wallace to Newt Gingrich: Race in the Conservative Counterrevolution, 1963–1994.* Baton Rouge: Louisiana State University Press, 1999.

————. *The Politics of Rage: George Wallace and the Transformation of American Politics.* Baton Rouge: Louisiana State University Press, 2000.

Chambers, Whittaker. *Witness.* New York: Random House, 1952.

Connolly, William E. *Capitalism and Christianity, American Style.* Durham, N.C.: Duke University Press, 2008.

Cosgrove, Kenneth M. *Branded Conservatives: How the Brand Brought the Right from the Fringes to the Center of American Politics.* New York: Peter Lang, 2007.

Coulter, Ann. *How to Talk to a Liberal (If You Must).* New York: Three Rivers Press, 2004.

Crespino, Joseph. *In Search of Another Country: Mississippi and the Conservative Counterrevolution.* Princeton, N.J.: Princeton University Press, 2006.

Critchlow, Donald T. *The Conservative Ascendancy: How the GOP Right Made Political History.* Cambridge, Mass.: Harvard University Press, 2007.

————. *Phyllis Schlafly and Grassroots Conservatism: A Woman's Crusade.* Princeton, N.J.: Princeton University Press, 2007.

————. "Rethinking American Conservatism: Toward a New Narrative." *Journal of American History* 98 (2011): 752–755.

Cunningham, Sean P. *Cowboy Conservatism: Texas and the Rise of the Modern Right.* Lexington: University Press of Kentucky, 2010.

Dean, John W. *Conservatives without Conscience.* New York: Viking Press, 2006.

Dean, John W., and Barry M. Goldwater, Jr. *Pure Goldwater.* New York: Palgrave Macmillan, 2008.

de Toledano, Ralph, ed. *Notes from the Underground: The Whittaker Chambers—Ralph de Toledano Letters: 1949–1960.* Washington, D.C.: Regnery, 1997.

de Velasco, Antonio, and Melody Lehn, eds. *Rhetoric: Concord and Controversy.* Long Grove, Ill.: Waveland Press, 2012.

Deutsch, Kenneth L., and Ethan Fishman, eds. *The Dilemmas of American Conservatism.* Lexington: University Press of Kentucky, 2010.

Diggins, John Patrick. *Ronald Reagan: Fate, Freedom, and the Making of History.* New York: W. W. Norton, 2007.

————. *Up from Communism: Conservative Odysseys in American Intellectual History.* New York: Harper & Row, 1975.

Doherty, Brian. *Radicals for Capitalism: A Freewheeling History of the Modern American Libertarian Movement.* New York: Public Affairs, 2007.

D'Souza, Dinesh. *Letters to a Young Conservative.* New York: Basic Books, 2002.

Dunn, Charles W., and J. David Woodard. *The Conservative Tradition in America.* New York: Rowman & Littlefield, 1996.

Durham, Martin. "On American Conservatism and Kim Phillips-Fein's Survey of the Field." *Journal of American History* 98 (2011): 756–759.

East, John P. *The American Conservative Movement: Its Philosophical Founders.* Chicago: Regnery, 1986.

———. "The Conservatism of Frank Straus Meyer." *Modern Age* 18 (1974): 226–245.

Easton, Nina J. *Gang of Five: Leaders at the Center of the Conservative Crusade.* New York: Simon & Schuster, 2000.

Eberstadt, Mary, ed. *Why I Turned Right: Leading Baby Boom Conservatives Chronicle Their Political Journeys.* New York: Threshold Editions, 2007.

Edelman, Murray. *Political Language: Words That Succeed and Policies That Fail.* New York: Academic Press, 1977.

———. *The Symbolic Uses of Politics.* Urbana: University of Illinois Press, 1985.

Edwards, Lee. *The Conservative Revolution: The Movement That Remade America.* New York: Free Press, 1999.

———. *Educating for Liberty: The First Half-Century of the Intercollegiate Studies Institute.* Washington, D.C.: Regnery, 2003.

———. *The Power of Ideas: The Heritage Foundation at 25 years.* Ottawa, Ill.: Jameson Books, 1997.

———, ed. *Reading the Right Books: A Guide for the Intelligent Conservative.* Washington, D.C.: Heritage Foundation, 2007.

———. *William F. Buckley Jr.: The Maker of a Movement.* Wilmington, Del.: ISI Books, 2010.

Edwards, Mickey. *Reclaiming Conservatism: How a Great American Political Movement Got Lost—and How It Can Find Its Way Back.* New York: Oxford University Press, 2008.

Eliade, Mircea. *Myth and Reality.* New York: Harper Colophon Books, 1975.

Evans, M. Stanton. *The Future of Conservatism: From Taft to Reagan and Beyond.* New York: Holt, Rinehart, & Winston 1968.

Farber, David, and Jeff Roche. *The Conservative Sixties.* New York: Peter Lang, 2003.

Feulner, Edwin J., ed. *The March of Freedom: Modern Classics in Conservative Thought.* Dallas: Spence, 2004.

Feulner, Edwin J., and Doug Wilson, *Getting America Right: The True Conservative Values Our Nation Needs Today.* New York: Crown Forum, 2006.

Fish, Stanley. *Is There a Text in This Class? The Authority of Interpretive Communities*. Cambridge, Mass.: Harvard University Press, 1980.

Fleming, John V. *The Anti-Communist Manifestos: Four Books That Shaped the Cold War*. New York: W. W. Norton, 2009.

Franke, David, ed. *Quotations from Chairman Bill*. New Rochelle, N.Y.: Arlington House, 1970.

Fried, Charles. *Modern Liberty and the Limits of Government*. New York: W. W. Norton, 2007.

Friedman, Milton. *Capitalism and Freedom*. 40th anniv. ed. Chicago: University of Chicago Press, 2002.

Frohnen, Bruce, Jeremy Beer, and Jeffrey O. Nelson, eds. *American Conservatism: An Encyclopedia*. Wilmington, Del.: ISI Books, 2006.

Frum, David. *Comeback: Conservatism That Can Win Again*. New York: Doubleday, 2008.

———. *Dead Right*. New York: Basic Books, 1994.

———. *What's Right: The New Conservative Majority and the Remaking of America*. New York: Basic Books, 1996.

Galewski, Elizabeth. "The Strange Case for Women's Capacity to Reason: Judith Sargent Murray's Use of Irony in 'On the Equality of the Sexes' (1790)." *Quarterly Journal of Speech* 93 (2007): 84–108.

Genovese, Eugene. *The Southern Tradition: The Achievement and Limitations of American Conservatism*. Cambridge, Mass.: Harvard University Press, 1994.

Goldberg, Jonah, ed. *Proud to Be Right: Voices of the Next Conservative Generation*. New York: Harper, 2010.

Goldberg, Robert Alan. *Barry Goldwater*. New Haven, Conn.: Yale University Press, 1995.

Goldwater, Barry. *The Conscience of a Conservative*. 30th anniv. ed. Washington, D.C.: Regnery Gateway, 1990.

Gorak, Jan. *The Making of the Modern Canon: Genesis and Crisis of a Literary Idea*. London: Athlone, 1991.

Gottfried, Paul. *The Conservative Movement*. Rev. ed. New York: Twayne, 1993.

Green, David. *The Language of Politics in America: Shaping Political Consciousness from McKinley to Reagan*. Ithaca, N.Y.: Cornell University Press, 1987.

Halbertal, Moshe. *People of the Book: Canon, Meaning, and Authority*. Cambridge, Mass.: Harvard University Press, 1997.

Hariman, Robert. *Political Style: The Artistry of Power*. Chicago: University of Chicago Press, 1995.

Hart, Jeffrey. *The American Dissent: A Decade of Modern Conservatism*. Garden City, N.Y.: Doubleday, 1966.

———. *The Making of the American Conservative Mind: National Review and Its Times*. Wilmington, Del.: ISI Books, 2007.

Hart, Roderick P. "The Rhetoric of the True Believer." *Speech Monographs* 38 (1971): 249–261.

Hart, Roderick P., Sharon E. Jarvis, William P. Jennings, and Deborah Smith-Howell. *Political Keywords: Using Language That Uses Us.* New York: Oxford University Press, 2005.

Hartz, Louis. *The Liberal Tradition in America.* New York: Harcourt Brace Jovanovich, 1955.

Hayek, Friedrich A. *The Constitution of Liberty.* Chicago: University of Chicago Press, 1978.

———. *The Road to Serfdom.* 50th anniv. ed. Chicago: University of Chicago Press, 1994.

Hayward, Steven F. *The Age of Reagan: The Conservative Counterrevolution: 1980–1989.* New York: Random House, 2009.

Heller, Anne C. *Ayn Rand and the World She Made.* New York: Doubleday, 2009.

Hendershot, Heather. *What's Fair on the Air?: Cold War Right-Wing Broadcasting and the Public Interest.* Chicago: University of Chicago Press, 2011.

Himmelstein, Jerome. *To the Right: The Transformation of American Conservatism.* Berkeley: University of California Press, 1990.

Hirschman, Albert O. *The Rhetoric of Reaction: Perversity, Futility, Jeopardy.* Cambridge, Mass.: Harvard University Press, 1991.

Hofstadter, Richard. *The Age of Reform: From Bryan to F.D.R.* New York: Vintage, 1960.

———. *The American Political Tradition and the Men Who Made It.* New York: Vintage, 1989.

———. *The Paranoid Style in American Politics: And Other Essays.* Boston: Harvard University Press, 1996.

Ivie, Robert. "Fighting Terror by Rite of Redemption and Reconciliation." *Rhetoric & Public Affairs* 10 (2007): 221–248.

Jacoby, Susan. *Alger Hiss and the Battle for History.* New Haven, Conn.: Yale University Press, 2009.

James, William. *The Varieties of Religious Experience: A Study in Human Nature.* New York: Penguin Books, 1982.

Jamieson, Kathleen Hall, and Joseph Capella. *Echo Chamber: Rush Limbaugh and the Conservative Media Establishment.* New York: Oxford University Press, 2008.

Jarvis, Sharon. *The Talk of the Party: Political Labels, Symbolic Capital, and American Life.* Lanham, Md.: Rowman & Littlefield, 2005.

Jasinski, James. "The Forms and Limits of Prudence in Henry Clay's (1850) Defense of the Compromise Measures." *Quarterly Journal of Speech* 81 (1995): 454–478.

————. "Instrumentalism, Contextualism, and Interpretation in Rhetorical Criticism." In *Rhetorical Hermeneutics: Invention and Interpretation in the Age of Science*, edited by Alan G. Gross and William M. Keith, 195–224. Albany: State University of New York Press, 1997.

————. *Sourcebook on Rhetoric: Key Concepts in Contemporary Rhetorical Studies*. Thousand Oaks, Calif.: Sage, 2001.

Johannesen, Richard L., Rennard Strickland, and Ralph T. Eubanks, eds. *Language Is Sermonic: Richard Weaver on the Nature of Rhetoric*. Baton Rouge: Louisiana State University Press, 1985.

Jones, John M., and Robert C. Rowland. "A Covenant-Affirming Jeremiad: The Post-presidential Ideological Appeals of Ronald Wilson Reagan." *Communication Studies* 56 (2005): 157–174.

Judis, John. *William F. Buckley, Jr.: Patron Saint of the Conservatives*. New York: Touchstone Books, 1988.

Kendall, Willmoore. *The Conservative Affirmation*. Chicago: Henry Regnery, 1963.

Kenny, Robert Wade. "The Phenomenology of the Disaster: Toward a Rhetoric of Tragedy." *Philosophy & Rhetoric* 39 (2006): 97–124.

Kermode, Frank. *History and Value: The Clarendon Lectures and the Northcliffe Lectures*. New York: Oxford University Press, 1989.

Kimball, Roger, and Linda Bridges, eds. *Athwart History: Half a Century of Polemics, Animadversions, and Illuminations: A William F. Buckley Jr. Omnibus*. New York: Encounter Books, 2010.

Kimmage, Michael. *The Conservative Turn: Lionel Trilling, Whittaker Chambers, and the Lessons of Anti-Communism*. Cambridge, Mass.: Harvard University Press, 2009.

Kintz, Linda. *Between Jesus and the Market: The Emotions That Matter in Right-Wing America*. Durham, N.C.: Duke University Press, 1997.

Kirk, Russell. *The Conservative Mind: From Burke to Eliot*. 6th rev. ed. South Bend, Ind.: Gateway Editions, 1978.

————. *Enemies of the Permanent Things*. Rev. ed. Peru, Ill.: Sherwood, Sugden, 1988.

————. "An Ideologue of Liberty." *Sewanee Review* 72 (April–June 1964): 349–350.

————. *John Randolph of Roanoke: A Study in American Politics*. Indianapolis: Liberty Fund, 1997.

————. "Libertarians: The Chirping Sectaries." *Modern Age* 25 (1981): 345–351.

————. *The Sword of Imagination: Memoirs of a Half-Century of Literary Conflict*. Grand Rapids, Mich.: William B. Eerdsmans, 1995.

Kruse, Kevin M. *White Flight: Atlanta and the Making of Modern Conservatism*. Princeton, N.J.: Princeton University Press, 2005.

Lanham, Richard A. *A Handlist of Rhetorical Terms*. 2nd ed. Berkeley: University of California Press, 1991.

Levine, Norman. *Dialogue within the Dialectic*. London: George Allen & Unwin, 1984.

Lichtman, Allan J. *White Protestant Nation*. New York: Atlantic Monthly Press, 2008.

Lind, Michael. *Up from Conservatism: Why the Right Is Wrong for America*. New York: Free Press Paperbacks, 1997.

Lindlof, Thomas R. "Interpretive Community: An Approach to Media and Religion." *Journal of Media and Religion* 1 (2002): 61–74.

Lowndes, Joseph E. *From the New Deal to the New Right: Race and the Southern Origins of Modern Conservatism*. New Haven, Conn.: Yale University Press, 2008.

Lundberg, Christian. "Enjoying God's Death: *The Passion of the Christ* and the Practices of an Evangelical Public." *Quarterly Journal of Speech* 95 (2009): 387–411.

Machlup, Fritz, ed. *Essays on Hayek*. New York: New York University Press, 1976.

Machor, James L., and Philip Goldstein, eds. *Reception Study: From Literary Theory to Cultural Studies*. New York: Routledge, 2001.

MacLean, Nancy. *Freedom Is Not Enough: The Opening of the American Workplace*. Boston: Harvard University Press, 2006.

———. "Neo-Confederacy versus the New Deal: The Regional Utopia of the Modern American Right." In *The Myth of Southern Exceptionalism*, edited by Matthew D. Lassiter and Joseph Crespino, 308–330. New York: Oxford University Press, 2010.

Marietta, Morgan. *The Politics of Sacred Rhetoric: Absolutist Appeals and Political Persuasion*. Waco, Tex.: Baylor University Press, 2012.

Mattson, Kevin. *Rebels All! A Short History of the Conservative Mind in Postwar America*. New Brunswick, N.J.: Rutgers University Press, 2008.

McCrum, Robert. *Globish: How the English Language Became the World's Language*. New York: W. W. Norton, 2010.

McDonald, W. Wesley. *Russell Kirk in an Age of Ideology*. Columbia: University of Missouri Press, 2004.

McGirr, Lisa. "Now That Historians Know So Much about the Right, How Should We Best Approach the Study of Conservatism?" *Journal of American History* 98 (2011): 765–770.

———. "Piety and Property: Conservatism and Right-Wing Movements in the Twentieth Century." In *Perspectives on Modern America: Making Sense of the Twentieth Century*, edited by Harvard Sitkoff, 33–54. New York: Oxford University Press, 2000.

———. *Suburban Warriors: The Origins of the New American Right*. Princeton, N.J.: Princeton University Press, 2002.

Medhurst, Martin J. "Resistance, Conservatism, and Theory Building: A Cautionary Note." *Western Journal of Speech Communication* 49 (1985): 103–115.

———. "Writing Speeches for Ronald Reagan: An Interview with Tony Dolan." *Rhetoric & Public Affairs* 1 (1998): 245–256.

Meyer, Frank. *The Conservative Mainstream*. New Rochelle, N.Y.: Arlington House, 1969.

———. *In Defense of Freedom: A Conservative Credo*. Chicago: Henry Regnery, 1962.

———, ed. *In Defense of Freedom and Related Essays*. Indianapolis: Liberty Fund Press, 1996.

———. *The Moulding of Communists: The Training of the Communist Cadre*. New York: Harcourt, 1961.

———, ed. *What Is Conservatism?* New York: Holt, Rinehart, & Winston, 1964.

Micklethwait, John, and Adrian Wooldridge. *The Right Nation: Conservative Power in America*. New York: Penguin Press, 2004.

Miller, John J. *A Gift of Freedom: How the John M. Olin Foundation Changed America*. San Francisco: Encounter Books, 2006.

Moore, Mark P. "To Execute Capital Punishment: The Mortification and Scapegoating of Illinois Governor George Ryan." *Western Journal of Communication* 70 (2006): 311–330.

Morrissey, Lee, ed. *Debating the Canon: A Reader From Addison to Nafisi*. New York: Palgrave Macmillan, 2005.

Murphy, John M. "Domesticating Dissent: The Kennedys and the Freedom Rides." *Communication Monographs* 59 (1992): 61–78.

———. "Inventing Authority: Bill Clinton, Martin Luther King, and the Orchestration of Rhetorical Traditions." *Quarterly Journal of Speech* 83 (1997): 71–89.

———. "Power and Authority in a Postmodern Presidency." In *The Prospect of Presidential Rhetoric*, edited by James Arnt Aune and Martin J. Medhurst, 28–45. College Station: Texas A&M Press, 2008.

Nash, George. *The Conservative Intellectual Movement in America since 1945*. New York: Basic Books, 1976.

———. *Reappraising the Right: The Past and Future of American Conservatism*. Wilmington, Del.: ISI Books, 2009.

National Review, ed. *Tear Down This Wall: The Reagan Revolution—A National Review History*. New York: Continuum, 2004.

Nisbet, Robert. *Conservatism: Dream and Reality*. New Brunswick, N.J.: Transaction, 2008.

———. *The Quest for Community*. New York: Oxford University Press, 1970.

Novak, Robert. *The Prince of Darkness*. New York: Crown Forum, 2007.

O'Neill, William L. *Max Eastman: The Last Romantic*. Oxford: Oxford University Press, 1991.

Ott, Brian L., and Eric Aoki. "The Politics of Negotiating Public Tragedy: Media Framing of the Matthew Sheppard Murder." *Rhetoric & Public Affairs* 5 (2002): 483–505.

Panichas, George A., ed. *The Collected Works of Russell Kirk*. Wilmington, Del.: ISI Books, 2007.

———. "Restoring the Meaning of Conservatism." *Modern Age* 47 (2005): 195—200.

———. "Restoring the Meaning of Conservatism (Part Two)." *Modern Age* 48 (2006): 3–5.

Perelman, Chaim, and Lucie Olbrechts-Tyteca. *The New Rhetoric: A Treatise on Argumentation*. Notre Dame, Ind.: University of Notre Dame Press, 1969.

Perlstein, Rick. *Before the Storm: Barry Goldwater and the Unmaking of the American Consensus*. New York: Hill & Wang, 2001.

Person, James E., Jr. *Russell Kirk: A Critical Biography of a Conservative Mind*. Lanham, Md.: Madison Books, 1999.

Phillips-Fein, Kim. "Conservatism: A State of the Field." *Journal of American History* 98 (2011): 723–743.

———. *Invisible Hands: The Making of the Conservative Movement from the New Deal to Reagan*. New York: W. W. Norton, 2010.

Pocock, J. G. A. "Concepts and Discourses: A Difference in Culture? Comment on a Paper by Melvin Richter." In *The Meaning of Historical Terms and Concepts: New Studies on Begriffsgeschichte*, edited by Hartmut Lehmann and Melvin Richter, 48–59. Washington, D.C.: German Historical Institute, 1996.

———. *Politics, Language, and Time: The Transformation of the Study of Political Thought*. New York: Atheneum, 1971.

———. "The Reconstruction of Discourse: Towards the Historiography of Political Thought." *MLN* 96 (1981): 959–980.

———. "Texts as Events: Reflections on the History of Political Thought." In *Politics of Discourse: The Literature and History of Seventeenth-Century England*, edited by Kevin Sharp and Steven N. Zwicker, 21–34. Berkeley: University of California Press, 1987.

———. "Verbalizing a Political Act: Toward a Politics of Speech." *Political Theory* 1 (1973): 27–45.

Raimondo, Justin. *Reclaiming the American Right: The Lost Legacy of the Conservative Movement*. Wilmington, Del.: ISI Books, 2008.

Reagan, Ronald. *Speaking My Mind: Selected Speeches*. New York: Simon & Schuster, 1989.

Regnery, Alfred S. *Upstream: The Ascendance of American Conservatism*. New York: Threshold Editions, 2008.

Regnery, Henry. *Memoirs of a Dissident Publisher*. New York: Harcourt Brace Jovanovich, 1979.

————. *A Few Reasonable Words: Selected Writings.* Wilmington, Del.: ISI Books, 1996.

————. *Perfect Sowing: Reflections of a Bookman.* Wilmington, Del.: ISI Books, 1999.

Reichley, James. "The Conservative Roots of the Nixon, Ford, and Reagan Administrations." *Political Science Quarterly* 4 (1981–1982): 537–550.

Reinsch, Richard, II. "Two Faiths: The Witness of Whittaker Chambers." *Religion & Liberty* 22 (2012).

Ricci, David M. *Why Conservatives Tell Stories and Liberals Don't.* Boulder, Colo.: Paradigm, 2011.

Richter, Melvin. "Appreciating a Contemporary Classic." In *The Meaning of Historical Terms and Concepts: New Studies on Begriffsgeschichte,* edited by Hartmut Lehmann and Melvin Richter, 7–19. Washington, D.C.: German Historical Institute, 1996.

Roberts, James. *The Conservative Decade: Emerging Leaders of the 1980s.* Westport, Conn.: Arlington House, 1980.

Rodgers, Daniel T. *The Age of Fracture.* Cambridge, Mass.: Harvard University Press, 2011.

Rothbard, Murray N.. *The Betrayal of the American Right.* Auburn, Ala.: Ludwig von Mises Institute, 2007.

————. "Conservatism and Freedom: A Libertarian Comment." *Modern Age* 5 (1961): 217–220.

————. *For a New Liberty: The Libertarian Manifesto.* New York: MacMillan, 1973.

————. "Frank S. Meyer: The Fusionist as Libertarian Manque." *Modern Age* 25 (1981): 352–363.

————. "The Laissez-Faire Radical: A Quest for the Historical Mises." *Journal of Libertarian Studies* (Summer 1981): 237–253.

Rove, Karl. *Courage and Consequence: My Life as a Conservative in the Fight.* New York: Threshold Editions, 2010.

Rowland, Robert, and John Jones. "Entelechial and Reformative Symbolic Trajectories in Contemporary Conservatism: A Case Study of Reagan and Buchanan in Houston and Beyond." *Rhetoric & Public Affairs* 4 (2001): 55–84.

Rusher, William A. *The Rise of the Right.* New York: William Morrow, 1984.

Russello, Gerald J. *The Postmodern Imagination of Russell Kirk.* Columbia: University of Missouri Press, 2007.

Sager, Ryan. *The Elephant in the Room: Evangelicals, Libertarians, and the Battle to Control the Republican Party.* Hoboken, N.J.: John Wiley & Sons, 2006.

Scarborough, Joe. *The Last Best Hope: Restoring Conservatism and America's Promise.* New York: Crown Forum, 2009.

Schiappa, Edward. *Defining Reality: Definitions and the Politics of Meaning.* Carbondale: Southern Illinois University Press, 2003.

Schlesinger, Arthur, Jr. *The Politics of Hope and the Bitter Heritage: American Liberalism in the 1960s.* Princeton, N.J.: Princeton University Press, 2008.

Schneider, Gregory L. *Cadres for Conservatism: Young Americans for Freedom and the Rise of the Contemporary Right.* New York: New York University Press, 1999.

———. *The Conservative Century: From Reaction to Revolution.* New York: Rowman & Littlefield, 2009.

Schoenwald, Jonathan M. *A Time for Choosing: The Rise of Modern American Conservatism.* Oxford: Oxford University Press, 2001.

Schulman, Bruce J., and Julian E. Zelizer, eds. *Rightward Bound: Making America Conservative in the 1970s.* Boston: Harvard University Press, 2008.

Schweizer, Peter, and Wynton C. Hall, eds. *Landmark Speeches of the American Conservative Movement.* College Station: Texas A&M University Press, 2007.

Sipiora, Phillip, and James S. Baumlin, eds. *Rhetoric and Kairos: Essays in History, Theory, and Praxis.* Albany: State University of New York Press, 2002.

Smant, Kevin J. *Principles and Heresies: Frank S. Meyer and the Shaping of the American Conservative Movement.* Wilmington, Del.: ISI Books, 2002.

Smith, Mark A. *The Right Talk: How Conservatives Transformed the Great Society into the Economic Society.* Princeton, N.J.: Princeton University Press, 2007.

Smith, Ted J., III, ed. *Steps toward Restoration: The Consequences of Richard Weaver's Ideas.* Wilmington, Del.: ISI Books, 1998.

Strauss, Leo. *Natural Right and History.* Chicago: University of Chicago Press, 1953.

Striphas, Ted. *The Late Age of Print: Everyday Book Culture from Consumerism to Control.* New York: Columbia University Press, 2009.

Stromberg, Peter G. *Language and Self-transformation: A Study of the Christian Conversion Narrative.* Cambridge: Cambridge University Press, 1993.

Sullivan, Dale L. "*Kairos* and the Rhetoric of Belief." *Quarterly Journal of Speech* 78 (1992): 317–332.

Swan, Patrick A., ed. *Alger Hiss, Whittaker Chambers, and the Schism in the American Soul.* Wilmington, Del.: ISI Books, 2003.

Tanenhaus, Sam. *The Death of Conservatism.* New York: Random House, 2009.

———. *Whittaker Chambers.* New York: Random House, 1997.

Tanner, Michael. *Leviathan on the Right: How Big-Government Conservatism Brought Down the Republican Revolution.* Washington, D.C.: Cato Institute, 2007.

Trilling, Lionel. *The Liberal Imagination*. Boston: Harvard University Press, 1950.

Tyrell, R. Emmett. *The Conservative Crack-Up*. New York: Simon & Schuster, 1992.

Vaughn, Samuel S., ed. *The Right Word*. New York: Random House, 1996.

Viereck, Peter. *Conservatism Revisited: The Revolt against Ideology*. New York: Transaction, 2009.

———. *Conservatism Revisited: The Revolt against Revolt, 1815–1949*. New York: Charles Scribner's Sons, 1949.

Viguerie, Richard. *Conservatives Betrayed: How George W. Bush and Other Big Government Republicans Hijacked the Conservative Cause*. Los Angeles: Bonus Books, 2006.

Viguerie, Richard, and David Franke. *America's Right Turn: How Conservatives Used New and Alternative Media to Take Power*. Chicago: Bonus Books, 2004.

Voegelin, Eric. *The New Science of Politics*. Chicago: University of Chicago Press, 1952.

Warnick, Barbara. "Conservative Resistance Revisited: A Reply to Medhurst." *Western Journal of Speech Communication* 46 (1982): 373–378.

———. "The Rhetoric of Conservative Resistance." *Southern Speech Communication Journal* 42 (1977): 256–273.

Weaver, Richard. *The Ethics of Rhetoric*. Chicago: Henry Regnery, 1953.

———. *Ideas Have Consequences*. Chicago: University of Chicago Press, 1984.

———. *The Southern Tradition at Bay*. New Rochelle, N.Y.: Arlington House, 1968.

———. "Up from Liberalism." *Modern Age* 3 (1958–1959): 21–32.

———. *Visions of Order: The Cultural Crisis of Our Time*. Baton Rouge: Louisiana State University Press, 1964.

Wiker, Benjamin. *Ten Books Every Conservative Must Read: Plus Four Not to Miss and One Impostor*. Washington, D.C.: Regnery, 2010.

Wilentz, Sean. *The Age of Reagan: A History, 1974–2008*. New York: HarperCollins, 2008.

Will, George F. *One Man's America: The Pleasures and Provocations of Our Singular America*. New York: Crown Forum, 2008.

Williamson, Chilton. *The Conservative Bookshelf: Essential Works That Impact Today's Conservative Thinkers*. New York: Citadel Press, 2004.

Wills, Garry. *Confessions of a Conservative*. Garden City, N.Y.: Doubleday, 1979.

Yergin, Daniel, and Joseph Stanislaw. *The Commanding Heights: The Battle for the World Economy*. New York: Free Press, 2002.

Zelizer, Barbie. "Journalist's as Interpretive Communities." *Critical Studies in Media Communication* 10 (1993): 219–237.

Zelizer, Julian E. "Reflections: Rethinking the History of American Conservatism." *Reviews in American History* 38 (2010): 367–392.

Index

⌘